BUILDING THE NEW EUROPE
Volume 2: Eastern Europe's Transition to a Market Economy

CENTRAL ISSUES IN CONTEMPORARY ECONOMIC THEORY AND POLICY

General Editor: **Mario Baldassarri**, *Professor of Economics, University of Rome 'La Sapienza', Italy*

This new series is a joint initiative between Macmillan and SIPI, the publishing company of Confindustria (the Confederation of Italian Industry), based on the book collection MONOGRAFIE RPE published by SIPI and originated from the new editorial pro-gramme of one of the oldest Italian journals of economics, the *Rivista di Politica Economica*, founded in 1911. This series is intended to become an arena in which the most topical economic problems are freely debated and confronted with different scientific orientations and/or political theories.
The 1990s clearly represent a transition period in which the world economy will establish new international relationships and in this context, new challenges and new risks will have to be faced within each economic system. Fundamental issues on which economic theory and policy have long based their reasoning over the last two or three decades have to be critically reviewed in order to pursue new frontiers for theoretical development and economic policy implementation. In this sense, this new series aims at being a "place of debate" between professional economists, an updated learning tool for students and a specific reference for a wider readership aiming at understanding economic theory and policy evolution even from a non-specialist point of view.

Published

Mario Baldassarri (*editor*)
KEYNES AND THE ECONOMIC POLICIES OF THE 1980s

Mario Baldassarri (*editor*)
INDUSTRIAL POLICY IN ITALY, 1945–90

Mario Baldassarri (*editor*)
OLIGOPOLY AND DYNAMIC COMPETITION

Mario Baldassarri, John McCallum and Robert Mundell (*editors*)
DEBT, DEFICIT AND ECONOMIC PERFORMANCE

Mario Baldassarri, John McCallum and Robert Mundell (*editors*)
GLOBAL DISEQUILIBRIUM IN THE WORLD ECONOMY

Mario Baldassarri and Robert Mundell (*editors*)
BUILDING THE NEW EUROPE
VOLUME 1: THE SINGLE MARKET AND MONETARY UNIFICATION
VOLUME 2: EASTERN EUROPE'S TRANSITION TO A MARKET ECONOMY

Mario Baldassarri, Luigi Paganetto and Edmund S. Phelps (*editors*)
INTERNATIONAL ECONOMIC INTERDEPENDENCE,
PATTERNS OF TRADE BALANCES AND ECONOMIC POLICY
COORDINATION

Mario Baldassarri, Luigi Paganetto and Edmund S. Phelps (*editors*)
WORLD SAVING, PROSPERITY AND GROWTH

Building a New Europe

Volume 2: Eastern Europe's Transition to a Market Economy

Edited by

Mario Baldassarri
Professor of Economics
University of Rome 'La Sapienza'

and

Robert Mundell
Professor of Economics
Columbia University, New York

St. Martin's Press

in association with
Rivista di Politica Economica,
SIPI, Rome

First published in Great Britain 1993 by
THE MACMILLAN PRESS LTD
Houndmills, Basingstoke, Hampshire RG21 2XS
and London
Companies and representatives
throughout the world

A catalogue record for this book is available
from the British Library.

ISBN 0–333–58703–0

Printed in Great Britain by
Antony Rowe Ltd
Chippenham, Wiltshire

First published in the United States of America 1993 by
Scholarly and Reference Division,
ST. MARTIN'S PRESS, INC.,
175 Fifth Avenue,
New York, N.Y. 10010

ISBN 0–312–08976–7

Library of Congress Cataloging-in-Publication Data
Eastern Europe's transition to a market economy / Mario Baldassarri
and Robert Mundell.
p.   cm. — (Building the new Europe; v. 2)
Published in association with *Rivista di Politica Economica*.
Includes index.
ISBN 0–312–08976–7
1. Europe, Eastern—Economic policy—1989– 2. Post-communism—
–Europe, Eastern.   I. Baldassarri, Mario, 1946–   .   II. Mundell,
Robert A.   III. Series.
HC240.B84   1993 vol. 2
[HC244]
338.94 s—dc20
[338.947]   92–189384
                                                                  CIP

Contents

Preface

Building the 'New Europe' lies at the core of the new international economic and political phenomena leading the world through the nineties and towards the twenty-first century.

The end of the bi-polarity between the United States and the Soviet Union, originally begun at Yalta and underscored over the years by the cold war, has led to a re-emergence of Europe. Indeed, the Continent finds itself at a crossroads fraught with challenges, and yet replete with opportunities for growth and development. Such are the complex economic and political transitions from East to West and from North to South that shape the world today.

Against this background, building the 'New Europe' is probably 'the' challenge of the decade. This challenge rests on dual processes: on one hand the European Community-wide single market and monetary integration; and, on the other, the East European transition to the marketplace and integration with Western economies. The former process was analysed at length in Volume 1.

This volume refers to the latter of the two processes, the transition and integration of ex-communist, centrally planned economies.

This study is divided into two parts. The first section, *From Planned to Market Economy* includes essays on the general and specific topics linked to the transitions to a market economy and to a pluralist political system.

These essays have been written by: Hirofumi Uzawa, University of Tokyo; Rueven Brenner, University of Montreal; Yves Balasco, University of Geneva and the University of Paris; Mario Baldassarri, Università 'La Sapienza', Rome; Jan Winiecki, University of Aalborg; Ronald I. McKinnon, Stanford University; Charles Wyplosz, Insead, Delta and Cepr; Alessandro Giustiniani, Francesco Papadia and Daniela Porciani, Banca d'Italia; James W. Dean and Aihua Xu, Simon Fraser University, British Columbia; and Franco A. Grassini, Università Luiss, Rome.

The second section comprises essays on individual countries by Béla Kádár, Minister of International Economic Relations and Otto Hieronymi, Battelle Europe, Geneva (Hungary), Grzogorz W. Kolodko, Warsaw School of Economics and Institute of Finance

8

(Poland), Mate Babić, University of Zagreb (Yugoslavia), Claudio De Vincenti, Università 'La Sapienza', Rome; Nikolai Shmelyov, Economic Commission of the Soviet Parliament, Oleg T. Bogomolov, Moscow Academy of Sciences and EugenioAmbarzumov, Moscow Institute of World Economics (Soviet Union).

Hirofumi Uzawa's paper, *'Rerum Novarum' Inverted: Abuses of Socialism and Illusions of Capitalism*, opens the volume with a keen, thought-provoking assessment of the events at centre stage in the West during this century. In the final years, the twentieth century is witnessing a reversal of the issues which existed one hundred years ago, at the time of the *Rerum Novarum* of Leo XIII. At the turn of the twentieth century, the illusions of socialism almost matched the abuses of capitalism. The historical experience of decades past has transposed the terms of the problem. The 'abuses' are embodied in the dramatic and sometimes tragic experienceof socialism in practice: however, capitalism, which emerges the victor, should not give rise to too many 'illusions'.

In the opening essay of Volume 1, James Meade clearly posed the problem of the victory of capitalism, whose component parts we must now assess as we approach the year 2000. *What is capitalism?* is the provocative question asked by James Meade. Hirofumi Uzawa opens this second volume on the *New Europe* in perfect counterpoint. The central theme, in Uzawa's view, remains the inalienable need for fixed capital formation, whatever form a free society may wish to take. As a consequence, the question of 'institutionalism' arises. The main issue then becomes how to maximise 'freedom' by minimizing 'government', making for the efficient and effective management of corporate investment capital. Visible signs exist even today (and, more and more often, we can experience first-hand situations in individual areas throughout the global village) of the slippery slope that lies between economic progress and environmental destruction. This topic will figure prominently in firms' fixed capital in the decades ahead. Here, too, the interaction between market economy and institutionalism begins to surface. Basically, Uzawa concludes, the real 'excess' of socialism lay in believing, and forcing others to believe, that institutionalism and fixed capital formation were two opposite extremes. However, now there is the danger of making the opposite mistake.

A surprising psychological and behavioural perspective is taken by Reuven Brenner in *From 'Envy and Distrust' to 'Trsut and Ambition'*,

Eastern Europe's Problems: How to Solve It and Why It May Take Long.

Central to the birth of Marxism is the abolition of private property. This should serve as the starting point for reform, observes Brenner. Reintroducing the concept of private property is the first stepping-stone' of the transition.

Precisely for these reasons, the 'missing element' in East European economies, especially in the Soviet Union, is entrepreneurial skill. Oddly enough, the only risk-taking 'entrepreneurs' who flouted law and state-run institutions are those who in decades past ran the black markets of socialist economies. Perhaps today the regulatory and legislative changes under way will turn to black marketeers as a source of entrepreneurial talent. Legal reforms, however, are not enough. In fact they can lead to a false liberalization process. In the past, freedom of the press was non-existent. Today, the new laws provide for sch freedom, but there may not be enough available paper for the printing presses! Far from being merely a question of legislation, the issue at hand is a complex web of institutional reforms, modes of production, micro- and macroeconomic phenomena, patterns of behaviour. It is precisely these trends in behaviour that form the basis of Brenner's analysis, which centres more specially on what he calls the 'dominant Russian mindset' that brought about the social stagnation of several decades. Centralization. collectivization, and the absence of private property 'by law' have led to individual behaviour characterized by the envy of those who could be better off, and by the mistrust of any person or institution. The profound feeling of envy leaves people with the absurd thought, 'I don't care if I lose one eye, as long as my neighbour loses both of his.' These conditions. says Brenner, cannot but lead to the 'triumph of mediocrity' and the 'Leonardo da Vinci' syndrome. It is as though the Pareto-optimality of the market economy had become a 'Pareto-pessimality': it is better for everyone to be worse off ratherthan one household to be better off.

Trust and ambition, and not envy and mistrust, must form the basis of the transition. Hope for the future and the drive to achieve better things will be the true 'minister of industry' in all ex-socialist economies. As Brenner provocatively points out, new laws must be made to protect 'the first, the best, the Leonardo da Vincis'. The real risk is that former bureaucrats, ever the chameleons, will disguise themselves as budding entrepreneurs and become the 'new ruling class', the 'new rich'. But in this case, very little would really be new. To be sure, those who fail deserve a second chance, but without detracting unduly from those who suceed.

After these first two insightful essays, which offer a wide range of economic, political, sociological, psychological and ethical analysis, it seemed appropriate to present the study by Yves Balasko, *On the Economic Reforms in Eastern Europe: a Theoretical Viewpoint.*

In this theoretical study, Balasko deals with two main issues: the link between efficiency and reasoning and its central role in the transition; and financial market formation and its effect on conditions of economic efficiency.

After the initial euphoria of political liberalization and that 'magic 1989', East European countries face the ever-increasing difficulties, costs and sacrifice of their long journey towards market economies. Hardly surprising, then that the danger of backsliding attempts to return to a 'boring bur tranquil' past — even if that tranquillity was won at the cost of hope for the future — should surface here and there. Economic indicators in all East European countries are sending negative signals: production is down, goods are in short supply, prices are spiralling and unemployment is rising out of control.

It is hard to imagine that a transition of these proportions, this almost biblical exodus towards the marketplace, can be achieved at zero cost. Thus it is necessary to view these indicators with a critical eye, and with more than a few reservations.

Mario Baldassarri, in *No Free Lunch, No Free Market, No 'One' East European Economy: Thoughts on the Transition to a Market Economy* sharply points out three chimera, then he underlines a 'missing' resource, i.e. the necessary human capital to manage the economic and political transition to a market economy and pluralistic democratic systems and concludes with an economic policy proposal, i.e. the need to create a 'free trade area' among Eastern Eropean countries rather than the individual pursuit of entry to the EEC, and an agreement on the exchange rates leading to an Eastern European monetary union as a useful instrument of transition.

Baldassarri opens his essay by underlining the nonexistence of a 'free lunch'. But, on the other hand, there might be costs that are not costs and output reductions that are not losses. From this point of view, Jan Winiecki, in *Costs of Transition that are not Costs: on Non-Welfare-Reducing Output Fall,* and Ronald I. McKinnon, in *Liberalizing Foreign Trade in a Socialist Economy: The Problem of Negative Value*

Added, makes two important concrete contributions which enable us to more correctly assess both the past and the present. To a large extent, East European countries have not suddenly become impoverished because of the transition. Indeed, this process is only bringing to light poverty which already existed, masked by artificial price systems, by values measured in central planning offices using back-of-the-envelope calculations, or even by falsified accounts and other forms of statistical fraud, a common practice among firms and central planning offices in the pricing and reporting of industry data.

A fall in production was and is probably inevitable. Nonetheless, that does not necessarily translate into an equal loss of welfare, according to Jan Winiecki. Forstly, today's assessments are being made on production that was previously non-existent. Numerous tricks were used by firms to prove that they had reached or surpassed the objective of the plan: the quantitative production measures were thus arbitrarily influenced by qualitative measures over which they had exclusive control and which could never be truely tested on the market by the consumer. One striking example is what is known in the West as an equivalent unit of output: the objective set out in the plan is to produce five kilograms of soap, but the facility produces only half that amount because, in the producer's view, since the quality has doubled, the quantity is equal to five kilograms, and thus deserves double the price. The transition will therefore produce a lot of 'soap that won't wash'. Secondly, goods were produced that 'should not have existed' but in no way served to increase welfare. For example, the intricate web of raw materials, semi-finished and final products, coupled with the enormous difficulties involved in organizing this imposing logistical system in an efficient way, induced firms to purchase and maintain an inordinate number of trailer trucks to ensure speedy delivery of all necessary equipment and/or to maintain abnormal amounts of inventory. Production levels were therefore kept artificially high. However, more efficient organization makes this store of trailer trucks redundant, and brings about a decline in their production. Another example involves households. Discontinuity and uncertainty concerning the availability of goods in shops compels households to hoard excessively. In many cases, the stock of perishable goods is never actually consumed. Per capita meat consumption figures in the Soviet Union reveal an appreciable percentage of meat 'gone bad'. Once again, increased efficiency leads to lower production and lower consumption.

Implicit in all of these examples is a warning. Although declines in supply and demand reveal these 'statisical effects' — at least in part the consequence of the gains in efficiency achieved by firms and households, resulting in less hoarding — macroeconomic reinflation, if left unchecked, can produce uncontrollable inflationary effects.

Ronald I. McKinnon analyses in depth the potential effects of freer foreign trade and lists the precise strategic implications for East European policy.

The artificial Eastern price systems must be taken into account: low-cost inputs and raw materials, high-priced final products. It follows thatthese same production systems, when 're-valued' at international market prices, still show negative value added. According to McKinnon, the first step is to clearly expose the degree of protectionism implicit in a traditional Stalinist economy, which in many cases produces goods that no consumer in a competitive market would be willing to buy.

Yet another important illustration may be made here. In order to fulfill the quantitative requirements of plans for the production of detergent, it was 'in the interest of firms' to generate poor-quality product to boost profit. Consumers' protests about the low-quality detergent reached the planning office, which would ask the producer firm to improve quality. The firm would accept, but would charge a higher price for the 'improved product'. This scenario would unfold time and time again: quality would worsen, consumers would protest, the firm's price would rise, and so on. Clearly, in this context, sudden freer trade would reveal negative value added in various forms, with disastrous effects on the entire systems. That is why it seems advisable to adopt a gradual approach that brings protectionist measures to light from the outset by means of explicit tariffs. Within a reasonable time, the concurrent drive inherent in the economy would foster the technological developments needed to lower and in time reduce to zero tariff protection and to enhance the country's prospects of success when embarking on the open waters of international competition.

Today, all eyes are on the 'transition', the reforms yet to be made. But what about 'after the reforms'? This is the main premise of the paper written by Charles Wyplosz, *Post-Reform Eastand West: Capital Accumulation and the Labor Mobility Constraint*. Let us imagine, says

Wyplosz, that reforms have aleady come to pass in Eastern Europe, and that East European economies are now shaped by market forces. Let us begin by measuring the factors of production. It seems clear that no major constraints exist as far a labour-force availability and, in part, professional skills are concerned. What stands out in sharp contrast is the shortage of capital..The corollary is a situation of low labour productivity and high marginal productivity of capital. There is thus a need to keep wages low over the medium to long term. However, in an 'open' market economy, how long would Eastern workers remain patient and long-suffering before pushing wage levels upward, thereby worsening the already grave problems associated with integration? After all, the '1989 revolution' is one step toward liberalization, in spite of short-term aspirations towards Western-style consumption, if not consumerism. In a liberalized economy, the necessary wage differences between East and West will undoubtedly set in motion massive migration flows. In one way or another, Western countries will witness radical 'domestic' change. This transverse flow, not easily identifiable or measurable today, especially in relative terms, will cut across Europe: capital flows will move eastward as labour moves westward, working its way into the folds of wage rigidity and other characteristics of the industrial relations fabric of Western countries.

The impact of East European reform on the West is discussed by Alessandro Giustiniani, Francesco Papadia and Daniela Porciani in their paper titled *The Effects of the Eastern European Countries' Economic Reform on the Western Industrial Economies: a Macroeconomic Approach*. The simplifying assumption at the basis of this paper excludes migration flows.

Viewed from this angle, the effects of East European economic reforms, especially in Western Europe, would be disastrous: a sudden wave of demand, given the negligible productive capacity of the East, would exert appreciable upward pressure on prices. To be sure, this effect would be partially offset if at the same time government expenditure were to decline overall. There is clearly a need. conclude Giustiniani, Papadia and Porciani, for a serious strategy concerning structural economic policy. In this sense, the authors add, the freer-trade processes initiated by the EC single market and the Uruguay Round of GATT could be of extreme importance in spreading the new East European demand to the largest number of countries in the rest of the world.

One specific problem of importance to East European countries is the high level of external debt. James W. Dean and Aihua Xu centre their analysis on this theme in *Debt Relief and Eastern Europe: Why Poland is a Special Case.*

Their paper describes in detail the debt position of each country, indicating the level, creditors, duration. size in proportion to the economy, prospects for settlement and potential to attract international capital. A major portion of the study deals with the special case of Poland; this section is followed by brief analyses of economic phenomena in Bulgaria, Czechoslovakia, the former German Democratic Republic, Hungary, Romania and Yugoslavia.

This first section closes with the study of a particularly Western experience which, if carefully evaluated and if its negative features are corrected, could serve as a useful tool to remedy the problematic experiences of East European countries. This objective is pursued in the paper written by Franco A. Grassini, *The Experience of West Euriopean Public Enterprise for the Transition of Eastern European Economics.* The presence of the public sector in the entrepreneurial activity of market economies is as diverse as it is controversial, ranging from firms which offer public services to state-controlled companies which, though a successful experiment, are replete with crises and contradictions.

The long and complex debate on the private–public-sector mix in market economies now tends to shy away from ideological extremes. A modern economy should be based on the rules of market competition which create the necessary conditions of productive and allocative efficiency. In a modern economy, however, the problem is not so much to achieve zero state participation as it is to redefine, perhaps within tighter, clearer limits, the strategic role of the state for the purposes of equitable distribution and greater economic development. In modern market economies, state involvement is 'better or more efficient'. The many negative experiences of public-sector firms in the West are often linked, as Grassini points out, to the setting of a wide range of diverse and, in some cases, contradictory goals. Policymakers have saddled public-sector firms with any and every objective: safeguarding employment, developing technology, fostering growth in less developed areas, and so on. However, with careful analysis and if the strategic focus is more limited and better defined, the Western experience of state-controlled firms is likely to be of great interest to East European countries during the transition phase.

Grassini uses great insight and analytical skill to examine the major issues that arise when public-sector firms operate in the marketplace: their organizational structure, their relationship with government and public institutions, their financing. Again, no one generic model exists; conditions vary with the type of public-sector firm involved. A direct link exists between these issues and the problem of privatizations in Western countries.

The second section touches on various important experiences of individual countries.

Béla Kádár, in *Transition to a Market Economy: the Experience of Hungary*, underscores the 'singularity' of the case of Hungary. With the revolution and repression of 1956, the Hungarian economy started down a road of slow but steady change. As a consequence, the economic developments have by far preceded the political change which occurred in 1989. In this sense, Hungary considers itself capable of moving more rapidly than other countries toward some form of association with the EEC. Hence Kádár's conclusion, that to achieve this end, Hungary's capacity to control inflationary pressures without unduly worsening employment conditions will play a crucial role.

The case of Hungary is also examined in the paper written by Otto Hieronymi, *The Development of the Social Market Economy in Hungary and the Opportunities Resulting from Future Entry into the European Community*, which describes that country's experience as an interesting example of a social market economy, similar in some ways to the Western market economies with heavy public-sector intervention.

In Poland, too, economic changes were brought about well before institutional and political reforms. Grzegorz W. Kolodko, in *Inflation Stabilization in Poland: A Year After*, describes in detail the events which occurred, from the protests in Danzig of the early eighties, to the Mazowiecki government, its defeat, and the formation of the new government which also faced a choice between so-called 'cold-shower' and 'gradualist' policies.

Historical differences exist in the case of Yugoslavia which, since the fifties under Marshal Tito, has attempted to create another type of socialism, characterized by a large number of cooperatives. Nonetheless, grave structural problems are inherent in the Yugoslav economy.

Add to these the ethnic and regional unrest that has erupted in military conflict among Yugoslav's various republics. This theme is discussed in an excellent piece written by Mate Babić, *The Problems of Transition from a Socialist to a Market Economy in Yugoslavia*.

Economic reform, new industrial stances, conflict among different cultures and republics: these form the potentially explosive mixture present in the former Soviet Union.

Claudio De Vincenti's paper, *Planning Authority and Enterprise in the Soviet Transition: A Principal-Agent Model*, proposes a theoretical model analyzing the relationships between planning authorities and individual productive units, showing how the incentives scheme used in the past produces adverse effects in the transition phase. It is absolutely necessary to alter the incentives model in such a way as to guide the former Soviet Union toward behaviour similar to that of a market economy.

Three 'voices and testimonies' are collected in this volume to describe first-hand the difficult political and economic transition of the former Soviet Union. Nokolai Shmelyov deals with the interaction between the Soviet economy and international markets. Oleg T. Bogomolov analyzes from within the transformation of the Soviet Union's economic and industrial apparatus. Finally, Eugenio Ambarzumov explores the complex process that links political changes with developments in the area's economic structure.

Given the continual change and uncertainty associated with economic transition, most of which will be defined 'as it happens', this collection can scarcely be considered an exhaustive array of analyses and indicators which provide all of the answers for political and economic reform of a sizeable portion of Europe. Nonetheless, building the 'New Europe' means guiding what seemed to be a monolithic bloc of centrally planned, communist countries towards pluralism and the marketplace. This is essential to meet the peaceful challenges that have arisen since the end of bi-polarity and that require increasing international stability. At the centre of the new-found balance, not only will Europe represent the point of physical contact between East and West, but it will also play the leading role in new North–South relations which reveal entire continents suspended in limbo between solid prospects for development and conditions of backwardness beyond all hope. If the latter conditions should prevail, then this would seriously jeopardize that 'global village', destined to remain a key issue in the decades ahead. Once again, history calls on Europe to be a 'source of ideas', a laboratory for experimentation', a 'protagonist in economic and social progress'.

Mario Baldassarri

I - FROM PLANNED
TO MARKET ECONOMY

"Rerum Novarum" Inverted: Abuses of Socialism and Illusions of Capitalism

Hirofumi Uzawa
Tokyo University

1. - Introduction

In his historic 1891 Encyclical, *Rerum Novarum,* Pope Leo XIII addressed himself to the most pressing problems of the times the abuses of capitalism and the illusions of socialism. He called the attention of the world on "the misery and wretchedness pressing so unjustly on the majority of the working class" and condemned the abuses of liberal capitalism, particularly the greed of the capitalist class. At the same time, he vigorously criticized the illusions of socialism, chiefly on the ground that private property is a natural right indispensable for the pursuit of individual freedom. Exactly one hundred years after *Rerum Novarum,* the problems which plague the world may be identified as the abuses of socialism and the illusions of capitalism.

Contrary to the classical Marxist scenario of the transition of capitalism to socialism, the world is now faced with the entirely different problem of how to smoothly transform a socialist economy to a capitalist economy. In order for such a trasformation to result in a stable, well-balanced society, however, we have to be explicitly aware of the short-comings of the decentralized market system as well as the deficiencies of the centralized planned economy.

The centralized planned economy has been plagued by the enormous power which has been exclusively possessed by the state and has been arbitrarily exercised. The degree of freedom bestowed upon the average citizen has been held at the minimum, while human dignity and professional ethics have not been properly respected. The experiences of socialist countries during the last several decades have clearly shown that the economic plans, both centralized and decentralized, which have been conceived by the government bureaucracy, have been inevitably found untenable either because of technological deficiencies or in terms of incentive incompatibility. The living standard of the average person has fallen far short of the expectations, and the dreams and aspirations of the majority of the people have been left unfulfilled.

On the other hand, the decentralized market economy has suffered from the perpetual tendency toward an unequal income distribution, unless significant remedial measures are taken, and from the volatile fluctuations in price and demand conditions, under which the maintenance of productive ethics has been found extremely difficult. Profit motives often outrun moral, social, and natural constraints, while speculative motives tend to dominate productive motives, unless proper regulatory measures are administered.

We may now have to search for an economic system in which stable, harmonious processes of economic development may be realized with the maximum degree of individual freedom and with due respect to human dignity and professional ethics. I may term such an economic system as institutionalism, to emphasize that it is not defined in terms of a certain unified principle, but rather the structural characteristics of an institutionalist economy are determined by the interplay of moral, social, cultural, and natural conditions inherent in the society, and they change as the process of economic development evolves and social consciousness correspondingly transforms itself. It explicitly denies the Marxist doctrine that the social relations of production and labor determine the basic tenure of moral, social, and cultural conditions of the society in question. Adam Smith emphasized several times in his *Wealth of Nations* that the design of an economic system conceived of purely in terms of logical consistency inevitably contradicts with the diverse, basic nature of human being, and instead he chose to advocate the merits of an economic system evolved through the democratic processes of social and political development. It is in this Smithian sense that I should like to address myself to the problems of the restoration of market economies in

Eastern and Central European socialist countries and their possible integration into a Greater Europe.

2. - Institutionalism and Social Overhead Capital

Institutionalism is characterized by the concept of social overhead capital and by the nature of social institutions which manage various social overhead capital.

In an institutionalist economy, all the scarce resources which are limitational in the process of production and consumption are classified into two categories: social overhead capital and private capital. Social overhead capital comprises those scarce resources that are not privately appropriated, but held as common property resources, to be managed by social institutions of various kind. Private capital, on the other hand, consists of privately owned or managed scarce resources, of which the ownership rights are transacted in the market. The criteria by which scarce resources are classified between these two categories are not necessarily technological, but rather social and cultural, to be dependent upon the nature of the functions they perform in relation to the fulfillment of the minimum standard of life for the average citizen.

Natural environments such as atmosphere, soil, water, forests, rivers, and oceans are important constituents of social overhead capital, so are social infrastructure such as roads, bridges, public transformation systems, communication systems, medical, educational, and cultural institutions, financial and monetary institutions, and administrative and judicial systems.

Scarce resources are classified as social overhead capital when the social consensus is attained that the services derived from them play a crucial role in order for the average citizen to be able to enjoy the minimum, still dignified life. Each type of social overhead capital is to be managed by an autonomous institution, which is subject to professional codes of ethics in deciding how to maintain the social overhead capital in charge and how to distribute the services derived from it. This does not necessarily mean that services derived from social overhead capital are freely distributed to the members of the society, nor does it imply that each autonomous institution in charge of social overhead capital is in financial equilibrium. Indeed, the aggregate of the current expenditures of all these institutions is nothing but the current governmental expenditures, while the aggregate of investments expenditures is the governmental capital formation.

It should be emphasized that the way in which the management of social overhead capital is entrusted to each autonomous institution is fiduciary. If social overhead capital is efficiently and equitably managed, the level of the minimum income which would be required for the average person to live the minimum standard of living will be held to the minimum, thus implying the intrinsic stability of the distribution of real income.

In an institutionalist economy, every citizen is accorded a maximum degree of freedom, constrained only by the moral and ethical codes of behaviour, while the power bestowed upon the government is held to the minimum, largely consisting of the fiduciary functions for the management of social overhead capital.

I should like again to emphasize that the role of the state is not to control and govern the people, but rather to maintain and put an order in the management of social over-head capital, which are fiduciarily entrusted by the people.

The processes by which scarce resources are designated as social overhead capital to be fiduciarily managed by autonomous social institutions are necessarily political. However, the economist has to play a pivotal role in the assessment of the functions of various scarce resources in terms of their effect upon the stability, equity, and efficiency of the allocative mechanism.

It may be noted that private capital and produced outputs are in principle to be transacted in the perfectly competitive market. Each product has levied an excise tax corresponding to the extent of the marginal social costs incurred by its production and use. The network of social overhead capital serves as the environment in which all the social and private activities of the members of the society are conducted. The economic activities are centered around the market system, and the stability, equity, and efficiency of the market mechanism crucially hinge upon the structure of social overhead capital and the way in which services from social overhead capital are distributed among the members of the society. Thus a group of countries having diverse social overhead capital structure are united to form a common market, a distortion may occur in the processes of resource allocation even in the perfectly competitive situation.

3. - Economic Growth and Environmental Degradation

Economic growth is typically defined as a sustained growth in real national product or in related aggregative statistical indices. However, growth in the per capita level of real national income does not necessarily mean that the level of living standard or the degree of satisfaction the average individual enjoys is improving at the same rate as the rate of increase in per capita national income. This is particularly the case when the disruption of natural environments occurs accompanying the process of economic growth, as has been the case with the processes of post-war economic development in many countries, both capitalist and socialist.

Natural environments constitute an important part of social overhead capital. The real level of living standard or the degree of satisfaction is influenced by the quality and quantity of social overhead capital, as well as by the per capita level of real national income. Indeed, those scarce resources that play an indispensable role in producing the services required in maintaining the minimum living standard are likely to be designated as social overhead capital, and accordingly the elasticities of the real level of living standard with respect to various social overhead capital are high. This is particularly the case with natural environments, and, if the process of economic growth involves the degradation of natural environments, the rate of increase in the real level of living standard would be significantly lower than athe rate at which the per capita level of real national income is increasing. Depletion of social overhead capital, particularly degradation of natural environments, implies not only a worsening of the welfare of the current generation, but it also affects the welfare of all the future generations. In order to ensure the pattern of economic

growth which is optimum from a social paint of view, it is necessary
to obtain the optimum balance between the increase in per capita
national income and the resulting degradation of social overhead
capital, particularly of natural environments.

The optimum balance between economic growth, as defined in
terms of the increase in per capita real national income, and the
degree of degradation of social overhead capital, particularly of
natural environments, may be obtained by applying the concept of
imputed price associated with social overhead capital. The imputed
price of a particular type of social overhead capital measures the
extend to which the marginal decrease in the stock of social overhead
capital conduces to the decrease in the real level of living standard for
the entire future. The concept of imputed price also takes into account
the equity aspect of the allocative mechanism, not only between the
current and future generations, but also between the individuals or
countries involved.

Within the framework of an institutionalist economy, when each
economic activity has levied by the autonomous social institutions in
charge of social overhead capital the amounts evaluated at the
imputed prices of social overhead capital which are degrated by such
an activity, then the economy will be able to sustain the path of
optimum balance between economic growth measured in the narrow
sense and the degradation of social overhead capital, particularly of
natural environments.

In the actual calculation of imputed prices for various social
overhead capital where the equity aspect of the resulting pattern of
resource allocaiton is explicity taken into consideration however, one
would have to be satisfied with obtaining approximated values. I
should like to refer to an illustrative example with regard to the
problem resulting from the anthropogenic concentration of radiative
forcing agents in the atmosphere, as reported in a recent paper of
mine (1).

The atmospheric concentrations of radiative forcing agents, in
particular carbon dioxide, methane, nitrous oxide, and chloro-

(1) See Uzawa H.: "Global Warning Initiatives: the Pacific Rim", in DORNBUSH R. -
POTERBA I. (eds.): *Global Warning: the Problem and Economic Policy Responses*,
forthcoming.

fluorocarbons (CFCs), have significantly increased since the times of the industrial revolution, resulting in a drastic increase in the global average surface air temperature. It is estimated that if the current trend were to continue, the global average surface air temperature would be increased by 2° C from the pre-industrial level within fifty years. The increase in the global average surface air temperature the earth has experienced in the period of 10,000 years since the last ice age to the times of the industrial revolution was about 1° C.

The phenomenon of global warming is largely of anthropogenic origin, particularly due to the combustion of fossil fuels and the depletion of terrestrial forests, particularly of tropical rain forests. The magnitudes of imputed prices of carbon dioxide and terrestrial forests take values quite different from those obtained within the traditional theory of imputation where only the efficiency aspect of the allocative mechanism is taken into consideration. The estiamtes I have obtained in the paper referred to above are based upon the method of imputation where the ratios of the imputed prices of carbon dioxide and terrestrial forests over the per capita level of national income are identical between the countries involved. Thus the imputed price of carbon dioxide in both the United States and Japan is $30 per metric ton of carbon content, while it is $1.00 for the Philippines and $3.00 for Brazil. As for terrestrial forests, the imputed price in both the United States and Japan is $3,000 per hectare, while it is $300 for the Philippines and $900 for Brazil.

The optimum pattern of the allocation of scarce resources including social overhead capital will ensue when each economic acativity is levied the amounts evaluated at the imputed prices for the degradation of social overhead capital, while privately owned or managed scarce resources are transacted in the perfectly competitive market.

The theory of social overhead capital explained above has been developed in Uzawa [2], [3] (*).

The concept of institutionalism as developed here is closely related to that of social market economy introduced by Professor Horst Siebert [1].

(*) *Advise:* the number in square brackets refer to the Bibliography in the appendix.

4. - Institutionalism and Market Economy

The processes of resource allocation in a market system are closely related to the institutional arrangements within which it works. A particularly important role is played by the structure of social overhead capital and by the way the services derived from social overhead capital are distributed among the members of the society.

As indicated in paragraph 2 above, public transportation systems, communication systems, educational, medical, and cultural institutions, monetary and financial institutions, and administrative and juridical systems constitute important components of social overhead capital, and they are crucial determinants for the stability of market mechanism and the optimality of the resulting resource allocation. One of the economic criteria by which scarce resources are classified as social overhead capital is that the elasticities with respect to the minimum level of living standard are close to zero, and if the scarcity of these social overhead capital relative to the endowment of private capital is increased, the prices of those goods and services that are indispensable to the maintenance of the minimum living standard will become higher, resulting in an increase in the level of the minimum income. The distribution of real income then becomes more unstable and the percentage of those who are not able to earn enough income to sustain the minimum level of living standard will be increased.

In order for the existing stock of social overhead capital to be efficiently utilized, the price corresponding to the marginal social cost has to he charged for the use of each type of social overhead capital. Each society then has to maintain the stock of social overhead capital in such a manner that the magnitude of marginal social costs remains below a certain critical level, thus ensuring the stability of the market mechanism and the dynamic optimality of resource allocation.

The introduction of a market stystem in a socialist country may now be discussed within the theoretical framework of institutionalism. A purely centralized socialist country may be regarded as an extreme form of an institutionalist economy where all scarce resources are classified as social overhead capital and the allocation of scarce resources, including labor, is dictated by the state authorities.

None of the East and Central European socialist countries naturally have been purely centralized socialist countries in this sense. However, the major implications of the introduction of a market system may be discussed within the context of such a purely socialist economy. On the other hand, the performance of capitalist countries has been crucially dependent upon the nature of social overhead capital. The relative excellent performance of West Germany and Japan during the 1980s may be attributed to the well-balanced structure of social overhead capital these two countries have suceeded in maintaining, while the poor performance of the United States seems to me to be due to the degradation of the social overhead capital structure, particularly since the end of 1960s.

Thus, the introduction of a market system in a socialist country has to be done in such a manner that the structure of social overhead capital ensures the stability of the market mechanism and the dynamic optimality of resource allocation in the institutionalist economy evolved.

Among the most important constituents of social overhead capital to ensure the proper working of market mechanism are public transformation systems, communication systems, educational, medical and cultural institutions, and fiscal and monetary institutions. The proper maintenance of these social infrastructure is indispensable in order for the allocative mechanism in any market economy to yield a dynamically efficient pattern of resource allocation and a stable distribution of real income. The prices to be charged for the services of these infrastructure are evaluated at the marginal social costs incurred by the use of such services. The revenues of the social institutions in charge of these infrastructure do not necessarily match the costs, both current and capital, they incur with respect to the maintenance of these infrastructure and the rendering of the services derived from them. In general, the larger the social evaluation of the services rendered by each type of social infrastructure, the larger will be the deficit incurred by the social institution in charge.

There is another category of social overhead capital which plays a crucial role in the stable maintenance of the allocative mechanism. It is related to the production and distribution of the basic foodstuffs. In the productive activities in the agricultural sector of the society, some of the factors of production, such as land, cultivation and husbandry techniques, distribution systems, and natural environments are better to be classified as social overhead capital to be fiduciarily managed by autonomous institutions in order to ensure adequate and stable provision of basic foodstuffs. This does not mean that the modes of production in the agricultural sector are either nationalized or collect-ive organizations, nor does it imply that those who are engaged in the agricultural sector are coerced to do their work. The financial and institutional arrangements have to be devised in such a manner that the productive and distributive organizations are so set that they are compatible with private incentives and at the same time the adequate and stable supply of the basic foodstuffs is maintained.

When a group of counatries having diverse structures of social overhead capital get together to form a common market, it should be emphasized that proper policy measures have to be adopted to counter inefficient price fluctuations and volatile changes in the production of the basic foodstuffs which occur as the result of differences in the structure of social overhead capital between the countries involved. At the same time, investment in social overhead capital in each counatry is so arranged that differences in the struc-ture of social overhead capital between the countries would gradually disappear. The efficiency function of the market system then would be fully realized, without having an undesirable effect upon the distribu-tion of real income.

It should be noted, however, that the transactions based largely upon speculative motives should be curtailed as effectively as possible. The experiences China had during the process of introducing the market system into the otherwise centralized society beginning in the early 1980s have taught us that, if speculative motives dominate the choice of economic activities, the allocative function of the market system will not properly work, occasionally with disastrous impli-cations upon the processes of resource allocation and income distribu-tion for the society as a whole. In the absence of efficient distribution and transportation systems, the speculative hoarding of the basic foodstuffs had increased and the price movement had become vola-tile, with an extremely unstable pattern of real income distribution and the spread of political unrest in the cities. The disruption of economic activities and the political unrest resulting from it finally threatened the legitimacy of the central power structure, with a tragic end for the brief period of the democratization in China.

The Chinese experiences during the same period also teach us another lesson on the privatization of land tenure. The gigantic structure of the peoples' communes had been abruptly dismantled to be replaced by the system of bidding on land tenure, with, however, the political control by the Party apparatus kept intact. The members of the Communist Party or those associated with them had come to exclusively possess the land tenure which had previously been control- led by the peoples' communes or similar organizations, and the majority of rural people had to become hired laborers, with extremely low wages. On the other hand, the introduction of market mechanism in land ownership in a previously socialist country would involve processes which would seem to be unsurmountable; namely, the processes of dividing the land ownership or tenure which previously had been collectively controlled between the people. At the same time, the system of allocating land ownership or tenure through a market mechanism would involve a significant degree of disturbance due to the speculative motives. It would be more desirable, both from the viewpoints of the efficiency and equity of allocative mechanism, to classify land as social overhead capital and to set up autonomous institutions to which the management and allocation of land tenure would be fiduciarily entrusted.

I should like to conclude my paper with a brief remark on the role of the central banking system. The central banking system provides each country with the institutional framework within which not only the efficient and stable working of the monetary and financial systems is ensured, but also all the economic, social, and cultural activities of the society are smoothly organized. Thus the central banking system may be regarded as an important component of social overhead capital in each country, and the management of the central banking system has to be discretely and prudently organized so that the stability of the whole society is not disturbed. It involves a political process in the genuine sense of the word and seems to be primarily delicated to preserving the economic and social welfare of the country concerned, with a due respect to the interests of all the countries involved. The concept of a unified, common central banking system for a group of countries would work well only if the countries involved have similar social overhead capital structure or appropriate measures are adopted to nullify the disturbances which would arise out of differences in the structure of social overhead capital between the countries involved.

BIBLIOGRAPHY

[1] SIEBERT H.: «Principles of the Economic System in The Federal Republic - An Economist's View», presented at the German-American Conference on *Federal Republic of Germany - 40 Years of the Basic Law, Experience, and Prospects*, 1989.

[2] UZAWA H.: *Sur la Théorie Economique du Capital Collectif Social*, Cahiers du Seminaire d'Econométrie, 1974, pp. 101-22; translation «On Economics of Social Overhead Capital», in H. UZAWA: *Preference, Production and Capital: Selected Papers*, New York, Cambridge University Press, 1988, pp. 340-62.

[3] — —: «Social Stability and Collective Public Consumption», in MATTHEWS R.C.O. - STAFFORD G.B. (eds.): *The Grant Economy and Public Consumption*, London, Mac Millan, 1982, pp-. 23-37, reprinted in UZAWA H.: *Optimality, Equilibrium and Growth: Selected Papers*, Tokyo, University of Tokyo Press, 1988.

From «Envy and Distrust» to «Trust and Ambition» Eastern Europe's Problems: How to Solve it and Why it May Take Long

Reuven Brenner
University of Montreal

The monetary and fiscal problems that the Soviet Union and other Eastern European countries face today are important, but not only are they marginal relative to others, but also their solution depends on making credible legal reforms enabling private property righrs to emerge, be defined and be enforced first, before trying to implement other reforms (1). Unless this is done, no monetary, no fiscal policy and no exchange rate policy in the world will put these societies back to the road leading toward a better life. Recall that idea of communism could be — and was — summed up (in its *Manifesto*) in one sentence: the abolition of private property. This is at the root of their problems, and this is were the treatment should start. All the rest of the communist regimes' undeniably big problems are only symptoms. Treating them rather than the sickness will not cure the patients. But even if such steps are firmly taken — and meanwhile in most Eastern bloc countries they are not: the symptoms are being treated, rather than the sickness — prosperity will not be around the corner. It will take years until credibility in the new legal system is established.

When euphoria prevailed about the prospects of the crumbling communist societies advancing in leaps and jumps, I was far more

---

(1) See BRENNER, [3], [4].

Advise: the numbers in square brackets refer to the Bibliography in the appendix.

pessimistic. Unfortunately all the pessimistic predictions, made more than a year ago, seem to be now confirmed (2). One reason for making such predictions was that it will take years for societies to make the transition from a state where the arbitrary rule of an enormous bureaucracy prevailed (consisting of an estimated 17 to 20 milion people in the USSR), to a State where the *tradition* of the rule of law is eventually established, and within which much of this bureaucracy would become obsolete. Another reason for the pessimistic prediction was that behind the mask of a communist ideology and its obscure vocabulary, a cruel, ordered state of lawlessness prevailed, shaping attitudes — profound envy and lack of trust among them — that will take years to overcome. Until people start to be cured from such attitudes, prosperity will be slow in coming. How does a move toward both a credible legal system promising enforcement of property rights, and decentralization provide the cure for both these attitudes are among the questions dealt with in this presentation.

1. - Black Markets and Property Rights

At first sight there seems to be a contradiction between «tyranny» and «lawlessness». But there is not.

The tyrannical power of bureaucracy and the arbitrariness in decisions — the rule of men rather than laws in every facet of people's lives — was, in part, due to the fact that many of the laws in these countries prohibited, and still do, activities required for normal, everyday life. The bureaucracy got many of its privileges not only because they either had first crack at many commodities and got items «under the counter», or because decisions at the workplace depended on their goodwill, but also because of the power to disregard black markets and widespread stealing at the workplace, and to enforce prohibitions selectively (3). Both the black markets and the widespread stealing were themselves the consequence of laws pre-

---

(2) See those predictions in BRENNER, [3] an article written more than a year ago.
(3) And even collaborate with the black markeeters in ways that would leave little trace.

venting the recognition of private property, and such laws turned almost everyone into a lawbraker (4). Thus bribes and lawlessness were common, and the young generation was taught to adjust to the system. If some did not, back-to-back shifts, denial of vacation, falling to the end of the waiting lists for an apartment, false accusations and threats of being exiled to far-away places, were among the incentives to teach the great majority the lesson. The bribes did not necessarily take the monetary form one would expect in the West. Rather, in a society where to obtain most commodities, be it food, clothing, housing, electronic appliances, or cars takes much time, either getting the products themselves, or being informed about their availability and having a priority claim to them, were privileges, not unlike monetary bribes in other societies (5).

The solution to this problem of lawlessness is not to enforce the still existing bad laws which prevented the establishment of private enterprises and were the source of the problem, but to decriminalize much that was and still is illegal. This would mean allowing laws to be gradually adjusted through the experience of, unpleasant as this may sound, the «black and informal marketeers» and the «speculators». They have been and can be the entrepreneurs in the reforming countries, being the only ones with experience about how decentralized systems work. They were the ones taking risks and producing, supplying and distributing agricultural products when it was illegal. They were supplying «private» transportation when doing so was illegal. They were the «intermediaries» between buyers and sellers, an occupation forbidden by law. And since these black marketeers were operating in the shadows, they were among the few who trusted one another, in a society where trust was a rare commodity and who, as one would expect, were frequently organized around an ethnic base. Whereas in the West, oral contracts are rare, in the Soviet Union's black economy (as in black economies everywhere), such contracts are the rule, and they are based on both trust and ostracism from the informal network if contracts are violated (6). But, apparently, only

---

(4) See BRENNER [3].

(5) Much more detailed discussion about the relationship between bad laws and bureaucracy can be found in BRENNER [3], GROSSMAN [15], O'HEARN [31].

(6) See BRENNER [6], chapter 2 on trust and contracts.

rarely is a «mafia» type of enforcement applied, though due to the close interaction between the legal and black sectors, a criminal prosecution for past breaches of the law may follow a breach of contract (7).

Indeed, when Gregory Grossman asked «black marketeers» in the Soviet Union how large and complicated operations can be done by relying on the spoken word only, «the answer has been "trust", sometimes followed by "after all, we are businessmen, not *apparatchiks*"» (8). These businessmen operated on the same principless as their Western counterparts, that is the recognition of property rights which, as Grossman notes, received enforcement from «the customary law of the Soviet underground, nurtured by a philosophy of live and let live, and even with its adjudication arrangements; the informal networks plus corrupt patronage by officialdom; [and the] widespread corruption all around» (9).

Yet instead of legalizing much that was illegal, and letting the black market's customary law serve as the seed of the new legal system, one of the first laws of the perestroika was the May 1986 law *against* «non-labor» income. Its aim was the black market, and, as one would expect, it turned out to be, eventually, ineffective: nobody knew what the meaning of «non-labor» was, and how it would be interpreted (10). Would the incomes of hard working «construction gangs» be considered illegal, since it was known that get their supplies from the black market? Would winnings from state lotteries and interest on state bonds be viewed illegal? Would high-paid, lazy, unproductive bureaucrats be fired (11)? Would anybody with relatively high incomes be accused of earning them «illegally»?

Though the enforcement of the law started with much enthusiasm, the consequences were not as expected: though a few-paid bureaucrats lost their jobs, food and medical services disappeared from the customarily tolerated «markets», since the enterprising

---

(7) See GROSSMAN [16], p. 85. On black market in general also see LOS [24], where one can find descriptions how black markets in Angola, Tanzania etc. were tolerated, got unofficial support. and helped maintain the system, Also see GROSSMAN [15].

(8) See GROSSMAN [16], p. 85, italics in original.

(9) See GROSSMAN [16], p. 82.

(10) See GROSSMAN [16], p. 89.

(11) These were some of the questions raised, according to GROSSMAN [16].

people were afraid that the law will be used against them, Thus more food than before was sold through the black market's channels. The black marketeers, taking on now bigger risks, sold them at higer prices. The results were increased shortages in the legal places and higher black market prices. The outcry was such that it led to a decision to relax the enforcement of the law, and everything returned to «normal», that is, to the pre-1986 law situation. By now this whole episode is known in the Soviet Union as «the excessive zeal of July» (12). The law thus turned out to be just an addition to the long Russian tradition of changing things on paper, with no consequences whatsoever on people's everyday lives (13).

In spite of this experience, in November 1990 Gorbachev ordered the creation of worker vigilante committees with power to monitor the food industry and punish people involved in theft and speculation. These committees, elected at workplaces, were given authority to shut down guilty enterprises, and demand both the dismissal of personnel and criminal proceedings. Also, under Gorbachev's instructions a special Kgb unit was to combat black markets, and the police was ordered to collaborate with the worker's committees (14).

It has been at times argued that the problem of the reforming communist countries will be lack of «entrepreneurship». But all the evidence suggests that this is not their problem. All the «informal marketeers» — and, I have to admit that, while growing up there, members of my family belonged to this category — took great personal risks, had to be quick and sharp, and trusted those who were worthy of trust. These are some of the characteristics required for becoming and being «legal» entrepreneurs too, and there are many

---

(12) See GROSSMAN [16], pp. 89-90.

(13) See another such episode discussed in BRENNER [3].

(14) .The plan seems to be ignored by independently elected governments of some republics and cities. A signed letter in the *Komsomolskaya Pravda* said that the writers organized armed lynch mobs to patrol stores and food distribution centers, and were apparently not afraid that such acts will bring criminal accusations against them. Nobody was alarmed by the letter and many expressed solidarity with the writers. On the first of December large scale food-rationing was introduced for the first time in Leningrad since its siege during World War II. The ration coupons gave the right to buy: one kg. of salami or cold cuts, 1.5 kg. meat, 0.5 kg. butter, 10 eggs, 0.2 kg. oil, 0.5 kg. of flour and 1 kg. cereal or pasta for a month. See «Vigilantes to Monitor Soviet Stores», *New York Times*, as reprinted in *The Gazette*, December 2, 1990: B6.

such people in the reforming communist countries. The problem of these countries is not lack of potential entrepreneurship, but the power of the mediocre collectivity which, as everywhere else and under every regime, tries to slow down the entrepreneurs and the innovators. The difference between the reforming communist countries and the West is not in lack of entrepreneurship, but that in the West the law has been on the innovators' and entrepreneurs' side for a long time, whereas in the reforming Communist countries laws and other policies have been against them for a long time, if not always in word then always in the spirit in which laws and statements have been implemented (15).

2. - Envy, Incentives and the Law

Anatoly A. Sobchak, the mayor of Leningrad, has recently told Hedrick Smith that: «Our people cannot endure seeing someone else earn more than they do. Our people want equal distribution of money, whether that means wealth or poverty. They are so jealous of other people that they want others to be worse off, if need be, to keep things equal. We have a story: God comes to a lucky Russian peasant one day and offers him any wish in the world. The peasant is excited and stars dreaming his fantasies. "Just remember", God says, "whatever you choose, I will do twice as much for your neighbor as I do for you". The peasant is stumped because he cannot bear to think of his neighbor being so much better off than he his, no matter how well off he becomes. Finally he gets an idea and he tells God, "Strike out one of my eyes and take out both eyes of my neighbor". Changing that psychology is the hardest part of our economic reform. That psychology of intolerance toward others who make more money, no matter why, no matter whether they work harder, longer or better — that psychology is blocking economic reform» (16).

---

(15) Another difference is that whereas in the West the selfish motivations of the mediocrity fearing to fall behind have to be hidden behind much, sometimes confusing, double speak, in the reforming communist countries the demands for redistribution can be openly stated.

(16) See SMITH [34], p. 71.

Nicolai Shmelev made similar observations in a speech before the Congress of People's Deputies, saying that: «The blind, burning envy of your neighbor's success has become the most powerful brake on the ideas and practice of perestroika. Until we at least damp down this envy, the success of perestroika will always be in jeopardy» (17).

Yet it is on this fundamental issue that leaders of the Soviet Union caved in again and again: whereas slogans, bills, laws seemed all to go in the direction of guaranteeing remedies to the situation, the practice was different, as the law concerning «non-labor» incomes already has suggested, and, as both the continuing rhetoric against «speculators» and the way other decisions were counteracted, suggests too. Moreover, nobody made the point that the remedy for such envy can be found in making credible moves toward emphasizing property and contract as the basis of the new order, whatever the name by which it will be called.

For example. the USSR's laws governing cooperative entreprises allows them autonomy in setting wages, in marketing and in making their financial arrangements. This does not mean, however, that the firms can now engage in all type of activities, or that they can be expected to flourish. The Council of Ministers' resolution of 29 December 1988 prohibited cooperatives from making vodka, weapons, drugs, publishing books and newspapers, making films, establishing schools, dealing in foreign currency and providing major medical services (though they are allowed to engage in the sale of video and audio services), They must stick to activities that appear in its «bylaws», a document that had to be approved by the local Soviet authority: to engage in any activities not described in the «bylaws» is illegal. But their taxation has changed every two years. In 1987, the suggested tax rate was 3% of taxable profit for the first two years, 10% thereafter. There was widespread protest against the high incomes of the new entrepreneurs, and the Minister of Finance increased the rates to 10 to 75% of taxable profit. The Supreme Soviet rejected this plan, allowing since August 1989 the Soviet republics to determine

---

(17) See SMITH [34], p. 71. Alexander N. Yakovlev, [one] of Gorbachev's closest allies said that «psychological dependence on state paternalism leads to mass inertia, a Soviet habit of mind he calls the "most debilitating obstacle" to reform». Also see SHMELEV [32], [33].

their own tax rates. Yet without general guidelines, the tax rates turned out to be the result of the attitudes toward business of those in policy-making positions in the different republics, and they vary between 10 to 45% in the Baltic republics to 70% and more in the central Asian ones, the highest being imposed on the wholesale sector (18).

Martin Malia, singing his article in *Daedalus* under the pseudonym «Z», also noticed that the cooperatives have become the focus of popular hostility since «the people» viewed them as benefiting only the speculators and the privileged, the prices of their products being high, as were the incomes of the partners in these co-operatives (19). But the co-operative's success was prevented not only by high taxation, a consequence of much vocal, opposition, but also by less visible, but equally deadly opposition. Malia notes that in practice «the law on State enterprises has remained a dead letter ever since it took effect in January 1988, because the silent resistance of legions of *apparatchiki* has kept industry operating at 90% on "state orders" that is' on the old plan» (20), thus preventing cooperatives from flourishing. But recently, on the 9th of December 1990, Gorbachev caved in even formally, issuing a decree effectively banning all republics and entreprises from trading directly with each other and with foreign partners, thus making it far more difficult to steer around the centrally controlled bureaucracy. Whether or not the decree will be effective in practice, or will stay on paper only, is another question. But there is no doubt that such behavior prevents the cooperatives' success. Similar tactics have been adopted in Romania too, as I was by Adrian Popescu-Necsesti and Dinu Zamfirescu, two Rumanian profesors. According to them, though in principle «free speech» is now permitted and people can publish newspapers, the practice is that publishers who tried to do so, but were critical of the new leaders, were simply not sold paper by the still state-owned enterprises.

Thus, part of the «public» hostility against the successful co-operatives should be discontinued since it comes from members of the

(18) See KISELEV [23], p. 78.

(19) See MALIA [25], p. 328.

(20) See MALIA [25], p. 329. By doing so they prevent co-operatives getting their supplies.

State bureaucracy and state-enterprises whose monopoly they threaten, and is not clear that «the public», rather than just a small fraction of it, is behind it. But there is no doubt that the opposition of a large segment of the public toward successful co-operatives and individuals are rooted in envy, as the miners' reactions in the Soviet Union made clear during their strike, and other people's reactions, frequently reported by the press, show too (21).

3. - A Russian Frame of Mind

People are always envious when suddenly outdone by their fellows, be it by chance or due to another reason. But, in a decentralized society, while envious, one will not harbor a grudge and feel maltreated if this happened by chance, by others taking more risks, by being more entrepreneurial, or by demonstration of undoubted talent (22). People' know that they, or their children, are given second chances. Not so in communist regimes: there bureaucrats and political administrators made decisions on advancement, and, since alternative ways toward achievement were absent, nobody being able to «make it on his own», the odds were always in favor of a belief that it is good contacts, opportunism, regulation passed by those already in power or plain stealing, rather than skills which led to one's rise in the ranks. While talent sometimes helped, being a party member was far

---

(21) But co-operatives are not new: they were already re-legitimated once by Stalin, reaching a membership of two million in 1955. But then they were absorbed by state-owned firms, the official reason being given that they were bribing the officials. If people in the Soviet Union do not come forward with great enthusiasm, it may be also because of this precedent. See GROSSMAN [16], p. 91. As to more recent events concerning co-operatives and personal success, SMITH ([34], p. 62), reports the following: «From Valentin Bershkov, a former Soviet diplomat, I heard of a farmer outside of Moscow whose horse and few cows were set free and whose barn was set afire by neighboring farm workers jealous of his modest prosperity. The Soviet press is full of stories about attacks on privately owned cooperative restaurants and other small service shops by people who resent seeing others doing well. In the debates at the Supreme Soviet, the most passionate arguments involve accusations that the free market enable speculators to get rich by exploiting the working class».

(22) See implications of these arguments in BRENNER [6], [7], [8], and BRENNER and BRENNER [9]. In all of them much attention is paid to matters concerning envy, trust, and their observable implications linked with risk-taking and entrepreneurship in particular.

more important, and, under Brezhnev, the higher positions became far better protected than ever before, diminishing the chances of moving up in the communist hierarchy (23). But let us make a historical detour, and look first at the more ancient, and later at some more recent, sources of this deeply rooted envy in the particular Russian context.

There are basically two different kinds of society and of inequality. In one society there is great mobility and change, and the position of families in the wealth or status hierarchy varies from year to year. In another there is rigidity, and each family stays in the same position, year after year, generation after generation. The inequality resulting in the first case is a sign of dynamism, of social mobility, inducing fears of falling behind and envy, yet also ambition and hope. The inequality resulting in the second case is that of a status society, and it induces mainly fear and envy, and, among those kept at the bottom, very little ambition and hope. The latter type society may be founded — and was founded — on institutions justified by a communist vocabulary in particular. Under Brezhnev, more than under other communist rulers, the Russian society turned even more than before into just such a society, the grounds being fertile for such a turn of events.

The grounds were fertile for a number of reasons. For centuries the *mir* was the main institution around which the Russian peasant communities were organized. As in many poor, peasant societies its roles were, among others, insurance, maintenance of traditions, helping those who fell behind and also providing for the upkeep of roads, bridges, wells (24). But, in contrast to other peasant societies,

---

(23) SMITH ([34], p. 62), intervewed Andrei Smirnov, a film maker, who described his union «as a microcosm of Soviet responses to greater economic freedom, adding that everyone was enthusiastic about overthrowing the old dictatorial system, but our directors and producers are fearful of the new system of competition. If we have a choice between the free market and a guaranteed salary, the majority will pick a guaranteed salary. Those who cannot compete on the market are unhappy at the prospect of being unemployed. Others who are more talented are unhappy because they think that studio directors will pick friends and favorites to make films, not the qualified people. They want the union to protect them and go after the studio directors».

(24) See HOSKING [17], p. 22, KENNAN [22], MIRONOV [30], FELDBRUGGE [13], KLOSE (1984) in the Russian context, and BRENNER [6], chapter 2, on similar institutions in peasant and primitive societies in general. HOSKING ([17], p. 22), also notes that the

this institution, which in Russia also held the ultimate ownership of land, was eventually used by the authorities «for tax-collecting, recruitment and local administration», increasing their power and leading to much arbitrariness and intolerance, rather than letting private property rights emerge when the population and its mobility increased (25). For similar reasons, even when peasants left their villages and moved to cities, they continuated to organize themselves around institutions that resembled the *mir:* the widespread *artel*'s. These institutions, as Hosking emphasizes, «displayed no democracy or civil freedom in the western sense. They encouraged no concept of citizenship, individual ownership or individual rights. The predominant force in them was not rule of law, but that of custom and authority» (26). But I do not wish to argue, as some observers of the Soviet scene have done, that the Soviet Union's centralized regime derives «locally» from the existence of such institutions: the grounds were fertile, but the consequences were not inevitable. Rather the contrary: the survival and influence of these institutions in Russia were due to the absence of credible moves toward institutions emphasizing individual property and contract (and maintaining «communal» laws instead), as well as to the fact that other institutions, that in the West limited the power and authority of rulers and the state for a long time — the Church being one of them — have been missing from the Russian scene (27).

---

mir held «the ultimate ownership of the land, and could redistribute holdings, assigning more to families who had new mouths to feed, and reducing the holdings of those whose members had recently died or left the village». But SMITH [34] analyses concerning the Russian people's passivity is inaccurate. They do want the reforms. Only, as shown over and over in this presentation, the lack of credible reforms still keeps them passive, and with very good reasons as the recentralization of power and the reliance on military since December 1990 suggests.

(25) See HOSKING ([17] p. 23), who also notes, however, that «in times of real need or difficulty, the community could and would help out. The notion of *pomochi*, or mutual aid, was fundamental. When a household suddenly lost its breadwinner, or was struck by illness, or its home was burnt down, then the *shkod* [the gathering of heads of households] would decree that their neighbors, or perhaps even the whole village, should turn out to help them with the heaviest or more urgent work». Similar traditions existed, however, in many peasant societies: see BRENNER [6], chapter 2.

(26) See HOSKING [17], p. 24.

(27) Peter the Great weakened the Church with the *Ecclesiastical Regulation* in 1721. After that, the Church ceased to be independent of the government, and its administration became a function of the state. HOSKING ([17], p. 21) also notices that Peter the Great also weakened the nobility «depriving them of the autonomy which enabled them, in most European societies, to make their own distinctive input into the political process». See discussion in BRENNER [3], pp. 212-5, MASSIE [27], p. 793.

These are circumstances that statesmen could have altered, but in the Soviet Union they did not.

The lack of any effective opposition had the consequence of giving rulers and governments discretionary power, leading to much arbitrariness and misfortune. Expecting them, the informal institutions either flourished or survived, reflecting, respectively, either individual initiative — as far as black markets and circumventing the government's regulations were concerned — or collective insurance. But becoming accustomed to the man-made disasters of arbitrariness and misfortune is different from facing them occasionally, as we all do in the West. Life under such trying circumstances induced deeply ingrained envy and fear. It is such fear, in turn, which has weakened resistance to excesses, leading to either obedience or, at least, passive resistance, and also prolonging the lives of «primitive», communal institutions. Ambitious rulers have thus been on fertile grounds, and their eventual ascent to power has reinforced beliefs in arbitrariness and the rule of men (28). This sequence of events reflects the accuracy of Alexis de Tocqueville's observation, who once wrote that «men are not corrupted by the exercise of power, or debased by the habit of obedience; but by exercise of power which they believe to be illegit-

---

(28) HOSKING ([17], p. 24) wrote that «the dogged radicalism of Russian workers and peasants in 1917 derived not from Marxism, but from the unusually late survival into the industrial world of popular institutions of primitive solidarity, accustomed to steering round governments, offering their officials passive resistance or profiting by their inadequacies». HOSKING [17], p. 29: «the peasant *mir* served both as the lowest rung in the ladder of authoritarian control, and yet also as a means by which ordinary people could cushion themselves against the excessive demands of the state». One may now raise the question: what caused what? Did laws shape the character of societies, or was such character the cause of the choice of laws and ideologies? The Communist regimes tried to abolish the whole idea of private property rights and of civil liberties, thus letting theory take its chance and forgetting all about tradition, custom and experience, their own as well as others'. The idea that this can be done can be traced back to the French Revolution which showed that political institutions and authorities, as well as social and economic ones were man-made, and might be subject to choice. When people thus get rid of all previously held ideas, weakening traditional bonds, customary and legal, the arbitrary rule of men will prevail, for a while, leading rulers to excesses when teaching the unconverted. In turn, this arbitrariness, and the uncontested authority further weakens the community, predisposing it toward the follies of ideological certainties of rulers. In this sense one can speak about the law as being one of the causes, rather than just one of the results of changes in society. More on this point can be found in BRENNER [3].

imate, and by obedience to a rule they consider to be usurped and oppressive (29).

The consequence of such beliefs are suspicion, distrust, malice and ill-will toward those leapfrogging «the collectivity» in every domain of life, and not just toward those chose to make their careers in the party or the security forces. Such torments and attitudes are particularly destructive in every society. But, as was the case in communist and other regimes, when envy has been coupled with fear and a belief in arbitrariness on one hand, and increased rigidity, on the other, the two have brought about a deeply ingrained sense on injustice, frustration and nihilism, and led to continuous attempts to undermine people's success. But the attempt to level down everybody who rises above the crowd — what the often approvingly told Russian warning describes as «the tallest blade of grass being the first to be cut down by the scythe» — should not be confused with some firm beliefs in «collectivism» and egalitarian principles. The attitude is the consequence of a long history of both lack of private property rights, lack of tradition of law and lack of opportunities to advance in society, opportunities that became even scarcer under Brezhnev's rule.

It was Khrushchev who stopped Stalin's regime of terror. With it, however, as Martin Malia noted «he gave away his leverage against the apparat and thus his own safeguard ... [and gave] the *apparatchiki* not only security of their persons; he inadvertently gave them life tenure in their positions as well ... The result of Khrushchev's failed reform, therefore, was the triumph of the nomenklatura ... and it is only in the late 1970s that the world learned of this new term and the privileged caste it designated. Brezhnev and his allies prudently drew from Khrushchev's fate the lesson that this group's privileges must forever remain inviolate» (30). Thus, under Brezhnev, the security police was brought under the party's control too, and it could no longer control members of the party. Though the beneficial effect was that the ruler's power diminished, the unanticipated impact was that the additional power being now vested in the bureaucracy led to the "stability of cadres". «This policy was — Malia concludes — the origin

---

(29) As quoted in MALIA [25], pp. 315-6.
(30) See "Z" (*alias* MARTIN MALIA [25]), p. 321.

of the extraordinary gerontocracy, led by Brezhnev himself, Suslov.
Andropov, and Chernenko, who dominated the Soviet scene in the
last decade before Gorbachev and whose longevity compounded the
arteriosclerosis of all other aspects of Soviet life (31). In other words,
the typical thing happened: the increased monopoly power led to
stagnation, the increased security bred increased timidity, a common
phenomenon across countries, time and all human activity (32).

But it is this increased rigidity and lack of hope of mobility, that
was also the source of the heightened sense of envy prevailing in the
Soviet Union during the last twenty years more than even before —
and to varying degrees in the other now-reforming communist countries as well — and which puts probably the severest constraints on
the policies its leaders might adopt. Among the working class it led to
«minimal but universal welfare safety net and comforted by the
socialist ethos of egalitarian leveling ... At a higher social level, the
officially stigmatized entrepreneurial ethos expressed itself in a growing "second", or "black" economy, which was indispensable to the
functioning of the official "first" economy» (33). Hosting [17] quotes
Alexander Zinoviez, the Russian emigrant's views, according to whom
Soviet society became a «web of material dependence, servility toward
superiors, and mutual support adulterated by mutual jealousy and
supervision ... Their inescapable result ... is a tendency to make
everyone mediocre. Be like everyone else: that principle is the very
cornerstone of a society in which communal laws are paramount ... A
person who can live in society independently of a primary collective is
a threat to the very foundations of society» (34). Many talented people
thus decide not to stick their neck out, and resign themselves to a life

---

(31) See MALIA [25], p. 321, and similar points in HOSKING [17], chapter 1. Thus
although the nomenklatura as a "caste" flourished under Stalin, it became rigid only
later. The nomenklatura had the privileges of better housing, superior medical care,
special stores with cheap, good food supplies. Higher in the hierarchy they had their
dacha, best doctors and apartments, holiday abroad etc. They also had better access to
higher education at a time when, as HOSKING ([17], p. 4) notes: «the chances of getting
into university, a prerequisite of moving up in the Russian hierarchy, [became] half of
what they were». Thus privileges were not measured in monetary terms, but their
perfect equivalents.

(32) See BRENNER (1987) about the impact of monopoly in business, and BRENNER
[4] about the impact of monopoly power in science.

(33) See MALIA (1989), p. 321.

(34) See HOSKING [17], pp. 29-30.

of sad, but safe, mediocrity. If they do not — Kapitsa, Medvedev, Engelhart and numerous other Russian scientists did not — then they found themselves committed to the gulags and to mental institutions, leading one of them to congratulate the state's psychiatrist for having discovered a new illness — the Leonardo da Vinci syndrome» (35). Other innovators did not fare much better. When Vladimir Kebanov, a coalmining engineer, established the first independent trade union in the Donbass, and began by protesting violations of the legal rights of employees, most of the union's members were detained soon after the foundations of the Union, and Klebanov himself was confined in a mental hospital (36). Indeed, in obscurity and obedience lie people's safety in such societies.

4. - The Remedy

Although these basic, destructive human impulse can be checked, and be even transformed into a striving that becomes valuable and a basis of culture — and then be called "ambition" — the transformation can no longer be achieved in the reforming communist countries by mere moralizing, as done now (37). How can it be achieved?

Instead of envying other people's successes and brooding over them, one may try to emulate them. Instead of doing everything in one's power to lessen others' financial or professional achievements, one may use the achievements themselves as a source of information, as revealing possibilities for future courses of action that may not have crossed one's mind. If this is some people's reaction, who were suddenly outdone by their fellows, "envy" is indeed transformed into "ambition", and becomes, as Bernard de Mandseville said, «a minister of industry». But what happens if those outdone do not have talent or discipline? How can their envious reactions and malice be contained and be channelled into their most benign form?

---

(35) See JACOBY [18], p. 313. Also see JOHNSON [19], p. 681-2.
(36) See HOSKING [17], p. 43.
(37) «Envy itself and vanity/were ministers of industry» wrote Bernard de Mandeville and in his *Fable of the Bees*, and he wanted this sentence to be taken seriously. He did not use the word "ambition" in the fable: behavior induced by "envy" covered for him the same ground.

The remedy for such negative attitudes would be to move with determination toward legal reforms guaranteeing the enforcement of private property rights and freedom of contract, protecting the successful entrepreneurs and "speculators" against the outdone fellows' "evil eyes". At the same time, however, bureaucrats who benefitted from the system in the past should be punished and kept on their toes. Only when people realize that some laws cannot be changed, that advancing in ranks and acquiring wealth has become more often a matter of talent, of entrepreneurial insight and of chance, rather than "contacts" can one expect to slowly extirpate these attitudes.

The fact that people in the reforming communist countries do not yet grasp that definitive moves toward establishing a legal framework should come first and that punishments are necessary to establish the new regimes' credibility, is evident when one considers events now taking place in Poland, Czechoslovakia, Hungary and Romania. Entrepreneurs fron the West were offered in Poland a rapid triple return on their investment by bribing local officials and factory managers to set artificially low valuations on Polish factories possessing land, machinery and stocks, buying them thus cheaply and selling them later at a higher price. When the entrepreneurs reacted that in the West that is "illegal asset-stripping" the members of the *nomenklatura* shrugged. Lech Walesa is also right in his attacks on the Polish Social Democratic Party (the new name for the former Communist Party), for appropriating vast properties — land, buildings, sport complexes, resorts, camps and others — that belonged to the Communist Party, and which today enrich the same people who had monopoly power before, and who obtained this power not because of entrepreneurial talent, however perversely used, but simply because they had the right contacts (38). It would be hard to establish credibility in a new system, and get rid of the deep-rooted distrust and envy, unless the reforming regimes will be able to show that among the successful people now there is a significant fraction of those who previously were excluded from the system. Unless this happens, people will reach the conclusion that, once again, behind the

---

(38) The same problem appeared in Romania, where the National Salvation Front appropriated the assets of the Communist Party. See BRENNER [3].

veil of words, the new vocabularies, the changes on paper, not much in fact has changed.

That is why Havel's strategy makes sense, and Martin Feldstein's observations on his policies do not (39). Havel seems determined to fight government officials who became rich illegally under the communist regime, and whom he denounced in his August 21st speech, on the occasion of 1968 invasion, making particular reference to «the extremely dark Slusovice-type practices» (40). Before 1968, Slusovice was a small, poor agricultural community. But after the invasion, large computer and chemical industries were built there, and as Joseph [21] notes, «under its director, Frantisek Cuba, the cooperative conducted its own foreign trade, amassed huge hard-currency reserves and ... laundered perhaps hundreds of millions of dollars for Communist cronies» (41). A day after Havel's speech, Cuba resigned. In December 1990, a law designed to confiscate illegally acquired assets is supposed to take effect. When Havel was later asked whether or not it was time to turn over the marketplace to entrepreneurs, Havel answered: «Right now we are in a transitional period, where individual businesses are acting as though they were private, but without legal standing. The law must be articulated before we proceed». Feldstein's reaction to Havel's policies was that he could hardly believe that Czech administration's highest priority was finding out who has accumulated capital illegally, and added «Their biggest problem is that after 40 years under a command economy, a lot of their businesses just cannot compete» (42).

Of course, Feldstein is right that the reforming countries' biggest problem is that the people there still do not work harder, are still cautious, conservative, do not take risks, and thus are not yet able to compete. But this lack of will is linked with the fundamental issue that Havel is struggling with, namely how to restore trust and promote entrepreneurship, and ensure that, to a large extent, people's success will not be attributed to political patronage but to talent and ambition. Only when the odds are in favor of the belief that political patronage is

---

(39) See JOSEPH [21].
(40) See JOSEPH [21], p. 34.
(41) See JOSEPH [21], p. 34.
(42) See JOSEPH [21], p. 34.

no longer the root of success, can entrepreneurship's and competition's rewards be legitimately protected. If the odds are against such beliefs, the «entrepreneur» will be viewed as a criminal, trust is not rebuilt and, as a result, businesses will not be able to compete since the legitimacy of acquiring wealth will be contested at every turn. If in the transition to the new system only the beneficiaries of the previous regime were the biggest winners of reforms, it would thus spell disaster.

That it is not easy to establish such credibility, recall just how difficult it is to reestablish credibility once it is lost even in matters far less serious than the protection of property rights. The difficulties that central banks all over the world experienced when trying to restore stable price levels after periods of high and varying rates of inflation are well known. Most recently this problem was perfectly illustrated when after years of trying — without success — to establish the pound sterling's credibility, the UK finally decided to peg it to one world's most reliable currencies, the Deutsche mark. The mark became reliable not because the German governors of the central bank or German politicians are smarter than the English ones, but because German law explicity requires the Bundesbank to maintain the mark's purchasing power (a requirement that the Germans have adhered to not so much because it is the law, maybe, but because of the sharp memories of the terrible consequences of their hyperinflation). Once the British did that, the value of the pound sterling rose.

However much the new leaders might be trusted (but whereas Havel is, Gorbachev is not), the fact is that the communist bureaucracy is still very much in power in the Soviet Union, Romania, Bulgaria, and to lesser extent elsewhere. With the deep-rooted envy and distrust prevailing in these countries, the continuing success of those who were already successful in the previous regime is interpreted by the population as implying that behind the change in vocabulary not much else has changed. In such an atmosphere it matters very much who are and stay the richer people, since this is what gives people information both about who is still in power, and about chances of success in the future.

The way to destroy the bureaucracy's and State-owned enterprises' monopoly power is not only by punishments, but also by letting competition come it. This, as already pointed out can come in to these societies from its entrepreneurs who previously carried out their businesses in the informal markets (43). If the writers and artists, who, under the Communist regimes, traded their fare — ideas — illegally, became respected and were even trusted with high positions, including the presidency, why should the previously outlawed businessmen be viewed with greater suspicion?!

Also, the best way to carry out legal reforms is not only by imposing them from above, but also by letting the «customary laws» of informal markets become the core of laws concerning private property and contracts. It would be a mistake to either impose such laws «from above», or transfer Western laws to countries in which there is no legal tradition, and where there is disrespect for many official documents, For, with good reasons, as shown next, people do not know the spirit in which such laws might be interpreted (44).

During the first week of March 1990 the Soviet legislature passed legislation that would permit citizens to own businesses and hire employees. But the language of the law is such that it is open to many interpretations and leaves much to the discretion of local bureaucrats. The fact that the law does not mention the term «private property», but calls it instead something that in translation approximates the term «personal property», is not a serious problem. The banking industry in Europe flourished when «usury» was illegal: the word «interest» was invented, and was legally charged (45). It is easier to invent a new word and use it with the older ones, than acknowledging that the metaphors of the past became totally useless. Although this leads to some confusion, whether businesses can develop will depend on what will become the spirit of the law through the coming interpretations. Neither should much attention paid to the fact that there is a provision in the law saying that the use of any form of ownership should «rule out workers' alienation from the means of production and the exploitation of man by man». The first part of the sentence does not mean anything, and the second is not different from a requirement to outlaw slavery and discrimination.

---

(43) Time is on the black market's side anyway: the bureaucracy's uncertainty weakens their power, the power to extort bribes in particular.

(44) Also see BRENNER [3] for additional examples.

(45) See BRENNER [6], chapter 3.

The problem lies in other parts of the law: in the fact that although permitting foreign ownership (and not just joint ventures as until now), it adds that this may be done only in the manner stipulated by the authorities; in the fact that although it gives the republics nominal ownership of natural resources, it also says that expropriation can be done only with the permission of the Soviet Union. The land-leasing law is also problematic because it establishes a new bureaucracy — «the farm committees» — which will supervise land leasing to farmers. This is the last thing that the Soviet Union needs, giving additional discretionary power to another bureaucracy. Indeed some legislators already warned that local officials would make only their worst land available.

5. - On Laws and Credibility

It is not enough to have laws and charter of rights. Laws defining property rights and «Charter of Rights» are only words, concepts and paper: recall that also Stalin's 1936 constitution was very liberal — on paper. What matters is how they are implemented: what will be the legal *tradition* — the jurisprudence — that will be established when decisions have to be made in cases when individual property rights conflict with collective outcries, whose roots may be found in deep-rooted fear and envy. It must be clear, however, that tradition and credibility have never been established either in days, or even years, but took decades or more.

Credibility cannot be established by just passing laws (although, as noted in the previous section, carrying out punishments under new laws can help establish credibility). At the conference on *Transition to Freedom*, organized by the Cato Institute, Alexei Yemelyanov, member of Russia's Supreme Soviet, [said] that «Mr Gorbachev refuses to talk about property rights. Instead, he and other Kremlin leaders are obsessed with creating more laws. Yesterday, they created 33 new ones. Gorbachev wants to shield the power center with paper» (46).

---

(46) Edward Lazear from the Hoover Institute told me that he was impressed that during his one week visit to Romania, some of the ideas he suggested found their way, already during that week, into some bills. He should not have been impressed, but very sceptical of what such ease might mean.

Yet Larisa Piyaseva, a Russian economist participating at the conference, added that with all the laws, «There has been not one step toward a real free market ... Gorbachev says he favors the coops, but he continues to support legislation that works against them [like 75% tax rates the moment they become profitable]. There is no independent wholesale market for retailers. And since the ruble is not convertible, retailers cannot buy on the world market» (47). No wonder Russians are sceptical (48). How to convince people that the new laws will be different? The best signal would be to let them act freely *now*, and so we arrive back at the remedy proposed in the previous discussions. The recommendations made here, as far as laws are considered, are therefore not in favor of «gradualism»: on the contrary, the movement toward laws enforcing property rights should be swift and made credible (49).

But Gorbachev did not intend to move toward the private property system, and, all the recent events and pronouncements suggest that many in the West have misinterpreted his goals. What he hoped to achieve was «economic efficiency» while still maintaining the large power of central institutions, without any major loss of the communist party's monopoly power in particular (50). The idea behind such a policy seemed to be that just as there totalitarian, centralized regimes in South Korea, Chile, Spain under Franco and others, which did better than the Soviet Union, why not try same and do it with a communist party at helm? The Soviet leaders did not take

---

(47) See ASMAN [2]. At the same conference, Gavriil Popov charged that the nomenklatura tried to turn private property over to themselves, an observation that reinforces Havel's strategy and the arguments developed in the previous section.

(48) On the language used in the Soviet Union, in general, MICKIEWICZ [29] notes that «commentary was mired in opaque bureaucratic language, causing the real events to dissappear into abstraction». In the West people said that the Eastern bloc was "crumbling". In the Soviet Union the same events were being described as victories of the process that Gorbachev set into motion. In the West the Eastern bloc was presented as abandoning communism, whereas in the Soviet Union as repairing the deformations of "socialism" and eliminating the command system. The fact that the leading role of the Communist Party, its monopoly power were canceled in these countries, were not announced, In the Soviet Union it was emphasized that the changes are "natural" and "logical", whereas in the West disorder and disintegration were the themes. Does this mean that the Soviet leaders never intended to abandon communism, or are the words used to disguise intentions?

(49) Other recommendations are, however, in favour of a gradual approach: see BRENNER [3], [5].

(50) See GOMULKA [14].

into account one difference between these countries and theirs: that centralized as such countries might have become, laws concerning property rights were not abolished, and state and ideology did not become confused — these are, in essence, the things that made communist regimes different from other forms of despotism (51). This did not make the other regimes more sympathetic, but they made transitions to a civil society easier.

The fact that promises are now being made in some of these countries — and the Soviet Union is not among them — to go in the direction of enforcing private property rights, eventually, does not mean that people can now safely assume that will indeed be the case. Even if today's politicians, be it Gorbachev, Havel or others now in power in the reforming countries, are viewed as honest, just and competent men, they are mortal. Their words and promises are important today, since there is little else to be guided by, but it should be clear that laws should not be written with them in mind, but with the fact that long-term expectations and the population's well-being are formed by looking at the *spirit* of the laws, and not at particular politicians' skills, honesty, and their ingenuity in using discretionary power (52).

In other words: one problem that these reforming countries will face, even if they had already their new laws and Charters of Rights, is that the spirit in which these laws will be interpreted is not known. They all have, and will have, «loopholes» in their constitutions permitting «exceptional» curtailment of individual rights. There is nothing special about this: the UK, the US, Canada, for example, have such loopholes too, and used them, though very infrequently. But it takes time until people learn how such discretionary power is used in countries where such powers were much abused in the past.

---

(51) See BRENNER [3] on this point. Also see MELLOAN [28].

(52) Bureaucrats may divert the process toward their own interest, distorting the new "legal" language. AGANBEGYAN [1], Mr Gorbachev chief economic adviser on economic matters, admits that they do not have a tradition of preparing formal, legal documents, and when recently a government commission on restructuring the management of enterprises was formed not one lawyer was among the participants. Governments officials continue to prepare such documents, and, AGANBEGYAN ([1], p. 203), added, they still «consider their own word to be law and not trouble themselves unduly with formulation». He recognized that this is why Russian laws are not thought through, are often changed, abound in contradictions, and can often be given many interpretations (thus maintaining the bureaucracy's hold on society).

Conclusions

When dealing with the problems facing the reforming communist countries, western economists should go back to the roots of their profession. The early economists, up to about 1870, wrote much less about the exchange of goods and services, than about the conditions necessary for the production of wealth. Among these conditions they emphasized the legal and institutional framework, the pillars being property and contract. Once the framework was accepted, one main question economists examined was whether or not new laws strengthened or weakened this framework, and another was the exchange of goods and services, neglecting the institutional questions which were assumend to be solved. But in the Soviet Union and other eastern bloc countries the issue concerning the appropriate institutional-legal framework is not solved, and it is not at all clear that without changing the principles and making the new ones credible, new laws going halfway toward the idea of «property» and «contract» can be expected to improve the situation. In the West the problem we try to solve is to maintain some institutions and the legal framework flexible enough to adjust to change, but make others inflexible enough so as to diminish the vulnerability of intertemporal transactions. What the Soviet Union and some of the Eastern European countries are missing is the backbone of the inflexible framework.

Making this transition from arbitrariness to laws suggesting permanence — from envy and distrust to credibility and ambition — is one of the major problems, if not the major one, that the reforming communist countries' leaders are facing. Trust and ambition are necessary for a system to work well: if the new leaders want their people to take business risks, to become entrepreneurial, to become innovative, to work hander (and what else than the appearance of such attitudes may eventually lead to the production of wealth), they must assure them that the rules of the game will now be stable; that people can trust their co-workers rather than suspect them of spying on them and of sabotaging their efforts; that they may come to realize that the odds are that achievement is due to talent rather than to being picked up for being a party member; that people are allowed to take chances and succeed or fail on their own merits, and that the resentment against achievement will not take the forms it took in the past. Simultaneously, they have to establish conditions in which there is a relatively firm answer to the question: When are the fruits of risk-taking legitimate and changes in social ranking consequent upon them deserved?

What distinguishes the reforming communist countries from the Western ones is not that in the latter envy has been eradicated — envy and resentment toward achievement are partners of competition too — but that reactions induced by these instincts have been channeled into «civilized» behavior which diminishes their harmful consequences.

Justice Holmes was right indeed when he said that «Taxes are what we pay for civilized society», although he did not mean by it the «tax» imposed by the rechanneling and mitigation of the losers' reactions, who are envious and more numerous. And yet it should be clear that it is the mitigation of such reactions, whatever the slogan used to disguise them, that we discuss in the West when we argue about taxation: we have to compensate some who, in the games of life, fell behind, providing them with second chances, but we want to do that without diminishing too much ambition's rewards. These are the conditions of a civil society, and it is this balancing act that statesmen in the reforming communist bloc too must look for.

BIBLIOGRAPHY

[1] AGANBEGYAN A.: *Inside Perestroika*, New York, Harper and Row, 1989.

[2] ASMAN D.: «Moscow Prepares for Its Own Boston Tea Party», *The Wall Street Journal*, 18 September 1990, p. A30.

[3] BRENNER R.: «The Long Road from Serfdom, and How to Shorten It», *Canadian Business Law Journal*, December 1990.

[4] — —: *Making Sense Out of Nonsense: Bad Science, Bad Policies and What to Do About Them*, manuscript, 1990.

[5] — —: «The Eastern Bloc: Legal Reform First, Monetary and Macroeconomic Policies Second», forthcoming in English and Spanish, in CLAASSEN E.M. (ed.): *Exchange Policies in Socialist Countries*, San Francisco e Panama, International Center for Economic Growth, February 1991.

[6] — —: *History- the Human Gamble*, Chicago, University of Chicago Press, 1983.

[7] — —: *Betting on Ideas: Wars, Invention, Inflation, 1985*, Chicago, University of Chicago Press, 1989.

[8] — —: *Rivalry: in Business, Science, among Nations, 1987*, Cambridge, Cambridge University Press, 1990.

[9] BRENNER R. - BRENNER G.A.: *Gambling and Speculation*, Cambridge, Cambridge University Press, 1990.

[10] CLINES F.X.: «From Moscow, a Plan to Junk Communism in 500 Days», *New York Times*, par. 4, 9 September 1990.

[11] DE JONG E.: «Statute on Handicraft-Artisan Trade», *Review of Socialist Law*, n. 4, 1976, pp. 266-7.

[12] DE MANDEVILLE B.: *The Fable of the Bees*, 1714, New York, Capricorn Books, 1962.

[13] FELDBRUGGE F.J.M.: «The Soviet Second Economy in a Political and Legal Perspective», in FEIGE E.L.: *The Underground Economy*, Cambridge, Cambridge University Press, 1989, pp. 297-339.

[14] GOMULKA S.: «Gorbachev's Economic Reforms in the Context of the Soviet Political System», in GOMULKA S. - YONG-CHOOL HA - CAE-ONE KIM (eds.): *Economic Reforms in the Socialist World*, Armonk (NY), Sharpe, 1989, pp. 59-78.

[15] GROSSMAN G.: «The Second Economy of the USSR», *Problems of Communism*, n. 5, 1977, pp. 25-40.

[16] — —: «The Second Economy: Boon or Bane for the Reform of the First Economy?», in GOMULKA S. - YONG-CHOOL HA - CAE-ONE KIM (eds.): *Economic Reforms in the Socialist World*, Armonk, (NY), Sharpe, 1989, pp. 79-96.

[17] HOSKING G.: *The Awakening of the Soviet Union*, London, Heinemann, 1990.

[18] JACOBY S.: *Wild Justice*, New York, Harper and Row, 1983.

[19] JOHNSON P.: *A History of the Modern World*, London, Weidenfeld and Nicholson, 1983.

[20] JONES A. - MOSKOFF W. (eds.): *Perestroika and Economy*, Armonk (NY), Sharpe, 1989.

[21] JOSEPH L.E.: «Prague's Spring into Capitalism», *New York Times Magazine*, part 2: «*The Business World*», December 2, 1990.

[22] KENNAN E.: «Muscovite Political Folkways», *Russian Review*, vol. 45, n. 2, April 1986, pp. 115-82.

[23] KISELEV D.: «New Forms of Entrepreneurship in the USSR», *Journal of Small Business Management*, vol. 28, n. 3, July 1990, pp. 76-80.

[24] LOS M.: *The Second Economy in Marxist States*, New York, St. Martin's, 1990.

[25] MALIA M. (signed under 'Z'): «To the Stalin Mausoleum», «Daedalus», 1990, pp. 295-344.

[26] ——: «The Soviet Union Is Dead: Thus Spoke "Z"», *The Herald Tribune*, September 1-2, 1990, p. 4.

[27] MASSIE R.K.: *Peter the Great*, New York, Ballantine Books, 1980.

[28] MELLOAN G.: «Private Property: Will Russia Permit It?», *The Wall Street Journal*, February 12, 1990, p. A15.

[29] MICKIEWICZ E.: «How Soviet TV Focuses Its Cameras on Eastern Europe», *New York Times*, December 31, 1989, p. H29 (also author of *Split Signals: Television and Politics in the Soviet Union*, Oxford, Oxford University Press).

[30] MIRONOV B.: «The Russian Peasant Commune After the Reforms of the 1860s», *Slavic Review*, vol. 44, 1985, pp. 438-67.

[31] O'HEARN D.: «The Customer Second Economy: Size and Effects», *Soviet Studies*, n. 2, 1980, pp. 218-34.

[32] SHMELEV N.: «Supporters and Opponents of Perestroika: the second Joint Soviet Economy Roundtable», *Soviet Economy*, vol. 4, October-December 1988.

[33] ——: «Economics and Common Sense», in JONES A. - MOSKOFF W. (eds.): *Perestroika and Economy*, Armonk (NY), Sharpe, 1989, pp. 267-77.

[34] SMITH H.: «The Russian Character», *New York Times Magazine*, October 28, 1990, p. 31.

[35] ——: *The New Russians*, New York, Random House, 1990.

[36] ZINOVIEV A.: *The Reality of Communism*, London, Victor Gollanz, 1984.

On the Economic Reforms in Eastern Europe: a Theoretical Viewpoint

Yves Balasko (*)
University of Geneva - University of Paris I

1. - Introduction

The market-oriented economic reforms in Eastern Europe tend to substitute what were basically centrally planned processes for the allocation of resources with a instantaneous highly decentralized market mechanism. Since the implementation of complete markets cannot be instantaneous, transition periods cannot be avoided and are likely to take time. The transition phase takes different forms depending on where and when the market mechanism and, more generally, competition are implemented.

A good deal of theoretical and applied work has already been pursued by the many economists involved in the design of these delicate transition processes. The scenarios that have resulted often coincide with common wisdom and follow more or less the following pattern: the pace of the transition to a competitive market economy is going to be voluntarily slow at the consumption level because of distributional issues would which make the competitive solution not socially acceptable given the current levels of resources; modernizing

(*) I am grateful for valuable discussions and encouragements from Giorgio Garau, Christian Ghiglino, Martino Lo Cascio, Jose Montano, Martine Orélio, Christophe Préchac, Gilbert Ritschard and Daniel Royer.

Advise: the numbers in square brackets refer to the Bibliography in the appendix.

the production sector and increasing the production of consumption goods get first order priorities while complex management rules are changed to profit maximization (this independently of the issue of privatization). Given the standards of living afforded by the market economies in the West, no one seems to doubt any more that the standards of living that will be reached once these reforms have successfully been implemented will be superior to those of the pre-reform period.

It is therefore very unfortunate that, in the meantime, the move towards a market economy may be threatened by the decrease in the overall well-being at the consumer level, a phenomenon currently observed in the Soviet Union for example. Shortages in many essential products have either popped up or dramatically increased. These shortages are not only felt at the consumption level but they also disorganize production by being random, which worsens the problem. As a result, the economy behaves so poorly that it seems to be on the brink of collapsing. There are now people who begin to regret the standard of living they used to endure before the political and economic reforms started. If this phenomenon develops, this will threaten the whole political and economic program of reforms.

In this paper, I address two issues pertaining to the common wisdom scenario. The first one is about the economic hardship that seems to be inevitably associated with the transition period. It is argued that the current shortages and the decrease in the overall well-being are not evidence that the current reforms are failing to reach their goals but, on the contrary, that they are, given the initial political and economic conditions, the necessary economic conse-quences of the successful political liberalization. As a consequence, the introduction of rationing on a grand scale is the only solution until production picks up and gradually enables supply to equal demand. The second issue relates with the fast implementation of competition at the production level. This means that there will be a huge demand for new investments and that funds will have to be found somewhere. This unavoidably raises the issue of financial markets. Implementing competition at the production level should be put on a par with the introduction of competitive financial markets. Competitive markets can operate efficiently only if they are complete in a theoretical sense to be recalled later on. If the role played by market incompleteness and restrictions to market participation has been understood only recently, it is, nevertheless, of the utmost importance. It turns out that if suitable financial markets do not exist, the economy is subject to inefficiency and to price volatility. These two consequences of market incompleteness are already undesirable in otherwise healthy economies. Their impact will be devastating on fragile economies. Completeness can be achieved if the variety of financial instruments is large enough and competition active. This means that banks, insurance companies, brokerage firms and pension funds must exist and operate on a competitive basis. This has two consequences. Since the size, the activity and, therefore, the efficiency of financial markets will depend on the extent of privatization, this provides us with a clue in the debate on how fast and how far privatization should go. In another direction, it must be observed that pension funds are usually the biggest players in financial markets in the West, a role that can be justified on theoretical grounds. Anyway, they greatly contribute to the efficiency of the financial markets. Therefore, the efficiency argument only is sufficient to suggest switching the currently state-funded retirement schemes to capitalization schemes that would be put in the hands of privatized pension funds for the sake and the benefits of competition. Combining these two remarks suggests that these impending pension funds should be major partners in the privatization game.

2. - From Efficiency to Rationing: the Success Story of Political Liberalization

2.1 *The Centrally-Planned Economy and the Fixprice Set-Up*

The main feature of centrally planned economies, the one that makes them most easily amenable to theoretical modelling, is the property that prices in these economies are administered, i.e., centrally regulated. By this it is meant fixed independently of (or at least without necessarily making explicit reference to) the adjustment of supply and demand. This makes such economies best described by fixprice models. Quite surprisingly, most of the fixprice models in the literature have been aimed at understanding unemployment in market economies with the avowed goal of putting Keynesian analysis on firmer grounds by providing it with some sorts of microeconomic foundations. This undertaking has been successful to the extent that prices can safely be regarded as fixed in a market economy, an issue that remains debatable. On the other hand, there is no problem of this sort when dealing with centrally planned economies. There is no question that prices are best described in such set-up by being fixed. Using the fixprice model as a proxy for centrally planned economies leads one to issues of a nature not encountered in the undertaking of proving proper microeconomic foundations to Keynesian macro-economics. These issues can broadly be organized around the following two themes: 1) the compatibility of the fixprice set-up with economic efficiency; 2) the quantity adjustment processes between supply and demand, i.e. the possible rationing schemes, if any, and their properties.

2.2 *Efficiency in the Fix-Price Set Up*

The issue of the economic efficiency of fixed price economies has often been debated. One should not forget that, for a time, the centrally-planned economies have achieved growth rates led many people to believe that these economies might outgrow some day the market economies and, therefore, be more efficient. This view has been supported by empirical studies. See, e.g. Whitesell [17] for a recent study that argues that (at least until recently) these countries were not far from efficiency given a stable technological environment. Other people have tended to regard the use of fixed prices for the sake of distributional justice as being a sin against efficiency by which they meant, I suppose, some vague concept of efficiency of the market mechanism where prices are determined by the equality of supply and demand, not the usual concept of Pareto efficiency used by the theorists. That observation on the lack of efficiency, would it be true, would easily explain the current inefficiencies of the fixprice economies of Eastern Europe.

This view is not only too simplistic, it is simply wrong. In fact, contrarily to some sort of pro-market oriented common knowledge, the fixprice set-up is not incompatible with Pareto efficiency. The concept of Budget-Constrained-Pareto-Efficient allocation (from now on the *BCPE* allocations) introduced in Balasko [2], and then studied by Keiding [12], Polterovich [13], [14] and Svenson [16] (see also Balasko [5]) is precisely aimed at describing efficient allocations that would be compatible with an exogenously given fixprice system and an exogenously given distribution of incomes. The research on BCPE allocations has shown that, for any arbitrary price-system and distribution of incomes (compatible with the total resources), there always exist (under standard assumptions) Pareto efficient allocations that are compatible with the given prices and incomes. This existence property proves that efficiency is not incompatible with fixed prices. Therefore, one cannot conclude from the only fact that prices are administered that the economy is necessarily going to be inefficient. But this raises the related issue of how to implement the BCPE allocations that are now known to exist. This role cannot be fully devoted to the price mechanism and, therefore, quantity adjustments of some sort have to be introduced.

2.3 - *The Convergence to Efficient Allocations in the Fixprice Set-Up*

By definition, if one is not at a Pareto optimum, this means that there exist allocations that make everyone better off. This implies that in an economy where there are no trade restrictions, the final allocation of resources is one where no one can be made better off through voluntary exchange. This is basically the meaning of the first welfare theorem of economic theory. In the fixprice set-up, voluntary exchange often means trade pursued at prices that are different from the fixed prices. Its effect is therefore to modify income distribution and some way of redistributing the gains associated with voluntary trade at unofficial prices must be considered if income distribution is to remain fixed. Assuming such processes exist is easy from a theoretical point of view. They are called "constrained" Pareto improving processes. The theory tells us that BCPE allocations are locally stable for the constrained Pareto improving processes: Balasko [3]. Not only does this define an algorithm that ends up at BCPE allocations but this also explains how, in an economic environment where prices are fixed, final allocations can be Pareto efficient.

The constrained Pareto improving processes are, from a theoretical point of view at least, a way of stabilizing a fixprice economy at a BCPE allocation. Can these processes be of any relevance for real economies? And how do they fit with the economic situation in Eastern Europe? The answer follows from a straightforward interpretation of these processes. Basically, Pareto improving processes are equivalent to voluntary trade. This can be interpreted as trade on (black) markets at prices that are not the official (administered) prices. Now such exchanges imply a redistribution of income because they are hardly compatible with a fixed distribution of income. This is where the "constrained" part of the constrained Pareto improving processes comes into play. According to the theory, the individual incomes or wealths have to be adjusted after black market transactions in order for the original distribution of income to be reestablished. The feasibility of such redistributing mechanism in real economies is debatable though there is a clear role for fiscal policy here. But it is plain that no sophisticated fiscal policies in Eastern Europe can be credited for such redistribution mechanism.

The solution is often found in another direction. Chasing profiteers and their illegal gains is a sport and a speciality of strong police States that turns out to be incompatible with individual freedom. There are degrees, however, in the level of police or state intervention. For example, the purpose of a fixed income distribution may be achieved if the money gains can be frozen in a way that makes them almost useless. It suffices that people are practically unable to buy consumption goods with the gains they make on the black markets. This certainly requires a form of State intervention that makes people wary of the ways they spend the money they have earned in more or less illegal ways. This also implies that quantity constraints of some sort must be part of the allocation process.

This solution is far from perfect. Besides taking some level of State intervention for granted, this approximation to constrained income distribution makes sense only to the extent that the amount of unspent incomes remains moderate compared to the allocated income. My point is that this kind of situation has been prevailing until recently in the Soviet Union and in some other countries. It follows from this discussion that "constrained Pareto-improving" processes in the fixprice set-up did have indeed a real world equivalent in Eastern Europe. This helps explain the relative efficiency of these economies under past totalitarian rule. This also raises the obvious questions: are the current inefficiencies only a consequence of political freedom and can a reversal to totalitarism bring back efficiency (of the sort illustrated by BCPE allocations)?

2.4 *The Current Situation: Inefficient Fixprice Equilibria*

The first question is easy to answer. The unleashing of political pressures materialized by the introduction of widely defined individual freedom has made totally obsolete the "constrained" part of the constrained Pareto improving processes described previously. This deprives them from the effect of stabilizing the economy at BCPE allocations. This means that, once the political reforms have been implemented, the only formulation that remains relevant is one of an economy with fixed prices, with a parallel free or black market and large amounts of cash reserves while the final allocations are fixprice equilibria that are not necessarily efficient. Anywise equilibrium in such models is characterized by the inequality of supply and demand that materializes through numerous visible shortages, a situation totally at variance with the case of BCPE allocations. Therefore, the answer to the first question is an unequivocal yes. The current shortages and disorganization of the economy are not only the direct consequences but also the best economic evidences that the implementation of individual freedom is working at last.

Therefore, and this is what the second question is about, some people might be tempted by a reversal to totalitarism for the sake of economic efficiency. This would be a dangerous fallacy if it is based on the idea that constrained Pareto improving processes would then bring back efficiency to the economy. It should be remembered that the implementation of these processes was based on the assumption that the effect of the unspent cash reserves could be neglected as a first approximation. This is true, for a given level of totalitarim, only up to some threshold value. The larger this value, the stronger State intervention and totalitarism have to be. These reserves have added up with time. Their huge build up (associated with unsatisfied demand) described by Soviet economists points to that direction.

Therefore, attempting to restore efficiency in the old ways would necessitate political oppression and State intervention of a form that, in order to match unsatisfied demand, will have to be far worse than what has been endured during the last two decades or so.

Incidentally, this line of reasoning leads one to wonder whether, in the case of the Soviet Union at least, a point where economic efficiency was becoming more and more difficult to sustain had not been reached with the build-up of these cash reserves a few years ago already. Then, according to this analysis, either the State had to become more and more totalitarian (for the sake of economic efficiency), or the way the economy is organized had to be changed. But *status-quo* could not be maintained in the long run. Choosing not to strenghten State intervention opened the way to political freedom. At variance with China where the economic reforms have preceded political liberalization, the timing in the Soviet Union has led to political freedom developing in a still centrally planned economy. This economy is not efficient anymore; but spurning political freedom would not bring back efficiency.

2.5 *The Necessity and Urgency of Rationing During the Transition to a Market Economy*

Rationing of one form or another cannot be avoided and in fact is urgently needed in the face of large disequilibria. The theoretical literature shows us that there exist rationing schemes that perform better, more efficiently, than others. For example, the papers by Drèze-Müller [10] and Balasko [4] describe rationing schemes which are relatively Pareto efficient. These schemes, based on coupon money, can even reach BCPE allocations within the fixprice set-up. But achieving the latter result would require, however, sophisticated redistribution schemes or fiscal policies, the feasibility of which is far from having been established yet. With less sophisticated or even without such fiscal policies, however, one would still get second-best Pareto efficiency using these rationing schemes based on coupon money. That outcome is definitely superior to what the old-fashioned quantity rationing schemes can achieve. But the urgency of the situation is such that time may be too short for the grand scale implementation of the former efficient rationing schemes.

Rationing is, given the current situation, better than just doing nothing even if this is achieved by way of "inefficient" quantity rationing schemes. In the Soviet Union, for example, shortages are pervasive. Their extent varies randomly. Making any serious forecast of where and when the shortages are going to develop is impossible. Already quite unpleasant at the consumption level, these shortages, by being highly unpredictable, disorganize production. This effects may be so devastating that production may never be able to catch up with the major disequilibria, making the goal of a complete market economy even more remote, if not hopeless. Signs of this reduction in the volume of production are already showing up. For example, GNP data clearly point to a reduction of production in the Soviet Union during the last year or so.

It may seem paradoxical that the transition to competitive markets may generate inefficiencies on the one hand and necessitate the implementation of rationing schemes on the other hand. The previous analyses help us understand why the transition period creates inefficiencies of its own, inefficiencies that are in no way evidence of failure of the reform process. Quite the contrary, the current inefficiencies illustrate how totalitarian the pre-reform period has been. Rationing is therefore a necessary feature of the transition period: it enables the economy to cope with the huge disequilibria which, as a consequence, will help reduce the length of the transition period.

3. - Financial Markets and Efficiency

3.1 *Markets for Contingent and Dated Commodities*

The standard approach to the comparison of competitive markets versus alternative forms of economic organization is based on the so-called welfare theorems and on the analysis of the relevance of these theorems for real-world economies. The first welfare theorem, the most interesting to us, simply states that every equilibrium or market allocation is efficient. This property can be established under one of the weakest set of assumptions one finds in economic theory. Basically, all that is required is: 1) competitive equilibrium exists (otherwise one could hardly discuss whether an equilibrium is efficient or not); 2) consumers are maximizing preferences subject to one budget constraint. The first assumption essentially amounts to having convex production sets or, equivalently but stated in less mathematical terms, to production being subject to constant or decreasing returns to scale. Violations of this assumption may of course have important consequences. But the consequences of increasing returns at the production level are rather well understood and well documented. For example, the argument in favor of the protection of infant industries (which usually display increasing returns) is standard. Therefore, there is no special need to develop this issue here.

It is the second assumption, namely the unique budget constraint, that really lies at the core of the efficiency of competitive equilibrium. To what extent can this assumption be taken as granted? In the discussion of the Arrow-Debreu general equilibrium model, one usually interprets commodities as dated and contingent to the states of nature. Considering then a unique budget constraint amounts to the assumption that every consumer is capable of transferring income or wealth across time periods and across state of nature. The problem is that such transfers require, in real world economies, contracts of a specific nature which fit into the broad category of financial instruments.

3.2 From Contingent and Dated Commodities
to the Definition of Financial Instruments
and the Equivalence with the Arrow-Debreu Model

A theoretical model that is more realistic than the standard Arrow-Debreu model in the description of the ways income can be transferred across time and states of nature has been proposed by Arrow [1], in a famous paper whose first version was published in 1953. In other words, were it not for the financial instruments, every economic agent would face as many dated budget constraints as there are time periods. The role of money and of the financial instruments is therefore to relax the liquidity or dated budget constraints. Arrow shows that, provided there is a complete set of financial instruments, his formulation is equivalent to the standard Arrow-Debreu model and therefore conveys the same implications in terms of economic efficiency at equilibrium.

The concept of a complete set of financial instruments can rigorously be defined only in the set-up of Arrow's model. This would take us far beyond the scope of this paper. The intuition of it, however, is quite simple and can be stated as follows: there are enough financial instruments (like stocks and bonds for example) to enable every consumer to buy (or sell) at every date a portfolio of financial instruments so that the various liquidity constraints are relaxed and merged into a unique global budget constraint. The analysis of the case of complete financial markets is straightforward because of the equivalence with the Arrow-Debreu formulation. The basic message that markets are efficient therefore remains unchanged.

Completeness of the set of financial instruments has been reduced to having consumers facing only one budget constraint. However, such reduction will not work if the financial markets are incomplete. Intuition confirms that, if there are too few financial instruments, or if these instruments are too similar in their characteristics, then consumers will not be able to design portfolios that can merge all liquidity constraints into a single budget constraint. Going back to the Arrow-Debreu formulation, having incomplete financial markets becomes equivalent to consumers facing multiple independent "budget con-

straints". For such models, the insight provided by the standard
Arrow-Debreu model with one budget constraint becomes misleading
because it does not extend to the case of multiple budget constraints.
Then, equilibrium allocations become indeterminate and, furthermore, they are not efficient anymore. (See, for example, the papers by
Balasko and Cass [7] and Geneakoplos and Mas-Colell [11]). The real
meaning of indeterminacy may seem somehow obscure at first sight.
This does not mean that indeterminacy is unimportant. It implies that
there is an infinite number of equilibria and that these equilibria
generate what mathematicians call a continuum. Therefore, equilibria
may widely fluctuate under random forces or shocks like those that
are continuously exerted on any economy. Unsurprisingly, this type of
unstability is closely related to, and actually implies, inefficiency. In
other words, what is most appealing in the market mechanism,
namely the efficiency of market allocations, simply vanishes whenever
financial markets fail from being complete.

Now it may happen that financial markets are complete but that
not all agents can have access to them. Using once again the
Arrow-Debreu formulation, this means that some consumers would
maximize their preferences subject to only one budget constraint
while other consumers, those who are denied access to some financial
markets, end up facing multiple budget constraints. These models
have led to the concept of sunspot equilibrium (Shell [15], Cass and
Shell [9]) in the uncertainty framework. The role of the extent of
restricting market participation on the properties of those equilibria is
described in Balasko, Cass and Shell [8]. The main lesson to be
learned from this literature is that restricting access to financial
markets of enough people (and there is no need for many people to be
restricted) lead to equilibria, the sunspot equilibria of Cass and Shell,
that are not efficient anymore. A similar analysis can be developed in
the intertemporal framework without uncertainty. The analysis then
relates market participation to business fluctuations, but the message
remains essentially the same: restricting market participation creates
new equilibria that are not efficient (Balasko [6]).

Economic theory teaches us that a necessary condition for
efficiency is the existence of a complete set of financial instruments
with full participation of every economic agent. Is this really feasible?

3.3 *Real World Implementation*
of Complete Financial Markets: Insurance Companies,
Banks, Pension Funds and Stock Markets

The implementation of financial markets proceeds through a number of financial institutions. For example the possibility of transferring income through states of nature is the essence of insurance contracts. These contracts are issued through insurance companies. Therefore, insurance companies can be expected to offer a variety of contracts that provides some form of approximation to markets for contingent commodities.

Now, experience shows that, even under the fiercest competition, insurance companies are not banks. Even if life insurance is often associated with some form of savings, it is usually not the role of insurance companies to lend money. And all savings are not made in the form of life insurance. This means that banks have a role of their own in lending and borrowing money. Now this activity, wheter it is the role of banks or of more specialized brokers, should not be limited to pure money but should include all known forms of financial instruments like bonds and stocks.

Financial markets could be limited to a few hardly competitive insurance companies, banks and brokers, the financial instruments being bonds and stocks issued by the various firms. This view of financial markets would miss the point because there would be no guarantee that the financial markets would then be complete. In order to be so, these markets must be highly competitive for the following reason. Completeness requires that there are enough financial instruments and the easiest way to achieve this result is through product competition that leads to maximum product differentiation. Now, this process works better with big markets than with small ones. Therefore, for the sake of maximal efficiency, financial markets should have the biggest size possible and the actors on these markets should behave competitively. There remains the issue of market participation. It is clear that there are categories of small consumers that are unlikely to directly operate on the stock exchange. There again, financial institutions like banks and insurance companies can play an important role by offering intermediary products accessible to small consumers. But the role of competition in ensuring full market (indirect) participation is even more important here than elsewhere. Last but not least one also finds in the role of ensuring (indirect) full market participation the pension funds. Their importance make them the biggest players on Wall Street. They should be part of any financial markets that would aim at unrestricted participation.

3.4 *The Economic Reforms and the Financial Markets*

The current pace of reforms in Eastern Europe rightly focuses on modernizing the production sector and on implementing market competition at the production level. It follows from the discussion on the importance of having complete financial markets with full participation that full-scale implementation should be considered at once.

This means that private banks and insurance companies should be allowed to participate in the economy. Stock exchange markets should be created. This also implies that privatization, a necessary condition for having a significant stock market, must be implemented. The speed of privatization and its priorities can be debated. But a clear goal stands out: creating a stock market of a size compatible with pure competition. The larger the market the better is the approximation to pure competition.

The crucial role played by pension funds in disseminating market participation illustrates, would this be necessary, their contribution to global efficiency. Therefore, despite the fact that retirement schemes are not provided through pension funds in Eastern Europe, this is clear indication that it is only time to switch systems and to implement retirement schemes based on capitalization. This requires creating appropriate pension funds from apparently nothing. It is therefore only fitting that a large part of the assets created through the privatization process be allocated to these pension funds. Not only would this imply a smoother transition to retirement schemes based on capitalization, but it would further solve most of the difficulties involved with privatization and the ownership of capital.

To sum up, a necessary condition for global market efficiency is to have the large competitive financial markets. My point is that the implementation of financial markets in Eastern Europe has to be pursued in conjunction with the modernization of the production sector. This necessary development makes sense only if competitive behavior of the financial institutions is warranted. The best insurance one can get is to resort to private ownership of the financial institutions.

4. - Conclusion

The two themes explored in this paper relate to very different issues. One issue is about a situation that is currently observed and that may threaten the reform process. The second issue deals with consequences of the incomplete implementation of competitive markets that cannot and therefore have not been observed yet. In both cases, however, the analysis suggests immediate and full scale action.

The first theme deals with the current situation that is characterized by a huge increase in the size of shortages. It has been argued in several places that these shortages are only temporary and that they will disappear thanks to the more or less gradual implementation of competitive markets. This type of analysis pertains more to common sense than to economic analysis. Though there is nothing fundamentally wrong with it, it is hardly satisfactory because it does not really explain the origin of the shortages and, most of all, why they have developed so suddenly. The current shortages are seen more as a temporary accident than the expression of deep-rooted disequilibria. By understating the importance of the shortage problem, this analysis induces people to believe that no long-run specific action is needed, the problem being only a matter of time, the time necessary for the market mechanism to take the place of the centrally planned system.

It follows from this paper that economies where prices are fixed always feature significant and durable shortages once there is enough individual freedom. The size of these shortages is such that they are likely to disrupt production on a permanent basis. Since it is only

through an increase of production that enough wealth will be created
to make market allocations socially acceptable, this implies that the
ultimate goal of a market economy will be severely delayed if no
action is taken to make production immune or at least the least
sensitive to shortages. There is no solution other than implementing
large-scale rationing.

The second theme developed in this paper focuses on an issue
that has been overlooked in most analyses of the economic reforms.
Recent developments in economic theory tell us that the incomplete
implementation of competitve markets may be far more harmful by
being inefficient than one had ever thought before. Financial markets
are the real world solution to the intertemporal and contingent
markets whose existence is posited in the welfare theorems that help
explain the efficiency of the market mechanism. Therefore, one can
hardly think of an efficient organization of the economy that would
bypass the introduction of financial markets. The practical importance
of having well-organized and flourishing financial markets in the
special set-up of Eastern Europe has quite unfortunately been somewhat neglected. It undoubtedly raises major political issues wherever
Marxism has remained a contender in the political game. Marxism
has tended not do be too friendly with the very idea of the market
itself of which the stock exchange is the epitome. But once the
political barriers to having a market economy have disappeared, the
logic is to get maximal efficiency from this form of organization of the
economy. This necessary condition of market efficiency can be satisfied anly through the full-scale implementation of financial markets on
the models of those of the United States or of Western Europe.

Finally and as a word of caution, it may be worth recalling that
markets and competition require some forms of regulation if one
wants to extract maximum efficiency. This means intervention of the
state. But, at variance with the centrally planned economies, state
intervention can in principle be achieved through and need nothing
more than the legal system whose role is to define the proper rules of
the game for market competition through regulation. Extremes in
deregulation have probably been reached in the United States lately.
Their troubled financial institutions illustrate what may happen without the proper legal frame. This applies to Eastern Europe: the

successful implementation of efficient financial markets will be a highly complex process that will require expertise that is not currently available in the East. The stakes, however, are so important that this reason is not sufficient to hinder the fast implementation of financial markets and of financial institutions.

BIBLIOGRAPHY

[1] ARROW K.J.: «The Role of Securities in the Optimal Allocation of Risk-Bearing», *Review of Economic Studies*, n. 31, 1964, pp. 91-6, French version: «Le Role des Valeurs Boursières Pour la Répartition la Meilleure des Risques», *Cahiers du Séminaire d'Econometrie*, n. 11, 1953, pp. 41-8.

[2] BALASKO Y.: «Budget Constrained Pareto Efficient Allocations», *Journal of Economic Theory*, n. 21, 1979, pp. 359-79.

[3] ——: «Equilibria and Efficiency in the Fixprice Setting», *Journal of Economic Theory*, n. 28, 1982, pp. 113-27.

[4] ——: «Budget Constrained Pareto Efficient Allocations: a Dynamic Story», *Journal of Economic Theory*, n. 27, 1982, pp. 239-42.

[5] ——: *Foundations of the Theory of General Equilibrium*, Boston, Academic Press, 1988.

[6] ——: *Economic Fluctuations as a Consequence of Restricted Participation in Financial Markets: a Finite, General Equilibrium, Viewpoint*, draft, University of Geneva, 1988, revised September 1989.

[7] BALASKO Y. - CASS D.: «The structure of Financial Equilibrium with Exogenous Yields: the Case of Incomplete Markets», *Econometrica*, n. 57, 1989, pp. 135-62.

[8] BALASKO Y. - CASS D. - SHELL K.: «Market Participation and Sunspot Equilibria», Department of Econometrics, University of Geneva, *Working Paper*, 1988.

[9] CASS D. - SHELL K.: «Do Sunspots Matter?», *Journal of Political Economy*, n. 91, 1983, pp. 193-227.

[10] DRÈZE J.H. - MULLER H.: «Optimality Properties of Rationing Schemes», *Journal of Economic Theory*, n. 23, 1980, pp. 131-49.

[11] GEANAKOPLOS J. - MAS-COLELL A.: «Real Indeterminacy with Financial Assets», *Journal of Economic Theory*, 1989.

[12] KEIDING H.: «Existence of Budget Constrained Pareto Efficient Allocations», *Journal of Economic Theory*, n. 24, 1981, pp. 393-7.

[13] POLTEROVICH V.M.: «Optimal Allocations of Commodities under Disequilibrium Prices» (in Russian), *Economic and Mathematical Economies*, n. 16, 1980, pp. 746-59.

[14] ——: «Equilibrated States and Optimal Allocations of Resources under Rigid Prices», *Journal of Mathematical Economies*, n. 19, 1990, pp. 255-68.

[15] SHELL K.: «Monnaie et Allocations Intertemporelles», CNRS, *Séminaire d'Econométrie*, 1977.

[16] SVENSSON L.G.: «The Existence of Budget Constrained Pareto-Efficient Allocations», *Journal of Economic Theory*, n. 32, 1984, pp. 346-50.

[17] WHITESELL R.S.: «Why Does the Soviet Economy Appear to be Allocatively Efficient?», *Soviet Studies*, vol. 42, n. 2, 1990, pp. 259-68.

No Free Lunch, No Free Market, No "One" East European Economy: Thoughts on the Transition to a Market Economy

Mario Baldassarri
Università "La Sapienza", Roma

1. - Introduction

After the fall of the Berlin wall, after the reunion of the two Germanies, after the democratization process of the former socialist countries of Central Europe, after perestroika and glasnost in the USSR, enthusiasm about free and pluralistic institutions and about a market economy has convinced eastern economies (and maybe western economies too) that this transition could occur at zero cost and could determine, even in the short run, a sudden jump in both individual and collective economic welfare.

The difficulties of the transition process are now weakening that enthusiasm. Nonetheless, we must remember that democracy and the market economy are a decisive strategic choice, and that the difficulties involved in the transition process must be realistically perceived. In the long run, eastern and western countries will face a positive non-zero-sum game, but in the short-to-medium term the "individual and collective costs" may be even higher than the immediately collectable benefits.

I am not an expert of socialist economies and so it is not that easy to me to appraise fully the problems of the transition. I will therefore limit my analysis to one or two basic concepts.

2. - Three Chimera

I will start my analysis with three arguments which, though well known and maybe banal, are always worthy of note: *a)* there is no "free lunch"; *b)* there is no "free market"; *c)* there is no "one" socialist economy of eastern Europe.

a) Any transformation process determines costs and benefits and, if the latter are higher than the former, it becomes necessary to allow for both the time frame (which is never the same for different transformation processes, and more often than not the burden of the costs is borne at the beginning and the benefits are collected later on) and the distribution among the components of society. Thus, there is no magical free lunch, and the situation cannot be considered the same across the board.

b) A formerly planned economy cannot be patterned after a model of a market competitive economy. In the world there is no "free market economy", no model of perfect competition as described in textbooks. Modern markets are characterized by oligopolies, internationalization, technological innovation, productive diversification, and different financial and managerial structures. Besides this microeconomic feature, macroeconomic aspect is to be considered: the public sector involvement in both demand and supply. For at least half century, these features have created differences in the public-sector/private-sector mix and in legislative and institutional organization. For example, one need look no farther than Sweden, the US, Italy, Germany, Japan, France, Labour-government England, Thatcherist England (1).

Small wonder, then, that in response to a progressive globalization of economic relations (the global village), institutional rules will have to be extended at first from a national to an all-European context

_____

(1) See PRODI B.: «In quale capitalismo c'è posto per l'Italia», *Il Mulino*, n. 1, 1991 and RONCHEY A., *I limiti del capitalismo*, Milano, Rizzoli, 1991.

and then worldwide. Certainly the Chernobyl crisis or the ozone layer simply show the "globalization of problems" and the need to globalize agreements and solutions. Another important example is the need for international antitrust laws.

Since there is no "one" free market economy, it is not possible to choose abstractly one of the several models of market economy. This is in fact the result of historical conflict of different istitutional orders, of political and economic leadership which, over decades, have created a sort of magma that characterizes modern market economies.

Therefore at the outset, the transition must rely on some basic rules common to any market economy; private capital accumulation, entrepreneurial freedom, financial markets, autonomous trade unions, definite limits and roles for public firms and more generally, limits to public intervention in the economy. Nonetheless, the other steps will have to ensue from experiments and not from a bad copy of other experiences different in time and space.

c) The old "iron curtain" has for a long time caused the "optical illusion" that a homogeneous area (from Berlin to Prague, from Budapest to Vladivostok) could well represent a homogeneous socialist economy. In practice the USSR has tried to make homogeneous and to exploit the different economic and productive realities of eastern European countries and this has left a heavy burden.

Although this attempt had, on political grounds, a good outcome, economically and socially it failed completely. Different histories and traditions, which had characterized the industrial development of countries like Czechoslovakia, Hungary and Gdr, relatively to the experiences of Romania, Bulgaria and of the heterogeneous Soviet republics, have been covered by the "ashes" of homogeneous regimes but maybe they have never stopped smouldering in them. As soon as the liberalization process set out, such cultural-historical and economic-productive differences exploded, creating problems which at a first glance may seem similar but which will assume peculiar features in each country.

This is the reason why there is no "one" economy for eastern Europe and maybe there will be neither "one" transition nor "one" solution.

3. - The "Missing" Resource: a Step Back in History

In my opinion there is a basic element which appears to occur in every national experience and which is becoming more and more relevant to the Western industrial democracies as well: I mean the limits and scarcities of "human" capital.

What characterized indeed the industrial development of Western countries was the fact that the downfall of ancient aristocratic oligarchies left room for the ascent of a large industrial and professional bourgeoisie, whose very existence refutes the hypothesis of the development of working classes (and lower classes) with "nothing to lose but their chains" in a collective revolt. The birth of this industrial bourgeoisie has been the driving force of development and welfare. However the progressive widening of its branches may prevent extreme processes of concentration, which could recreate the conditions of XVIII century aristocratic oligarchies for a new XXI century oligarchy.

This process marking the XX century's industrial development, widespread in vast areas and several continents since the last world war, has been virtually absent or "stillborn" in East European nations.

The Russia of the Tsars, in spite of the late attempt at industrialization by Alexander III, passed "in a matter of days" from an absolute aristocratic power to the proletarian revolution, to the absolute power of who appeared as the leader and the rescuer of the proletariat. And, instead of in the widespread industrial middle classes, the power was concentrated at first in a proletarian aristocracy of "leaders", then in the middle classes of party members and bureaucrats, aiming almost only at preserving their new powers and privileges. In the countries of Central Europe, however, the industrialization process had already taken flight in the first half of this century on the ground of unification of the Austro-Hungarian empire. Before the second world war a few countries, such as Czechoslovakia and Hungary, were already industrial economies with several sectors that were technologically very advanced. But the accession of communist regimes, and their definitive settlement sanctioned in Yalta, has stopped that process and has substituted the young industrial bourgeoisie with middle classes of party bureaucrats, twisting their productive/industrial complex which was driven, after the reconversion to the primary industry, to serve the strategy of collectivized planning led by the USSR.

As a matter of fact, in all East European countries, at least for the last three or four generations, people have no idea of a market operating firm, nor do they know what it means to be a manager, or what constitutes the healthy and functional striving of industrial relations, driven however by competition in production and markets. Neither grandfathers, nor fathers nor sons have had experiences as "entrepreneurs", nor unfortunately of personal freedom, in an institutional order which insisted on planning the very lives of individuals. And those great-grandfathers who remember another way of life will never be able to lead the transition. That is why, in my opinion, what is most important is to narrow the gap in terms of human capital. And human capital is a resource as crucial as it is expensive and difficult to accumulate.

4. - Equity, Development and "Public" Human Capital

I would now like to stress a key *economic* aspect: that is the need to implement during the transition a policy of stabilization. The latter must however be capable of enhancing the hope of more sustained and widespread economic development, i.e. the starting factors of the fall of the Wall. The true challenge is one of obtaining more equity along a common path of growth. The eastern regimes fell because of a weird and unacceptable concept of equity that, in a process of relative involution, has produced economies that are maybe more equitable but with the presence of poorer economic subjects overall and furthermore with the presence of a restricted *bourgeoisie d'état*. So what will become one of the core problems to be faced with boldness is an initial apparent loss of equity and of old certainties (job, wage, health benefits, free education, housing) that will be accepted only if the growth of the economy will be obtained relatively quickly and substantially. Actually, the lower standards of living associated with this period facilitate on the one hand huge waves of speculative accumulations of wealth, whether legal or illegal, and on the other enhance the temptation for a "new captain", that would quickly bring the ship in the safe and old harbour of state *dirigisme.*

It appears therefore clear that the lack of human capital does not refer exclusively to the entreprenerial and managing skills needed for the realization of a market economy but also to the capabilities of a political class able to implement the "new state" and to guide it over the difficult seas of the market economy.

It is my opinion that what we need is not only to drive the state out of the economy but also to build a "new and different state". The transition cannot be implemented by a complete liberalization that would lead to a chaotic mix of an extreme "old" and an infant "new". A Russian economist has recently told me: "we have been living for decades in the artificial conditions of a zoo and we cannot all of a sudden adapt ourselves to the market-jungle. We are born and we have lived in captivity and we are not capable of finding the food by ourselves".

Under this point of view one can understand, but not share, the temptation to accelerate and arrive first in the "west". This is a competitive race among the eastern countries maybe even towards the illusion of a western liberalism of the previous century or the simplistic indications of a monetarist neo-classical economic policy that not even Mr. Reagan or Mrs. Thatcher have been able or capable of implementing and that maybe only General Pinochet has been able to afford.

This temptation may certainly have solid roots. The eastern countries are characterized by repressed inflation that can explode towards hyperinflation. The accumulation of savings is due to a lack of supply of goods, not to the excess of income over the needs of consumption. It therefore hides a potentially huge amount of ex-penditure that new productions or imports may well stimulate up to explosive levels. Furthermore, updated industrial relations may end up in unbounded wage spiralling, until now repressed and governed by central planning authorities. It is therefore clear that a demand-push exists: if allowed to emerge before the productive capacity has been upgraded quantitatively and qualitatively it will inevitably create a crazy rise of prices. At that point one would need the only remaining instruments, the monetary ones, at the expense of halting the growth process and also of a heavy reduction of production and employment.

5. - An Economic Policy for the Transition

It is therefore my opinion that eastern European countries must control the demand but mainly act on the supply-side. For the latter I suggest two streams of action: one internal to the individual countries and another external.

The internal policy could take suggestions from the important historical experience of Italy of a state that shares the ownership of enterprises with the private sector. This can be done by taking those aspects that have contributed to the Italian post-war economic development and avoiding those negative aspects that have characterized the waste of resources and the inefficiencies of those last two decades. Where there is no market who do you sell the previous state-owned firms to? A public holding with a strategic goal of letting the firm "run" for the market can be useful as long as it is associated with a will towards the selling (also to big western enterprises) of chunks of the national industry.

The external policy pushes towards the creation of a free-trade area among eastern countries rather than the individual pursuit of entry in the EEC. This area would allow for a transition period with positive effects whether real, monetary or financial.

On the real side it can guarantee integration and specialization capable of improving the conditions of productivity and efficiency. By taking place among homogeneous countries it can be realized and constitute the benchmark for a successive and final catch-up with western Europe. Furthermore, seen from outside, this homogeneous area can represent a critical mass, a reference for the western firms that would be pushed to base themselves in the East. Because of their small dimensions and low levels of income, the existing single states may often represent a non-appealing site for the transfer of the advanced western technologies. Under those conditions one could see, rather than a process of integration, only a localization of production due to the low costs of labor which will however be constrained by the low level of productivity and doomed to end with a more or less rapid closing of the cost-differentials per unit of product.

On the financial and monetary side, one cannot question the necessity for the determination of a monetary unit "credible" on the international markets. It is however equally clear that the old single currencies cannot satisfy this requirement. On the other hand one cannot jump all of a sudden to the dollar, the yen, the mark or the ECU. An agreement on the exchange rate, first, and an Eastern Monetary Union could therefore be a useful instrument of transition: it would help the member countries to learn how to use the exchange rate, i.e. not as an administrative act, but as a true and proper instrument of economic policy that would guide them in entering the financial-monetary international system through a coordinated fluctuation also controlled towards the other big world-monetary blocs.

The old state has fallen apart but I believe that the transition towards the market economy requires not a state of economic anarchy but the construction of a new state, with defined and non-demagogic goals, effective instruments and steps, even slow ones, towards the market economy and democracy.

But this requires, in the East and in the West, that level of human capital able to guide firms and governments.

It is in this direction that Western Europe must bear some responsibility which, if managed with wisdom, will also prove to be a common historical chance of development.

For everyone the future requires, in relative terms, fewer raw materials and ever increasing amounts of grey matter.

Costs of Transition That Are Not Costs: On Non-Welfare-Reducing Output Fall

Jan Winiecki
Aalborg University

The steep fall of industrial output in Poland after January 1, 1990, and even steeper one in East Germany after July 1, 1990, as well as smaller declines elsewhere even before the beginning of transition programmes generated a lot of criticism. This criticism came from the not so numerous defenders of the communist order and more numerous believers in painless transition to the market.

Beside hand-wringing and complaints that the cost of transition was "too high" or even "unnecessary", output fall also created strong pressure for reflation. In Poland many demanded it as early as in January, after a few weeks of the beginning of "shock therapy". In the recent presidential election these demands played also an important role. Since East Germany became a part of a larger economic entity, these reflationary pressures were (fortunately) diluted there.

Everywhere, however, the fall of output became a source of serious concern. But are the criticism and concern justified? Is it true that the costs of transition are "too high" or that we could even shift to another economic system painlessly, without any cost whatsoever? And if there are some causes of concern what are their policy implications?

1. - The Real Economic Cost:
Output Fall Due to Macroeconomic Restraint

In order to begin answering the questions posed in the introduction we remind the audience what "big bang" or "shock therapy" or
any other stabilization cum liberalization programme is aiming at in
the case of post-Soviet-type economies (*post*-Stes for short) in transition to the market.

First of all, *post*-Stes always enter the transition period in the
state of a larger or smaller disequilibrium. Excess demand and
shortages are typical features of the Soviet-type economy (Ste for
short), well known from the literature on the subject. This disequilibrium need not approach the level of Polish hyperinflation of the
second half of 1989 or may even be manifested by lengthening queues
rather than open inflation (as in the USSR today) but whatever the
extent and form of disequilibrium, it is always there.

So are, larger or smaller forced savings.

Therefore, stabilisation measures envisage restrictive monetary
policy and reduction (ideally: elimination) of budget deficit. They are
expected to eliminate forced savings by wringing out excess money
supply from the economy.

The attention is usually focussed on forced savings but this focus
is not justified. After all, if stabilisation is coupled with liberalisation
(as it should!), the price rise that reveals "true" (at the start only
"truer") relative prices is going to wipe out forced savings anyway.

What really matters is not so much actual disequilibrium but
attitudes of economic agents shaped by 40 years (in the USSR 60
years) of the Soviet-type economy and accompanying excess demand,
shortages and the uncertainty of supply. Volumes were written on the
subject of excess demand of enterprises for everything: investment,
labour, material inputs under the conditions of "soft" budget constraint, that is lack of financial responsibility of enterprises for their
performance. Households, in spite of the fact that they did not enjoy
"soft" budget constraint, also adjusted somehow to the Ste reality and
made, whenever possible, precautionary purchases of consumer
goods (more about this below). It is the sharp break with the past in
terms of attitudes that is crucial for the success of the transition

programme. What macroeconomic restraint aims at is to impose such a break by drastically changing the supply/demand relationship.

After a few decades of persistent excess demand, shortages and supply uncertainty, the fall in demand caused by monetary squeeze and elimination or reduction of subsides is to discipline economic agents. For the first time in decades they will face the situation of being forced to look for purchasers of their products. In the past the reverse was the norm, as shown for example by sharply differing input-to-output inventories ratio in Stes and market economies (see, e.g. Winiecki [5](*)).

To complete the picture, macroeconomic, especially monetary restraint is expected also to reduce the pressure for wage increases, In the past any price increases exogenous to enterprises were compensated by wage increases and both passed on to customers. This gave rise to continuous inflationary pressures often increasing over time as accomodative macroeconomic policies continued. Macroeconomic squeeze makes it much harder to validate cost increases by price increases. Under the circumstances fall in demand makes credible the threat of bankruptcy which restrains wages.

It is the fall in demand resulting from macroeconomic restraint that — translated into fall in output — constitutes the real cost of transition to the market. That is economic cost because, as it will be shown later, there is also a social cost associated with the transition.

The policy of macroeconomic restraint is absolutely necessary. The belief that economic agents will change their behaviour to one that requires much more effort without (in the early phase) extra reward should be seen as a new variety of the perennial quest for "free lunch". In real life, possibilities of getting something — in this case a more efficient economic system — for nothing (without paying the adjustment price) are nonexistent.

The foregoing should not be construed to mean that output fall was caused in its entirety by macroeconomic restraint. Nor should all output fall be seen as a cost of transition. The present writer posits that output fall is inevitable at the start of the conversion from Soviet-type to market-type economy.

(*) *Advise:* the numbers in square brackets refer to the Bibliography in the appendix.

There are certain system-specific features that reduce demand once macroeconomic restrictions are introduced. Moreover, only a part of output fall may be seen as a cost of transition. Another part, maybe an even larger one, does not reduce the aggregate welfare of the population. The latter stems from two different sources.

2. - Output That Was Not

Let us with a simpler case of output that never was. In the literature in Stes, central planning, etc., an interested reader will find a lot of evaluation of the phenomenon called pripiski (write-ins). This Russian word describes higher reported output than that actually produced, done in order to obtain higher premiums and bonuses by enterprise managers and employees.

Beside this crude method of doctoring the reports sent from enterprises to their superiors in the planning hierarchy, there are more subtle ones that yield similar results, that is increase reported output relative to actual one. Among the most often used by enterprises are pseudo-innovations, i.e. production of goods only minimally (or not at all) better than standard goods in the same class but at disproportionately higher prices. Another are goods from lower quality inputs but at unchanged prices.

In a shortage economy both kinds of goods will eventually find their buyers. Both give at the same time the appearance of increased output value, while in fact it is only the prices that increased. This phenomenon is called hidden inflation in the literature on Stes.

These fictitious figures are aggregated as they move upwards from enterprises to higher levels of planning hierarchy and later appear as official statistics of economic growth, industrial output, etc. It is not surprising, then, that independent Western and more recently also Eastern estimates are always lower — sometimes much lower — than official figures published in Stes (see examples of unofficial estimates showing real growth to be at times as little as one fifth of official growth figures in Winiecki [6]).

If, for example, Soviet economic growth was in the 1980s at below one per cent level annually (Khanin, 1989) and official figures ranged between 3.5-4% per annum, then an overwhelmingly large part of economic growth was paper growth only. But the Soviet Union is a long way off the transition to the market. Therefore another example will refer to an economy in transition.

East German communists published every year figures showing annual growth of national product (more precisely: net material product according to Mps classification) within the 4-4.5% range. And those were figures for a country with a long stagnant economy, high foreign debt, real wages falling already since the early 1970s, etc. These figures were obviously fictitious (although often taken seriously by many, including "expert" Sovietologists). The GDR's growth was most probably not higher than that of the Soviet Union — that is near zero. The remainder, approaching 100%, was again paper growth.

Now with the monetary union and disappearance of a border between the Eastern and Western parts of Germany something important happened also with respect to statistics. East German enterprises realised the difference between being paid by what they report to their superiors and by what they sell. The incentives to cheat disappeared, and with them paper output growth.

But this was a purely statistical fall of output that changed nothing: after all that part of output did not exist earlier in any case. The level of welfare of the population did not change in the aggregate. Life — in contrast with statistics — went on as if nothing happened. And in reality it did not.

3. - Output That Was But Should Not

Now, I suggest shifting attention from output that was not to output that was but should not. In any Ste there exists a part of output produced by such economy that simply would not have existed in a less wasteful economic system. This output, although it contributes to the economic growth of every Ste does not contribute to economic welfare. Some examples may help to better capture the nature of this unique non-welfare-increasing output.

From time to time in the 1980s Polish official press wrote scandalising stories about the Warsaw car factory (FSO) that brought some car parts from a supplier in Szczecin (about 500 km) by helicopters. There was — in the system as it then existed — an obvious incentive to engage in such a shocking waste. On the one hand output plan figures were most important for enterprises managers (whose bonuses and goodwill of their superiors depended on fulfilling output plan), on the other enterprises enjoyed the so-called "soft" budget constraint, that is their superiors generously helped subordinated enterprises that exceeded costs (Kornai [2]).

Shipping car parts by helicopters was unusual even for a Soviet-type-economy. Therefrom stemmed the attention of the official press. However, the dispatching of enterprise trucks or vans to snatch small quantities of subassemblies, parts and components not delivered on time by unreliable suppliers has been a way of life in all Stes. In the Ste world, where uncertainty reigned supreme and the costs of plan fulfillment did not matter, every enterprise tried to keep as large a fleet of lorries, trucks, vans and pick-ups as possible to cope with all the contingencies of that sort.

Now, with the fundamental realignment of supply/demand relationship under the impact of restrictive macroeconomic policies, i.e. falling demand, it is suppliers who begin to look for customers — not the over way round as before. Under such circumstances suppliers, however reluctantly, become more disciplined and input deliveries become less of a problem.

One of the most important outcomes of changed attitudes is a marked fall in the state enterprise sector's demand for transport equipment. This is what happened, e.g., in Poland, where domestic output of that equipment fell in the first quarter of 1990 by 34.8%. In fact, state enterprises adjust even faster by selling transport equipment they acquired earlier: at the end of the third quarter of 1990 the private enterprise sector owned already 60% of all transport equipment.

Another examples are buses. Under the Ste regime with its excess demand for everything, enterprises used buses to bring labour from distant small towns and villages. As fall in demand for output reduced demand for labour as well, enterprises sharply reduced their demand for buses. The outcome: fall in output in the first quarter of 1990 by 54.9%

In the normally performing economy, a fall in domestic demand is usually partly or fully compensated by increased exports. But Stes have been far from normal. Their products are quite often unsaleable on the world market or are saleable there at a heavy discount. Therefore a fall in output in many cases is unavoidable in the short run. This applies to both our examples as well.

Capital goods are not a category for which a wasteful economic system generates artificial demand. Ste enterprises are noted for their extremely high inventories of inputs (Kornai [3], and Winiecki [5] for data). To insure themselves against possible non-fulfillment of planned output targets, enterprises tried to maintain as large and wide a range of input as they could get (again, regardless of cost due to "soft" budget constraint).

With the changed supply/demand relationship after the introduction of macroeconomic restraint, enterprises begin to adjust their inventory-to-output ratios downard. An outcome is a temporarily lower demand for their inputs. And again, before input suppliers find other customers domestically or abroad output of these inputs is expected to fall in the short run.

This is what happened in Poland, where inventories of industrial enterprises fell in the first quarter by 7.8% in real terms, that is by almost 30% on annual basis. This attitude change may be compared with the behaviour of the same enterprises in 1989, where they increased inventories by over 20% (also in real terms) in spite of the fall in industrial output of 3%.

Not only producers' behaviour has been affected by the wasteful system but also that of consumers. This has happened in spite of the fact that households do not enjoy "soft" budget constraint *à la* Ste enterprises. Nonetheless decades of shortages forced households to make "precautionary" purchases. Food products are the best example. Households in Stes make larger purchases of food products than their current needs because they do not know when they will be able to buy the next batch. A lot of that food gets spoiled afterwards in the households' refrigerators. Therefore, as this author stressed elsewhere (Winiecki [4] and Winiecki [6]), 67 kg of meat allegedly consumed by the average Pole or 59 kg by a statistical Russian amount to much less than the 67 kg consumed by a Greek or 57 kg by a Finn. The supply/demand realignment changed very quickly the pattern of food purchases. With the disappearance of shortages, overly large "precautionary" purchases all but disappeared. Let it be noted that the low quality of Polish (and other East European) processed food products makes them by and large unsaleable on the world market. Thus, the possibility of compensating the fall in domestic demand by sales abroad has been very limited, too.

4. - Some Consequences of Shift to More Efficient Economic System

What has been most interesting in the phenomena analysed in the preceding two paragraphs, is the fact that the output fall which occurred in the case of all categories of goods (capital, intermediate and consumer goods) took place without reducing the aggregate welfare of the household sector. Enterprises are using less input (both capital and intermediate) per unit of output under the more efficient market system.

Households, too, are using less input per unit of consumpion. Buying, say, less meat by the amount that used to get spoiled in the past does not affect real consumption, although it obviously affects statistical consumption. This reasoning finds an indirect support in households surveys. Although the Polish food industry's output fell by 30-40% in the first few months of 1990, a survey of households' budgets revealed the fall of consumption in all basic categories of food products by 11%. Part of the difference might have come from households' attempts to maintain the level of food consumption by cutting purchases of non-food products and services in the face of falling real incomes but undoubtedly part of the difference stems from the adjustment of households to the reduction or elimination of food shortages.

Now, if the short-run downward adjustment of demand resulting from a shift to a more efficient system is not reducing welfare, then why there is so-much hand wringing? Part of it is ignorance. A kind of heritage of real socialism's fascination with output figures, no matter how fictitious.

But there is another part of the explanation that is associated with the uneven distribution of income losses due to the adjustment in question. Everybody gained from the lower use of inputs per unit of consumption (plus from eliminating the disutility of queueing). But these gains are dispersed, while income losses are concentrated. They are paid to a much greater extent by those made redundant than by those earning somewhat less but remaining employed.

The foregoing means that short-run quantity adjustment is to a large extent a social problem to be alleviated by social policy measures, as well as by judiciously applied employment policy measures (skills' upgrading or skills' changing measures). This should not be confused with macroeconomic reflationary measures demanded insistently from various quarters in Poland.

Furthermore, the non-recoverable nature of the lost output should be stressed in this context. Once the economy has shifted to the market system (however imperfect at the beginning), enterprises will not by more lorries, trucks, vans, buses, or will not increase their inventories bought for "precautionary" reasons. Nor will households revert again to similarly "precautionary" purchases once shortages have disappeared.

To the extent that reflation is aimed at recovering the output level without changing in any way output structure, that is without responding to new domestic and foreign demands, macroeconomic reflation may be not only useless for the reasons explained in the preceding paragraph but highly inflationary. Support for existing firms trying to do what they did in the past will only be reflected in higher prices undermining a degree of discipline that has been imposed upon enterprises by the market as a result of the changed supply/demand relationship.

BIBLIOGRAPHY

[1] BLACKWELL SELUNIN V. - KHANIN G.: «Lukavaya Tsifra», *Novy Mir*, n. 2, 1987.

[2] KORNAI J.: «Resource-Constrained vs. Demand-Constrained Systems», *Econometrica*, vol. 47, n. 4, 1979.

[3] ——: *Growth, Shortage and Efficiency*, 1982.

[4] WINIECKI E.D. - WINIECKI J.: «Quality Differences in America-Soviet Consumption Comparisons», Washington (DC), American Institute for Public Policy Research, A paper prepared for the Conference on *Comparing the Soviet and American Economies*, mimeo, 19-22 April 1990.

[5] ——: «Distorted Macroeconomics of Central Planning», Banca nazionale del lavoro, *Quarterly Review*, n. 157, 1986.

[6] ——: «How It All Began: Sources of the Recent Breakdown of the Soviet Economic System», *Ekonimsk Debatt*, in Swedish, October 1990.

Liberalizing Foreign Trade
in a Socialist Economy:
The Problem of Negative Value-Added

Ronald I. McKinnon (1)
Stanford University

In their remarkably swift adoption of free trade with full current account convertibility in 1990, both East Germany and Poland experienced rapid industrial decline: the collapse — or threatened bankruptcy — in an astonishing wide variety of manufacturing and agricultural industries that turned our *expost facto* not do be internationally competitive. Are there constraints on how fast currency convertibility, and free arbitrage between domestic and foreign markets for goods and services, is best achieved in a liberalizing socialist economy?

At first glance, the great difficulty of East Germany and Poland in expanding (new) export activities as import substitution industries contract seems to refute the Ricardian law of comparative advantage. Whether under free trade or economic autarky, the Ricardian model of comparative advantage assumed that all goods are, or can be, produced according to predetermined production technologies from basic labor. Even if average labor productivity was low, therefore, conventional textbook wisdom had it that the comparative efficiency

(1) This paper was not presented at the International Economic Conference *Building the New Europe*. It is a shortened, adapted version of Chapter 12 in the author's forthcoming book *The Order of Economic Liberalization; Financial Control in the Transition to a Market Economy* to be published by the Johns Hopkins Press in July of 1991. I would like to thank John Hussman, David Robinson, John Williamson and Michael Treadway for their help in preparing this paper.

of at least some major domestic industries soon would assert itself if the real wage could be set sufficiently low, i.e. the real exchange rate was sufficiently devalued. And some reasoning such as this lay behind the willingnbess of the Polish and German policy makers to move so quickly towards unrestricted foreign trade.

Alternatively, this paper considers the circular flow of production in a "typical" socialist economy. Goods are produced from intermediate products such as energy and other material inputs as well as from labor and capital, and there are substantial substitution possibilities for combining them. In this substitution model, technological capabilities — including labor productivies — are conditioned by the pre-existing structure of protection before liberalization occurs. By taking this *implicit* protection in the traditional Stalinist economy properly into account, I will *(i)* show that, no matter how the exchange rate is set, most manufacturing and food processing industries need not be viable under free trade at pre-existing combinations of factor inputs: in the short run they might well exhibit negative valued added at world market prices; and *(ii)* propose a more gradual program of trade liberalization based on temporary tariff protection and the repricing of material inputs so as to winnow out those industries that cound not survive in the long run under free trade from those that could (2).

1. - Implicit Protection
in the Traditional Stalinist Economy

In the traditional Stalinist economy for which the Soviet Union will be our leading prototype, virtually all domestic production of

---

(2) Behind the scenes in this paper is the presumption that the liberalizing socialist economy has strong domestic fiscal and credit controls in place that prevent enterprises from overbidding for scarce resources. Thus, the national government need not resort to blocking the cash balance positions of enterprises, i.e. to "commodity inconvertibility" WILLIAMSON JOHN [15], in order to prevent domestic inflation. To avoid this syndrome of commodity inconvertibility, however, the whole structure of domestic taxation and money and credit may have to be reformed at the outset of the liberalization see (MCKINNON [6] e [7]. Here, I simply assume that liberalization has proceeded to the point where enterprise money can be spent freely for domestic purpose.

more or less "finished goods" — those sold directly to consumers or sold back to industry as plant and equipment — was insulated from foreign competition. Because the ruble was inconvertible into foreign exchange on current account, protection for domestic manufacturers — including processed agricultural goods — was absolute: the State trading agency refused to authorize competing imports unless there were pronounced domestic shortages of similar produts.

Although there were no formal tariffs or quota restrictions in any legal codes, the *implicit* rate of protection was very high as if quantitative restrictions had eliminated competitive pressure from abroad. At some "equilibrium" exchange rate (to be discussed below), domestic prices for finished goods — after discounting for their normally poorer quality in the protected setting — were typically higher than their foreign counterparts. Thus, in its general repercussions on economy-wide resource allocation, this price wedge is similar to the effect of a high tariff on the importation of competing finished goods.

At the same time, exports of energy, raw materials, and limited amounts of manufactures (largely militar equipment in the Soviet case) were largely determined centrally by "a vent-for-surplus" doctrine. That is, after domestic "needs" for, say energy, at low domestic prices had been more or less satisfied, the residual (quite a large residual in the Soviet case) was then sold abroad at much higher world market prices. The effect was similar to imposing an export tax on, say, energy that drives the domestic price below that paid by foreign buyers. Energy in all forms — together with non-food raw materials which were similarly "taxed" — amounted to over 60% of Soviet exports in 1989, and over 75% if one omits "protected" military sales from the export base.

In order to approximate how these relative prices in the Stalinist economy differ from those prevailing in the world economy, therefore, let us partition the tradable goods produced and consumed into two categories: *finished goods*, which are largely manufactures and processed foodstuffs; and *material inputs*, which are largely energy products and non-food raw materials.

For modelling purposes, assume that all finished goods are largely import substitutes or imports and are not exported; whereas material inputs are either exported or used up in the domestic manufacture of finished goods. Reinterpreting the notatation and methodology of Tan [13] (3), denote the gross output of finished goods industry i by Z_i, where the corresponding production is:

(1) $Z_i = Z_i (L_1, L_2, \ldots, L_m; M_1, M_2, \ldots M_r)$

GRAPH. 1

VALUE ADDED AND PROTECTION
IN FINISHED GOODS

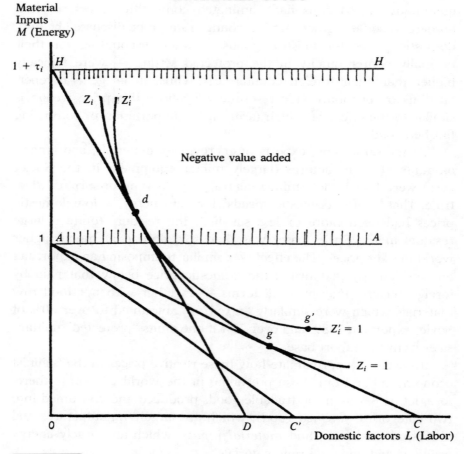

The L_i's refer to the primary factors such as labor or land, and then M_a's are intermediate material inputs. In considering the production choices facing industry i (Graph 1), however, let us dispense with all but one intermediate input, M, and one domestic factor L. We can then denote value-added in domestic prices of finished goods industry i as:

$$(2) \qquad\qquad V_i = P_i Z_i - P_m M$$

where P_i and P_m are the domestic currency prices of the finished product and material imput respectively. The value added by the domestic factor *(s)* is simply gross value minus the cost of intermediate inputs, and the normal presumption is that value added at domestic prices is positive (4). But what determines the relative prices of Z_i and M in domestic commodity markets, and how is that linked to domestic factor costs?

2. - The Coefficient of Protection for Finished Goods

Consider relative commodity prices first, presuming that one unit of the domestic currency exchanges for one foreign. Because we are dealing with an economy that is a small part of the world economy, foreign currency prices — denoted with asterisks — are fixed. Let t_i represent the *implicit* tariff protecting domestic production of the finished product — the gap between the foreign and quality — adjusted domestic price — such that:

$$(3) \qquad\qquad P_i = (i + t_i) P^*_i$$

intermediate inputs entered duty free. For our analysis of the Soviet Union, I treat the taxed export good as the relevant intermediate product. However, for the smaller Eastern European economies where material inputs are imported, one might want to introduce an untaxed importable as a third commodity in the analytical model — as per MCKINNON [10].

(4) In any market economy, value added being positive at domestic prices is a necessary condition — although by no means sufficient to assure profitability — for the firm to exist. In a socialist economy, in extreme cases one could imagine a degree of public subsidy that enabled an enterprise to keep going even when it was not covering the costs of its material inputs. But I am ruling out this unlikely possibility.

and let t_m represent the similarly calculated implicit export tax on material inputs such that:

$$(4) \qquad\qquad P_m (1 + t_m) = P_m^*$$

In order to see the divergence between domestic relative prices and their foreign counterparts, divide *(3)* by *(4)* and rearrange to get:

$$(5) \qquad\qquad P_i/P_m = (1 + t_i)(1 + t_m)(P_i^*/P_m^*)$$

(5) captures the dual aspect of the overall protection to the gross output of finished goods: the effect of restricting competing imports and of subsidizing the use of material inputs. Indeed, from Lerner's *Symmetry Theorem* (Lerner [4]), we know that restricting imports or taxing exports have "equivalent" protective effects in long-run equilibrium — as worked out more fully in the presence of intermediate products by McKinnon [10]. For industry *i*, we thus define the overall "coefficient of protection" to be:

$$(6) \qquad\qquad 1 + \tau_i = (1 + t_i)(1 + t_m)$$

On the vertical of Graph 1, the coefficient of protection shows the domestic relative price of finished goods in terms of material inputs. To better interpret Graph 1, however, let us first consider domestic value added at world prices

$$(7) \qquad\qquad V_i^* = P_i^* Z_i - P_m^* M$$

From *(5)*, we can rewrite V_i^* in terms of domestic prices to get

$$(8) \qquad V_i^* = [P_i Z_i - (1 + t_m)(1 + t_i) P_m M]/[(1 + t_i)]$$

Although we presume V_i remains positive, there can be no presumption that domestic value added at world prices is positive. Indeed, if either t_m ot t_i are sufficiently high, and if the relatively cheap M is substituted for other factors of production, equation *(8)* tells us that $V_i^* < 0$

These relationships are depicted in Graph 1, which is a modified version of that used by Tan [13]. For a "typical" finished goods industry i (which is one of many), the unit isoquants Z_i and Z_i' portray alternative possibilities for substituting the tradable material input for the domestic factor of production in the long run, i.e., not taking transitional adjustment costs into account. The distance OA on the vertical axis represent the material inputs which are equivalent to one unit of finished goods at world prices. For example, at the hypothetical free trade equilibrium at point g, where the new budget line AC (whose slope now relects the relatively higher world cost of energy in terms of labor) is tangent to the unit isoquant Z_i, one unit of final output could buy OA in material inputs.

Going one step further, we can scale our measure of output in Graph 1 so that one unit of the finished good is worth just one dollar of foreign exchange: the unit isoquants Z_i or Z_i' denote just one dollar's worth of finished good i. Similarly, we can scale our measure of material inputs on the vertical axis so the one unit of, say, energy is worth just one dollar: the distance OA in Graph 1 is one.

Then, under the preexisting system of implicit protection and using this scaling, equation *(5)* tells us that the *domestic* relative price of the final output in terms of material inputs — the distance OH in Graph 1 — is simply our coefficient of protection $1 + \tau_i$. The higher domestic price of finished goods compared to that prevailing on world markets (and compared to the price of material inputs) reflects both the implicit export tax on material inputs and the implicit tariff on competing imports.

3. - The Overuse of Material Inputs and the Shoddy Product Syndrome

Under protected domestic prices, all feasible input combinations — feasible in the sense of domestic value added being positive in the production of one unit of finished goods — must lie below the horizontal line *HH* in Graph 1. Below *HH*, the domestic value of finished goods output exceeds the domestic cost of the material inputs used in their production.

At world relative prices, on the other hand, all feasible input combinations must lie below *AA* if domestic value added is to be positive. Indeed, all production points in the shaded area lying above *AA* in Graph 1 show negative value added at world prices. For example, the point *d* is profitable under the existing mantle of protection: the budget line *HD* (whose slope shows relatively cheap energy and expensive labor) is just tangent to the unit isoquant Z_i (or its alternative Z_i'). Nevertheless, *d* shows negative value added if the final output had to be sold, and material inputs had to be purchased, in unrestricted world markets.

Why is this phenomenon of negative value added at world prices probably commonplace in Soviet (and Eastern Europe) industry?

First, as drawn in Graph 1, the relative prices of energy and other material inputs to most sectors of the Soviet economy have been kept very low — causing them to be used intensively. In addition, the old Stalinist system of rewarding managers by whether they (over) fulfill gross output targets encourages them to waste material inputs. «According to the calculations of the Soviet Institute of World Economy and International Relations, we use 1.5 times more materials and 2.1 times more energy per unit of national income than the United States ... Our agricultural production is 15% less than the United States but we use 3.5 times more energy» (Shmelev and Popov [12], p. 128).

Second, the Stalinist planning system based on gross output targets tends to produce manufactured or processed outputs of uncertain quality. «The quality of Soviet produce appears to have been declining steadily since the 1960s, as a result of permanent excess demand, regardless of technical progress» (Asland [2], p. 76). For example, take a common household product like detergent that is introduced at a certain benchmark standard. The (protected) domestic producer will have continual incentive to degrade product quality if, by so doing, more units can be produced. After complaints roll in, the enterprise might get permission to introduce a new and "improved" benchmark detergent at a higher price and for which it gets more weight in its gross output target (5). Then the slippage in quality begins all over again. For short, I will call this process the shoddy product syndrome.

In Graph 1, the shoddy product syndrome affects the position of the unit isoquant because material inputs at world prices — or, equivalently, units of foreign exchange — is the numeraire by which final output is measured. The shoddier the product or more uncertain the product quality, the further to the northeast will be the unit isoquant, say at Z'_i rather than Z_i. In the sudden German trade liberalization of 1990, for example, the adverse signalling from simply knowing that a good had been produced in East Germany was sufficient to induce East German consumers to reject it in favor of higher-priced West German goods, thus increasing the distress in East German industry.

In a sudden move to free trade at any exchange rate, therefore, a finished goods industry chosen at random would likely show negative cash flows under the (pre)existing combination of factor inputs and low valuation of the finished product in world markets. A devaluation, coinciding with the (hypothetical) move to free trade, would simply raise material input prices in tandem with the prices of shoddy finished goods. In the short run before input combinations and product quality could be adjusted, negative value added would persist. Because manufacturing absorbs a much higher proportion of the labor force in the Soviet Union than in the United States (Shmelev and Popov [12]), a wholesale industrial collapse would be intolerable.

4. - The Adjustment Problem

In "long-run" free-trade equilibrium, however, could industry i, as depicted in the substitution model of Graph 1, be viable? Suppose our

---

(5) This absence of a market test for valuing final outputs is one important reason why the growth in Soviet GNP may have been significantly overstated in the postwar period. Continual decline in product quality did not reduce measured GNP, while the continual introduction of "new and improved" products was allowed to increase it.

putative reformers observe the "protected" starting point d, a combination of output and inputs with negative (or very low) value added at world market prices. Yet they do not know whether industry i (and similar finished goods industries) would be sufficiently productive, and capable of ultimately shifting away from its current heavy dependence on material inputs while improving product quality, to become profitable under free trade. In the long run, whether industry i was on an "efficient" unit isoquant such as Z_i running through the point d, or on an "inefficient" unit isoquant such as Z_i' also running through the point d is uncertain. In the former case, output at world prices would ultimately be sustainable at the point g. In the latter case, the best industry i could manage in the long run after energy became more expensive was a production point like g': the value of gross output at g' remains less than the local cost of production.

Notice that the long-run viability of the industry i depends not only of its production efficiency, i.e., whether it is on the unit isoquant Z_i or Z_i', but also on the prevailing costs of the domestic factors of production after a new free-trade equilibrium is established. Suppose labor is the principal domestic factor of production. Then the budget line AC shows the real wage (in terms of material inputs) to be sufficiently low under free trade so that the point g tangent to Z_i profitable. However, if the equilibrium real wage is higher, so that AC' is now the relevant budget for producing one unit of the finished good, then industry i will not be profitable under free trade. AC' lies to the left and below Z_i. The real wage in long-term equilibrium facing any particular industry i will be the outcome of a complex macroeconomic interaction as all industries liberalize simultaneously.

Given this fundamental uncertainty about substitution in production, product quality, and equilibrium real factor costs when all industries are finally liberalized in the long run, could the reformers devise a system of *interim* protection at "correct" relative input prices that: 1) initially sustains the profitability of most existing production of manufactures and processed goods; and 2) when systematically reduced over the next several years, allows market mechanisms to phase out inefficient finished goods industries while encouraging "learning by doing" in others so that they eventually thrive under free trade.

5. - From Implicit to Explicit-Tariff Protection:
The Case of Chile

The trade liberalization in Chile after 1973 was perhaps the most comprehensive and draconian (before the Polish and East German experiences in 1990) of modern times, see Edwards and Edwards [3] for putting the remarkable empirical details into a solid analitical perspective. Chile's tariff and foreign exchange policies provide useful clues of what to do, or what not to do, in a similarly comprehensive trade liberalization program in a socialist economy like the Soviet Union's.

In 1973, Chile had some very high formal tariffs protecting finished goods, averaging over 90% with some, improbably, going as high as 500%, as shown in Table 1. However, these numbers conceal the fact that much protection in Chile in 1973 was from non-tariff barriers. Quota restrictions or absolute prohibitions on imports of finished goods were commonplace, along with restrictions on the export of food and industrial raw materials. In addition, the government refused to allocate foreign exchange for imports that didn't suit its immediate social objectives, and set multiple exchange rates across different categories of imports and exports so that many tariff rates themselves had become rather meaningless.

Therefore, the first order of business in the Chilean liberalization of foreign trade in 1974 and 1975 was to: *(i)* unify the exchange rate so that all exporters and importers transacted at the same rate; then *(ii)* convert all quota restrictions into some rough tariff equivalent-lumping similar commodities together in the same tariff category; then *(iii)* move to unrestricted foreign exchange convertibility on current account.

The net effect of these first steps taken in 1974 and 1975 was to convert implicit protection by direct controls into explicit protection by tariffs — albeit still very high tariffs as Table 1 shows. By 1976, this conversion into a system of explicit tariff protection in Chile was virtually complete. Then the government proceded to phase out the explicit protection slowly over a period of several years by *(iv)* reducing the higher tariffs, in preannounced small steps, to converge to a modest uniform import tariff at a prespecified future date.

In the event, Chile speeded up this process slightly and converged to uniform 10% tariff on all imports (for revenue) by July of 1979 (Table 1) with no other significant import restrictions. The uniform tariff was justified on revenue grounds, and from Lerner's *Symmetry Theorem*, we know such a tariff is equivalent to a 10% tax on all exports in long-run equilibrium.

TABLE 1

PROFILE OF THE CHILEAN TARIFF REFORM

	Average nominal tariff rate (percentages)	Maximum nominal tariff rate (percentages *)
1973 July - December	94	500 +
1974 January - June	80	160
July - December	67	140
1975 January - June	52	120
July - December	44	90
1976 January - June	38	70
July - December	33	60
1977 January - June	24	50
July - December	18	35
1978 January - June	15	20
July - December	12	15
1979 June 30 onwards	10 (**)	10
1980	10	10
1981	10	10
1982	10	10

(*) With a few exceptions for some (but not all) automotive vehicles. Small cars may be imported at the standard tariff rates.

(**) Of the 4,301 commodities or tariff lines that are classified for customs purposes, only 12 are exempt from any duties.

Source: CENTRAL BANK OF CHILE.

Note that after 1973 Chile also removed all controls and other significant taxes on exports *per sé*. However, in parallel with what should be the case for the natural-resource based exports of the Soviet Union, the Chilean government continued to tax the profits and other economic rents associated with natural-resource based industries rather systematically. For example, in Chile's huge copper industry, which dominated Chile's exports much like petroleum now does the Soviet Union's, the government retained ownership and control of a number of major mines; and concessions given to private mining companies, whether international or domestic, were rather carefully taxed. The important point for our purposes, however, is these were "profits" taxes rather than export taxes. Hence, after liberalization, they did not drive a wedge between the price seen by domestic users and by foreign buyers of exportable material inputs, unlike the Soviet energy industry today.

In summary, in difficult political circumstances, Chile in late 1973 eschewed the "cold turkey" approach to free trade adopted by (forced on?) Poland and East Germany in 1990. Instead, Chilean producers of finished goods had some years in which to adjust. The one major mistake was to allow excessive capital inflows that forced a severe overvaluation of the Chilean peso in 1978-1982 and caused widespread bankruptcy in the newly opened tradable goods sectors (McKinnon [6], Chapter 6). Despite this early trauma, Chile's trade liberalization itself, and political commitment to free trade, have been successfully sustained into the 1990s.

6. - A Transition Parable for Soviet Foreign Trade

Suppose the spirit of the deliberate Chilean approach to free trade — as summarized in steps *(i)* to *(iv)* above — can be depicted within the confines of our two-commodity substitution model of the Soviet economy. How might an "idealized" Soviet approach to free trade be worked out?

The Soviets go off on the wrong foot in 1989 by decentralizing foreign exchange contracting by domestic enterprises before their budget contraints were hardened so that domestic commodity prices could be decontrolled, and before the regime of multiple exchange rates was unified. In 1990, hundreds of individual exchange rates, ranging from the old official rate of 0.64 rubles per dollar to more than 20 rubles continue to proliferate. Thus, as a practical matter, the Soviet government might have to recentralize foreign exchange allocations until the domestic financial controls necessary for supporting a market economy have been established (McKinnon [6]) and until the exchange rate is unified as per phase *(i)* above.

But how should this single (unified) nominal exchange rate be set when unrestricted commodity or financial arbitrage with the outside world does not yet exist? We know that the price of exportable material inputs — inclusive of the huge energy sector — must rise sharply relative to domestic factors of production including labor. Moreover the ruble prices of these fairly homogeneous material inputs can be directly compared to those prevailing on world markets, which are typically quoted in dollars. Thus, the exchange rate, in rubles per dollar, can be set according to a limited version of the principle of purchasing power parity as follows.

Take the prevailing domestic wage level in rubles as a starting point. Then estimate the average increase in the relative price of energy (and other material inputs) against wages that would prevail in long-run equilibrium if the economy were to move towad free trade. Accordingly, adjust the domestic ruble price of energy (and other material inputs) sharply upwards — doubling or trebling it in terms of wages at the outset of the trade liberalization process. In Graph 2, the *slope* of the budget line *BB'*, running through the old production point *d*, now represents this higher price of energy relative to labor; whereas *HD*, also running through *d*, represents the old budget line when energy was previously underpriced.

Simultaneously, to make the new ruble price level for material inputs effective, set the exchange rate in rubles per dollar to equate (average) domestic prices of material inputs to those prevailing in world markets. This new unified exchange rate would now apply to all current account transacting, on either the import or export sides, for material inputs, finished goods, or services. Once established, this nominal ruble/dollar exchange rate would be invariant to further ups and downs of world prices for material inputs. At the fixed exchange rate, continual minor changes in the domestic ruble prices of in- dividual material inputs (and other tradables) would keep them aligned with their counterparts on world markets.

What have we accomplished by this exercise in exchange rate unification? First, the implicit export tax on energy and other material

INTERIM TARIFF PROTECTION
IN THE TRANSITION TO FREE TRADE

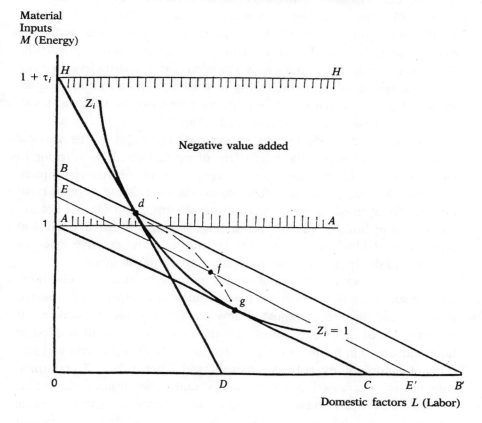

inputs has been eliminated as their ruble prices rise sharply to world levels. (Note, however, that the revenue position of the government would be greatly enhanced if it retained a full claim on the profits or surpluses being generated by natural resource based industries at the higher domestic prices). In the short run, producers in industry i would have immediate incentive to begin economizing on energy and other material inputs.

Second, this nominal exchange rate is now capable of sustaining the real purchasing power of domestic money in terms of material inputs — a very broad class of primary commodities produced, traded, and consumed throughout the economy — once full current account convertibility is achieved. This potentially stable "real" exchange rate also provides a benchmark for converting the implicit tariff protection associated with quota restrictions and with the existing system of exchange controls into *explicit* tariff equivalents. That is, the authorities may now calculate the t_i's sufficient to keep most finished goods manufacturing in existence, a calculation requiring a stable real exchange rate if effective protection by tariffs is, itself, to remain operative at some prespecified level.

For finished goods indistry i portayed in Graph 2, the vertical scale at point H shows the coefficient of protection, $1 + \tau_i$, prior to this elimination of the domestic subsidy to the use of material inputs. This total implicit protection depends on the preexisting implicit tariff on imports of finished goods and on the old input subsidy. As before, the resulting budget line for producing one unit finished good i at point d is HD, whose steep slope reflects the low relative price of energy and other material inputs relative to domestic labor.

After the price of material inputs increase to world levels, however, explicit tariff protection from competing imports of finished goods would have to be adjusted upwards from its old implicit rate if industry i is to survive. Suppose t'_i is the new explicit tariff needed to keep industry i in business once exchange controls were removed and current account convertibility was achieved. Then $t'_i > t_i$. To compensate for the increased price of energy and other inputs, the initial explicit tariff would have to be somewhat higher than the previous quality-adjusted differential between the foreign and domestic price of finished good i.

The vertical distance AB in Graph 2 shows the level of this new (hypothetical) explicit tariff relative to the (newly increased) prices of material inputs. Insofar as the domestic price of material inputs now equals the world level of one dollar, AB also represents the actual *ad valorem* tarif needed to protect the domestic industry. BB' is the corresponding new budget line just sufficient to sustain production at point d (at the old combination of domestic factors and material inputs). BB' is somewhat flatter that the old budget in line HD in order to reflect the newly increased price of material inputs relative to labor.

Because the price of material inputs has also increased relative to that of the finished goods, the distance AB is correspondingly less than AH.

But this is not the end of the parable. Because the slope of the new budget line BB' is flatter (reflecting higher energy costs), BB' now cuts the unit isoquant Z_i at point d rather than being tanget to it. This induces the manager of industry i to raise profits by increasing the demand for domestic factors and reducing energy dependence, i.e., to start moving along the new budget line from d in the direction of B' as fast as the re-equipment of the enterprise permits. The great advantage of raising material input prices rather sharply at the outset of the trade liberalization is that firms immediately see the "right" relative factor costs for inducing them to economize on material inputs, exports of which will then slowly increase.

Nevertheless, our controlled liberalization differs from a strategy of jumping directly to free trade. Under immediate free trade with no interim protection for domestic finished goods, industry i would face the budget line AC in Graph 2, which could not support existing production at point d. Because the world market would bid them away from domestic uses, exports of material inputs and energy would jump sharply and so cause the collapse of most domestic manufacturing and goods processing activities.

That said, our parable based on interim tariff protection should leave no doubt in the minds of domestic industrialists, merchants, and farmers that the economy will eventually move to free trade as in stage *(iv)* of the Chilean program cited above. Simultaneously with the introduction of explicit tariff protection for finished goods industries, the liberalizing socialist government could announce that the higher tariff rates would be scaled down by small steps until, say 10 years hence, all rates had converged to some low uniform level. Further reductions in this resulting "revenue tariff" would then depend on the government's fiscal position.

Graph 2 nicely illustrates the nature of this declining tariff protection in smoothing the transition to free trade. Starting with the high explicit tariff equal to the vertical distance AB, the relevant budget line supporting production at point d is BB'. Then, some years later, formal tariff protection for our representative finished good is reduced to AE so as to support production at point f along the new budget line *EE'*. Finally, tariff protection for finished goods industries is phased out altogether; the relevant budget line becomes *AC*: that prevailing under free trade. (For diagrammatic simplicity, Graph 2 does not show the process ending with a low revenue tariff; and I have simply assumed that the initial guess of the authorities in raising the price of material inputs relative to domestic factors turns out to be correct in free-trade equilibrium).

During this transition, successful in the particular case of industry *i* shown in Graph 2, the combination of factor inputs for producing one unit of the finished good shifts along the locus shown by the arrows from *d* to *f* to *g*. Only at the beginning point *d*, and the end point *g*, are these production combinations actually on the unit isoquant Z_i. That is, the unit isoquant traces out efficient production points in long-run equilibrium after the industry has the necessary time to rebuild its capital stock and restructure its labor force when relative prices change. The other points on the locus *dfg* are above the efficient long-run unit isoquant; and their "excessive" use of material inputs and domestic factors represents the real (social) costs of the transition. These costs are covered by the interim tariff protection and thus are shifted forward to the final user of the finished good in question.

However, the change from implicit quota restrictions and import prohibitions to explicit tariff protection could still benefit users of finished goods.

First, even over high tariffs, the new threat of import competition would curb the monopoly power of concentrated domestic manufacturers. Manufacturing industries in the Soviet Union are indeed highly concentrated. For example, 100% of Soviet sewing machines are produced by a single state enterprise; the same is true for such diverse goods as tram rails, locomotive cranes, and coking equipment. All hydraulic turbines produced in the country come from a small number of plants run by a single government ministry; the same can be said for tin plate production and certain consumer goods such as color photographic paper and freezers (*The Economist* [14]).

Second, the shoddy product syndrome would be immediately alleviated: the worst domestic products would not survive in the face of even modest competition from abroad. Indeed, the successful transitional production locus in Graph 2, the movement from *d* to *f* to *g*, implicitly incorporates improvements in product quality.

7. - A Generalized Cascading Tariff?

These advantages from the move to explicit tariff protection presume that the government does not precisely tailor individual tariffs to keep each finished goods producer in business at the outset of the liberalization. Rather, the vertical distance *AB* in Graph 21 is best interpreted as simply a representative initial tariff — a common levy — that applies to imports of all finished goods in a similar category. Following the Chilean experience described earlier and that of other primary products producing countries such as Canada which once had quite high tariffs, one could start off with fairly broad tariff categories: a "cascading" tariff scaled downwards according to the distance from the final consumer and degree of manufacturing complexity. Ranked from highest to lowest, a single tariff rate could apply to each of the following or similar categories: 1) consumer durables: autos, home appliances, and so forth; 2) consumer nondurables: textiles and highly processed foods; 3) capital goods and manufactured intermediate products; 4) industrial materials and basic foods.

The highest tariff in category 1) could be over 100% depending of how one computed their average survival capability after the prices of material inputs had been raised sharply; whereas the lowest would be the final uniform tariff of say, 10%, on imports of material inputs in category 4). As far as possible, the government would set a simple across-the-board "yardstick" tariff in each category. Not only would this general approach weed out the most inefficient producers (basket cases) at the outset, but "rent seeking" by individual industries petitioning for protection especially geared to their own needs would be minimized.

Then, over, say, a ten year interval similar to that used in the recently concluded Canadian-American free trade agreement, the rates in categories 1), 2), and 3), would be gradually but firmly reduced to those prevailing in category 4) again without accepting special pleading for exceptions. In order to facilitate adjustment in his own mix of inputs and outputs, each producer should know the cumulative tariff reductions (6) at the end of every year until virtual free trade was established.

A cascading tariff schedule, but one that is not adjusted downwards, is often used by LDCs to protect "infant" industries for producing finished goods. In our transition parable, by contrast, the purpose is quite different: to make explicit and then phase out already very high levels of implicit protection for domestic manufacturing. Moreover, with the degree of uncertainty involved as to which firms would ultimately survive and which not, it is simply not feasible for those firms that would be viable in the long run to jump immediately to free trade and to cover their losses and transition costs by borrowing. Indeed, such massive borrowing by socialist enterprises would undermine the hard budget constraints, based on limited access to external capital, which were pivotal for achieving domestic financial control (McKinnon [6] and [7]). Instead, temporary tariff protection, which increases the internal cash flows of manufacturing firms, is fully consistent with keeping self finance as the main financial mode for liberalized enterprises in a transitional socialist economy.

8. - Are Foreign Capital Inflows Necessary?

Because a properly orchestrated move to free trade presents no inherent problem of foreign exchange shortages for the Soviet Union, our parable of step-by-step trade liberation did not discuss the role of capital inflows from abroad. Quite the contrary, the country abounds with energy and other material inputs that are overused at home. Thus the elimination of implicit export taxes should allow exports to increase rather easily. Indeed, flooding the economy with foreign exchange by borrowing abroad could well worsen the adjustment problem. Domestic finished goods industries would face additional

---

(6) The authorities don't have to reveal any exact dates on which tariffs would be discretely adjusted thereby inviting inventory speculation, Continual adjustment by very small amounts to yield a prespecified cumulative change would be much preferred.

competition from "subsidized" manufactured imports that reduced their international competitiveness (McKinnon [9]).

Are there circumstances where one might want to mitigate this seemgly harsh judgement against heavy reliance on foreign capital inflows to "ease" adjustment to free trade?

Unlike the Soviet Union, some of the smaller countries of Eastern Europe are not particularly rich in natural resources that are easily traded internationally. Worse, their extensive manufacturing and agricultural industries have also become addicted to cheap material inputs, particularly energy. Before 1990, at least, the close trade links among the countries of Eastern Europe simply extended the ambit of the old Stalinist industrial system. Through the trading apparatus of the CMEA (the Council for Mutual Economic Assistance), the Soviet Union sold relatively cheap energy and other material inputs to smaller Eastern European economies in return for manufactured goods of a lesser quality than those traded in Western markets. In fact, the extensive trade among the CMEA countries (Table 2), albeit largely bilateral because of the absence of a freely convertible trading currency, also included the mutual exchange of (shoddy) manufactured goods through direct bargaining by state trading agencies.

The problem for CMEA countries to then adjust to full-scale trade liberalization with the West is obvious. The smaller ones that have not much in the way of primary products (what we have been calling material inputs) exports would find themselves with an immediate shortage of foreign exchange. First, they stand to lose the subsidies for their Soviet-produced material inputs: the willingness of the Soviet authorities to accept their manufactured products at very favorable terms of trade. Second, the syndrome of negative value-added (at world market prices) means they can't sell their manufactures, without significant improvements in product quality, to the West. In effect, they are currently producing at a point like d in Graph 1; but where the vertical showing material inputs now reflects actual imports rather than potential exportables as in the Soviet case. Hence, a highly industrialized country like Czechoslovakia, where in 1988 about 80% of its exports went to other Socialist economies (Table 2), faces an immediate foreign exchange shortage if the CMEA trading umbrella collapses.

TABLE 2

TRADE FLOWS FOR THE CMEA (1988)
(PERCENT OF TOTAL EXPORTS AND IMPORTS)

	Six (*)	USSR	Developed market economies	LDCs	Rest (**)
			Exports		
Bulgaria	18.1	62.8	6.4	9.1	3.6
Czechoslovakia	29.9	43.1	16.3	4.7	6.0
German Dem. Rep.	26.1	34.8	29.9	3.6	5.6
Hungary	17.0	39.5	39.5	9.9	6.0
Poland	16.2	24.5	43.3	10.2	5.8
Romania	16.8	24.0	33.7	19.0	6.5
USSR	48.9	—	21.9	14.2	15.0
			Imports		
Bulgaria	20.1	53.7	15.5	7.8	2.9
Czechoslovakia	32.3	40.3	18.6	3.5	5.3
German Dem. Rep.	25.3	36.8	31.8	2.7	3.4
Hungary	18.7	25.0	43.3	7.7	5.3
Poland	17.2	23.4	45.7	7.1	6.6
Romania	24.6	24.0	13.5	18.8	19.1
USSR	54.1	—	25.1	8.2	12.6

(*) Six: Bulgaria, Czechoslovakia, German Democratic Republic, Hungary, Poland and Romania.
(**) Rest of the world (predominantly Yugoslavia and China).
Source: Finance and Development, Sept. 1990, p. 29. Based on official statistics yearbooks of the reporting countries and UN estimates.

In a general equilibrium model based on just two highly aggregated commodities, the Stalinist system of protection under the prototypical "Soviet" case can be distinguished from the prototypical "Czech" case. In the Soviet case, exports of primary materials are heavily (albeit implicitly) taxed with the domestic government collecting the tax revenue, whereas potential imports of finished manufactures face very high (implicit) tariffs. In the Czech case, imports of material inputs such as energy are subsidized by an outside agent (the Soviet Union); and so are exports of finished manufactures subsidized (7): first by the cheap energy inputs, and second insofar as they can be unloaded in other CMEA countries.

---

(7) I am greatly indebted to Peter Kenen for suggesting this point to me.

The distinction between these two cases is important. In the Soviet case, a natural method of easing the transition to free trade is to impose temporary explicit tariffs on competing imports of finished manufactures — as sketched above — in order to give domestic producers of these goods time to adjust as the price of energy and material inputs increases to world levels. But that would be insufficient in the Czech case. Czech producers of finished goods need some temporary protection in their export markets when their energy subsidies are removed. And, even if such export subsidies to Czech manufactures were allowed under the GATT, they would be a big drain on the Czech government's budget. Perhaps continuing with CMEA trade for some years into the transition would be a partial solution.

However, converting the CMEA into a full fledged common market with convertible currencies and a common external tariff (in the mode of Western Europe) seems completely out of the question (Schrenk [11]). This is a much more difficult task than reforming each socialist economy individually. Nevertheless, apart from the schema for tariff-based liberalization sketched above, continuing the bilateral exchange of manufactured products through state trading agencies on an interim basis could be helpful for some years before each socialist economy is fully liberalized. Very likely, however, the net debits or credits arising out of bilateral imbalances in such trade would have to be settled in convertible Western monies rather than inconvertible trade rubles as is presently the case (8).

In proceeding with the main task of liberalizing its foreign trade with the West, therefore, a smaller Eastern European country might well require carefully crafted bridging finance from some international agency, such as the European Bank for Reconstruction and Development set up in 1990. However, the conditionality imposed by this agency for lending the money might well follow our parable sketched above and reflected in Graph 2: a discrete increase in the domestic price of energy and other material inputs to world levels coupled with conversion from implicit protection through exchange controls to an

---

(8) The possibilities for hardening the trade ruble, making it convertible into Western monies, are discussed in McKINNON [8], Chapter 3.

interim system of explicit protection for finished goods through tariffs or special export subsidies. At the beginning of such a liberalization with otherwise free convertibility on current account, the agency might well provide the foreign exchange necessary for, say, Czechoslovakia, to continue buying material inputs until its manufactured exports become more competitive in world markets.

But accepting official bridging finance based on strict conditionality is. not tantamount to a general relaxation of controls over private capital movements. Only after the domestic capital market is fully liberalized, with unrestricted borrowing and lending at equilibrium domestic interest rates, should the socialist economy's currency be made convertible into foreign exchange on capital account. Many years hence, individuals and enterprises, including joint ventures with foreign firms, could be allowed to choose freely between domestic and foreign sources of finance. But this is the last, rather than the first, step in the optimum order of liberalization (9).

9. - Summary of Main Conclusions

Let us now return to summarize the main results of the paper.

In a traditional centrally planned Stalinist economy, protection for domestic manufacturing is almost entirely implicit. Through exchange controls and the apparatus of state trading, disguised subsides to users of energy and other material inputs are coupled with virtually absolute protection from competing foreign manufactures. Although no formal tariffs appear in any legal codes, the implicit structure of tariff equivalents "cascades" downward from very high levels for the domestic production of finished consumer goods through manufactured intermediate products through industrial raw materials and energy, whose production is negatively protected because of implicit export taxes (or import subsidies).

This highly cascaded structure of implicit tariffs in socialist economies raises effective protection in finished goods to the point

---

(9) That the international convertibility of the ruble on capital account comes last rather than first in the optimum order of economic liberalization is well recognized by Academician AGANBEGYAN ABEL [1] and is discussed at some length in McKINNON [6].

where most manufacturing will exhibit negative (or very low) value added at world market prices. In such circumstances, a precipitate move to free trade could provoke the collapse of most domestic manufacturing industries no matter how the exchange rate is set, and no matter that some of this industry might eventually be viable at world market prices.

Thus, reforms to make commercial policy more explicit should accompany efforts to make the currency convertible on current account. This paper suggested the simultaneous "tarification" of quantitative restrictions on competing imports and the elimination of implicit export taxes on energy and material inputs as the economy moves quickly to a market-based system. Once made explicit, the highest tariffs in the cascade can then be phased down step-by-step to zero (or a low uniform level) over a preannounced five- to ten-year time horizon. The newly marketized economy would then converge to free foreign trade at a more deliberate pace, one that better recognized the problem of overcoming distortions from the preexisting system of protection.

BIBLIOGRAPHY

[1] AGANBEGYAN ABEL: *The New Stage of Perestroika*, Institute for East-West Security Studies, 1988, pp. 25-44.

[2] ASLUND ANDERS: *Gorbachev's Struggle for Economic Reform*, Ithaca, (New York), Cornell University Press, 1989.

[3] EDWARDS SEBASTIAN - ALEJANDRA COX EDWARDS: *Monetarism and Liberalization: The Chilean Experiment*, Cambridge (Mass), Ballinger, 1977.

[4] LERNER A.P.: «The Symmetry Between Import and Export Taxes», *Economia*, n. 111, August 1936, pp. 308-13.

[5] LIPTON DAVID - SACHS JEFFREY: «Creating a Market Economy in Eastern Europe: The Case of Poland», *Brookings Papers on Economic Activity*, n. 1, 1990.

[6] McKINNON RONALD I.: *The Order of Economic Liberalization: Financial Control in the Transition to a Market Economy*, Baltimore, The John Hopkins University press, forthcoming 1991.

[7] — —: «Financial control in the Transition from Classical Socialism to a Market Economy», *Journal of Economic Perspectives*, forthcoming 1991.

[8] — —: *Money in International Exchange: The Convertible Currency System*, New York, Oxford University Press, 1979.

[9] — —: *Money and Capital in Economic Development*, Washington (DC), Brookings Institution, 1973.

[10] — —: «Intermediate Products and differential Tariffs: A Generalization of Lerner's Symmetry Theorem», *Quarterly Journal of Economics*, vol. 80, November 1966, pp. 584-615.

[11] SCHRENK MARTIN: «Whither Comecon?», *Finance and Development*, set. 1990.

[12] SHMELEV NIKOLAI - VLADIMIR POPOV: *The Turning Point: Revitalizing the Soviet Economy*, Doubleday, New York, 1989.

[13] TAN AUGUSTINE: «Differential Tariffs, Negative Value-Added and the Theory of Effective Protection», *American Economic Review*, vol. 60, n. 1, March 1970.

[14] THE ECONOMIST: *Industrial concentration in the Ussr*, August 11, 1990, p. 67.

[15] WILLIAMSON JOHN: «Convertibility, Trade Policy, and the Payments Constraint», in WILLIAMSON J. (ed.): *Currency Convertibility in Eastern Europe*, Institute for International Economics, forthcoming 1991.

Post-Reform East and West: Capital Accumulation and the Labor Mobility Constraint

Charles Wyplosz (*)

DELTA, INSEAD and CEPR

1. - Introduction

The reform process in several Eastern European countries is clearly directed at the freeing of domestic markets, along with the opening to trade in goods and capital. Out from the cold mantle of centralized planning will emerge a continent of more than a hundred million people. This cannot fail from affecting the world as the whole, first and foremost Western Europe. While attention is focused on the steps which must be taken to implement such a program, this paper looks beyond the reform process itself. Assuming that reform has been successfully enacted, I ask what happens next and attempt to map out some of the key features of the ensuing process, the economics of post-reform.

Once reform has taken hold, the East should function like the West. What matters then is the difference in initial conditions. A key, obvious, difference is the living standards. Table 1 illustrates this point: GDP per capita in Eastern Europe is much lower than in most

(*) I have benefited from useful comments from Michael Burda. Financial support from the Commissariat General du Plan and INSEAD R&D budget is acknowledged with thanks. This research is part of CEPR's program on Economic Transformation in Eastern Europe. None of these institutions is responsible for the views expressed in this paper.

Advise: the numbers in square brackets refer to the Bibliography in the Appendix.

of Western Europe, by a factor of 3 to 10 or more. At best, the East looks like the South. The situation reminds us of the immediate post-war period: then, Western Europe was 3 to 6 times poorer than the US. We know that catchup was slow, took the form of capital inflows and relatively little outmigration from Europe. West Europeans showed, in retrospect, a high degree of patience, facing years of restraint, for example extensive rationing. To be sure, political turmoil erupted in a number of countries, in effect prompting the *Marshall Plan*. Yet, in the aftermath of a long war, the dominating feeling, fed by either the enthusiasm of victory or the shame of defeat, was that countries had to re-establish themselves and endure sacrifices. Eastern Europe seems to be in a different mood. The feeling

TABLE 1

GDP PER CAPITA
(1988 US Dollars) (*)

Bulgaria	1,500	Germany	18,480
Czechoslovakia	3,500	UK	12,810
GDR	4,000	Spain	7,740
Hungary	3,000	Portugal	3,650
Poland	2,000		
Romania	1,000		

(*) Data for Eastern Europe are notoriously unreliable. The numbers used here are estimates by CREDIT SUISSE FIRST BOSTON.
   Source: BEGG *et* AL. [1].

TABLE 2

GDP PER CAPITA IN 1950
(US Dollars)

Belgium	790
France	690
Germany	470
Italy	320
UK	740
US	1,890

Source: INTERNATIONAL FINANCIAL STATISTICS.

of four decades of deprivation and of abandonment to dark forces, together with an extraordinary proximity of the West, seems to result in a more subdued, if not recriminatory, public opinion.

The sources of Eastern poverty are too well known. One of them is inefficiency on a grand scale. Hopefully, this is what reform will eliminate. In principle, faced with the right set of incentives, Easterners will find the ways of operating their economies as efficiently as elsewhere. This will bring to the forefront the post-reform challenge, namely the closing of the gap in productive resources. Hamilton *et Al.* [5] show that Eastern Europe is generally well endowed with relatively highly skilled labor while Begg *et Al.* [1] conclude that its stock of productive (at world market prices) physical capital is extremely limited. The challenge then mostly takes the form of the accumulation of productive capital.

The combination of a low productive capital endowment and abundant human capital has a very clear implication: the marginal productivity of capital is potentially very high while the marginal productivity of labor is very low. An obvious consequence is that wages in particular, and standards of living in general, must be low in the East. That this is the case at the outset is clearly established by Table 3 (1). Another implication is that the key to economic success in

TABLE 3

WORK TIME REQUIRED TO PURCHASE
SELECTED GOODS. 1988
Index numbers: West Germany = 1.0

	Bulgaria	Czechosl.	GDR	Hungary	Poland
Pork (1kg)........	4.1	3.4	1.3	2.4	2.0
Beef (1kg)........	5.9	3.7	1.0	2.6	1.7
Butter (1kg)........	6.0	3.6	1.9	2.5	3.5
Sugar (1kg)........	7.1	3.3	1.4	3.2	3.6
Motor car	4.0	2.5	2.4	2.3	9.2
Color TV..........	5.3	6.6	5.6	4.0	13.4

Source: UN ECONOMIC COMMISSION FOR EUROPE: *Economic Survey of Europe in 1989-1990.*

---

(1) Note that these numbers underestimate the true differences between East and West as it does not account for queues and delivery lags.

the East is the accumulation of productive capital, justified by its potentially high marginal productivity. This is how a patient population can expect to see its standards of living grow, and eventually catch up with the West.

But how patient will the population be? I assume here that the combination of economic frustrations accumulated over decades and some degree of political instability in the early democratic period will fan out powerful incentives to migrate. Indeed, the returns from migration are considerable, and this is the other point made by Table 3. By merely walking across the border, an Eastern European stands a reasonable chance of doubling, tripling, or quadrupling his income level. The mere threat of large-scale migration suggests a central difficulty of the transition period.

No matter how well-crafted the reform will be, it is likely that the East will share with the West the continuing existence of market distortions, in particular in the labor market. The coexistence of strong incentives to migrate and labor market distortions suggests that some degree of real wage rigidity is a good departure point to think about the transition. The paper is entirely devoted to a study of real wage rigidities in both the West and the East. Because the transition process is fundamentally dynamic, intertemporal considerations need to be emphasized. Paragraph 2 provides the simplest possible model which captures the elements sketched above, with real wage rigidity and a Ramsey model of capital accumulation. Convergence without labor market distortions, the benchmark case, is studied in Paragraph 3. Paragraph 4 is devoted to the effect that migration may exert, via real wage rigidities in the East. It is assumed that, to stem outmigration, workers are offered real wages not too far below those in the West. The result is unemployment of course, but also lower capital accumulation. Interestingly, we find an hysteresis effect: the steady state unemployment and capital stock levels in the East depend on the level of real wages during the transition. This hysteresis also concerns the level of indebtedness of the East, and therefore the West's increase in wealth. Paragraph 5 considers briefly the case where real wages are also rigid in the West while Paragraph 6 concludes by discussing some policy options.

2. - An Intertemporal Model for the Transition

2.1 *The Firm*

It is assumed that the world consists of two "countries", the East and the West. The West is denoted with a star. Each country is described by an infinitely lived representative consumer. External debt is allowed to vary, but it is assumed that there are no constraints on borrowing abroad. Complete integration in trade is represented by the assumption that there exists a single good, which can be used for consumption or putty-clay investment. Thus all variables are written in real terms without any ambiguity. The cost of this simplification is that the terms of trade are constant throughout the transition period and that there are no gains from trade. Full financial integration implies that the same real interest rate r applies to both the East and the West. Because the emphasis is on labor market distortions in the East, real wages are, for the time being, taken to be fully flexible in the West, so that full employment obtains there. It is further assumed that know-how accrues freely to the East so that it has access to the same technology — the same production function — as in the West, right after economic reform is implemented, that is at the point where the present story starts out. Finally, there is no technological progress or population growth, and constant returns in production eliminate the plausible scope for endogenous growth. Thus we look at deviations from what would have happened without reform in the East.

Let N be the size of the population in the East, L of which are working supplying each one unit of work. There are as many firms as people in this country, all of them perfectly competitive and identical. If K is the total capital stock, total profit is (2):

$$(1) \qquad \pi = F(K, L) - wL - I$$

where w is the real wage and I investment. Each firm is $1 / Nth$ the total. Using the assumption that production exhibits constant return to scales so that $F(K, L) = Kf(K/L)$, and denoting per capita

---

(2) The time variable is omitted unless required to avoid ambiguity.

variables in lower case (e.g. $k = K/N$), each firm's profit can be written as:

$$(2) \qquad \pi = (1-u) f(k/(1-u)) - i - (1-u) w$$

where $u = 1 - (L/N)$ is the rate of unemployment. Note the distinction between k — capital per citizen — and $k/(1-u)$ — capital per employed worker. It is assumed that the firm finances its investment through retained earnings. All the firms' capital stock belongs to the consumers, and is equally shared among them.

What prevents the transition from being instantaneous is the fact that capital accumulation takes time. To obtain this, I follow Hayashi [6] and assume that there are costs of adjustment in installing capital. Precisely, it is assumed that to install $k = dk/dt$ units of capital, the representative firm must spend the amount:

$$(3) \qquad i = \dot{k} + \phi(\dot{k}), \qquad \phi(0) = 0, \; \phi'(0) = 0, \; \phi''(0) > 0$$

The firms chooses optimally its inputs. If $r(t)$ is the instantaneous real interest rate, the representative firm solves the following program:

$$(4) \qquad \underset{i,\,u}{\text{Max}} \int_0^\infty e^{-\int_0^t r(s)ds} \, [(1-u) f(k/(1-u)) - i - (1-u) w] \, dt$$

subject to (3) and the initial condition $k(t) = k_0$. The first order conditions are:

$$(5) \qquad w = f(k/(1-u)) - (k/(1-u)) f'(k/(1-u))$$

$$(6) \qquad \dot{k} = h(q-1) \;\; \text{with} \; h() = [\phi'()]^{-1}, \text{so } h(0) = 0 \text{ and } h' > 0$$

$$(7) \qquad \dot{q} = rq - f'(k/(1-u))$$

2.2 *The Supply of Labor*

As noted above, a central purpose of this paper is to study the effect of labor mobility between East and West, given the incentive for Eastern workers to settle in the West to increase their standards of living. To capture this effect, it is assumed that each worker may always choose between supplying his work domestically and earn a wage w, or to supply it abroad to earn w^*. But there is a fixed cost to migration, both to move and to stay abroad (3), so that the net return to migration is $(1 - \alpha) w^*$, with $\alpha(t)$ a measure of the cost of migration, $1 > \alpha > 0$. As will be noted below, to get any dynamics at all, we need $\alpha(t)$ to converge to zero as t goes to infinity. The total supply of work by each person is totally inelastic and normalized at unity as already noted, but can be supplied to the domestic firm in proportion v and abroad in proportion $(1 - v)$.

In addition, although there may be unemployment, each worker believes that he can get a job if she supplies it. This assumption greatly simplifies the analysis but is far from innocuous. A useful extension would be to allow for wage bargaining or for a trade union to set wages. A possible interpretation, which is adopted here, is that the wage is set domestically by a monopolist trade union which cares only for the employed insiders. As will be shown, this results in hysteresis effects.

2.3 *The Consumer*

The consumers jointly and equally share the firms, one each. They derive income from their work and from their firm profit. In addition they can freely borrow and lend abroad. Thus their budget constraint is:

$$(8) \qquad \dot{b} = rb + \pi + \gamma w + (1 - \gamma)(1 - \alpha) w^* - c$$

---

(3) An alternative specification would be a once-and-for-all cost of moving.

where b represents net per capita foreign assets. In addition, the consumer must satisfy the solvency condition:

$$(9) \qquad \lim \int_0^\infty e^{-\int_0^t r(s)ds} \, b(t) \, dt \geq 0$$

The West is described by the same set of equations, except that there is no unemployment so that the equivalent of *(5)* determines the real wage w^* taken as a reference in the East. Initially, the West is assumed to be initially in steady state. Since there are two countries in the world, the West net per capita asset position b^* is related to b as follows:

$$(10) \qquad b(t) + b^*(t) = b_0 + b_0^* = 0$$

where b_0 and b_0^* are the initial positions of b and b^* when the East comes into play after a successful economic reform. Note that in *(10)* it is assumed, for simplicity and no loss of generality, that the population size is the same in the East and in the West.

The representative consumer is assumed to choose consumption and investment so as to maximize her intertemporal utility function (4):

$$(11) \qquad \int_0^\infty e^{-\delta t} \, \log(c(t)) \, dt$$

subject to *(8) (9)*, and the initial condition $b(0) = b_0$. The optimal plan follows the following equations:

$$(12) \qquad \dot{c}/c = r - \delta \quad \text{and} \quad c = \delta \Omega$$

---

(4) The solution will be particular because of the logarithmic instantaneous utility function. It is not possible to solve explicitly the model for more general functions.

where Ω is the country's per capita wealth (5):

$$\Omega(t) = b(t) + \int_t^\infty e^{-\int_t^s r(v)dv} [(1-u)f(k/(1-u)) - i]\, dt$$

(13) $\qquad\qquad w = (1-\alpha)w^* \qquad \lim_{t\to\infty} \alpha(t)\, 0$

Equation *(13)*, the labor mobility constraint, states that real wages in the East are indexed to those in the West, the wedge between them being just the cost of migration. As it is assumed that α eventually becomes nil, in the long run standards of living converge between the East and the West. The fact that *(13)* is satisfied implies that there is no actual migration (6).

Similar equations hold for the West, with $u^* = 0$ by assumption (7). To complete the model, we need to add the good market equilibrium condition:

(14) $\qquad (1-u)f(k/(1-u)) + f(k^*) = c + c^* + i + i^*$

and the financial market integration condition:

(15) $\qquad\qquad r(t) = r^*(t)$

Given the evolution of the state variables k and k^*, the goods market equilibrium condition determines at each point in time the world real rate of interest, and therefore wealth and consumption.

---

(5) This is obtained by substituting the profit function in the consumer budget constraint but noting that only a proportion $(1-u)$ of them will be employed, while workers abroad do not contribute to domestic wealth, i.e.:

$$db/dt = rb + \pi(1-u)w - c$$

(6) Two extensions are worthwhile and deferred to latter work. One is that Eastern workers take into account the probability of being unemployed. The second is that unemployment in the East triggers outmigration to the West and possibly unemployment there.

(7) It might be noted that the labor mobility constraint *(13)* together with *(5)* may yield a negative unemployment rate. While this could be interpreted as imports of foreign workers, in what follows it is clear that we always have $u > 0$.

2.4 *Steady State*

The steady state, represented by a bar over each variable, is easily derived. Denoting $z = k / (1 - u)$, capital per employed worker, we have:

$$f'(\bar{z}) = f'(\bar{k}^*) = \bar{r} = \delta, \qquad \bar{q} = \bar{q}^* = 1$$

(16)

$$\bar{w} = f(\bar{z}) - \bar{z}f'(\bar{z}) \qquad w^* = f(\bar{k}^*) - \bar{k}^* f'(\bar{k}^*)$$

While most of the implications are standard features of the Ramsey model, it is worth noting that what is determined in the steady state is z, the capital/employed labor ratio, not k, capital per capita:

(17) $$\bar{z} = \bar{k}/(1 - \bar{u}) = \psi(\bar{w}) \qquad \text{with: } \bar{w} = \bar{w}^*$$

Thus the steady state values of $\bar{k}$ and $\bar{u}$ are not uniquely determined (8). Any pair of values which satisfies *(17)* is *ex-ante* possible, as represented in Graph 1. What determines unemployment in the long run, therefore, is capital accumulation which, by *(6)*, depends on the whole path of q — the shadow price of investment or Tobin's marginal q — during the transition. This case of hysteresis underscores the link between the labor and goods markets which lies at the center of the present analysis. Note that if α were to be constant, the unemployment rate would immediately jump to a level such that *(17)* is satisfied for any value of $w = (1 - \alpha) w^*$, and nothing else would happen. This is why it is assumed that α is gradually vanishing.

3. - **The Full-Employment Case**

In this paragraph, the real wage in the East is assumed to be perfectly flexible and satisfies *(5)* for $u = 0$. This case is interesting in

---

(8) This is a consequence of the fact that with constant return to scale, the level of production is not determined.

GRAPH 1

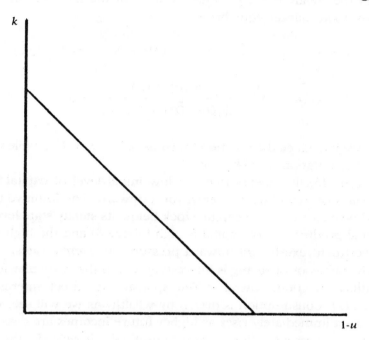

its own right as it sheds light on the links between East and West as the East converges to become identical to the West. It will be useful as a benchmark for the next paragraph since the simplicity of this case allows for an easy graphical solution, which is not possible with rigid real wages.

The experiment designed to represent the effect of economic reform in the East consists in assuming that at $t = 0$, East Europe starts with k_0 much lower than the West full employment level defined by $f'(\bar{k}) = \delta$, while West Europe is initially at its steady state position $(k^*_0 = \bar{k}^* = \bar{k}$ such that $f'(\bar{k}^*) = 0)$. Given the symmetry of the situation — both "countries" are identical in all respects except for the starting position — it is convenient to solve the model in sums and differences. Interaction between the two countries occur through the goods market equilibrium condition *(14)* which affects only the sums, and through the financial market condition *(15)* which affects only the differences. Differentiating *(14)*, using *(6)*, *(7)* and *(12)*, and linearizing around the steady state, we find the level of the interest rate which ensures good market equilibrium:

$$(18) \qquad r = \delta - \gamma \left[(k - \bar{k}) + (k^* - \bar{k}^*)\right] = \delta - \gamma (k^+ - 2\bar{k})$$

$$\text{with: } \gamma = - \frac{h'(0) f''(\bar{k})}{\delta (\bar{\Omega} + \bar{\Omega}^*) + 2h'(0)} > 0$$

where we introduce the notation for sums: $k^+ = k + k^*$, while we use below the notation $\bar{k} = k - k^*$.

From *(18)*, it appears that the low initial level of capital in the East will push world-wide interest rates upward. The intuitive reason should be clear: with the capital stock below its steady state level, the marginal productivity of capital is high (above δ) and the high return on investment exerts and upward pressure on interest rates.

The behavior of saving is interesting. Given the particular form of the utility function, saving is unresponsive to direct interest rate effects *(12)*. Consumption is driven by wealth. As we will see, wealth in the East immediately rises as higher future incomes are discounted back to the present. Thus private households *dissave*. In the West, wealth too increases and saving declines. This implication of the model is backed by the lack of empirical evidence linking household saving to the real interest rate, see e.g. Blanchard and Summers [2] (9).

Substituting *(18)* in *(6)* and *(7)*, and linearizing we find the following systems for the sums and differences:

$$(19a) \qquad \begin{cases} \dot{q}^+ = \delta (q^+ - 2) + \dfrac{\delta \gamma (\bar{\Omega} + \bar{\Omega}^*)}{h'(0)} (k^+ - 2\bar{k}) \\[2mm] k = h'(0)(q^+ - 2) \end{cases}$$

$$(19b) \qquad \begin{cases} \dot{q}^- = \delta q^- - f''(\bar{k}) k^- \\[2mm] \dot{k}^- = h'(0) q^- \end{cases}$$

---

(9) This is to be contrasted with Giustiniani *et* Al. [4].

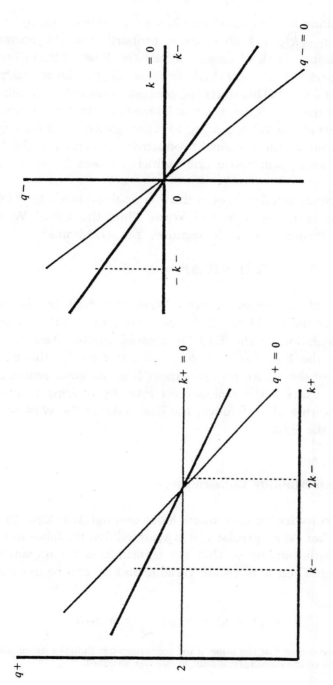

GRAPH 2

The transition is shown in Graph 2, staring from k_0^+ above $\bar{k}^*$ and k_0^- larger than $-\bar{k}^*$, in both cases in proportion to the economic value of the initial stock of capital. When the East embarks on the transition process, q is very high because of the large marginal productivity of capital. This starts the process of capital accumulation in the East. At the same time, the real interest rate increase pushes q^* downward (10) in the West, leading to a decumulation of the capital stock. Over time, as the marginal productivity of capital in the West rises, q^* increases again above unity which restores k^* to its initial value.

As k^* declines initially, so does the marginal productivity of labor, and therefore real wages in the West. Thus the initial Western perception of Eastern reform is negative. Yet, *(12)* implies:

$$(20) \qquad \dot{\Omega}/\Omega = \dot{\Omega}^*/\Omega^* = r - \delta$$

Thus wealth increases in both West and East in the same proportion. For the world as whole, the source of wealth increase is capital accumulation in the East. It accrues to the West through borrowing by the East ($\dot{b} = -\dot{b}^* < 0$). It pays for the East to borrow because the return on investment (the marginal productivity of capital) far exceeds the real interest rate. By offering a return r larger than the rate of preference, the East induces the West to save and invest in the East.

4. - The Labor Mobility Constraint

We now consider the case where labor outmigration leads to rigid wages in the East. More precisely, it is assumed that the labor mobility constraint *(13)* is binding so that the transition is accompanied by unemployment. Then w is a state variable and *(5)* can be inverted to give:

$$(21) \qquad z = k/(1 - u) = \psi(w) \qquad \psi' > 0$$

---

(10) It can be shown that the slope of the convergence path in the minus diagram exceeds the slope of the convergence path in the plus diagram.

With k another variable driven by *(6)*, unemployment is determined trivially by:

$$(22) \qquad 1 - u = k / \psi(w)$$

The good market equilibrium condition still determines the real interest rate, but the evolution of the capital stock in the East ceases to be an independent driving variable. Indeed, the capital labor ratio is now driven by real wages which are exogenous to the East because of *(13)*. This is seen by substituting *(21)* and *(22)* in *(18)*, differentiating and linearizing around the steady state to get:

$$(23) \qquad r = \delta - \gamma \frac{\bar{w}/\bar{z}}{f''(\bar{k}^*)}(q - 1) - \gamma(k^* - \bar{k}^*) - \gamma \psi'(\bar{w})(w - \bar{w})$$

$$- \gamma \frac{\bar{w}/\bar{z}\,\psi'(\bar{w})(1 - \bar{u})}{h'(0)\,f''(\bar{k}^*)}\,\dot{w}$$

The real interest rate rises in response to any pressure for higher capital accumulation in the East or in the West, i.e. when q exceeds 1 (note that $f'' < 0$), or when k^* is below its steady state level, or when wages in the East grow as w rises because it is below $\bar{w}$ or because of its own dynamics ($\dot{w} > 0$).

From *(7)* and *(23)* we have, after linearization:

$$(24) \qquad \dot{q} = \left[\delta - \gamma \frac{\bar{w}/\bar{z}}{f''(\bar{k}^*)}\right](q - 1) - \gamma(k^* - \bar{k}^*) + \gamma_1 \psi'(\bar{w})(w - \bar{w})$$

$$- \gamma \frac{\bar{w}/\bar{z}\,\psi'(\bar{w})(1 - \bar{u})}{h'(0)\,f''(\bar{k}^*)}\,\dot{w}$$

$$(25) \qquad \dot{q}^* = - \gamma \frac{\bar{w}/\bar{z}}{f''(\bar{k}^*)}(q - 1) + \delta(q^* - 1) + \gamma_1(k^* - \bar{k}^*)$$

$$- \gamma \psi'(\bar{w})(w - \bar{w}) - \gamma \frac{\bar{w}/\bar{z}\,\psi'(\bar{w})(1 - \bar{u})}{h'(0)\,f''(\bar{k}^*)}\,\dot{w}$$

where: $\qquad\qquad \gamma 1 = - \gamma - f''(\bar{k}^*) > 0$

This case cannot be solved graphically since real wages in the East are driven by wages in the West via the labor mobility constraint *(13)* (11). Yet it is possible to characterize the transition in relation to the benchmark case of the previous paragraph. With flexible real wages and therefore full employment in the East, wage convergence was the result of capital accumulation up to the Western level. If the labor mobility constraint imposes excessively high real wages (12) in the East, firms enter the post-reform transition period by immediately raising the capital labor ratio with the only degree of adjustment available, that is by reducing employment.

Thus, early on, high unemployment in the East is the channel through which the marginal productivity of labor is brought up to the real wage level. Over time, capital accumulation takes on part of the pressure, as discussed below. The high effective capital labor ratio thus achieved in the East forces up the real interest worldwide *(23)* with $w < \bar{w}$), which depress Tobin's q in the West and leads to a temporary decumulation of capital. The falling capital labor ratio means that real wages in the West decline. The fall in k^* further increases the real interest rate worldwide as the marginal productivity of capital rises in the West too. This crowding-out process in the West is eventually reversed when rising capital productivity exerts enough upward pressure on Tobin's q. In the East, the very high initial marginal productivity of capital ensures that capital accumulation occurs throughout the transition, possibly relieving the need for unemployment to be the main balancing variable. Thus, qualitatively, the transition process is accompanied in the West by the same evolution as in the full-employment benchmark case.

What is the role of the labor mobility constraint, represented here by $\alpha(t)$? It is instructive to consider the other polar case, i.e. when real wages in the East are immediately aligned on those in the West, which occurs when there is no labor mobility cost i.e. when $\alpha(t) = 0$ $\forall t \geq 0$. Then unemployment in the East is immediately driven to a level such that, at the initial per capita capital stock the capital labor ratio establishes equality between the real wage and the marginal

---

(11) The analytical solution for a special case is given in the Appendix.
(12) Precisely $w(0) > f[k(0)] - k(0) f'[k(0)]$.

productivity of labor. But then the capital labor ratios are the same in the West and the East ($z = k^*$) and so are the marginal productivities of capital, both equal to the initial steady state rate of interest $r = \delta$. There is no further incentive for Eastern firms to invest and the transition is instantaneous. Nothing other than unemployment happens anywhere, East or West. Unemployment and per capita capital (in this model) stay at their initial post-reform levels forever. Of course, the West remains unaffected and world wealth does not change either.

Thus in the long-run we find that the tighter the labor constraint, the less capital accumulation occurs in the East and the larger the unemployment rate. As a low level of capital accumulation means a limited increase in world wealth, the West lends less to the East, which undergoes lower current account deficits and lower foreign debt accumulation. Of course, if real wages were to become flexible, the long run would have the properties of the case studied in the previous section.

In the shorter run, the previous reasoning shows that a tight labor mobility constraint — a low value of $\alpha(t)$ — implies a limited increase in Tobin's q in the East and a limited decrease in the West. Thus, there is also less of an initial fall in investment and a lesser pressure on Western wages. By tying their real wages to the Western level, Eastern workers exert less of a downward pressure on their Western counterparts. In fact, the pressure falls progressively more on unemployed workers in the East. This makes it clear that the assumption of real wage rigidity, and the resulting hysteresis effect, must fundamentally be justified by a segmentation of Eastern labor markets. The unemployed must be unable to challenge the real wage rigidity (13).

Summarizing, the tighter the labor mobility constraint (the lower the coefficient $\alpha(t)$ during the transition), the less capital eventually increases in the East, and the less it temporarily declines in the West. There are two additional, permanent, effects of a strong labor mobility constraint. First, in the East, the low per capita capital k requires a comparatively larger rate of unemployment as seen in Graph 1. Second, on a per capita basis, world wealth and welfare benefit less

---

(13) This completes the implicit link with standard macroeconomic models which display hysteresis, see e.g. BLANCHARD and SUMMERS [3].

from the reform. This effects both the East and the West, and shows up as reduced borrowing by the East.

5. - Rigid Wages in the West

For completeness, and possibly realism, this section takes up the case when Western workers also peg their real wages. It is assumed that w^* is permanently set to a level such that there was unemployment in the West prior to reform in the East:

$w^* = \bar{w}^*$ such that $k_0^* = k^*(0) < \psi(\bar{w})$ so that $1 - u_0^* = k_0^*/\psi(\bar{w}^*) < 1$

It is clear that the West is now described by the same set of equations which applied to the East in the previous section. The goods market equilibrium condition sets the real interest rate as follows:

$$(26) \qquad r = \delta + \gamma^2 h'(0) [q - 1) + (q^* - 1)] +$$

$$- (1 - \bar{u}) \gamma_2 \upsilon'(\bar{w}) \dot{w} - \gamma \psi'(\bar{w}) (w - \bar{w})$$

All the qualitative results of the previous section apply with one, fairly obvious, exception. As Tobin's q initially falls in the West, the capital stock still declines initially, but it now keeps declining throughout the transition. In the long run, per capita capital has declined in the West and increased in the East. In both countries unemployment increases, from zero in the East, from u_0 in the West. These effects are smaller the tighter the labor mobility constraint in the East. Thus, even with rigid real wages, unemployment would not grow in the West if real wages were perfectly flexible in the East. Furthermore, capital accumulation in the East outweighs capital decumulation in the West so that world wealth increases, the more so the less tight is the labor mobility constraint (i.e. the lower α throughout the transition).

How does real wage rigidity in the West impinge on the transition in the East? In the special case studied in the Appendix it can be shown that if the cost of mobility does not converge too fast to zero

(14), there is *less* capital accumulation in the East when western wages are fully flexible. Wage rigidity in the West favors capital accumulation in the East because the initial rise in the worldwide interest rate is met in West by higher unemployment. When q^* recovers later on, the capital labor ratio in the West is partly restored by a fall in unemployment. Less capital accumulation needs to occur because there was less capital decumulation to start with. This means less pressure on interest rates from the West, which benefits capital accumulation in the East. In fact, under the same conditions, total world capital accumulation is larger with rigid wages in the West.

6. - Conclusion

As the East starts with a low level of productive capital per capita, workers face a low marginal productivity of labor. The prospect of low real wages until the transition is completed, which may take several years if not decades, will act as a powerful incentive for workers to migrate. Such migration is not desirable, neither for the East, for it would reduce the marginal productivity of capital and therefore its accumulation and wealth increase, nor for the West where an additional supply of labor would force wages down. A central question therefore is how to avoid migration.

A likely answer may be generated by the internal political dynamics of the new Eastern democracies. Time and again history has shown how major political changes are quickly accompanied by steep wage increases. This paper has studied the possible effects of such an outcome, deliberately overlooking a host of issues which would accompany a major wage push, chiefly inflation and external imbalances. Real wage rigidity is always a recipe for unemployment, and that is the case in the present case. In addition, it appears that capital accumulation itself is affected.

An important issue is how will the West respond. To tackle this question, it is useful to think in terms of incentives and to ask first how will the West be affected. As is clear, in any case, the West will have to

---

(14) The precise condition is given in the Appendix.

finance external balances, and should gladly do so in view of the potential high marginal productivity of capital (15). But the West and the East share two common interests in the process described here. Both have an interest in avoiding migration, which calls for high wages in the East. At the same time, worldwide wealth increase will be higher the lower are labor costs. This common externality suggests that some form of wage subsidies, financed by the West, may be a second best solution during the transition. Much work is required to give a precise content to this idea, particularly in view of severe moral hazards difficulties.

---

(15) On this point see BEGG *et* AL. [1] and WYPLOSZ [7].

1. - A Particular Case With an Explicit Solution

In this appendix, we derive the solution of the model used in the case when the cost of labor mobility declines exponentially. The key equations of the model are *(6)*, *(24)* and *(25)*, along with *(13)*. Here *(13)* is particularized in two ways. First, it is assumed that w is indexed to the steady state wage level in the West, i.e. $w = (1 - \alpha)\, w^*$. Second the mobility cost is assumed to decline exponentially, i.e. $\alpha\,(t) = \alpha_0\, e^{-\theta t}$. Under these assumptions, the labor mobility constraint can be linearized as:

(A1) $\qquad w - \bar{w} = -\,\bar{w}\,\alpha \qquad$ and $\qquad \dot{w} = \bar{w}\,\theta\,\alpha$

Note that: $\qquad\qquad\qquad \bar{w} = \bar{w}^*$

2. - Model of Paragraph 4

Under these conditions *(24)* and *(25)* become:

(A2) $\qquad\qquad \dot{q} = \gamma_5\,(q - 1) - \gamma\,(k^* - \bar{k}^*) - \gamma_3\,\alpha$

(A3) $q^* = \gamma_2 = h'\,(0)\,(q - 1) + \delta\,(q^* - 1) + \gamma_1\,(k^* - \bar{k}^*) - \gamma_4\,\alpha$

with: $\qquad\qquad \gamma_3 = [(1 - \bar{u})\,\theta\,\gamma_2 + \gamma_1]\,\psi'\,(\bar{w})\,\bar{w}$

$\qquad\qquad\qquad \gamma_4 = [(1 - \bar{u})\,\theta\,\gamma_2 - \gamma]\,\psi'\,(\bar{w})\,\bar{w}$

$\qquad\qquad\qquad \gamma_5 = \delta + \gamma_2\,h'\,(0)$

Along with *(6)* rewritten as:

(A4) $\qquad\qquad\qquad \dot{k} = h'\,(0)\,(q - 1)$

(A5) $\qquad\qquad\qquad \dot{k}^* = h'\,(0)\,(q^* - 1)$

these four equations fully characterize the system. Note that it is block-recursive, with *(A4)* solved in a second stage. The first block, comprised of *(A2)*, *(A3)* and *(A5)*, is saddle-path stable with one negative root λ. Given that $\alpha = \alpha_0 e^{-\theta t}$, we can guess that the solution is of the form:

(A6) $$q(t) - 1 = A_1 e^{-\theta t} + A_2 e^{\lambda t})$$

(A7) $$q^*(t) - 1 = A^*(\theta e^{-\theta t} + \lambda e^{\lambda t})$$

(A8) $$k^*(t) - k^* = -h'(0) A^* (e^{-\theta t} - e^{\lambda t})$$

where we have used the initial condition $k^*(0) = \bar{k}^*$. Then tedious computation shows that:

(A9) $$q(0) - 1 = A_1 + A_2$$

(A10) $$q^*(0) - 1 = (\theta + \lambda) A^*$$

(A11) $$\bar{k} - k(0) = h'(0)[(A_1/\theta) - (A_2/\lambda)]$$

The signs of these expressions are generally ambiguous and are given by the following conditions:

$$q(0) > 1$$

when: $$(\delta + \theta - \lambda)(\gamma_5 - \lambda)\gamma_3 + \gamma h'(0)\gamma_4 > 0$$

$$q^*(0) > 1$$

when: $$\gamma_2 h'(0)\gamma_3 - (\gamma_5 + \theta)\gamma_4 > 0$$

$$\bar{k} > k(0)$$

when: $(\gamma_5 - \lambda)[\gamma_1 h'(0) - \theta\lambda]\gamma_3 + (\gamma_5 + \theta - \lambda)\gamma h'(0)\gamma_4 > 0$

To interpret these conditions, it is instructive to see how they vary with the size of θ. As θ increases α becomes smaller yet positive, $q^*(0) - 1$ becomes negative while $q(0) - 1$ and $\bar{k} - k(0)$ become positive. Indeed, $\theta \to \infty$ is the limiting case where $\alpha = 0$ so that nothing happens in the West while unemployment jumps to its steady state level in the East. Furthermore, the absolute values of all the above expressions is proportional to the initial cost of mobility α_0.

3. - Model of Paragraph 5

Using *(A1)* and *(26)* we find that the model, linearized, is fully described by the two following equations:

(A12) $\dot{q} = \gamma_5 (q - 1) + \gamma_2 h'(0)(q^* - 1) - \gamma_3 \alpha$

(A13) $\dot{q}^* = \gamma_2 h'(0)(q - 1) + \gamma_5 (q^* - 1) - \gamma_4 \alpha$

Of course, *(A4)* and *(A5)* then determine k and k^*. The solution is of the form:

(A14) $q - 1 = A e^{-\theta t}$

(A15) $q^* - 1 = B e^{-\theta t}$

It can be shown that $A > 0$ but the sign of B is ambiguous. Total capital accumulation is:

(A16) $\bar{k} - k_0 = h'(0) A/\theta$ and $\bar{k}^* - k_0^* = h'(0) B/\theta$

To compare the models of paragraphs 4 and 5 we compute the following:

(A17) $(A_1/\theta - A_2/\lambda) - A/\theta = K_1 [(\gamma_5 + \theta) \gamma_4 - \gamma_2 h'(0) \gamma_3] \alpha_0$

(A18) $(A_1/\theta - A_2/\lambda) - (A + B)/\theta = - K_2 (\theta + \lambda) A^*$

where $K1$ and $K2$ are both positive expressions. Note that the condition for capital accumulation in the East *(A17)* depends on the same sign condition as $q^*(0) - 1 = (\theta + \lambda) A^*$ in paragraph 4. The same conditions also characterizes world capital accumulation in *(A18)*.

BIBLIOGRAPHY

[1] BEGG DAVID - DANTHINE JEAN-PIERRE - GIAVAZZI FRANCESCO - WYPLOSZ CHARLES: «The East, the Deutschmark, and EMU», *Monitoring European Integration*, London, CEPR, 1990.

[2] BLANCHARD OLIVIER J. - SUMMERS LAWRENCE: «Perspectives on High World Interest Rates», *Brookings Paper on Economic Activity*, n. 2, 1984, pp. 273-344.

[3] ————: «Hysteresis and the European Unemployment Problem», NBER, *Macroeconomic Annuals*, 1986.

[4] GIUSTINIANI A. - PAPADIA F. - PORCIANI D.: «The Effects of the Eastern European Countries' Economic Reform on the Western Industrial Economies: A Macroeconomic Approach», *Rivista di Politica Economica*, n. 4, 1991.

[5] HAMILTON CARL - NEVEN DAMIEN - NORMAN VICTOR - SAPIR ANDRE SMITH ALASDAIR - WINTERS ALAN: «Trade Patterns and Trade Policies», Londra, CEPR, *Monitoring European Integration*, 1990.

[6] HAYASHI FUMIO: «Tobin's Marginal and Average q: a Neoclassical Interpretation», *Econometrica*, n. 50, 1982, pp. 213-24.

[7] WYPLOSZ CHARLES: «The Real Exchange Rate Effect of German Unification», *Weltwirschaftkiches Archiv.*, forthcoming 1991.

The Effects of the Eastern European Countries' Economic Reform on the Western Industrial Economies: a Macroeconomic Approach

Alessandro Giustiniani - **Francesco Papadia** - **Daniela Porciani**
Banca d'Italia, Roma

1. - Introduction and Summary (1)

During the sixties, a quite vivid debate developed among economists and sociologists on the issue raised by Tinbergen ([58], p. 341) on the converging pattern shown by centrally planned and market economies, as each system was adopting elements of the other (2). In a nutshell, the thesis was that the two economic systems, considered less than optimal in the light of their difficulties, would move towards an intermediate "optimal" economic *regime*. However, Tinbergen concluded underlining that: «It is ... hardly conceivable that we will soon be able to indicate precisely where the optimum lies, or even to say whether 'East and West' will actually 'meet' in their attempts to find the 'welfare summit'».

---

(1) This paper is dedicated to the memory of Stefano Vona whose comments, criticism and help we missed so much. The authors are grateful to P. Catte, C. De Vincenti, A. Gelb, P. Kenen, T. Krueger, M. Marrese, G. Meredith, G. Szegö, U. Thumm, and C. Wyplosz for their helpful comments. G. Meredith and J.C. Martinez Oliva helped in handling the INTERMOD world model. The views expressed are those of the authors and do not necessarily reflect those of the Banca d'Italia. The authors are the only responsible for all remaining mistakes and drawbacks.

Advise: the numbers in square brackets refer to the Bibliography in the appendix.

(2) For a deeper analysis of the convergence theory see, for example, LAUTERBACH [28], SPULBER and HOROWITZ [55] and ELLMAN [16].

After thirty years, the current extraordinary developments in Central and Eastern Europe have probably answered Tinbergen's dilemmas. East and West are very near to meeting even though the picture is completely different from that imagined by Tinbergen. As it has been clearly stressed by Roland ([48], p. 385): «If a convergence process is taking place nowadays, it is not a convergence of both capitalism and socialism towards some median optimal order, but a one-side convergence of centrally planned economies towards Western-style market economies».

It is clear that Western industrial economies are not at all *laissez-faire* economies and that public policy covers very important functions; however, the superiority of the "regulated market economy" is now evident.

Since the reconstruction needs of these economies are by any standard large (3), extraordinary opportunities should open up for Western firms and therefore significant consequences for our economies should be expected. However, the substantial uncertainty about the pace and content of economic reforms in these countries, the difficulties that Eastern economies will face in re-orienting their exports from CMEA partners to Western markets may induce a more sober view. The aim of this paper, however, is to shed some light on the magnitude of the challenges that the world economy will face over the next several years even if the reform process in the East is successful and sustained. We adopt a simple neoclassical growth model where capital is perfectly mobile whereas labour is immobile. Hence, the possibility of large migration flows from East to West is ruled out (4). The relaxation of this last hypothesis would substantially change our results.

Our attempt to quantify the impact of reform in the East on Western economies differs from the approach adopted by the Project Link [47]. In that case, the analysis was based on evaluations of the likely scale of foreign-resource transfers (official capital flows and direct investment) to Central and Eastern European countries in

---

(3) European CMEA countries, including the Soviet Union, have broadly the same population as the European Community while their total product is about a half. This gives a rough idea of the gap that these economies are expected to fill in coming years.

(4) On this issue, see for example FITOUSSI and PHELPS [21] and WYPLOSZ [65].

coming years. Since these flows are likely to be modest in a macro-economic perspective, with the exception of those emanating from German unification, the impact of the reconstructing process of Eastern Europe and the Soviet Union on Western countries is esti-mated to be negligible.

The point of departure of our analysis is different. We try to assess the potential demand for foreign resources by the Central and Eastern European countries by estimating the investment require-ments for these economies to catch up with their Western counter-parts.

We are aware of the limits of this approach because of four basic problems. Firstly, the statistical information about the present state of Eastern economies is very uncertain: even for a statistic as funda-mental as national income, different sources give widely differing estimates (5). Secondly, since the Eastern economies are undergoing a very deep structural change, the parameters needed to obtain the required estimates cannot be derived from past information but must be obtained by educated guesses. Thirdly, for lack of a world model including the economies of Central and Eastern Europe, the exercise is essentially recursive: the import requirements of the East are estimated and these affect Western economies but there is no feed-back to the East. Fourthly, the very idea that the supply of capital is very elastic with respect to return differentials may be questionable: the trend is clearly in that direction but it is not at all warranted that flows of the size we estimate are realistic from a balance-of-payments perspective.

The present paper is organized in the following manner. Para-graph 2 tries to estimate the import requirements deriving from the reform process in the East. The starting point of the analysis is the illustration of the fact that human capital indicators in Eastern and Central Europe are broadly similar to those of Western Europe, in particular of its Southern part. Looking, country by country, at human capital indicators and geographical vicinity, each Eastern country is matched to a Western counterpart, represented by a single

---

(5) For an overview of the methods used to estimate GDP levels in Eastern Europe and Soviet Union, see HAVLIK [24].

country or by the average of a group of countries. It is assumed that the Eastern country will, in a number of years, achieve the same basic characteristics of its Western counterpart, in particular as regards labour productivity. This is brought about over the years by very rapid "technological progress" and by increases in the capital-labour ratio. The investment needed to achieve this increase in the capital-labour ratio is then transformed into import requirements by making some bold assumptions about the behaviour of fundamental national accounting variables, in particular consumption, in the East.

The resulting import requirements are huge, notwithstanding the fact that many choices were made, during the estimation, with a view to avoid their explosion. In the first year of the simulation the additional net import requirement is equal to about 300 billion 1989 constant dollars, the amount grows to 450 billion by the sixth year and to 800 billion by the thirteenth year, which is the end period of our simulation, corresponding to the time when the fastest Eastern country (the Eastern region of Germany) reaches its Western counterpart (the former FRG). The additional demand from the East is not only very large but also heavily concentrated on the former West Germany which would have alone to "export", by the thirteenth year, nearly 250 billion dollars more, i.e. about 30% of the total. At the other extreme of the range, the US would have additional demand for only 17 billion dollars by the end of the simulation period, equal to about 2% of the total shock.

In paragraph 3 the estimated import requirement shocks are applied, in the framework of the INTERMOD macroeconomic model, to the Western economies. The results are, as it could be expected, disruptive: a gargantuan increase in interest rates, large exchange-rate variations, a substantial increase in inflation, huge crowding out of domestic demands. A policy of deep cuts of government expenses offsetting a half of the additional demand shock mitigates, again according to INTERMOD simulations, some of the most extreme consequences by increasing national savings. However, severe macroeconomic strains persist; furthermore, the assumed cuts in government expenses are so large, especially in Germany, as to be politically unfeasible and economically undesirable.

What is also required, we conclude, is that Eastern countries finance a larger share of their investment needs with domestic resources by increasing national saving through a strong policy of reduction of public expenses. As an example, we calculate that if they managed to increase national saving by 3% of GDP, their import requirement would be reduced by about a fifth. In addition, Western countries should also pursue a determined policy of trade liberalization, as embodied, for instance, in the Uruguay Round and in the Single Market project within the EEC, in order to spread more evenly the demand shock across the industrial countries by increasing the substitutability of the goods they produce.

2. - Macroeconomic Characterization of the Reform in the East: A Scenario

As it has been clearly stressed by Hardt and McMillan ([23], p. 2), in Eastern Europe and the Soviet Union the traditional system of centralized planning and management have failed in three critical areas: «Long misallocation of resources had created inefficient production structures which the system then perpetuated and reinforced. Centralized administration of investment and material supply proved increasingly cumbersome, inefficient and prone to arbitrary decision (6).

The system proved unable to stimulate a rate of technical progress sufficient to offset the downward pressures on growth from the inefficient use of increasingly scarce resources. This in turn forced greater reliance on external sources of technology.

The poor operation of the system in these first two respects resulted in the inadequate development of economically competitive export sectors in the process of industrialization. This in turn led to chronic balance of payments problems, especially with the West, which became more critical with the increasing reliance on imported technology to maintain growth».

Despite these failures, «the potential quality of labour inputs in these economies is judged to be reasonably high, though massive

---

(6) On the issue of investment inefficiency and growth see the Appendix.

over-manning, lack of proper incentives, and general management failure have resulted in low work-effort and poor productivity» (OECD [42], p. 47).

These considerations represent the starting point of our exercise. The basic idea is that, since the return on human capital, which represents one of the fundamental driving forces of economic development, has been compressed by the distorted economic system prevailing in the East, the replacement of that system with a more efficient one should, over time, bring labour productivity towards the levels prevailing in the West. Graphs 1 and 2 illustrate the very low level of return on human capital in planned economies. Graph 1 shows the data on life expectancy at birth and (the log of) income per head reported by the United Nations Development Programme [61] for a group of about 130 countries. As shown by the interpolating line, there is a strong positive relationship between the two variables. It also appears that planned economies, especially those with relatively high income, have an income per head lower than it would be warranted by the level of their life expectancy. An analogous conclusion can be drawn from Graph 2 where the relationship, admittedly more sensational, between (the two log of) income per head and the literacy rate is reported.

It is obvious that human capital is a very complex variable that cannot be captured by simple indicators such as those used above (7) and not even by the more articulated ones used below to conclude that it is broadly comparable in Eastern and Western Europe. It is also obvious that there cannot be an instantaneous jump of the return to human capital and that substantial time is needed to let a learning-by-doing process develop. However, the idea that there is a basic relationship between human capital and growth is deeply radicated and the works by Romer [52] and Lucas [30] are breathing new life into it. Indeed, a new growth theory is developing, which, taking into account externalities, is based on increasing rather than decreasing returns to scale (8).

---

(7) See BECKER [7], MADDISON [31], DENISON [14] for an analysis of the many facets of human capital and for its relationship with economic growth.

(8) On the issue of increasing returns to scale see, also, ROMER [49], [50], [51] and BALDWIN [4], [5].

GRAPH 1

LIFE EXPECTANCY AND INCOME PER HEAD (*)

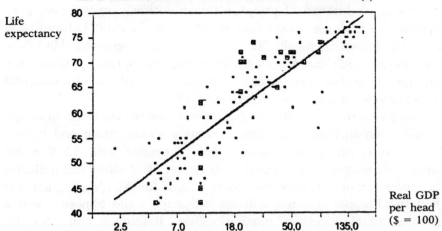

☐ Centrally planned economies.

(*) The values of the *X* axis have been calculated on a logarithmic scale.
Source: United Nations, Development Programme [61].

GRAPH 2

ADULT LITERACY RATE AND INCOME PER HEAD (*)

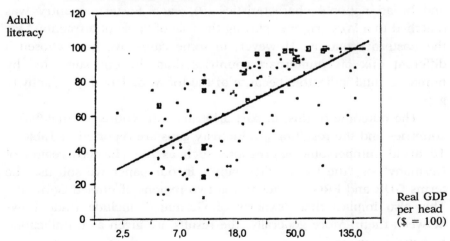

☐ Centrally planned economies.

(*) The values of the *X* axis have been calculated on a logarithmic scale.
Source: United Nations, Development Programme [61].

Our paper does not follow this line of thought, remaining in the Solowian tradition, but it is not inconsistent with it. Indeed, in our framework technological progress (albeit formally exogenous) goes together with intense accumulation, such that the capital-output ratio does not change drastically. This is an historical regularity (Maddison [32], Romer [52] that we maintain in our assumptions, without any attempt at explanation, which is instead one of the fundamental contributions, of the "new growth theory".

To give a more specific content to our idea we consider, in Graph 3, eight human capital indicators, relating to education and health. The Eastern European countries are compared with 12 Western European countries and 4 developing countries. A white cell indicates that the reference country has a better value for the specific indicator than the Eastern country, a black cell implies the opposite, and a question mark identifies missing values. Reference countries are ordered from top to bottom according to the number of white cells they have, i.e. according to their human capital endowment. Hence, it is observable that, overall, the human capital indicators of the Eastern countries are broadly comparable to those of middle ranking Western European countries, i.e. to countries of Southern Europe.

Taking into account the human capital information in Graph 3 and broad national characteristics (9), each Eastern country was matched to a Western one, playing the role of "pole of attraction" for the Eastern economy. However, in some cases, we have chosen a different mix of counterpart countries than the one suggested by human capital indicators because of the too wide labour-productivity gap.

The outcome of this, in part arbitrary, procedure of "matching" countries and the resulting productivity gaps are reported in Table 1. To avoid cumbersome expressions such as the "Eastern region of Germany" or "the former Germany", in our paper we still use the terms GDR and FRG to refer to the two regions of unified Germany. This also implies that "exports of Germany" include trade flows between them. More generally, the results are given as if unification had not occurred.

---

(9) As much as possible, also geographical vicinity has been taken into account in choosing the Western country to which a given Eastern country is to converge.

GRAPH 3

MAIN HUMAN CAPITAL INDICATORS

Countries: Denmark, Finland, Sweden, Italy, France, Austria, The Netherlands, FRG, Greece, Portugal, Spain, Turkey, Mexico, Brazil, India, Nigeria

Comparison groups: USSR, Romania, Poland, Hungary, RDT, Czechoslovakia, Bulgaria

Indicators: 1 2 3 4 5 6 7 8

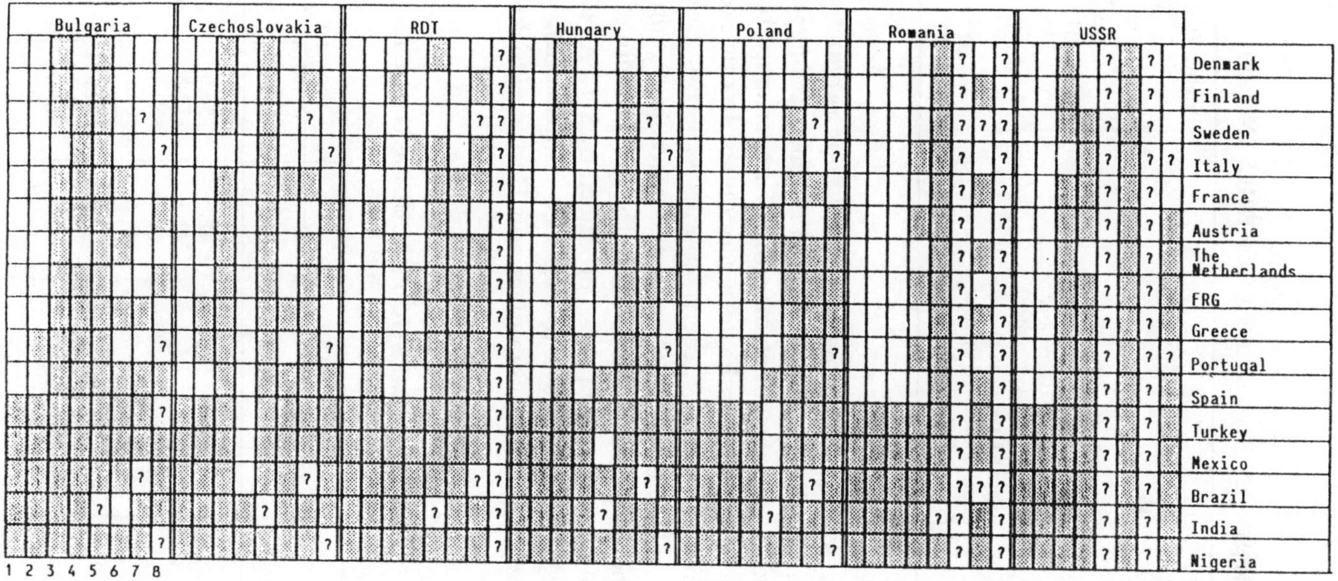

Legend:

1 Life expectancy at birth.
2 Infant mortality rate.
3 Population per physician.
4 Secondary school enrollment.
5 Science/engineering as % of tertiary students.
6 Pupil/teacher ratio (primary school).
7 Pupil/teacher ratio (secondary school).
8 Pupils reaching grade as % of the cohort.

Source: WORLD BANK: *World Development Report 1989*, Oxford, Oxford University Press.

TABLE 1

PRODUCTIVITY GAPS
OF THE EASTERN EUROPEAN COUNTRIES IN 1989

Eastern European country	Reference countries	Relative Productivity (East/West) (in %)
Bulgaria	Greece-Portugal	40
Czechoslovakia	Austria-Greece-Portugal	31
German Dem. Rep.	Fed. Rep. of Germany	35
Hungary	Austria-Greece-Portugal	23
Poland	Austria-Greece-Portugal	19
Romania	Austria-Greece-Portugal	24
USSR	France-Italy-Spain-Portugal	36

These figures, which show how low the labour productivity of these countries is, relative to that of their reference countries, are obviously surrounded by substantial margins of uncertainty because of the poor quality of statistics on Eastern economies. In our exercise, we use IMF estimates of the Eastern countries' Gross Domestic Product (GDP) converted into US dollars at the prevailing commercial exchange rates. These estimates, as shown in the first column of Table 2, turn out to be about one half of those produced by WEFA [62] and by Alton et Al. [2]; the figures we use also give substantially lower GDP per head than reported by Summers and Heston [56] for 1985

TABLE 2

ALTERNATIVE GROSS DOMESTIC PRODUCT ESTIMATES
(1989 - in billions of US dollars)

	WEFA			Alton et Al. [2]	
	(1)	(2)	(1/2) (%)	(3)	(1/3) (%)
Bulgaria	21.6	50.9	42.4	50.9	42.4
Czechoslovakia	50.1	121.4	41.3	122.8	40.8
German Dem. Rep.	130.8	188.0	69.6	159.4	82.1
Hungary	28.9	72.9	39.6	64.6	44.7
Poland	66.8	215.1	31.1	172.9	38.6
Romania	53.5	92.0	58.2	105.5	50.7
USSR	1,564.5	2,034.7	76.9	n.a.	...

within the International Comparison Project. The experience with the GDR after unification seems, however, to suggest that production potential in the East is closer to the lower rather than the higher estimates.

After this phase of "matching", we have supposed that each Eastern country will converge towards its Western counterpart as regards basic macroeconomic characteristics such as labour productivity, capital-labour ratio and total factor productivity (TFP). For lack of data on all Western counterpart countries and to avoid a mechanistic interpretation of this idea, the calibration of the assumptions necessary to carry out the exercise for each Eastern country was also based on economic judgement. For instance, to avoid unplausibly large productivity gains we took into account the experience of those Western countries which after World War II reconstructed their economies (Table 4).

More specifically, we assume that after T years the Eastern country reaches exactly the same labour productivity level of the reference country. Differences in the length of the "catching-up" period reflect differences in the progress of the reform process and in the initial width of the productivity gap. Therefore, T is fixed at 21 years for the USSR, 17 for Poland, 15 for Hungary, Czechoslovakia and Romania, 13 for the Eastern region of Germany and Bulgaria.

Having fixed the counterpart country and the time period required for the catch-up, we can easily derive the required rate of productivity growth:

(2.1)
$$g_q^E = \left(\frac{q_T^W}{q_0^E} \right)^{1/T} - 1$$

where q is the output per worker, g_q is the rate of growth of labour productivity, superscripts E and W indicate the Eastern and the Western country, respectively (10).

---

(10) In the case of the Western country, we extrapolate labour productivity by applying the average rate of productivity growth experienced in the period 1976-1989. If more than one Western country is taken into account, the rate of labour productivity growth of the "synthetic" reference country is given by a weighted average of the countries considered, where the weights are given by their respective labour productivity shares in 1989.

Therefore, given the required rate of labour productivity and assuming that employment in the Eastern country grows at a rate (g_L) equal to its average in the last twenty years, we can determine the required rate of output growth (g_Q):

(2.2) $$g_Q^E = g_q^E + g_L^E$$

Following the neoclassical tradition, output is supposed to grow as the result of the long-term effects of labour force expansion, capital formation, and technological change (11). In fact, by assuming that the production function in the Eastern countries can be represented by a standard Cobb-Douglas function, it is possible to write:

(2.3) $$g_Q = g_A + \alpha g_K + (1 - \alpha) g_L$$

where g_Q, g_K, g_L, and g_A are the growth rates of aggregate output, capital, labour and total factor productivity, and α is the share of capital in the total product, which has been assumed to be equal to 0.30 for all the countries on the basis of information reported in Nuti [38] and Maddison [32].

To achieve the required rate of productivity growth we can count on capital accumulation and technological progress.

To figure out the relative roles of these two factors, we first determine the initial value of the TFP of the Eastern country as a share of the absolute level of TFP of Italy in 1989 (12). Then, we assume a rate of TFP growth that satisfies the condition of maintaining the capital-output ratio in a range between 2 and 3 (13) and generates, by the end of the catch-up period, a TFP level consistent with that of the counterpart Western country. In doing so, we also looked at the experience of countries like Japan, Germany, Italy, and Greece which in the sixties experienced a period of very fast growth in their catch-up

---

(11) For sake of simplicity, we make the additional assumption that technical progress is neutral in the Hicksian sense that it raises the output achievable from a given combination of capital and labour without affecting their marginal product.

(12) The TFP of Italy in 1989 is just a scale factor, estimated assuming that, also in this case, the production function is a Cobb-Douglas with $\alpha = 0.30$.

(13) On the approximate constancy of the capital-output ratio see ROMER [52] and MADDISON [32].

towards the technological frontier represented by the United States (14). The analogy between these countries and the Eastern countries resides in the drastic political changes affecting both, and in the fact that these changes are associated with the reconstruction and the reintegration of the national economies into the world economy; for instance, from an economic point of view, the end of the fascist autarky in Italy can be assimilated to the demise of the CMEA in the case of the Eastern countries.

The average rates of TFP growth used in the estimation carried out with the straight converging path are quite high (Table 3), generally even higher than those recorded by top performers such as Japan, Germany, Italy and Greece in the sixties; so are the growth rates of labour productivity and, given the approximate constancy of the employment, those of output. In a sense, this is an important result *per se*: even scaling down the ambitions by choosing "easy" counterpart countries and assuming a fairly long catch-up period, the present economic performance of Eastern countries is so poor that extremely high growth rates are required to fill the productivity gap (Table 4).

TABLE 3

ASSUMED AVERAGE GROWTH RATES OF TFP, CAPITAL AND GDP IN EASTERN COUNTRIES DURING THE CATCH-UP PERIOD
(in %)

•	Bulgaria	Czecho-slovakia	GDR	Hungary	Poland	Romania	USSR
TFP	5.5	6.5	6.7	7.5	7.5	6.6	5.1
K	9.2	8.9	10.1	11.1	12.4	13.8	7.9
GDP	9.0	10.2	10.7	11.5	12.3	11.6	8.4

The methodology described so far also allows us to circumvent the problem that the available estimates of the existing capital stocks in the Eastern countries are unreliable, since they overestimate the stock of economically productive capital, reflecting obsolete tech-

---

(14) On this issue, see for example BAUMOL [6], GOLDSMITH [22], CHENERY [13], WOLFF [64], ENGLANDER [17], and ENGLANDER and MITTELSTADT [18].

TABLE 4

PRODUCTIVITY, OUTPUT AND INPUT GROWTH IN WESTERN
EUROPEAN COUNTRIES: 1960-1986
(business sector; average percentage changes at annual rates)

	Output	TFP	Labour productivity	Capital productivity	Capital growth
Japan					
1960-1973	9.7	6.1	8.6	−2.4	12.1
1973-1986	3.8	1.7	3.0	−2.5	6.3
Germany					
1960-1973	4.6	2.8	4.9	−1.1	5.6
1973-1986	2.0	1.3	2.7	−1.2	3.2
Italy					
1960-1973	5.6	4.7	6.5	0.4	5.2
1973-1986	2.4	1.1	1.8	−0.6	2.9
Greece					
1960-1973	8.4	6.6	9.1	−3.4	11.8
1973-1986	2.3	0.6	1.6	−3.3	5.9
OECD (average)					
1960-1973	5.2	2.8	4.1	−0.4	5.6
1973-1986	2.6	0.6	1.5	−1.4	4.0

Source: ENGLANDER and MITTELSTADT [18].

nologies and wrong relative prices. Anecdotal, but widespread, information is available on the poor state of much of the productive capital in the Eastern Europe and the Soviet Union. This information is broadly consistent with the findings of Bergson [8] that labour productivity in a group of Eastern countries (the USSR, Hungary, Poland and Yugoslavia) is between one third and one quarter lower than in the West, controlling for different levels of capital and land per worker (15). This evidence could be interpreted in the sense that part

---

(15) On the contrary, BURKETT and SKEGRO ([10] p. 1130), by estimating CES and translog functions for national income from data on 65 countries in 1975, conclude that: «while the relative productivity of socialist economies may decline as capital-labour ratios rise, the net effect of socialism on productivity is insignificantly different from zero at all observed levels of the capital-labour ratio».

of the physical capital which is available in the East is not economically productive and thus contributes to low labour productivity.

Having assumed the absolute level of TFP in each Eastern country for 1989 and in all following years, the "required" capital stock is estimated by simply inverting the production function (16), that is:

$$(2.4) \qquad K_{t-1} = \left[\frac{Q_t}{A_t \cdot L_t^{1-\alpha}} \right]^{1/\alpha}$$

The initial and final estimated capital-output and capital-labour ratios are reported in Table 5.

Eventually, given the estimated time series of the capital stock and imposing a declining rate of capital depreciation (under the

TABLE 5

CAPITAL-OUTPUT AND CAPITAL-LABOUR RATIOS
(1989 US dollars)

	Capital-labour ratio		Capital-output ratio	
	initial	final (*)	initial	final (*)
Bulgaria	11,937	48,255	2.4	3.0
Czechoslovakia	14,532	63,813	2.3	2.3
German Dem. Rep...........	39,349	177,609	2.6	3.0
Hungary....................	11,561	83,947	2.4	3.1
Poland	8,110	78,528	2.1	2.8
Romania...................	10,263	102,249	2.1	3.7
USSR	21,966	109,082	2.0	2.0
Memorandum:				
Federal Republic of Germany	128,860	187,749	3.0	3.1
France	99,960	167,604	2.3	2.6
Italy.......................	110,079	162,003	2.7	2.6
Greece	56,329	85,259	3.8	4.5

(*) For Bulgaria and German Democratic Republic: 13 years after the beginning of catch-up; for Czechoslovakia, Hungary, and Romania: 15 years; for Poland: 17 years; for the USSR: 21 years; for the reference countries: 15 years.

---

(16) In the specification of the production function, we have assumed that the capital stock relevant for the production at time t is that at the end of the previous period.

hypothesis that in the first years of the catch-up period the Eastern economies will have to scrap a significant part of their obsolete capital stock) (17), we get the required gross investment flows.

In principle, to transform these investment requirements into import requirements, nothing less than a macroeconomic model of each Eastern country would be needed, since the crucial issue is the proportion to which additional investment is to be financed by national savings or by a current account deficit. Two very simple assumptions have been used here to deal with this problem.

First, consumption is supposed to grow at the same rate as income, under the hypothesis that any saving which will be made in public consumption, maybe because of reduction in military expenses, will go into additional private consumption to satisfy pent-up consumer demand. Thus, the average propensity to consume is kept constant.

Second, exports are assumed to grow at a rate slightly higher than the average rate of growth of world trade in the period 1973-1990 (7 vs. 5.1%) under the conjecture that the Eastern countries will gain market share in the world market.

These assumptions allow us to determine imports as a residual, that is as the difference between production and demand. As a consequence of the way in which the exercise has been constructed, the time path of imports is dominated by required investment.

The resulting net import requirements are reported in Table 6. It is evident the extent of the resource transfer which, sooner or later, would be required to bring these countries towards productivity levels comparable to those of the market economies. In the first year of our simulation, the trade deficit of the Eastern European countries jumps from 10.4 to 310 billion 1989 US dollars, and reaches, in the last year considered, the astonishing peak of 791 billion, which represents about 14% of the estimated GDP of the whole region.

It may be useful to summarily compare our results with those obtained by the OECD [41] and Masson and Meredith [33] for the

---

(17) In the estimation exercise, we have assumed that the rate of depreciation linearly declines from 7 to 4% between the beginning and the end of the catch-up period.

TABLE 6

NET IMPORT REQUIREMENTS
(billions of 1989 US dollars)

Year	Bulgaria	Czechoslovakia	GDR	Hungary	Poland	Romania	USSR	Total
1989	− 0.9	0.7	3.6	1.0	3.0	2.4	6.9	− 10.4
1	− 5.0	− 7.7	− 36.6	− 7.9	− 21.1	− 9.2	− 222.9	− 310.3
2	− 5.5	− 8.2	− 40.1	− 8.8	− 23.9	− 11.1	− 235.8	− 333.3
3	− 6.0	− 8.7	− 43.9	− 9.9	− 27.1	− 13.4	− 249.5	− 358.4
4	− 6.5	− 9.2	− 48.2	− 11.0	− 30.7	− 16.0	− 264.0	− 385.8
5	− 7.1	− 9.8	− 53.0	− 12.4	− 34.8	− 19.2	− 279.3	− 415.7
6	− 7.8	− 10.4	− 58.3	− 13.9	− 39.5	− 23.0	− 295.6	− 448.4
7	− 8.5	− 11.1	− 64.1	− 15.6	− 44.9	− 27.4	− 312.8	− 484.4
8	− 9.3	− 11.8	− 70.6	− 17.5	− 51.0	− 32.7	− 331.1	− 523.9
9	− 10.2	− 12.5	− 77.8	− 19.7	− 57.9	− 38.9	− 350.4	− 567.4
10	− 11.1	− 13.3	− 85.8	− 22.1	− 65.8	− 46.2	− 370.9	− 615.2
11	− 12.2	− 14.1	− 94.7	− 24.8	− 74.9	− 54.7	− 392.7	− 668.1
12	− 13.4	− 15.0	− 104.6	− 31.5	− 85.1	− 64.8	− 415.7	− 690.6
13	− 14.8	− 15.9	− 115.6	− 35.4	− 96.8	− 76.6	− 440.2	− 791.3
14		− 16.9		− 39.9	− 110.1	− 90.5	− 466.1	
15		− 18.0			− 125.3	− 106.8	− 493.6	
16					− 142.7		− 522.7	
17					− 162.4		− 553.7	
18							− 586.5	
19							− 621.4	
20							− 658.4	
21							− 697.7	

GDR, and by the CEPR [12] and Fitoussi and Phelps [21] for the whole region excluding the Soviet Union. In the OECD exercise, when the catch-up period is set equal to 15 years, the estimates of net import requirement for the GDR (available for the first 5 years after German unification) are similar to those we derive. On the contrary, Masson and Meredith obtain figures (which span for 12 years after the unification) significantly lower than ours, even in their "less optimistic scenario". This reflects different hypotheses and, in particular, the fact that the Eastern region of Germany is assumed to reach only 80 or 66 per cent of the productivity level of the Western part by the end of the simulation period. The CEPR estimates, referring to the whole Eastern Europe excluding the Soviet Union, are presented as a range: the lower bound is 1,350 billion dollars in a decade, the higher bound is close to 3,000 billion dollars. Our corresponding estimates (1,806 billion dollars) are much closer to their lower than to the upper bound. A comparison with Fitoussi and Phelps is very difficult given the different nature of the exercise, but a rough comparison of our estimates with those they present for the aggregate excluding the USSR does not reveal large inconsistencies.

As was pointed out above, one crucial behavioural parameter in this exercise, given investment requirements, is the national savings rate. Our assumption of constant propensity to save is only a simplifying assumption resulting from the expectation of a decrease in the private component and an increase in the public one, thanks to a reduction of current public expenses.

Confronted with the huge demand for resources needed to reconstruct their economies, it would however be opportune if Eastern countries did even more in terms of reduction of public expenses to finance a larger part of capital accumulation through domestic resources. Of course, the possibility to raise the national saving by means of fiscal restraint must also take into account that, according to available statistics, the savings rate is already fairly high in Eastern countries ranging from a minimum of 23% in the USSR to a maximum of 33% in Hungary and 34% in Romania, against an average of about 20% in the OECD, with the US (among the G7) at the bottom, with 15%, and Japan and Germany at the top, with 33 and 25% respectively. However, we should also take into account that

Italy in the sixties (our golden period of economic growth), had a national savings rate of about 28%.

To give an order of magnitude, if the Eastern countries managed such a deep reduction of public expenses as to increase their national savings rate by 3%, their import requirement would be reduced by about a fifth, thus lessening significantly their demand for resources from the West.

3. - Macroeconomic Effects in the West of Reform in the East

In order to transform the additional net imports of Eastern countries into additional exports of the Western industrialized countries, some assumptions have to be made about East-East and East-developing countries trade. As regards the former, we assume that each Eastern country's trade balance with the rest of the CMEA area is in equilibrium. This assumption is made for convenience but probably is not the most unreasonable one, since, in the medium term, it is very difficult to predict how trade among the CMEA countries will develop after the shift to world prices and settlements in convertible currencies from the beginning of this year (18). As regards trade with developing countries, it is assumed that the trade imbalance existing in the base year, 1989, grows at the long-run growth rate of world trade, i.e. about 5%. The final result of these two hypotheses is that the bulk of the additional net imports of the Eastern countries has to come from the industrialized Western countries.

To distribute the additional net exports between each of the G8 countries (the G7 plus an aggregate made up of the remaining small industrial countries — "other industrial countries") a trade matrix relative to the period 1987-1989 was used, reflecting the exports of each of the eight Western countries to each of the seven Eastern countries. The additional net exports of each of the G8 countries (Table 7) thus result both from the import requirement of each Eastern country and from the historical bilateral trade pattern. The

---

(18) On the problems posed to Eastern countries by the shift to trade at world prices, see KENEN [26].

final manipulation was to transform the constant 1989 dollars of Table 7 into current dollars.

To get an idea of what the additional demand for the East may mean for Western economies, the shock was imparted to the exports of the G8 countries, in the framework of the INTERMOD world model (19). The exercise is analogous to those carried out for East Germany alone by the OECD [41] and Masson and Meredith [33].

Given that the export equation in INTERMOD has the share of the country concerned in world exports as the dependent variable, the shock to the residuals of that equation took the form of an increase in the export share. In a way, all G8 countries are assumed to gain market share; this occurs because they increase their exports to the Eastern countries which are outside the model. As the figures in Table 7 are very large so is the shock: in the case of Germany and "other industrial countries" it corresponds, by the end of the simulation, i.e. by the thirteenth year, to a 5% larger share of world exports; for Canada, Italy, Japan and France it corresponds to 1/1.5% gain of market share; the shock is instead smaller in the case of the UK, 0.8%, and the US, 0.4%, given the small trade linkages with Eastern countries.

It was argued above that our exercise does not seek to be "realistic" in terms of the required capital flows in that it assumes that capital moves unhindered across borders, only seeking the highest return, without any consideration of risk, institutional factors and all the other obstacles to perfect mobility.

The results, expressed in terms of deviations from the baseline show that, in macroeconomic terms, it would be utterly undesirable to have such huge demand for resources hitting the Western economies; indeed, the results are so undesirable as to be unrealistic also in macroeconomic terms. The effects on interest and exchange rates are disruptive. Nominal long-run interest rates increase, by the end of the simulation period when the shock is largest, from a "minimum" of 9.5

---

(19) INTERMOD as illustrated by MEREDITH [35] and MASSON-MEREDITH [33], is a PC version of MULTIMOD, the world model built at the IMF (see MASSON - MEREDITH - SYMANSKY [34]) and is a small model of the economies of the G8, especially thought for simulation purposes, as witnessed by the special care put in achieving acceptable long-run characteristics and in taking into account stocks together with flows. We always simulated the model under the hypothesis of adaptive expectations.

TABLE 7

ADDITIONAL NET EXPORTS OF THE G-8 COUNTRIES
(billions of 1989 US dollars)

Year	Canada	USA	Japan	Germany	France	UK	Italy	Other industrial countries
1989	0.4	0.1	0.5	1.5	0.3	0.2	0.4	1.6
1	29.1	7.3	28.9	83.3	21.7	12.4	26.0	96.0
2	31.1	7.8	30.7	90.0	23.4	13.4	27.8	103.1
3	33.4	8.4	32.7	97.5	25.2	14.5	29.8	110.8
4	35.8	8.9	34.9	105.7	27.1	15.6	32.0	119.3
5	38.4	9.6	37.2	114.7	29.2	17.0	34.4	128.5
6	41.2	10.2	39.7	124.6	31.6	18.4	36.9	138.6
7	44.4	11.0	42.3	135.6	34.1	20.0	39.7	149.7
8	47.8	11.8	45.2	147.7	37.0	21.8	42.8	161.9
9	51.6	12.7	48.4	161.2	40.1	23.7	46.1	175.3
10	55.7	13.6	51.8	176.1	43.5	25.9	49.8	190.1
11	60.3	14.7	55.4	192.6	47.3	28.3	53.9	206.3
12	65.3	15.8	59.4	211.1	51.5	31.0	58.3	224.4
13	70.9	17.1	63.8	231.6	56.2	34.1	63.2	244.3

percentage points in the US to more than 14 in Germany (Graph 4); real long-run interest rates increase by a minimum of about 7 percentage points in the US to a staggering 12 in Germany (Graph 5). As regards the exchange rates, the estimates show, again by the end of the simulation period, that the D-mark appreciates towards the US dollar by 34%, the Canadian and "other industrial countries" currency by more than 20%, the Lira, the French Franc and the Pound by about 15%, while the Yen appreciates by about 8% (Graph 6).

The huge increase of interest rates and, in all countries except the US, the appreciation of the exchange rate can not avoid serious inflationary tensions. The deflator of GNP is, in Germany, by the thirteenth year about 44% higher than in the baseline, corresponding to a higher average yearly rate of inflation of about 3 per cent, notwithstanding an unchanged money supply (Graph 7). The increase of the GNP deflator is about 40% higher by the end of the simulation period in Canada, "other industrial countries", France, the United Kingdom, Italy; 35 and 30% higher in Japan and the US respectively. In some years, for some countries, the increase in the rate of inflation reaches 4%.

By the end of the simulation period, in all countries the level of gross domestic product is lower than in the baseline because of the large drop of consumption and the even larger drop of investment brought about by the steep increase in interest rates. This is not the case with the GNP, which takes into account the income accruing to residents from the net foreign assets, which grow enormously. In fact, GNP is 15% larger in Germany (equivalent to an average yearly growth rate about 1% higher) by the end of the simulation period, albeit with large swings, 8% larger in "other industrial countries" and in Canada, 3% larger in Italy and Japan; it is lower, by 3.5 and 1% respectively, in the US and the United Kingdom (Graph 8). The large increase in GNP in the aggregate of the G8 countries underlines the positive effect, in the long run, of the reform process in Eastern countries that increases world efficiency. The problem is that the road to this positive long run is fraught with intolerable strains.

The problem resides not only in the huge size of the estimated import requirements of the Eastern countries, but also in their concentration on Germany and, to a lesser extent, "other industrial coun-

GRAPH 4

LONG-TERM NOMINAL INTEREST RATES
Increase in net exports
(deviation from baseline)

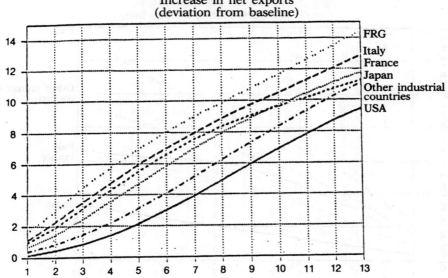

GRAPH 5

LONG-TERM REAL INTEREST RATES
Increase in net exports
(deviation from baseline)

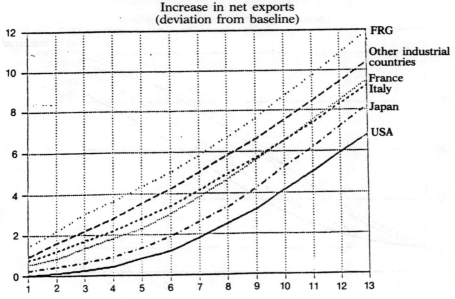

GRAPH 6

EXCHANGE RATE OF THE VARIOUS CURRENCIES
TOWARDS THE DOLLAR
Increase in net exports
(percentage deviation from baseline)

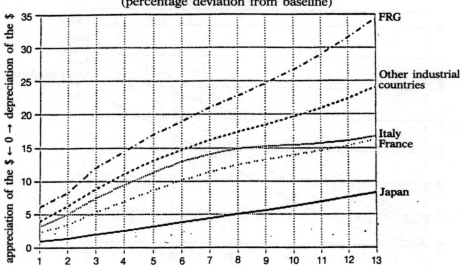

GRAPH 7

GNP DEFLATOR
Increase in net exports
(percentage deviation from baseline)

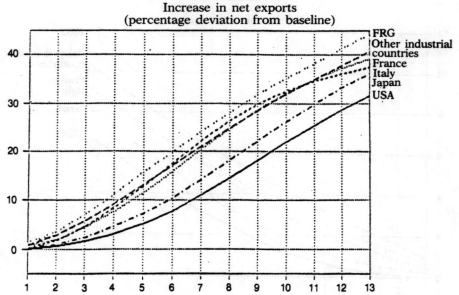

tries", Canada, Italy and France, while Japan, the United Kingdom and, particularly, the US are cut out of most the action because of their traditionally small trade flows with the Eastern countries.

The first, obvious line of defense confronted with an excess of demand is to resort to fiscal policy. To do this, it was assumed that government expenses are reduced by an amount equal to a half of the net-export shock.

The results of the simulation in which there is this "fiscal offsetting" are less dramatic but remain untolerable. The long-run rate of interest now increases by "only" 7 percentage points in Germany by the end of the simulation period, 6 in Canada and "other industrial countries", 5 in all other countries except the US, where it grows by 4 percentage points (Graph 9). Also the increase in the real long rate is less extreme, ranging by the end of the period between 6% in Germany and 3% in the US (Graph 10). The D-mark now appreciates by 20% with respect to the dollar on the thirteenth year, followed by the Canadian dollar (15%), the "other industrial countries" currency (13%), the Lira, the French Franc and the Pound (about 6%) and the Yen (5%) (Graph 11). Of course, such exchange rate movements, while more moderate, would still not be consistent with the constraints of the EMS, let alone with the irrevocably fixed rates envisaged in the European economic and monetary union. Also in terms of inflation the results are less outlandish: the deterioration in the average yearly rate of inflation in Germany is somewhat higher than 1%; it is on average around 1% in the other G8 countries and it never exceeds 2% (Graph 12). The behaviour of GDP is also more acceptable since in all countries there is practically no change with respect to the baseline by the end of the simulation period. Consumption is practically unchanged in the US, Japan and the UK, while it increases, in some cases substantially, in the other countries; investment is lower in all countries by the end of the simulation period, in some cases substantially (e.g. by nearly 10% in France). The change in GNP is about zero in the US, the UK and Japan, but, buoyed up by substantial income from foreign net assets, it is sizable in Germany (12%), Canada and "other industrial countries" (8%) and also in the remaining countries (Graph 13).

The problem is that, to achieve a "fiscal offsetting" of the size

GRAPH 8

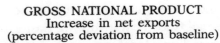

GROSS NATIONAL PRODUCT
Increase in net exports
(percentage deviation from baseline)

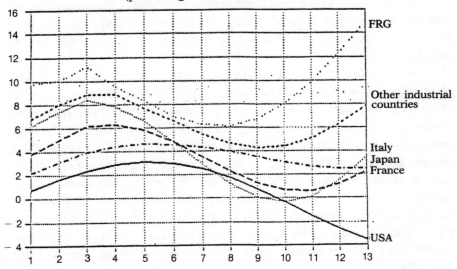

GRAPH 9

LONG-TERM NOMINAL INTEREST RATES
Increase in net exports and reduction of government expenses
(deviation from baseline)

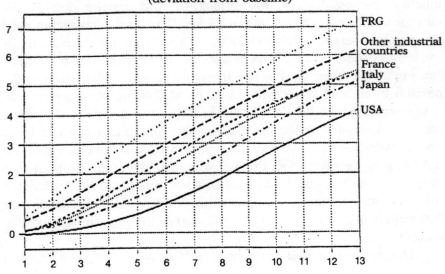

GRAPH 10

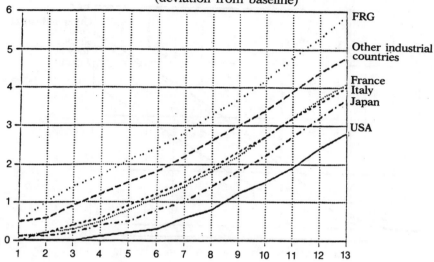

LONG-TERM REAL INTEREST RATES
Increase in net exports and reduction of government expenses
(deviation from baseline)

GRAPH 11

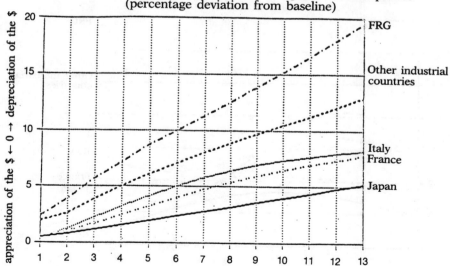

**EXCHANGE RATE OF THE VARIOUS CURRENCIES
TOWARDS THE DOLLAR**
Increase in net exports and reduction of government expenses
(percentage deviation from baseline)

GRAPH 12

GNP DEFLATOR
Increase in net exports and reduction of government expenses
(percentage deviation from baseline)

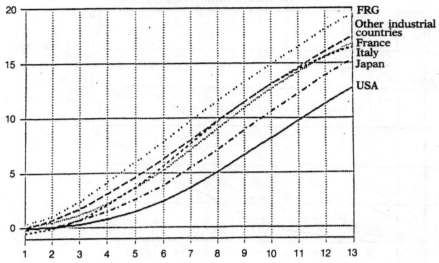

GRAPH 13

GROSS NATIONAL PRODUCT
Increase in net exports and reduction of government expenses
(percentage deviation from baseline)

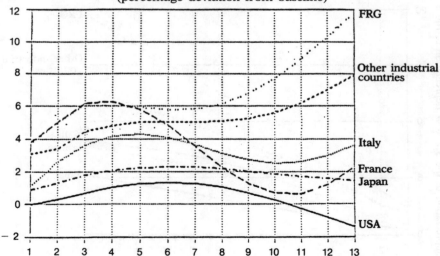

assumed above, government expenses must be reduced with respect to the baseline by about 50% in nominal terms, that is by more than 60% in real terms, in Germany, "other industrial countries" and Canada. The required reduction is smaller, but still sizable, in all the remaining countries except the US, Japan and the UK. The result of these cuts is that by the end of the simulation period all countries with the exception of the US and, marginally, Italy have a budget surplus, very substantial in the case of Germany (about 7.5% of GNP).

One economic policy conclusion emerges clearly from this second simulation: a drastic cut of government expenses and budget deficits helps freeing the resources necessary for the reconstruction of the economies of Eastern Europe but, surely, cannot be the unique answer: on one hand, cuts such as those assumed above are, for some countries, politically as well as economically unaffordable as they would require substantial reduction of necessary public services; on the other hand, they are not sufficient to reduce to an acceptable extent the large macroeconomic strains deriving from the additional Eastern countries' demand.

We have discussed in the previous section the possibility for the Eastern countries to generate a larger saving, essentially by reducing government expenses. But, of course, there are limits to what can be done in that direction. Monetary policy cannot lessen the pressure on available resources. Indeed, the only advisable course of action would be to take an even more restrictive stance to fight inflation, but this would exacerbate the rise in interest rates and the divergence of exchange rates. If we want to avoid the costly alternative of an impossibility for the Eastern countries to regain the standard of living they could attain with their human capital, the only tool left is structural policy. Unlike in many other cases, structural policy can take a very precise meaning in our setting.

Our exercise throws in full relief one aspect already noticed by the recent CEPR publication [12]: the problem of the sheer amount of resources needed to reconstruct the Eastern economies is compounded by the fact that, if the additional import flows follow the historical pattern, there will be a heavy concentration of demand on some countries, in particular on Germany. What a structural policy should do in this case is to increase the substitutability, say, between German goods and those produced by other industrial countries.

It is clear that, to a certain extent, substitutability does not have to do with policies but rather with the intrinsic characteristics of goods. However, policies matter a good deal in artificially differentiating products and making those produced by one country a poor substitute for those produced by another country. Take, as an example, procurement policies whereby national goods are administratively preferred over foreign goods or, as an other example, protectionist agricultural policies which treat much differently domestically produced goods from those produced abroad. Trade liberalization, in all fields and at all levels, is the obvious structural policy which can help spread more evenly the additional demand emanating from Eastern countries. Fundamental, in this respect, can be both the implementation of the single market in the European Community and, at last, a successful outcome of the Uruguay Round at the world level. The favourable effect of such moves would be enhanced by the efficiency gains, à la Cecchini-Baldwin (Cecchini Report [11] and Baldwin [4]), which increase available resources.

To give a quantitative idea of what could be the favourable effects of a structural policy which increased the substitutability of goods produced by the various industrial countries, we have carried out a further simulation in which the additional exports are divided among the G8 countries on the basis of their total exports, instead of the exports to the various Eastern countries as above. This could be dubbed a "world market" simulation, in the sense that we assume that structural policies have made the goods of industrial countries so substitutable one with the other that the additional demand from the East is distributed according to the size of each Western country, as approximated by its share in world exports, and not according to the bilateral export flows. It is clear that this is an extreme assumption; however, it can be useful as a standard of comparison.

As could be expected, the aggregate results for the G8 countries do not show large changes with respect to the preceding simulation (20): the deterioration of inflation performance in the US, Japan and the UK more than compensates the reduction in Germany, thus

---

(20) For the sake of brevity these results are not reported extensively and are available from the authors.

causing a slight overall deterioration of inflation; on the other hand, the improvement in real income growth in the US, the UK and Japan more than compensates the loss in Canada, Germany, "other industrial countries" and Italy. It is obvious, however, that exchange rate variations are much less extreme: the maximum appreciation towards the dollar in the previous simulation was nearly 20% (for the D-mark); in this simulation the maximum appreciation by the end of the simulation period is about 9% (for the Yen). More interesting is the fact that the "fiscal offsetting" policy in the West is now more easily achievable because it is much more equally distributed among industrial countries and thus does not require such extreme reductions as those seen above.

4. - Concluding Remarks

With all the large caveats which necessarily accompany an exercise like ours, the most interesting conclusions which emerge from our study can be briefly summarized in three points.

Firstly, if the economies of Central and Eastern Europe have to develop the full potential which would be warranted by their endowment of human capital and catch-up with their Western counterparts, they would need, in addition to very deep and difficult structural reforms which are outside the scope of this paper, a very large transfer of resources which would cause very substantial and sustained balance-of-payments deficits, much larger even than those recorded by the United States in the eighties.

Secondly, if the Western industrialized countries had to provide the vast amount of resources needed to reconstruct the economies of the East, the medium-run consequences would be unbearable in terms of interest rate increases, exchange rate changes, inflation and crowding out of local production, hence unemployment, even if in the long run the consequences would be favourable since the income on foreign assets would increase substantially. On the other hand, a scenario in which the countries of Eastern and Central Europe did not catch up with their Western counterparts would also be riddled by severe tensions. Without the Iron Curtain and given the geographical vicinity, the countries of Eastern and Central Europe will integrate more and more with Western Europe with which they share many fundamental characteristics. Persisting and large income differentials would inevitably create social unrest in the East which would inevitably spill over to the West, not least in terms of massive migration flows which it would be impossible, barring the erection of a new Iron Curtain, to stem.

Thirdly, the policy action necessary to mitigate the medium-run disruptive effects of the large increase in the demand for resources must include three components: i) a determined action of reduction of public expenses in the East such that it can accommodate the inevitable increase in private consumption and, nonetheless, bring about a substantial increase of the national savings rate; ii) a substantial increase in national savings also in the West, essentially through a reduction of public expenses; iii) an incisive structural policy which, by reducing the artificial differentiation of the products of the various industrial countries, would spread more evenly the demand shock originating in the East; examples of this kind of policies are the trade liberalization moves within the GATT and the completion of the single market in the European Community.

Investment Inefficiency and Reforms
in a Two-Country Model

What is particularly striking in the Eastern European economies, with respect to the Western ones, is the association of high rates of investment with low rates of output growth. As it has been stressed by the OECD ([42], p. 48), this evidence suggests that: «much investment has been largely wasted, so that the effective, potentially productive capital stock is small in relation to the cumulative investment effort undertaken».

In the present section, we present a simple growth model by which we try to enlighten, from a theoretical point of view, what are the consequences of the presence and of the removal of the above mentioned inefficiency in investment (21).

In the present model the world economy consists of two countries, the representative Western country and the representative Eastern country. For sake of simplicity, we make the "heroic" assumption that the two countries are identical in every respect except in investment efficiency (22). In particular, we assume that investment in the Eastern country does not translate entirely into capital accumulation because part of it is wasted due to the distortions mentioned in the previous section (23). Furthermore, we assume that the world has a life span of two periods.

Following Lipton and Sachs [29], we depart from the previous literature on two-country 'growth models because savings behaviour is

---

(21) The fundamental reasons for this inefficiency in investment have been emphasized by the UNITED NATIONS ECONOMIC COMMISSION FOR EUROPE [60], (pp. 1-6).

(22) However, the structure of the model allows to consider differences in other critical parameters.

(23) This hypothesis resembles that of costs of installing investment goods adopted, for example, by TOBIN [59], ABEL [1], and LIPTON and SACHS [29].

not determined by *ad hoc* assumptions, as for example savings proportional to disposable income and/or wealth (Fischer and Frenkel [19], [20], Oniki and Uzawa [45], and Ruffin [54]), but is derived by the intertemporal maximization behaviour of individuals.

Buiter [9], by adopting a similar approach in an overlapping generations framework, explains international capital movements in terms of different pure rate of time preference in the two countries. On the contrary, in our model, the critical determinant of international trade and of international capital movements is the presence of investment inefficiency in the Eastern country. Furthermore, as in Svensson and Razin [57], we explicitly take into account investment decisions by welfare-maximizing individuals. This hypothesis is similar to that of the Lipton and Sachs [29] model, where investment decisions are taken by value-maximizing competitive firms and hence investment depends upon Tobin's q. Instead, in our model, individuals are consumers and investors at the same time and they choose investment as to maximize their wealth defined as the present value of net output.

Since the two economies, linked together in an international commodity market and an international capital market, produce a single, identical good that can be either consumed or used for capital accumulation, the present model can be defined a "pure-absorption" model. Indeed, as stressed by Buiter ([9], p. 779): «international trade and international lending and borrowing (international capital mobility) are part and parcel of the same transaction. In a one-commodity model, the only way to pay for an extra unit of output today is with a promise of future output. Each trade balance transaction has to involve credit». Moreover, by assuming perfect capital mobility, we impose interest rates to be equalized in the world economy.

The Model

In both the Western and the Eastern country, output (Q) is given by a Cobb-Douglas production function in both the Western and Eastern country. There are only two productive factors, capital (K) and labour (L). In both countries, labour is equal to the population, which is assumed to be constant and therefore is normalized to one. Therefore, we can write:

(A.1) $$q_t = k^{\alpha}_t, \qquad t = 1,2$$

(A.1') $$q^*_t = k^{*\alpha}_t, \qquad t = 1,2$$

where all the variables are in lower case because they are expressed in per capita terms, α is the output elasticity with respect to capital, and t is the time index. All variables associated with the Eastern country are distinguished by a star surperscript.

In each country, individuals maximize an identical log-utility function subject to the present value budget constraint,

(A.2) $$\text{max. } U = \log c_1 \left(\frac{1}{1 + \theta} \right) \log c_2$$

$$\text{s.t.} \qquad c_1 + \left(\frac{1}{1 + r} \right) c_2 = W$$

(A.2') $$\text{max. } U^* = \log c^*_1 + \left(\frac{1}{1 + \theta} \right) \log c^*_2$$

$$\text{s.t.} \qquad c^*_1 + \left(\frac{1}{1 + r} \right) c^*_2 = W^*$$

where c_t is the consumption at time t, θ is the (constant) pure rate of time preference, r is the world interest rate, and W is the country's wealth. Wealth is defined as the present value of future net output (i.e., gross output minus investment):

(A.3) $$W = (q_1 - i_1) + \left(\frac{1}{1 + r} \right) q_2$$

(A.3') $$W^* = (q^*_1 - i^*_1) + \left(\frac{1}{1 + r} \right) q^*_2$$

where i denotes investment, which is zero in the second, and last period,

(A.4) $i_1 = (k_2 - k_1)$

(A.4') $i_1^* = (1 + z^*)(k_2^* - k_1^*)$, $z^* > 0$

where z^* is the inefficiency factor which affects investment in the Eastern country. Therefore, in that country it takes $1 + z^*$ units of output to increase the capital stock of one unit, because part of it is wasted during the investment process.

The model is closed by the commodity market equilibrium condition:

(A.5) $q_t + q_i^* = c_t + c_t^* + i_t + i_t^*$, $t = 1,2$

In summary, the decision problem is to determine the level of consumption in the two periods and that of investment, or more precisely the capital stock, in the second period, so as to maximize the intertemporal utility function.

Properties of the Model

Plugging investment into the budget constraint and performing the constrained maximization of the utility function, we determine consumption in period one and in period two for the two countries:

(A.6) $c_1 = \left(\dfrac{1 + \theta}{2 + \theta}\right)\left[q_1 + k_1 + \left(\dfrac{1 - \alpha}{\alpha}\right) k_2 \right]$

$c_2 = \left(\dfrac{1 + r}{1 + \theta}\right) c_1$

(A.6') $c_1^* = \left(\dfrac{1 + \theta}{2 + \theta}\right)\left[q_1^* + (1 + z^*) k_1^* + \left(\dfrac{1 - \alpha}{\alpha}\right)(1 + z^*) k_2^* \right]$

$c_2^* = \left(\dfrac{1 + r}{1 + \theta}\right) c_1^*$

Choosing the second-period capital stock so as to maximize wealth yields:

(A.7)
$$\alpha k_2^{-(1-\alpha)} = 1 + r$$

(A.7')
$$\frac{\alpha k_2^{*-(1-\alpha)}}{1 + z^*} = 1 + r.$$

The left hand side of equations (A.7) and (A.7') is the marginal productivity of capital in the second period. Since z^* is greater than zero, the second-period capital stock is lower in the Eastern country than in the Western country:

(A.8)
$$k_2 = \left[\frac{\alpha}{1 + r}\right]^{1/1-\alpha}$$

(A.8')
$$k_2^* = \left[\frac{\alpha}{(1 + z^*)(1 + r)}\right]^{1/1-\alpha}$$

The second-period capital stock is an inverse function of the world interest rate and, in the case of the Eastern country, of the investment inefficiency parameter.

The world interest rate is determined by the commodity market equilibrium condition (equation (A.5) at time 1), which states that world saving is equal to world investment. Hence: «the world pool of savings is channeled to profitable investment projects without regard to the national origin of the savings» (Lipton and Sachs [29], p. 138). Marking the necessary substitutions, we obtain:

(A.9)
$$r = \alpha \left(\frac{\Omega \cdot Z}{\Lambda}\right)^{(1-\alpha)} - 1$$

where:

$$\Omega \equiv \frac{1 + \alpha + \theta}{\alpha}$$

$$Z \equiv 1 + \left(\frac{1}{1 + z^*}\right)^{\alpha/1-\alpha}$$

$$\Lambda \equiv q_1 + k_1 + q_1^* + (1 + z^*) k_1^*$$

It is then possible to demonstrate that the derivative of r with respect to z^* is negative and that the elasticity is less than one. Hence, we can write:

$(A.10)$ $r = \rho (z^*)$, $\rho' (\cdot) < 0$, $\eta_{r,z^*} < 1$

Therefore, given the first-period factor endowment and the value of the investment inefficiency parameter, the model determines simultaneously the world interest rate, the Eastern and Western country's consumption, investment, production, and the trade balance in the first and second period.

Simulation of the Model

Since the dynamics of the model are not straightforward, we have simulated it numerically. In the exercise, we have assumed that the Eastern country differs from the Western country because it starts with a lower capital endowment inherited from previous periods that are not taken into account. This assumption is the direct consequence of the hypothesis of investment inefficiency that affects that country. Giving plausible values to the other parameters of the model, we obtain the results reported in Table $A.1$.

In the first period, the Eastern country is characterized with respect to the Western economy by a lower level of output and consumption but a higher investment level. The net result is a trade deficit which is equal to the current account deficit since we have assumed that the initial stock of foreign debt is nil. In the second period, the Eastern economy runs a trade surplus in order to service the foreign debt previously accumulated.

If we suppose that the reforms implemented in the East succeed in wiping out by magic the investment inefficiency, investment will be stimulated in the Eastern country because, *ceteris paribus*, the optimal second-period capital stock increases. This will determine an excess of world investment over world savings at the initial world interest rate, which will require an increase in the world interest rate, as shown in Table $A.2$. This, in turn, will induce Western households

EFFECTS OF INVESTMENT INEFFICIENCY (*)

	Western country	Eastern country
Time 1		
Capital-labour ratio	0.5	0.25
Output	81.2	65.9
Consumption	62.3	52.6
Investment	16.9	15.3
Trade balance	2.0	− 2.0
Wealth	120.6	101.8
Interest rate (%)	4.2	
Time 2		
Capital-labour ratio	0.169	0.123
Output	58.6	53.3
Consumption	60.7	51.2
Trade balance	− 2.1	2.1
Utility level	2.821	2.082

(*) $z^* = 20\%$. The other hypotheses are: $\alpha = 0.30$; $\theta = 0.07$; $L = 100$.

EFFECTS OF ECONOMIC REFORMS (*)

	Western country	Eastern country
Time 1		
Capital-labour ratio	0.5	0.25
Output	81.2	65.9
Consumption	61.4	53.5
Investment	16.1	16.1
Trade balance	3.7	− 3.7
Wealth	118.8	103.6
Interest rate (%)	7.7	
Time 2		
Capital-labour ratio	0.161	0.161
Output	57.8	57.8
Consumption	61.8	53.8
Trade balance	− 4.0	4.0
Utility level	2,897	2,218

(*) $z^* = 0$.

to postpone consumption in order to smooth spending over the two periods taking into account that the increase in the world interest rate will reduce the second-period capital stock and the second-period output in the Western country. The rise in savings and the decline in domestic investment will enlarge the trade surplus of the West in the first period. In fact, Western entrepreneurs will carry out direct investment in the Eastern country in order to take advantage of higher capital productivity.

As far as the Eastern country is concerned, the increase in the world interest rate will only in part offset the effect on the second-period capital stock of the decline in the investment inefficiency, because the elasticity of r with respect of z^* is less than 1. As shown in Table A.2, the growth in investment is partially financed by domestic savings (24). The additional financing will be provided by the Western economy, as we have already pointed out. At the end, the Eastern economy will catch up the Western economy as far as capital-labour ratio and output are concerned. This will allow the Eastern country to increase, with respect to the previous scenario, the second-period consumption notwithstanding the higher debt to serve. Also the Western country will increase spending in the second period, even though the production will decline with respect to the first scenario, because of the greater first-period accumulation of foreign assets.

In summary, the removal of the investment inefficiency in the Eastern country will imply an increase in world welfare because it will move both countries onto a higher indifference curve.

---

(24) It is possible to demonstrate that first-period consumption in the Eastern country will increase if $\eta_{r,z^*} < \alpha$.

BIBLIOGRAPHY

[1] ABEL A.: «Dynamic Effects of Permanent and Temporary Tax Policies in a q Model of Investment», *Journal of Monetary Economics*, n. 3, 1982.

[2] ALTON T.P. - BADACH K. - BAKONDI R. - BASS E.M. - BOMBELLES J.T. - BRUMARU A. - LAZARCIK G. - STALLER G.J.: «Economic Growth in Eastern Europe 1975-1989», Research Project on National Income in East Central Europe, New York, L.W. International Financial Research, Inc. *Occasional Papers*, n. 110, 1990.

[3] BAGNOLI P. - KRUUS A.: «Intermod Model User's and Developer's Guide for PC Systems», Ottawa, Canadian Department of Finance, *Working Papers*, n. 9, 1988.

[4] BALDWIN R.: «The Growth Effects of 1992», *Economic Policy*, n. 9, 1989.

[5] — —: «Measuring 1992's Medium-Term Dynamic Effects», NBER, *Working Papers*, n. 3166, 1989.

[6] BAUMOL W.J.: «Productivity Growth, Convergence and Welfare: What the Long-Run Data Show», *The American Economic Review*, n. 5, 1986.

[7] BECKER G.S.: *Human Capital*, New York, NBER, 1975.

[8] BERGSON A.: «Comparative Productivity: The USSR, Eastern Europe, and the West», *The American Economic Review*, n. 3, 1987.

[9] BUITER W.H.: «Time Preference and International Lending and Borrowing in an Overlapping-Generations Model», *Journal of Political Economy*, n. 41, 1981.

[10] BURKETT J.P. - SKEGRO B.: «Capitalism, Socialism, and Productivity: An Econometric Analysis of CES and Translog Functions», *European Economic Review*, n. 6, 1989.

[11] CECCHINI P.: *The European Challenge, 1992. The Benefits of a Single Market*, London, Gower, 1988.

[12] CEPR: *Monitoring European Integration. The Impact of Eastern Europe*, London, 1990.

[13] CHENERY H.: «Growth and Transformation», in CHENERY H. - ROBINSON S. - SYRQUIN M. (eds.): *Industrialization and Growth: A Comparative Study*, New York, Oxford University Press, 1986.

[14] DENISON E.F.: *Why Growth Rates Differ*, Washington, The Brookings Institution, 1967.

[15] — —: *Accounting for Slower Economic Growth*, Washington, The Brookings Institution, 1979.

[16] ELLMAN M.: *Collectivisation, Convergence and Capitalism: Political Economy in a Divided World*, London, Academic Press, 1987.

[17] ENGLANDER S.A.: «Tests of Total Factor Productivity Measurement», OECD, *Working Papers*, n. 54, 1988.

[18] ENGLANDER S.A. - MITTELSTADT A.: «Total Factor Productivity: Macroeconomic and Structural Aspects of the Slowdown», OECD, *Economic Studies*, n. 10, 1988.

[19] FISCHER S. - FRENKEL J.: «Interest Rate Equalization and Patterns of Production, Trade and Consumption in a Two-Country Growth Model», *The Economic Record*, December. 1974.

[20] — —: «Economic Growth and Stages of the Balance of Payments: A Theoretical Model», in HORWICH G. - SAMUELSON P.A. (eds.): *Trade, Stability, and Macroeconomics: Essays in Honor of Lloyd A. Metzler*, London, Academic Press, 1974.

[21] FITOUSSI J.P. - PHELPS E.S.: «Global Effects of Eastern European Rebuilding and the Adequacy of Western Saving: An Issue for the 1990s», paper presented at the Second Villa Mondragone Annual Conference on *World Saving: Prosperity and Growth*, Roma, July 2, 1990.

[22] GOLDSMITH R.W.: *Comparative National Balance Sheets*, Chicago and London, The University of Chicago Press, 1985.

[23] HARDT J.P. - MCMILLAN C.H. (eds.): *Planned Economies Confronting the Challenges of the 1980s*, Cambridge, Cambridge University Press, 1988.

[24] HAVLIK P.: «An Overview of the Methods Used for East-West GDP Comparisons», paper presented at the Conference on: *Statistics of Central and Eastern European Countries*, organized by the OECD and the United Nations, Paris, September 10-12, 1990.

[25] HELLIWELL J.F. - MEREDITH G. - DURAND Y. - BAGNOLI P.: «Intermod 1.1: A G-7 Version of the IMF's Multimod», *Economic Modelling*, January 1990.

[26] KENEN P.: «Transitional Agreements for Trade and Payments Among the CMEA Countries», IMF, *Working Papers*, n. 79, 1990.

[27] KRAVIS I.B. - HESTON A. - SUMMERS R.: *World Product and Income*, Baltimore and London, The Johns Hopkins University Press, 1982.

[28] LAUTERBACH A.: «The "Convergence" Controversy Revisited», *Kyklos*, fasc. 4, 1976.

[29] LIPTON D. - SACHS J.: «Accumulation and Growth in a Two-Country Model: A Simulation Approach», *Journal of International Economics*, n. 15, 1983.

[30] LUCAS R.E.: «On the Mechanics of Economic Development», *Journal of Monetary Economics*, n. 22, 1988.

[31] MADDISON A.:«Long-Run Dynamics of Productivity Growth», BNL, *Quarterly Review*, n. 128, 1979.

[32] — —: «Growth and Slowdown in Advanced Capitalist Economies: Techniques of Quantitative Assessment», *Journal of Economic Literature*, June 1987.

[33] MASSON P.R. - MEREDITH G.: «Economic Implications of German Unification for the Federal Republic and the Rest of the World», IMF, *Working Papers*, n. 85, 1990.

[34] MASSON P.R. - MEREDITH G. - SYMANSKY S.: «Multimod Mark II: A Revised and Extended Model», IMF, *Occasional Papers*, n. 71, 1990.

[35] MEREDITH G.: «Intermod 2.0: Model Specification and Simulation Properties», Ottawa, Canadian Department of Finance, *Working Papers*, n. 7, 1989.

[36] MEYER-ZU-SCHLOCHTERN F.J.M.: «An International Sectoral Data Base for Thirteen OECD Countries», OECD, *Working Papers*, n. 57, 1988.

[37] MORGAN GUARANTY TRUST COMPANY: «Eastern Europe: A Cautionary Note», *World Financial Markets*, n. 1, February 1990.

[38] NUTI D.M.: «Perestroika: Transition from Central Planning to Market Socialism», *Economic Policy: A European Forum*, n. 7, 1988.

[39] OECD: *Flows and Stocks of Fixed Capital, 1962-1987*, Paris, OECD, April 1989.

[40] — —: *Financial Market Trends*, Parigi, OECD, n. 45, February 1990.

[41] — —: *Impact of German Economic and Monetary Union in OECD Countries*, Note by the Secretariat, Paris, OECD, May 1990.

[42] — —: *Economic Outlook*, Paris, OECD, n. 47, June 1990.

[43] — —: *Labour Force Statistics: 1968-1988*, Paris, OECD, 1990.

[44] — —: *Quarterly Labour Force Statistics*, Paris, OECD, n. 3, 1990.

[45] ONIKI H. - UZAWA H.: «Patterns of Trade and Investment in a Dynamic Model of International Trade», *Review of Economic Studies*, January 1965.

[46] PAPOULIS A.: *Probability, Random Variables, and Stochastic Processes*, New York, McGraw-Hill, 1965.

[47] PROJECT LINK: *Global Economic Implications of Financial Transfers to Eastern Europe and the Soviet Union*, mimeo, April 1990.

[48] ROLAND G.: «Gorbachev and the Common European Home: The Convergence Debate Revived?», *Kyklos*, fasc. 3, 1990.

[49] ROMER P.M.: «Increasing Returns and Long-Run Growth», *Journal of Political Economy*, n. 5, 1986.

[50] ——: «Growth Based on Increasing Returns Due to Specialization», *The American Economic Review - Papers and Proceedings of the American Economic Association*, n. 2, 1987.

[51] ——: «Increasing Returns and New Developments in the Theory of Growth», NBER, *Working Papers*, n. 3098, 1989.

[52] ——: «Capital Accumulation in the Theory of Long-Run Growth», in BARRO R.J. (ed): *Modern Business Cycle*, Oxford, Basil Blackwell, 1989.

[53] ROSA G. - SIESTO V.: *Il capitale fisso industriale: stime settoriali e verifiche dirette*, Bologna, il Mulino, 1985.

[54] RUFFIN R.J.: «Growth and the Long-Run Theory of International Capital Movements», *The American Economic Review*, n. 5, 1979.

[55] SPULBER N. - HOROWITZ I.: *Quantitative Economic Policy and Planning*, New York, Norton, 1976.

[56] SUMMERS R. - HESTON A.: «A New Set of International Comparisons of Real Product and Prices: Estimates for 130 Countries, 1950-1985», *The Review of Income and Wealth*, n. 1, 1988.

[57] SVENSSON L.E.O. - RAZIN A.: «The Current Account and Productivity Changes: A Diagrammatic Note», Foder Institute for Economic Research, Faculty of Social Science, Tel Aviv University, *Working Papers*, n. 21, 1982.

[58] TINBERGEN J.: «Do Communist and Free Economies Show a Converging Pattern?», *Soviet Studies*, n. 4, 1961.

[59] TOBIN J.: «A General Equilibrium Approach to Monetary Theory», *Journal of Money, Credit and Banking*, n. 1, 1969.

[60] UNITED NATIONS, ECONOMIC COMMISSION FOR EUROPE: *Economic Survey of Europe in 1989-1990*, New York, 1990.

[61] UNITED NATIONS, DEVELOPMENT PROGRAMME: *Human Development Report*, New York, 1990.

[62] WEFA GROUP: *World Economic Outlook*, Bala Gynwyd (Pennsylvania, USA), 1990.

[63] WHITESELL R.S.: «The Influence of Central Planning on Economic Slowdown in the Soviet Union and Eastern Europe: A Comparative Production Function Analysis», *Economica*, n. 206, 1985.

[64] WOLFF E.N.: «Capital Formation and Long-Term Productivity Growth: A Comparison of Seven Countries», New York University, *Economic Research Reports*, n. 37, 1987.

[65] WYPLOSZ C.: *Post-Reform East and West: Capital Accumulation and the Labor Mobility Constrained*, mimeo, December 1990.

Debt Relief and Eastern Europe: Why Poland is a Special Case

James W. Dean - Aihua Xu
Simon Fraser University, Vancouver, Canada

Introduction

A key determinant of Eastern Europe's (1) prosperity under capitalism will be its ability to attract foreign loans and investment. Ironically, under socialism Eastern Europe's ability to attract international bank lending (though not equity capital) was high and its repayment record (excepting Poland's and Yugoslavia's) was uninterrupted. However, in recent years, secondary market prices for much of this debt has declined dramatically: a "debt overhang" has developed (2). Moreover, some bankers are worried that the prospects for repayment will deteriorate still further under the new, less authoritarian regimes (3). Whether the Eastern European countries can attract foreign capital in the 1990s despite their debt overhang from previous regimes is the focus of this paper. For some countries, the way to break the apparent impasse may be some form of debt relief.

---

(1) In this paper, we define Eastern Europe (properly, Eastern and Central Europe) to mean Bulgaria, Czechoslovakia, the former East Germany, Hungary, Poland. Romania and Yugoslavia.

Advise: the numbers in square brackets refer to the Bibliography in the appendix.

(2) A country's "debt overhang" is the difference between the nominal of "face" value of its debt and its expected value. Under (somewhat heroic) efficient market assumptions, expected values can be measured as nominal values times secondary market prices.

(3) Indeed, Poland's repayment record only began to deteriorate under the populist pressures of the Solidarity movement in the early 1980s; now, in 1991, the new President, Lech Walesa, has expressed great reluctance to recognize debt contracted by previous governments. Yet lenders will be loath to commit more capital if he does not.

We begin by summarizing the evolution of official and private creditors' strategies for dealing with the last decade's sovereign-debt repayment problems. We also briefly review some recent theoretical thought on the relationship between sovereign debt overhang and new lending. Next, we examine the Eastern European record of debt accumulation and debt burdens. We use secondary market loan price data and debt service statistics to fit "debt relief Laffer cuves" for 24 heavily-indebted countries pooled. We then locate seven Eastern European countries on this curve. Finding that only Poland seems to be on the "wrong side" of this curve, we examine that country's prospect for relief and new lending in more detail.

1. - Debt Overhang, New Lending and Debt Relief

When Poland, Yugoslavia, the Philippines and most Latin American debtors all began to experience repayment difficulties in the early 1980s, official and private creditors quickly improvised a holding strategy to keep service payments coming and forestall defaults. The strategy was two-pronged, involving rescheduling (lengthening and postponing repayment periods) on the one hand, and making new loans on the other. The rationale behind new lending was to provide liquidity to keep interest payments current: the strategy was equivalent to permitting interest arrears, but more acceptable to accountants and regulators since it maintained a facade of normalcy. Of course new lending had to be coordinated between the various creditors, since any individual bank had an incentive to free ride on new lending provided by others. Thus the new lending was "concerted", and involuntary from any individual bank's point of view. Moreover it was in general only the banks with significant outstanding claims from the past that could be persuaded to undertake such involuntary new lending (4). Thus the

---

(4) KRUGMAN [19] neatly summarized such banks' incentive to make new loans as the difference between the increase in the expected value of outstanding claims $(d - d^*) D$ and the expected cost of new loans d^*L, where d and d^* are expected default rates before and after new lending.

bulk of new lending to Latin America in the 1980s came from US banks, whereas most new lending to Eastern Europe was from Western Europe.

By 1985, the scheduling *cum* new lending strategy had been successful enough that private creditors felt less threatened. However, they were increasingly reluctant to lend more, whiuch meant that the debtors' economic prospects began to look even bleaker. In recognition of this, the then-Us Treasury Secretary James Baker III announced a new "plan" to pressure private and official creditors to lend more in return for commitments by debtor countries to liberalize their economies along free market lines.

The *Baker Plan* may have encouraged some countries to begin economic liberalization, but it also encouraged them to take on more debt. By 1988, the US Treasury as well as several prominent academics (for example, Kenen [17]; Sachs [24]) had begun to advocate a very different strategy: debt relief. Whereas rescheduling preserves the contractual present value of debt and new lending increases it, the defining characteristic of debt relief is that it reduces contractual present values.

By 1988, a secondary market in sovereign debt was well-established. Much of this market is inter-bank, but beginning in the mid 1980s, non-bank "investors" began to buy discontinued country debt and swap it for equity. "Debt equity swaps" have provided an important, and voluntary, mechanism for debt relief for several countries, including Chile, Brazil, Mexico, Argentina, the Philippines and Yugoslavia. In 1988, precedents for other forms of voluntary debt relief were set, when an externally-funded "buyback" of Bolivian debt took place, and Mexico issued collateralized "exit bonds" in exchange for part of its debt.

In March 1989, US Treasury Secretary Nicholas Brady, in a major departure from the *Baker Plan*, announced his support for an official strategy of debt relief (*Treasury News* [29]). By May, 1989 the *Brady Plan* had been endorsed by the IMF and the World Bank, which along with the US and Japanese governments have now committed some $40 billion to provide funding for debt buybacks and collateralization of exit bonds by debtor countries. As of the end of 1990, Mexico, the Philippines, Costa Rica and Venezuela had become the first four recipients of *Brady Plan* debt relief. A Moroccan settlment is underway, and Poland may be next on the list.

The theoretical rationale for debt relief is ambodied in the "debt relief Laffer curve" (DRLC), a phrase originated by Krugman [19]. In Graph 1 the expected value, *V*, of a country's outstanding debt is drawn as a function of its contractual value, *D*. At some point, indebtedness may so impede repayment prospects that *V* actually begins to decline. Beyond this point, debt relief, *X*, while writing off contractual claims, will raise the expected value of remaining claims above their pre-writeoff value. If a country finds itself on the "wrong side" of its DRLC at, for example, point *A*, both it and its creditors will be better off if anything up to (D^0 - D^*) of debt is simply forgiven.

GRAPH. 1

THE DEBT - RELIEF LAFFER CURVE

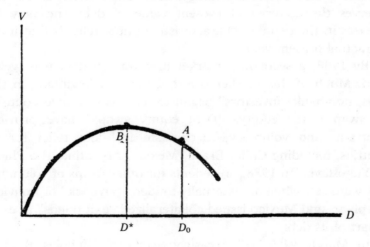

Debt relief on these grounds, espoused particularly by Jeffrey Sachs [24], [25] (who, incidentally, advises the Solidarity Government in Poland), has been opposed by others for several reasons. First, there seems little evidence that most countries are on the wrong sides of their DRLC. Indeed, Claessens [7] identifies only four such countries (Sudan, Peru, Zambia and Nicaragua) from a sample of 29.

Second, there is a serious free-rider problem. In general, an individual creditor cannot benefit by providing debt relief voluntarily; all creditors must be induced to provide it at once. Third, the so-called "voluntary" instruments for debt relief provide much less debt relief than they sometimes seem to promise. "Buybacks" by debtor countries at secondary market prices may cause such prices to rise sufficiently that the expected value of remaining debt is unchanged: this was more or less the case after Bolivia's 1988 buyback of $308 million of its $670 million debt. The country's debt price rose from 6¢ to 11¢, and the market value of its debt remained almost unchanged, falling only from $40.2 million to $39.8 million (Bulow and Rogoff [5], [6]).

Moreover, buybacks usually (unlike Bolivia's) use the debtor-country's own resources, which may have high opportunity costs (since real domestic interest rates are typically well above world levels). Although this argument is less applicable to Brady-funded buybacks (which are funded by loans to the debtor country at or below world interest rates), it remains questionable how much of the relief from a buyback will, in the end, be wholly "appropriable" by the debtor, in the sense that the debtor may not be able to subtract 100% of the funds used for the buyback from the reserve assets that it is expected to dip into to make debt payments when foreign exchange earnings are insufficient. Similar caveats apply to the presumed benefits from exit bonds. Debt equity swaps, in turn, are even less likely to benefit debtors and must be approached with even more caution when advocated as instruments of debt relief. Debt equity swaps can provide liquidity relief since they release the debtor from contractual payment obligations and replace them by performance-contingent obligations; however the expected present value of the debtor's obligations may actually increase (5).

In short, debt relief as a strategy for simultaneously reducing debtor's debt burden and raising the value of the bank claims is in its infancy in practice and is controversial theoretically. One thing is

---

(5) The drawbacks of debt equity swaps are discussed, for example, in KRUGMAN [19]. DI LEO and REMOLONA [9] show that debtors stand to benefit relative to creditors most from *buybacks* followed by *exit bonds*, and least from *debt equity swaps*.

clear, however: debtor and creditors cannot even in principle benefit simultaneously unless debt relief provides sufficient incentive for increased investment in and structural adjustment by the debtor country that the expected value of debt payments increases — that is, unless the debtor country lies on the wrong side of its DRLC (6). Recall, however, that the rationale behind concerted new lending was also to raise the expected value of debt payments (see footnote 4). Thus expected debt payments by a country like Poland that seems to be on the wrong side of its DRLC are likely to be increased maximally by some optimal combination of debt relief and new lending (7).

Finally, debt relief remains controversial because theorists and practitioners disagree on the appropriate degree of official coordination or underwriting. The *Brady Plan* is a compromise between advocates of the "hands-off" policy which would leave banks and debtors free to organize buybacks, exit bonds and debt equity swaps voluntarily, on a piece-meal basis, and advocates of coordinated official writedowns and wholesale buyouts of private creditors at discounts by international bodies, with creditors encouraged or coerced to sell by whatever carrots and sticks their home-country regulators and governments can devise. *Brady Plan* settlements have thus far offered commercial banks a menu of "voluntary" options (basically buybacks and exit bonds) enhanced by official funding, but have pressured "non-exiting" banks into committing fresh funds.

1.1 *Debt Relief or Liquidity Relief?*

Relief can take three forms. *Rescheduling* provides up-front liquidity relief, but no reduction in the debt's present contractual value. *New lending* also provides liquidity relief, but increases the debt's present value. *Debt relief* reduces the debt's present value.

Central to the choice between liquidity relief and debt relief is their relative impacts on investment. In the 1980s, investment in most heavily indebted countries, including Poland, declined dramatically.

(6) The necessary and sufficient condition for this is that $dV/dX = -G + (1 - G) f' (dI/dX)$, where G is the probability of full repayments before debt relief, I is investment, and f' is the marginal product (in terms of foreign exchange earnings) of investment (FROOT [14]).

(7) We discuss this optimal combination in Section 1.1.

A study by Cohen [8] shows that between 1982 and 1987, 20-50% of domestic expenditure reduction by the rescheduling countries came from investment (with the remainder from private and public consumption). Recent analysis by Froot [14] and Borenzstein [3] attributes the investment disincentive effects of a heavy debt burden to two factors: a *liquidity* disincentive and a *debt-overhang* disincentive. A country is "liquidity-constrained" if it is unable to attract voluntary new lending from abroad. As a result, domestic real interest rates exceed world levels, and investment declines or ceases altogether because it is costly in terms of foregone consumption. A country has a "debt overhang" if its nominal debt obligations exceed the amount it is expected to pay. This overhang acts as a disincentive to investment since any consequent increase in output up to the amount of the overhang would stand to be appropriated by foreign creditors. The overhang acts as a disincentive to investment since any consequent increase in output up to the amount of the overhang would stand to be appropriated by foreign creditors. The overhang can thus be thought of as an expected loss of future output to creditors and acts as a (nominally 100%) tax on new investment. It follows that liquidity relief — rescheduling or new lending — induces investment by lowering the domestic rate of interest, whereas debt relief induces investment by increasing expected marginal returns (since foreign creditors' "tax" on marginal increases in output has been removed) (8).

In Froot's [14] analysis, the optimal combination of debt relief and liquidity relief $\{D^*, L^*\}$, that which maximizes creditors' claims over two periods, is given by:

$$(1) \qquad f'(I^*) = 1 + \frac{U'(E + L^*)}{\beta}$$

$$(2) \qquad D^*(L^*) = \frac{U(E + L^* - I^*)}{\beta} - \frac{U_1(E + L^*)}{\beta} + f(I^*)$$

---

(8) DOOLEY *et* AL. [11] have attempted to model and simulate the link between relief and economic growth. Their link does not distinguish between liquidity and debt relief. Debt relief, they assume, lowers domestic interest rates because it is less likely that the debtor government's payments to foreign creditors will come at the expense of payments to domestic creditors. Therefore the return on domestic government securities will fall, and by arbitrage, so will the return on domestic private securities.

where:

D^* : optimal stock of debt: i.e. that resulting from optimal debt relief;

L^* : optimal new lending;

E : initial endowment of foreign exchange resources;

β : discount factor from period one to period two;

I^* : investment induced by the optimal combination of debt relief and new lending;

$f(I)$: output.

These conditions show that higher liquidity relief, L, raises the optimal level of investment, I^*, and therefore reduces the optimal amount of debt relief provided by creditors. This is obvious from Graph 2, where an increase in liquidity relief from L_0 to L_1 raises the DRLC and increases the level of debt which maximizes creditor's claims, V, from D_0 (at A) to D_1 (at B). It is also obvious from Graph 2 that countries that are more liquidity constrained are more likely to be on the wrong side of the DRLC.

GRAPH. 2

LIQUIDITY AND THE DEBT - RELIEF LAFFER CURVE

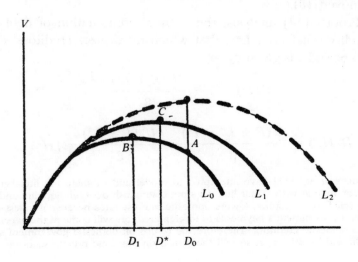

The intuition behind providing liquidity relief as well as debt relief can be spelled out by considering an initial position D_0 on Graph 2. Pure debt relief could move the country from point A to point B on the DRLC labelled L_0. This would raise the debtor's investment incentives by reducing the debt overhang. However investment could increase at the expense of current consumption. The consequent rise in the marginal utility of consumption would mean that the domestic interest rate would remain above world levels. Liquidity relief permits further investment to take advantage of this high marginal return, and shift the DRLC up to L_1. Creditors can thus capture a surplus above the world interest rate by making new loans while *reducing* their debt relief. However they can capture this surplus only if the debt and new lending are tied together. If debt relief and new lending were negotiated separately, creditors would end up worse off because then the new lending would be competitive. Froot ([14], p. 67), proves the following proposition: «The more liquidity-constrained the country is, the more creditors sacrifice with simple debt-reduction schemes in comparison with optimal relief...».

In section 4, we calculate some possible combinations of debt and liquidity relief for Poland.

2. - Eastern Europe's Debt

In the late 1970s, the heyday of sovereign lending, Eastern Europe accumulated debt to the point that its debt (9) to export ratio by 1981 had reached 195%, a ratio the OECD classifies as the top end of "medium" (10). The debt service ratio had risen even more sharply, to 63%, due to sharp increases in interest rates. Poland and Romania were already having to reschedule. In reaction, the creditor banks sharply cut back their lending. However, the various authoritarian regimes were able to curtail imports abruptly, and by 1985 their current accounts had turned around sufficiently that bank lending had

---

(9) All references to "debt" throughout this paper are to gross convertible-currency external debt.

(10) OECD [21] p. 22. A net debt to export ratio of less than 100 is considered "light"; 100 to 200, "medium" and more than 200, "heavy".

resumed. Between 1984 and 1989, their foreign debt rose again, from $59.6 billion to $100.2 billion (excluding Yugoslavia).

By 1989, the region's debt export ratio had climbed to a "heavy" 211%, although the debt service ratio, thanks to lower interest rates and rescheduling, had fallen to 46%. However, this figure masks a wide range of debt service burdens within the region, from Poland's 88% to Romania's 15%. Judging solely from their debt service ratios, Czechoslovakia, the former East Germany, Romania and Yugoslavia currently could all assume more debt, whereas Poland, Hungary and Bulgaria could not. Appendix 1 documents these various countries' debt status individually.

2.1 *Composition of Creditors*

Eastern Europe's total convertible currency external debt is about $117 billion. This compares with $405 billion for Latin America, $338 billion for the Asia/Pacific region, and $225 billion for Africa and the Middle East. Of the $117 billion, some 48% is owed to commercial banks, 39% to creditor governments, 7% to official international agencies, and 6% to non-bank private lenders. While the commercial bank's share is low relative to their share in Latin America and Asia/Pacific, it is high relative to their share in Africa. In Latin America, debt relief efforts have focussed on commercial banks; in Asia and the Pacific, debt relief (except in the Philippines) has been unnecessary; in Africa it has focused on official lenders.

2.2 *Maturity Structure*

Eastern Europe's $117 billion external debt is comprised of $56 billion in long and medium term debt, and $44 billion in short term. The latter has terms to maturity of one year or less and is largely trade credit. Other things equal, a country with a high proportion of short term debt is less likely to default on its long term debt since it is vulnerable to credit sanctions which could shackle its ability to export and import. For example, in recent years both Peru and Brazil discovered that the benefits from interrupting payments on their longer term obligations were largely or wholly offset by their losses in export revenues after their creditors withdrew trade finance.

2.3 *Debt Burden*

Various ratios measure different aspects of a country's debt burden. The ratio of total debt to GNP measures a country's potential ability to pay. The potential burden on individual citizens is given by the ratio of debt to GNP per capita. The actual burden is given by ratios of debt service payments to GNP or GNP per capita. The country's ability and/or willingness to pay is measured by ratios of debt service, either including or excluding principal payments, to hard currency export earnings, either gross or net of payments for imports. A potential burden becomes actual as debt service payments come due and are paid. A country is able to pay to the extent that it generates net foreign currency earnings. A country's ability to pay can be increased to the extent that either GNP or the export share of GNP is increased, or that imports are reduced.

In aggregate, Eastern Europe's debt burden is not high by international standards. Its D/GNP ratio in 29.8% and its iD/GNP ratio is 15.1% (where iD denotes interest payments). However, as we shall see, the burden varies widely between countries within Eastern Europe. The Appendix 1 outlines the external debt status of the six major Eastern European countries, excluding Poland.

2.4 *Prospects for Debt Relief*

Debt relief prospects in Eastern Europe differ from elsewhere for several reasons: *a)* except for Poland, Yugoslavia, and now Romania, debt service payments have not been interrupted: there has been no "crisis" from creditors' point of view; *b)* commercial banks' share is relatively low for the region as a whole, and exceptionally low for certain countries; *c)* US commercial banks' exposure is relatively small; their interest in "concerted" new lending to forestall default on oustanding exposures is less than it is in Latin American. On the other hand, European, particularly German, banks have greater stakes in the region, as well as more political interest, and have consequently shown more interest both in debt relief and new lending; *d)* official lending and debt relief must be a major part of the solutiuon, and indeed are probably a precondition for further private lending; however both bilateral and multilateral efforts hinge critically on political developments in the debtor countries.

The most likely candidates for debt relief are Poland, Bulgaria and Hungary. Debt relief for Poland is probably imminent, and is discussed in Section 4. Bulgaria is now in need of debt relief but as a brand-new member of the IMF it must prove that its commitment to economic reform is serious before *Brady* relief will be considered. Hungary may need relief in future but has not yet asked for it. Yugoslavia has already achieved some debt reduction independently of the *Brady Plan* via its debt equity swap program.

2.5 *Prospects for Private Capital Flows to Eastern Europe*

To date, Eastern Europe has relied most heavily for its private capital inflows on bank lending. In addition, both Bulgaria and Hungary in recent years have issued international bonds. In 1988-1989, four countries — the GDR, Hungary, Czechoslovakia and Bulgaria — were net borrowers from banks; Romania and Yugoslavia reduced outstanding debt, whereas Poland incurred interest arrears.

The prospects for future bank lending are mixed. The bond markets are now demanding increased risk premia, and secondary market loan prices (except for Yugoslavia) have fallen. However, official support has begun to turn these prices around: bilateral aid for the former GDR, IMF and World Bank credit for Poland, Hungary, and Yugoslavia, and promises of export guarantees. The banks are closely watching for signs of life from the new EBRD, particularly for prospects of cofinancing. The openness of the West to imports of Eastern European goods and labor will also influence the bank's willingness to lend. On the other hand, the banks warn that imposition of an involuntary debt reduction scheme would seriously undermine their future lending (11).

Prospect for bank lending to Eastern Europe also depend on the preference and constraints facing particular banks. Since North America banks' existing exposure is relatively small, their incentive to minimize default probabilities via concerted, involuntary lending is lower than the European and Japanese banks'. Moreover, since finance follows trade and direct investment, European and Japanese banks again are likely to be larger players. Finally, regulatory costs such as loan loss requirements, and official support via export credit guarantees and cofinancing, will influence banks from different countries differently. Analogously, regulatory treatment of foreign banks by the individual Eastern European countries will determine whether and how banks can establish local operations, which in turn will facilitate their willingness to lend. Moreover, days of voluntary, arms-length sovereign to developing countries are long gone: banks now look for specific projects or trade and leasing opportunities that generate appropriable hard currency cash flows, and that require on-the-spot assessment.

The prospect for borrowing on international bond markets are also mixed. Recent analysis by the OECD (12) points to recent sharp hikes in the risk premia demanded on sovereign bonds issued by Hungary and Bulgaria, and attributes them both to their rising debt overhangs and to the economic uncertainty created by political upheaval. Of course Poland's debt overhang is even larger (Table 2, Section 2.7).

Eastern Europe's ability to draw portfolio investment is limited by lack of capital markets. Only Hungary has a stock market, which is highly illiquid with very low volumes, and has low standards for investor protection and disclosure (13). However, if and when capital markets do develop, it is likely that large pools of expatriate funds can be mobilized, as well as the foreign-currency assets of Eastern Europe

---

(11) See INSTITUTE OF INTERNATIONAL FINANCE [15], p. 47.
(12) OECD [21].
(13) The $80 million gathered by Sarlos's Hungarian Investment Fund is still sitting on the US money market looking for a viable Hungarian outlet.

residents. Portfolio inflows and reversals of capital flight would help to reinforce resolve for painful economic reforms, as well as vice versa.

Finally, direct investment must play a crucial role in the recovery of Eastern Europe. Until 1989, such investment was negligible; most of the $305 million inflow in 1989 was accounted for by Yugoslavia and Hungary. However among all potential sources of finance, direct investment is what Eastern Europe needs most. First, it requires that payments be made only if profits materialize: unlike debt, it is performance-contingent. Second, it typically carries with it much-needed management expertise and technical know-how.

2.6 *Poland*

Poland's convertible currency debt, at $41 billion, is the highest in Eastern Europe. The fraction of that debt which is official is also the highest in the region, with more than two-thirds owed to western governments, and only 22% to commercial banks. Her debt-to-GDP ratio, at 53%, is the second highest in the region, and at 42%, her debt-service to exports ratio is by far the highest. Since 1981, despite frequent reschedulings, she has accumulated large interest arrears with her official, Paris Club creditors. Her principal obligations to commercial banks have been rescheduled seven times since 1982. Interest obligations were kept current until September 1989, but since then, no payments have been made. On secondary markets, Poland's debt price has plummetted from 40¢ in September 1989 to about 15¢ currently.

Since the outset of its repayment problems in the early 1980s, Poland's export performance has greatly improved, due to a combination of foreign trade reforms and a halving of the real effective exchange rate. However, in 1988 movements toward world levels for energy and other prices touched off a round of wage increases. By 1989, weak monetary restraint and a growing fiscal deficit had translated these wage increases into a 600% inflation rate. Consumer and intermediate imports increased and the current account deficit rose to $20 billion.

Since 1987, Poland's current account deficits and capital outflows

TABLE 1

FINANCING OF POLAND'S CURRENT ACCOUNT DEFICITS

	1985	1986	1987	1988	1989 (*)
Current account balance	− 618	− 665	− 417	− 580	− 2,000
Equity investment, net	0	0	0	0	15
International financial institutions, net	− 144	− 107	− 160	− 70	− 45
Official bilateral creditors, net ..	− 945	− 22	1,129	2,957	2,480
Commercial banks: credit flows, net	− 495	283	− 16	− 93	50
Commercial banks: Interest arrears	0	0	0	0	0
Other private creditors, net......	349	− 352	− 130	− 82	− 245
Resident lending abroad, net	17	− 228	− 280	− 153	0
Errors & omissions, net	1,599	918	670	− 1,419	− 100
Reserves	236	172	− 797	− 560	− 300

(*) Estimates.
Source: INSTITUTE OF INTERNATIONAL FINANCE [15].

have been financed by official bilateral loans. The IMF provided $710 million in stand-by credit for 1990. This agreement triggered further official commitments, including a $1 billion exchange stabilization fund, and substantial credits from the German and Japanese governments. Table 1 shows the sources of financing for Poland's deficit since 1985.

On January 1, 1990, Poland introduced dramatic "cold turkey" reforms that included 53% devaluation of the zloty, monetary restraint, tax increases, wage restraint, and sharp increases in real interest rates. By March, the monthly inflation rate had slowed to 6%, and real wages had fallen by one-third. Although measured real output has fallen sharply, it is debatable whether overall economic welfare has fallen *pari passu*, since the informal sector has grown rapidly and goods have appeared in markets and on store shelves almost overnight. In fact Sachs (Sacht-Lipton [28]) argues persuasively that, due to reduced queuing time and the like, consumer welfare has probably risen.

Nevertheless, in the first nine months of 1990, GNP fell by 15%, unemployment rose sharply (though at 7-10% it is still low by Western standards), personal consumption (according to official statistics) dropped 33%, gross investment fell by 13%, and the output of state industry by 17%. But private trading and small businesses have flourished, and the private sector has boosted its share of GDP by 35%.

The reforms have done wonders for Poland's trade balance. Stimulated by the zloty devaluation, hard-currency exports increased by 25% over the first nine months of 1990, to $7.6 billion, and drastically reduced domestic demand lead to a 24% fall in imports, to $4.2 billion. The hard-currency trade surplus increased sixfold, to $3.4 billion. A 40% drop in imports from Comecon countries, mainly due to lower Soviet oil deliveries, led to a 3.2 billion rouble surplus on soft currency trade as well (14).

Nevertheless, Poland's immediate external financial problems remain the most serious in the region. It is currently, in late 1990, negotiating with the IMF and the World Bank for official relief, but the form this may take is still unclear. With two-thirds of its debt official, some sort of precedent may have to be set. Indeed, Lech Walesa is calling for a 100%/ official writeoff.

There is of course some scope for the conventional Brady type of officially-backed, market-based debt conversion, since Poland owes $8.8 billion to commercial banks. However the only precedent for a buyback at prices as low as Poland's is Bolivia's in 1987. As already mentioned, that transaction raised Bolivia's debt price from 6¢ to 11¢, leaving the espected value of her debt obligations roughly unchanged. Thus even though the buyback was funded with external aid, Bolivia gained little if at all. Indeed Bulow and Rogoff ([5], [6]) argue that in general, buybacks and exit bonds which are partially or solely self-funded will impose losses on debtor countries.

Debt equity swaps would seem a natural option for Poland since its current ratio of debt to private equity financing is so high, and since short term repayment prospects seem so poor. However, it must be remembered that debt equity swaps are no more than buybacks

---

(14) The source of data in this and the preceeding paragraph is the *Financial Times*, November 20, 1990, p. IIb.

linked to subsidized foreign investment. Under some circumstances the link may be pragmatically justified. For example, an explicit, coordinated buyback may be legally impossible due to sharing, *pari passu* and negative pledge clauses on existing debt contracts; debt equity swaps are more piecemeal and discrete since the initial buyer of the debt is usually a third-party "investor", not the debtor country. However, subsidizing foreign investment must also be rationalized. Most importantly, perhaps, debt equity swaps *per sé* attract no new money inflows (unless they carry "new money" requirements); rather, they merely extinguish contractual obligations in exchange for new, contingent liabilities. For this reason Jeffrey Sachs (Sachs-Lipton [28] and Sachs [26]), who is well versed in both the economics of debt relief and Poland's problems, argues against debt equity swaps for Poland. On the other hand the banks (as usually (15)) are likely to advocate a debt equity swap program (Institute of International Finance [15]), and may, as they did for Mexico, insist on one in return for throwing their support behind *Brady* buybacks or exit bonds.

Whether or not debtors and creditors can *simultaneously* benefit from buy backs, exit bonds or debt equity swaps depends critically upon whether contractual debt relief raises the expected value of remaining debt above its pre-relief value. As explained in Section 1, this relationship can be summarized in a country's "debt relief Laffer curve". We estimate such curves, and locate Poland on them, in Section 3.

2.7 *Rescheduling Poland's Debt in the 1980s*

After extensive borrowing in the late 1970s, Poland was hit by several adverse events in 1979-1980. First, popular expectations raised by the capital inflows and access to imports were not realized: much of the imported capital was poorly invested or allocated. The result was the popular "Solidarity" uprising in 1980, which led to extensive strikes, plummeting output, and consumer uprisings. Second, Poland

---

(15) Dɪ Lᴇᴏ and Rᴇᴍᴏʟᴏɴᴀ [9] show that under fairly general theoretical conditions, creditors are more likely than debtors to benefit from debt equity swaps.

was hit, along with other indebted countries, by rising interest rates, and falling demand for her exports, thanks to credit-crunch and recession in the developed world. In 1980, Poland interrupted her debt payments for the first time.

Rescheduling Poland's official debt was far from an orderly process, due to the objections of Western governments, led by the US, to the crushing of Solidarity and the imposition of martial law. After a rescheduling agreement in 1981, Western official creditors suspended talks with Poland for nearly two years, and export guarantees were restricted. In one respect this redounded to Poland's advantage since she was able to accumulate interest arrears without being held in default. Official interest arrears between 1982 and 1984 averaged well over 20% of export earnings, and have not yet been cleared. Finally, between July 1985 and March 1986, the various maturities of official debt were rescheduled, with grace periods extending through 1989. In February 1990, the Paris Club of official creditors rescheduled accumulated interest arrears, as well as principal and interest payments, until March 1991.

The effect of official rescheduling has been to move all maturities originally due in 1982-1986, plus accumulated arrears, into 1991-1996. Thus, under present arrangements, payments due to Paris Club creditors will more than double in 1991, with over $23 billion due through 1996.

By contrast, commercial bank rescheduling throughout the 1980s proceeded rather smoothly. Agreements in 1984 and 1986 rescheduled virtually all maturities due 1984-1987. From 1982 until September 1989, there were no interest arrears on private debt (16). Although commercial banks did not extend any new medium or long term credit in the 1980s, they did regularly place 50% and more of interest actually paid into a six-month trade credit facility, which was regularly used.

In the end, the commercial banks have not fared badly: with

---

(16) This stands in contrast to over $18 billion in arrears to commercial banks accumulated since 1985 by some 14 other debtor countries. According to the INSTITUTE OF INTERNATIONAL FINANCE [16], Argentina now owes over $6 billion in arrears, Brazil well over $5 billion and Peru almost $3 billion. Poland's arrears to the commercial banks began only in 1989, and as of Dec 1990 are still under $1 billion.

modest repayments and as well as reimbursement under official guarantee programs, commercial bank exposure was reduced from $9.3 billion in 1987 to $8.8 billion in 1989. Official bilateral debt, by contrast, has accumulated because of interest arrears and recent new lending to $27.6 billion. Poland is now one of the largest debtors to the Paris Club.

It would be misleading to conclude from Poland's debt payment difficulties in the 1980 that impressive adjustment efforts were not made. After the Solidarity-led strikes and consumer protest of 1980-1981, Poland in a sense faced double jeopardy. On the one hand, it was sanctioned and boycotted by official creditors, particularly the US. It was cut off from export markets and export guarantees, denied strategic imports, and denied official credit. Even its IMF membership was suspended. All this was in response to General Jaruzelski's imposition of martial law in an attempt to suppress Solidarity and put the economy back on its feet. On the other hand, it was cut off from new lending by the banks for commercial rather than political reasons, in response to the chaos that precipitated the payments difficulties of 1980-1981, and therefore implicitly because of Solidarity itself rather than the Government's attempts to suppress it.

The result of this double jeopardy was a net transfer of hard-currency funds from Poland to the West of some $5.5 billion between 1982 and 1985. $6.5 billion was paid in interest and $2.5 billion in principal, whereas new credits came to only $3.5 billion. This is by contrast with net inward flows averaging $7-$8 billion per year from the late 1970's through 1980. Poland financed this dramatic reversal in its capital fortunes by imposing severe austerity, notably by sharply cutting Western imports and partially replacing them with imports from the USSR and Comecon. In 1982, Poland achieved its first trade surplus with the West in 11 years, and for the three years thereafter the trade surplus exceeded $1.0 billion each year. In 1984, per capita imports, at $288, were the lowest in Europe, some 30% lower than even Romania.

There are compelling augments for substantially forgiving Poland's debt. The sacrifices of the 1980s not only curtailed consumption, they impeded investment and growth because capital imports were often unavailable, and because the technical modernization process begun in the 1970s was truncated. The buffer provided by Soviet and Comecon trade and credit has come to an end. Indeed, the prices of imports from these countries, notably Soviet oil, are rapidly moving to world levels. As well, the stoicism with which the populace has weathered the sharp reduction in real income associated with the 1990 reforms needs to be rewarded. The ultimate tragedy would be for the reform program to be abandoned under popular pressure for wage increases: as Jeffrey Sachs has repeatedly warned, this could lead to the Latin Americanization of Poland, with round after round of hyperinflation.

If official creditors led the way with a major writedown of their two-thirds of the debt, private creditors might well benefit, even if they were persuaded to shoulder part of the burden by selling off or swapping part of their claims at current secondary market prices, or by committing more funds if they chose to hang on and take advantage of the inevitable rise in prices. In Section 3, using a debt relief Laffer curve, we estimate just how large that rise might be.

2.8 *Polish Debt Status Now*

One of the constraints on the newly launched Polish stabilization program and the blueprint for restructuring and privatizing the Polish economy, is its external debt. Unless handled properly, the serious debt problem may strangle the economic reform program in its infancy. As of the end of 1989, Poland's infancy. As of the end of 1989, Poland's estimated debt in convertible currency stood at $40.4 billion on which the annual interest bill was $3.6 billion. 68% of this debt was owed to Western governments, 22% to the commercial banks, 6% to international institutions and 4% to other creditors. Prospects for repayment on this debt seem dim, as evidenced by the sharp drop in its secondary market price, and accumulating interest arrears. Poland's recent economic performance has not helped to restore confidence. Table 2 presents major economic aggregates and relevant ratios for the period 1986 to 1989.

In general, the recent situation can be characterized as slow and sometimes negative growth, current account deficits, and an accumu-

TABLE 2

DEBT DATA, 1986-1989, POLAND
(all in US $ million, data for 1989 are estimated)
(long-term debt only)

years	Debt outstanding	GNP	Exports	Debt/Export (%)	Secondary market price (*)	Debt overhang	Current account balance
1986	31,931	71,221	14,129	259.5	43.00	18,201	−1,106
1987	36,050	60,990	14,459	294.7	43.13	20,502	− 379
1988	33,661	65,869	16,589	254.0	34.00	22,216	− 107
1989	32,342	63,893	17,916	259.1	19.00	26,197	n.a

(*) Estimates.
Source: WORLD BANK, [33], Suppl. 1.

lating debt overhang, The one bright spot is that current account has now turned into surplus, thanks to impressive export growth, especially in 1990, combined, of course, with the cessation of debt service payments.

Table 3 presents the composition of Polish debt by institutional nature of creditors, and Table 4 shows Poland's recent debt service record.

From Table 4, we can see that a major payment was made in 1989. This suggests there were problems in fulfilling contractual obligations in previous years. Therefore a brief glance at the past is to the point here.

TABLE 3

COMPOSITION OF DEBT STOCKS: BY CREDITORS
(US $ billion)

Type of creditors	1971	1984	1985	1986	1987	1988	1989	% 1989
International financial inst. ..			2.4	2.6	2.8	2.6	2.5	1
Western governments			17.5	20.3	24.9	25.9	27.6	68
Commercial banks			7.5	8.6	9.5	8.9	8.8	22
Other creditors			2.1	1.9	2.0	1.8	1.5	4
Total	1.00	26.9	29.5	33.4	39.2	39.2	40.4	100

Source: RYDZKOWSHI - ZAOLABKIEWICZ [23]; WORLD BANK, [33], Suppl. 1.

TABLE 4

COMPOSITION OF DEBT STOCKS: BY COUNTRIES OF CREDITORS
(US $ billion)

Creditors	% of Total debt December 31, 1983	% of Total debt June 30, 1984
West Germany	20.8	21.1
U.S.	18.1	18.0
France	12.8	12.8
Austria	10.8	11.2
Great Britain	10.0	9.9
Italy	6.6	6.1
Total	100.0	100.0

Source: RYDZKOWSHI - ZAOLABKIEWICZ [23].

TABLE 5

DEBT SERVICE FLOWS
(excluding IMF)
(US $ million)

	Principal Repayment	As % of TDS	Interest Payments	% of TDS	Total Debt Service (TDS)
1985	855	35	1,591	65	2,445
1986	780	42	1,097	58	1,877
1987	981	48	1,077	52	2,058
1988	969	51	932	49	1,901
1989	700	16	3,588	84	4,288

Source: WORLD BANK [33], Suppl. 1.

Poland's inability to service its payment obligations become evident as early as the late seventies. Accumulating debt coincided with social and economic disturbances, which in turn worsened the debt situation. Interest payments to private creditors were delayed. After December 13, 1981, Poland was not paying any service at all, either principal nor interest, to its official creditors. As a result, from March 1981, Poland began bilateral negotiations with Western governments and about 500 Western banks. This process resulted in the restructuring of some $17 billion of debt (including repeated restructuring), in \$1.3 billion of short-term credit maintenance aid, and in somewhat improved terms on earlier agreements. Ultimately, these agreements rescheduled the debt due between 1982 and 1987 to come due during 1988-1993. Agreements with official creditors took longer. Four agreements were finally signed, rescheduling almost all principal and interest to official creditors to fall due in March 1991.

However, a distinguishing feature of these reschedulings was the absence of new money, which is usually a part of such agreements. Except for the \$1.3 billion of short-term credit maintenance mentioned above, only \$2.5 billion in medium and long term credits were made available during 1982 to 1985. It was not until 1990 that the much needed official assistance showed up, as backup for the zloty stabilization program. One type of assistance took the form of balance-of-payments support loans from IMF and BIS. The other was a \$1 billion stabilization fund provided by the G-7 governments (Sachs [26]). But these are relatively small in amount and especially designed for the stabilization program. They therefore can not be expected to ease the debt situation substantially and directly.

3. - Debt relief Laffer Curves and Eastern European Debtors

The debt relief Laffer curve (DRLC) hypothesis asserts that the expected (market) value of a country's external debt is a funcion of its debt stock and perhaps other variables:

$$(1) \qquad V = f(D,X)$$

In terms of market prices, which are defined as the ratio of the market value to the debt, the DRLC can be represented as:

$$(2) \qquad P = V/D = g(D,X)$$

where:
V is the value of the debt; D is the total debt outstanding; X is a set of variables which explains the country's willingness to pay: that is,

credit-worthiness indicators; P is the secondary market price of the debt.

Various specifications of equation *(2)* have been estimated empirically. Claessens [7] estimated a debt relief Laffer curve based on a pooled cross-sectional regression using the December 1986, 1987 and 1988 secondary market prices of the bank debt of 29 high indebted and sub-Saharan African countries. His specification is as follows:

(3) $$P = \beta_0 + \beta_1 D/XGS + \beta_3 XGSGROWTH + {} + \beta_4 DUMMY_1 + \beta_5 DUMMY_2$$

where:
D/XGS is the debt-to-export ratio; $XGSGROWTH$ is the rate of real export growth over the 5 preceeding years; $DUMMY_1$ and $DUMMY_2$ are designed to capture year-to-year shock such as rescheduling rounds.

We have estimated a revised version of *(3)*, specified as *(4)*:

(4) $$P = \beta_0 + \beta_1 D/XGS + \beta_2 D/GNP + \beta_3 XGSGROWTH + \beta_4 DUMMY_1 + \beta_5 DUMMY_2 + \beta_6 DUMMY_3$$

where D/GNP is the debt-to-GNP ratio.

Following Claessens, we chose rates of real exports growth averaged over the 5 preceeding years as indices of creditworthiness. In addition, we made the following modifications in an attempt to improve the goodness of fit: 1) we up-dated data to 1989; 2) we added a regressor, the debt-to-GNP ratio, to help capture creditworthiness; 3) we re-estimated the model in terms of total debt rather than Claessens's medium-and long-term debt. This in turn makes it more appropriate when applied to Eastern European countries.

The estimated result support the notion of a DRLC because the secondary market prices have a significant negative relationship with the level of total debt. Our estimates are reported in Table 6, along with Claessens's original estimates for comparison.

Equation *(4)* can be used to carry out debt and debt reduction analyses. Given economic aggregates for certain countries, it can

TABLE 6

EMPIRICAL DRLC ESTIMATES

Coefficient	Claessens's estimates		Revised estimates	
	estimates	*t*-statistics	estimates	*t*-statistic
b_0 constant	58.9		84.6	
β_1 *D/XGS*	− 2.2	4.5	− 5.22	3.5
β_2 *D/GNP*			− 16.06	3.0
β_3 *XGSGROWTH*	2.05	4.5	0.44	1.4
β_4 *DUMMY1*	− 11.08	2.3	− 11.5	2.3
β_5 *DUMMY2*	− 17.8	3.4	− 21.4	4.1
β_6 *DUMMY3*			− 26.6	5.0
R^2	0.472		0.427	
Degrees of freedom...............	80		88	

predict the secondary market prices in future periods (or the shadow prices of the debt in the non-trading cases), on the (rather heroic) assumption that the market is efficient. Another way of looking at *(4)* is to note that $P = V/D$, as in *(1)*. Multiplying both sides of *(4)* by D, yields:

$$(5) \qquad V = 84.60D - 5.22D^2/XGS - 16.06D^2/GNP + $$
$$+ 0.442XGROWTH - 11.6DUMMY_1 - 21.4DUMMY_2 - $$
$$- 26.6DUMMY_3$$

Equation *(5)* expresses the expected value of debt as a function of the debt stock, depicted in the conventional DRLC diagram, Graph 1. Applying the first order condition to *(5)* yields the debt level D^* at which the debt Laffer curve reaches its maximum (provided the second order derivations of *(5)*, evaluated at D^*, are negative):

$$(6) \qquad D^* = \frac{84.6 + 0.44\ XGROWTH - 26.6\ DUMMY_3}{10.44/X + 32.12\ D/GNP}$$

Equation *(6)* offers a guideline for locating a country on the DRLC. A straightforward comparison of the country's actual debt-to-export ratio and the calculated D^*/Export should help identify countries which are on the wrong side of the DRLC and therefore support the argument for reduction of their debt. These comparisons are summarized in Table 7.

TABLE 7

LOCATIONS OF EASTERN EUROPEAN COUNTRIES
ON THEIR DRLCS, 1989
(US $ million)

Debtors	GNP	Export	Export growth (%)	D^*/ Export (%)	D/ Export (%)	Location on DRLC
Bulgaria	46,700	13,777	2.44	295	298.6	turning point
Czechoslovakia	52,300	25,625	3.36	227	93.5	right side
GDR	81,000	29,811	3.40	267	192.5	right side
Hungary	26,900	10,900	2.74	252	223.1	right side
Poland	72,900	13,550	5.50	368	470.9	wrong side
Romania	68,100	13,400	3.90	356	2.8	right side
Yugoslavia	77,100	13,800	6.75	377	110.2	right side

First and foremost, the empirical evidence in Table 7 seems to suggest that Poland is the only nation in the region that is currently on the "wrong side" of her Laffer curve. It is therefore in both the creditor's and Poland's interest to implement some forms of debt reduction. On the other extreme is the case of Romania, which has strikingly low debt-to-export ratio of 2.8%, far below her D ratio of 356%. The five other countries lie somewhere in between these two extremes. Two cases are worth mentioning. Bulgaria is roughly on the "turning point" of her Laffer curve, and Hungary is approaching hers.

These results are hardly surprising, but rather what we would expect from our case-by-case analysis in Appendix 1. Bulgaria may soon call for debt relief and a debt equity swap program may be advocated for Hungary, given her relatively favorable long term investment climate. More importantly, our results offer strong support for our earlier notion: some sort of debt reduction solution should be worked out more or less immediately for the Polish debt. It is to this problem that we now turn.

4. - Debt and Liquidity Relief Scenarios for Poland

4.1 *Debt Relief Without New Lending*

We now propose different levels of debt relief, X, in the absence of new lending, apply our estimated Laffer curve to them, calculate the implied secondary market price $\hat{P}$, and present it in Table 8.

TABLE 8

POLISH DEBT RELIEF WITHOUT NEW LENDING

Debt relief $(X/D_0 \%)$	($ bil) (X)	Remaining debt $(D_0 - X)$ ($ bil) *(b)*	Implied secondary market price $\hat{P}$ *(c)*	$V = (D_0 - X) P$
20	8.2	32.8	18.9	6.2
30	12.3	28.7	23.8	6.8
34.5 *(a)*	14.1	26.9 *(a)*	26.0	7.0
40	16.4	24.6	26.8	6.6
60	24.6	16.4	38.7	6.3
85	34.9	6.1	51.2	3.1

(a) This is the debt stock level D^* where the DRLC reaches its maximum. Consequently 34,5% corresponds to the extent of debt relief necessary to bring the expected value of the debt to its turning point.

(b) $D_0 = \$41$bn, the current total debt stock.

(c) P was calculated as follows. From *(4)*, predicted P is $P' = 38,63$ when $D = D_0 = 41$ bn. However eqn *(4)*, estimated from pooled cross-sectioned data, overpredicts Poland's actual debt price for 1989, $P = .19$. We therefore produced a country-specific adjustment factor for Poland of $19/38.63 = 0.49$. We then calculated P' for eqn *(4)* for the lower levels of debt $D = (D_0 - X)$ after debt relief, and produced $\hat{P} = 0.49 P'$.

It is rather straightforward in the case of no new lending to recommend 35% debt relief. This assumes that the shadow price of official debt is equal to that of private debt, that official creditors, like private, are solely self-interested, and that the burden of debt relief will be pro-rated between them (17). But this is not the end of the story. The question is: can creditors do better with the help of new lending? The answer is an unambiguous "yes".

---

(17) Official/private burden sharing is far more complex than this paper implies. A promising new analysis of burden sharing is DOOLEY [10].

PARETO-OPTIMAL DEBT RELIEF IN THE ABSENCE OF NEW LENDING
(US $ billion)

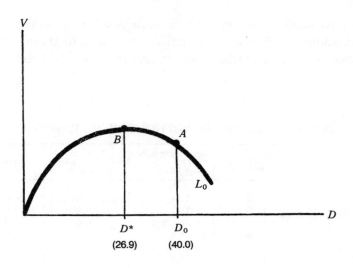

4.2 *Debt Relief With New Lending*

Krugman [19] argues that even with substantially depressed secondary market prices, it will generally be in exposed creditors' *collective* interest to lend more money — "throw good money after bad" — as long as the new money lowers the expected default rate. And as we saw in Section 1, Froot [14] further shows that for a liquiduty-constrained country such as Poland, new lending can actually shift up debt Laffer curves so that it is possible for creditors to expect more payment on their claims, and yet offer less debt relief.

In Graph 4 the Laffer curve labelled L_0 assumes no new lending or other liquidity relief. New lending shifts L_0 up to L_1. Point C on this new Laffer curve is an unambiguous creditors' welfare improvement from B. At C, creditors enjoy a higher expected value for claims, but with less debt relief. It follows that creditors' optimal choice, instead of the level of debt relief X_1 which maximizes the Laffer curve L_0, resulting in $D_1 = (D_0 - X_1)$, should instead be an optimal combination of debt and new lending (D^*, L^*), where $D^* > D_1$. In the Polish

COMBINATIONS OF DEBT RELIEF AND NEW LENDING
(US $ billion)

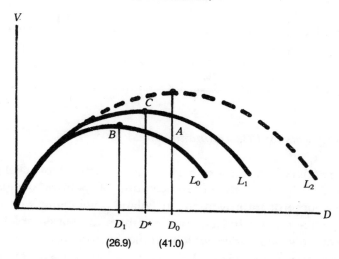

case, this implies that less than 35% of debt relief should be considered in conjunction with an optimal level of new lending, L^*.

Calculating the optimal (D^*, L^*) is beyond the scope of this paper. We simply offer upper bounds of new lending for possible levels of debt reduction. We define d and d^* as the probabilities of nonpayment before and after debt relief. The cost of the lending operation is therefore d^*L, where L is the amount of new lending. The benefit from improved repayment prospects after debt relief is $(d-d^*)D$, where D is the current debt stock. The condition to rationalize new lending in combination with debt relief is that the benefit exceeds the cost:

(7) $$d^* L < (d - d^*) D_0$$

which requires:

(8) $$L < (d/d^* - 1) D_0$$

We present the upper bounds for new lending according to equation (8) in Table 9. Any package that requires more new lending than the relevant L_{max} will leave creditors worse off.

TABLE 9

UPPER BOUNDS FOR NEW LENDING

X/D %	X ($ bn)	D ($ bn)	P	$d = 1 - P$	$Lmax$
25.0	10.3	30.0	21.3	78.7	1.2
30.0	12.3	28.7	23.8	76.7	2.6
34.5	14.1	26.9	26.0	74.0	3.9

4.3 *Conclusions and Recommandations*

Our results suggest a very partial and tentative debt relief package for Poland. We have taken no account of politics or any other potential source of improvement in Poland's willingness or ability to make debt payments. Indeed, our numbers are based solely on the rise in Poland's debt price which would be forecast by a *cross-sectional* estimate of the DRLC. This requires heroic assumptions about the "efficiency" of debt markets when the reality is that sovereign debt claims are anything but homogeneous financial instruments, and thus relief may well affect different countries' debt prices quite differently. Also, our estimates for maximum new lending — L_{max} — are *not* based on any estimates whatsoever of the extent to which new lending would shift up DRLCs: we do not have such estimates (nor does anyone else). Rather, what our L_{max} denotes is the maximum amount of new lending which existing creditors could be induced to make on the condition that *debt relief* lowers the default rate from d to d^*. This maximum would impose a default loss, $d^* L_{max}$, that would just be offset by the benefit from debt relief, $(d-d^*) D$.

However on Froot's [14] reasoning it is possible — indeed likely — that L would lower d^* still further, raising L_{max} above the levels shown in Table 9, and lowering optimal debt relief. As already noted, we have no way of estimating any impact of L on d^*; thus our estimate is in effect an upper bound for debt relief and a lower bound for associated new lending.

With these caveats in mind, we suggest the following debt relief package:

1) given their two-thirds share of the Polish debt and their relative cohesiveness, official creditors should take the lead via the Paris Club and agree to forgive about (2/3)*(35%), or 23% of Polish debt. They should also share the new lending of $3.9 bn (Table 9);

2) simultaneously, commercial banks should be offered the opportunity to chose from the debt relief menu now available under the terms of the *Brady Plan*. Banks which choose not to "exit" (18) — that is, sell off portions of their claims at the current market discount (81%) — should be required to commit new funds of about (1/3)*($3.9 bn) or $1.3 bn remembering that they stand to benefit from the rise in the debt price which will follow from debt relief offered by the exiting banks and by official creditors.

Of course there is no guarantee that bank participation in this *Brady* offering would yield (D^*, L^*) since their choice between debt relief and new lending would be voluntary. However, the rather dramatic nature of these DRLC results should be clear enough to banks to appeal to their self-interest. Perhaps the key to ensuring banks' collective participation in any debt and liquidity (19) relief settlement will be for the IMF and the Paris and London Clubs (20) to make their relief contingent on a prior commitment from the banks to sign on to a Brady settlement simultaneously, at current market prices. In short, the Polish settlement will require unprecedented coordination between official and commercial lenders.

---

(18) WILLIAMSON [31] suggests that the essence of "voluntary" debt relief options (such as buybacks and exit bonds) is that they break the free rider barrier by allowing banks with different preferences or constraints to choose between "exiting" or not.

(19) Here we are ignoring rescheduling possibilities, which at this level of analysis are alternatives to new lending as a form of liquidity relief.

(20) A quotation seems to the point here. "The Paris Club: clients visit it to discuss rescheduling and conditionality with OECD governments under the chaperonage of the IMF. Not to be confused with The London Club: where meeting one less public, more private and often take place without a chaperone". (BIRD GRAHAM: *Third World Debt: The Search for a Solution*, England, Edward Elgar Pub. Ltd., 1989).

1 - Single Countries' Position

1.1 *Bulgaria*

Since 1985, Bulgaria's total external convertible-currency debt rose from $3.6 billion to $10.0 billion largely due to sharp increases in imports. The bulk of this rise was financed by long and medium term loans from commercial banks, though other private creditors also contributed. Until 1989, Bulgaria was not a member of the IMF or the World Bank and thus borrowed nothing from them. By 1989, some $2.3 billion was owed to official creditors, $6.6 billion to commercial banks and $1.0 billion to other private creditors.

Between 1985-1989, the burden of Bulgaria's debt rose from 11.0% to 21.4% of GNP, and the debt service burden from 5% to 16.5%. By 1989, signs of trouble had begun to appear. Debt service payments were absorbing some 40% of export revenue, and reserves stood at 2.7 months' worth of imports. Commercial bank interest margins were rising. In March, the Foreign Trade Bank notified its commercial bank creditors that principal repayments would be frozen temporarily. Adding to Bulgaria's current account deterioration was substantial repayment of official bilateral creditors between 1985-1989, and considerable "lending" abroad by residents. High negative errors and omissions during 1985-1987 also point to capital flight.

Bulgaria's debt burden is now the third largest in Eastern Europe after Poland's and Hungary's. Moreover, its burden has increased by far the most rapidly. Nevertheless it is not yet being considered for *Brady* or other official relief. It has just joined the IMF and its political reform process is not well enough under way. Although private enterprise was legalized in January 1989, wage and prices are still controlled. Banking reform, begun in 1987, has not yet taken off.

(*) This appendix draws heavily on INSTITUTE OF INTERNATIONAL FINANCE [15].

Restrictions on consumer imports have been lifted but firms can still keep only 50% of hard currency revenues. Foreign ownership laws remain restrictive. In short, the combination of deteriorating external balance and rising debt burden means that Bulgaria may soon call for debt relief; whether it is forthcoming depends on the speed of political and economic reforms.

1.2 *Czechoslovakia (The Czech and Slovak Republics)*

Between 1985 and 1989, Czechoslovakia's debt rose from $4.6 billion to $7.2 billion, financed largely by commercial banks. The major part of this increase in bank credit was short term, financing considerable upturns in import volumes following sharp devaluation of the currency. Correspondingly, the current account balance deteriorated markedly. At 6% of GNP, Czechoslovakia's debt service ratio is the second lowest in the region (21).

From 1979-1986, Czechoslovakia ran large trade surpluses, largely with developing countries. However, these were financed with some $5 billion in export credits, about half of which were never collected. Since 1987, exports to developing countries have been curtailed, and hard currency imports from the West have increased. These trends account for the deterioration in the current account.

Commercial banks voluntarily lent an average of $500 million annually between 1987-1989, much of which was used to repay official bilateral creditors. As it still not a member of the IMF or IBRD, Czechoslovakia is not eligible for loans from them. However, non-bank private creditors have increasingly provided financing in recent years.

Due to its history of industrial and engineering prowess, and its lack of a debt burden, Czechoslovakia has maintained productivity and living standards at relatively high levels. Perhaps for this reason, it has shown less eagerness for market-based reforms than, say. Poland or Hungary. Privatization of state firms has not begun. Nor has

---

(21) The sharp jump in Czechoslovakia's debt to GNP ratio in 1989 is a statistical artifact due to a sharp fall in $ GNP after currency devaluation.

foreign equity investment appeared, although a joint venture law is now in place, However, the country's relatively low debt burden means that a call for debt relief is unlikely.

1.3 *German Democratic Republic*
(Since Oct. 1990, part of the Federal Republic of Germany)

In 1989, the GDR's external debt was $22 billion, $14 billion of it owed to commercial banks, most of it medium to long term. The debt and debt service ratios were relatively high, at 26.7% and 13% respectively.

In recent years the current account surplus had been deteriorating, most sharply in 1989 following the opening of the border with West Germany in November. There were substantial hard currency outflows due to repayment of official bilateral debt (about half of which was East German-West German trade credit), resident lending abroad and errors and omissions (probably capital flight). These outflows were financed by commercial bank loans and, in 1989, by a large, $2 billion drawdown of official hard currency reserves.

Still, at the end of 1989, the GDR's reserves deposited in western commercial banks were estimated at $8.1 billion. These assets, combined with political and economic union with West Germany, suggest that neither the former GDR's official or private creditors will be called upon to provide debt relief.

1.4 *Hungary*

Hungary's external debt is about $19.7 billion, up from $13.4 billion in 1985. Roughly $16 billion of this is due to commercial banks, most of it medium-to-long term. The $D/$GNP ratio at 69% is the highest in Eastern Europe, and the $iD/$GNP ratio, at 18,8% is the second highest. Real GNP growth has been slow.

Since 1985, Hungary's current account balance has been consistently negative. Moreover, there have been fairly large capital outflows. These current and capital account foreign exchange outflows have been financed mostly by commercial banks, though recent years have also seen both official lending and large drawdowns of official reserves. In 1989, fully one third of the current account deficit was financed via reserves.

The current account deficit increased sharply in 1989 after travel restrictions were removed. Simultaneously, domestic absorption rose due to increased monetary expansion and fiscal deficits. These prompted the IMF to interrupt its stand-by credit program, though it was restored in March 1989. In 1990, it was expected that the commercial banks' willingness to lend to Hungary would diminish, and official lenders would have to play a larger role.

Hungary began its economic liberalization earlier and until Poland's radical reforms in 1990 had carried it further than any other Eastern Europeen country except Yugoslavia. Price decontrol began in 1985, and recent legislation permits privatization. Joint ventures are well-established; since 1988 100% foreign ownership has been allowed. However ownership rights and contractual law are still ill-defined. Financial market reforms has been hampered by restrictions on foreign borrowing by Hungarian banks and by a reluctance to open domestic financial markets to full foreign competition. Foreign exchange regulations have been softened, import restrictions liberalized, and the official exchange rate brought closer in line with the uncontrolled parallel rate.

Hungary's debt management has been skilled, its repayment record unblemished, and until recently debt has traded at near par. However between the end of 1989 and April 1990, the price of its debt dropped from 98¢ to about 85¢. Private creditors are increasingly cautious about new lending because of relatively slow real growth and continued deterioration in the current account. Although exports have risen recently since 1987 due to a 15% real effective devaluation in the forint, imports have jumped sharply. Despite the only stock market in Eastern Europe and favourable joint venture laws, equity and direct investment inflows have been slow. At least two Canadian and American investment funds have been created since 1989, but the funds have mostly remained on US money markets awaiting outlets in Hungary. In the longer run, however, expatriates investing in such funds may prove a significant source of foreign capital.

Hungary would seem well poised for voluntary or official debt relief, given her established membership in the international financial agencies, her record of financial and political reform and her unblemished repayment record. By the same token, she has no urgent need for relief, nor has she called for it. Her high and rising debt service ratio but relatively favorable long term investment climate might nevertheless argue for a debt equity swap program. Moreover, such a program might, as in Chile, be used as a magnet to attract expatriate foreign currency or to reverse capital flight by domestic residents.

1.5 *Romania*

Romania has reduced its hard currency debt from $10 billion at the end of 1981 to $0.2 billion in 1989. Thus its debt service ratios are now by far the lowest in Eastern Europe: 3.6% and 1.8% respectively. Romania accomplished this feat by brutally cutting imports and generating huge current-account surpluses, which in 1989 stood at $3.3 billion.

Romania's low foreign indebtedness was achieved at the price of severely restricted consumer demand, The draconean discipline of the Ceausescu regime has not yet been replaced by market discipline, given the current government's fragile popular support. It is reasonable to predict that once political stability is restored and economic reform begun, Romania will begin to attract significant portfolio and direct investment from abroad (22). As a relatively long-standing member of the IMF and World Bank, with its previous debt to them fully paid off, Romania will also be eligible for official institutional credits. However, the new government is still far from coherent, and debt service payments have been frozen since Ceausescu's fall.

1.6 *Yugoslavia*

Yugoslavia foreign debt is $17.6 billion; 42% or $6.6 billion is owed to commercial banks, with the rest divided between interna-

---

(22) It is noteworthy that Romania is the only Eastern European country with a large and diversified enough stock of foreign investment that the US government feels free to publish numbers without fear of identifying individual corporation.

tional institutions and Western governments. As recently as 1985, its debt ratios were the highest in Europe, but since then they have fallen continuously. By 1989, the debt to GNP ratio at 23% was lower than Hungary's, Poland's, and the GDR's, and its debt service ratio at 10% was also below Bulgaria's and the former GDR's. Yugoslavia achieved its debt service reductions by a combination of strong current account surpluses, debt equity swaps and rescheduling. Debt equity swaps in 1989 cut commercial debt by $1.4 billion. Between 1983 and 1988, there were six Paris Club and four commercial bank rescheduling agreements. Yugoslavia has kept current in its commercial bank interest obligations. Between 1989-1990 its debt price rose substantially, from about 44¢ to about 58¢.

Yugoslavia's recent external financial success has not been matched domestically. Since 1987, real output has fallen or stagnated, and by the beginning of 1990 the inflation rate was close to 300%. Severe monetary and fiscal restraint was imposed, a new dinar was established (equal to 10,000 old dinars) and frozen against the Deutsch-mark, and wages and prices of essentials were frozen. In March 1990, the IMF provided stand-by credit for $600 million over 18 months.

Yugoslavia's immediate prospect for attracting foreign capital appears reasonably good. Although there are still threats of political and financial instability due to loose central control over the budgets of state enterprises and the individual republics, privatization and joint venture rules are now well established. Even the banking sector anticipates privatization, as well as joint ventures with foreign banks. Import restrictions are being rapidly removed, and resident convertibility for current transaction has now been established. Net inward equity investment at $150 million accounted for half of that for all Eastern Europe. However, unlike Hungary and Poland, Yugoslavia has not yet begun to establish capital market reforms.

2. - Restructuring Negotiations, Loans
   Relief and Aid Activities for Polish Debt, 1989-1990.

October 1989

Italy agrees to give Poland GBP 25 mil aid package offers to support Poland's case with IMF, EEC and Paris Club.

November 1989

Paris Club agrees to let US $3.6 bil Poland's official debt arrears due in 1989, built up while an agreement between Poland and the IMF over economic reforms is being negotiated.

December 1989

Poland reaches an agreement with IMF to receive up to US $700 mil in standing credit.

January 1990

1) US Treasury informs Poland that the country can be eligible for debt reduction under the *Brady Plan*;
2) creditors in Paris Club and the London Club meet for the first time to discuss Polish finances and the debt.

February 1990

1) Western govts. agree to Poland's request to suspend interest and capital payments on its debt until March 91. Payments due in 90 and the first quarter of 91 are rescheduled for 14 years with 8 years grace. This brings the total debt to US $9.4 billion;

2) the World Bank approves loans to Poland worth US $360 mil, pending decision by Paris Club and IMF's approval of a reform package.

March 1990

1) Japanese prime minister pledges to provide US $350 mil in trade insurance to Poland;

2) Poland's main bank creditors suggest that Poland should pay them 15% of the interest due on US $9.1 bil from start-1990 to end-May 91, with the remaining 85% of the interest being rolled into an existing US $1 bil short term trade credit.

May 1990

1) Poland seeks to cut its debt service obligations to an average interest rate of 2%, vs 10% currently, and therefore to cut the servicing burden by 80%;

2) US suggests official Polish debt relief of $32 bil in the Group of Seven meeting.

June 1990

1) Banks ease pressure to Poland for interest payment in 1990;

2) France reschedules FF 8.3 bil over 14 years with 8 years grace. But no forgiveness;

3) Finland demands Polish environmental protection in exchange for forgiveness of Fm 90 mil debt;

4) World Bank initiates an agreement for a US $300 mil structure adjustment loan to Poland.

July 1990

1) Group of Seven leaders urge the Paris Club to extent the IMF's *Toronto Terms* to Poland;

2) The UK Commons Treasury and Civil Service Select Committee oppose a Marshall plan for Eastern Europe. It instead proposes debt relief, especially for Poland;

3) Germany agrees to reschedule Polish debt worth DM 3 billion due March 31 1991, to 14 years.

November 1990

Poland pays no interest in 1990 to any of its creditors.

BIBLIOGRAPHY

[1] BALCEROWICZ L.: «Polish Economic Reform, 1981-1988: an Overview», in *Economic Reform in the European Centrally Planned Economies*, New York, Limited Nations Econimic Commission for Europe, 1989.

[2] BEKSIAK J. *et* AL.: *The Polish Transformation: Programme and Progress*, London, The Centre for Research Into Communist Economies, 1990.

[3] BORENSZTEIN E.: «Debt Overhang, Credit Rationing and Investment», IMF *Working Paper* n. 89/74, mimeo, September 1989.

[4] BOWE M. - DEAN J. W.: «Can the Market Solve the Debt Problem? The Theory and Practice of Sovereign Debt Relief», Simon Fraser University, mimeo, 1990, Outline for forthcoming in *Journal of Economic Literature*. Surrey.

[5] BULOW J. - ROGOFF K.: «The Buyback Boomdoggle», *Brookings Papers on Economic Activity*, n. 2, 1988, pp. 675-98.

[6] — — - — —: «Cleaning up the Third World Without Getting Taken to the Cleaners», *Journal of Economic Perspectives*, n. 4 (1), Winter, 1990.

[7] CLASSENS S.: «The Debt Laffer Curve: Some Estimates», World Bank, *Working Paper*, 1988.

[8] COHEN D.: «Is the Discount on the Secondary Market a Case for Debt Relief?» World Bank *PPR Working Paper*, n. 132, 1989.

[9] DILEO P. - REMOLONA E.M.: *Voluntary Conversions of LDC Debt*, New York, Federal Reserve Bank, mimeo, April (technical version), July (nontechnical version) 1989.

[10] DOOLEY M.P.: *Burdensharing Among Creditors when Repayment is Uncertain*, IMF, mimeo, 1990.

[11] DOOLEY M.P. - FOLKERTS - LANDAU D. - HAAS R.D. - SYMANSKY S.A. - TYRON R.W.: *Debt Reduction and Economic Activity*, Washington, International Monetary Fund, March, 1990.

[12] FISCHER S.: «Sharing the Burden of the International Debt crisis» *American Economic Review*, May, 1987.

[13] FRENKEL J. A. - DOOLEY M. P. - WICKHAM P. (eds.): *Analytical Issues in Debt*, Washington, International Monetary Fund, 1989.

[14] FROOT K.A.: «Buybacks, Exit Bonds, and the Optimality of Debt and Liquidity Relief», *International Economic Review*, n. 30, February, 1989, pp. 49-70.

[15] INSTITUTE OF INTERNATIONAL FINANCE: *Building Free Markets*, Washington, April, 1990.

[16] — —: *Improving the Official Debt Strategy: Arrears Are not the Way*, Washington, May 1990.

[17] KENEN P.: «A Bailout Plan for the Banks», *The New York Times*, 6 March 1983.

[18] KRUGMAN P.: «Financing vs. forgiving a Debt Overhang», *Journal of Development Economics*, n. 29, 1988, pp. 253-68.

[19] — —: *Market-Based Debt-Reduction Schemes*, in FRENKEL *et* AL., 1989.

[20] MARER P. - SIWINSKI W. (eds.): *Creditworthiness and Reform in Poland: Western and Polish Perspectives*, Bloomington (Ill.), Indiana University Press, 1988.

[21] OECD: *Financial Market Trends*, OECD, Paris, February, 1990.

[22] PURCELL J. - ORLANSKY D.: *Developing Country Loans: a New Valuation Model for Secondary Market Trading*, Salomon Brothers, New York, 1988.

[23] RYDZKOWSKY W - ZAOLABKIEWICZ K.: «Polish International Debt: Prospects for Repayment», *Eastern European Quarterly*, June 1989.

[24] SACHS J.: «Managing the LDC Debt Crisis», *Brookings Papers on Economic Activity*, n. 2, 1986, pp. 397-431.

[25] —— —: «New Approaches to the Latin American Debt Crisis», Princeton (NJ) Princeton University, *Essays in International Finance*, n. 174, July 1989.

[26] —— —: «Charting Poland's Economic Rebirth», *Challange*, January-February, 1990.

[27] SACHS J. - HUIZINGA H.: «US Commercial Banks and the Developing-Country Debt Crisis», *Brookings Papers on Economic Activity*, n. 2, 1987, pp. 555-601.

[28] SACHS J. - LIPTON D.: «Creating a Market in Eastern Europe: the Case of Poland», *Brooking Papers on Economic Activity*, n. 1, 1990.

[29] TREASURY NEWS: *Remarks by Secretary Nicholas F. Brady*, Washington (DC), US Treasury, 10 March, 1989.

[30] —— —: *Statement by Under Secretary David C. Milford*, Washington (DC), US Treasury, 21 March, 1990.

[31] WILLIAMSON J.: *Voluntary Approaches to Debt Relief*, Washington (DC), Institute for International Economics, September 1988, revised June 1989.

[32] WORLD BANK: «Poland: Reform Adjustment and Growth», vol. I, *A World Bank Country Study*, Washington, (DC), World Bank 1987.

[33] —— —: *World Bank Debt Statistics: Tables 1988-1989 and 1989-1990*, Washington (DC), World Bank.

The Experience of West European Public Enterprises for the Transition of Eastern European Economies

Franco A. Grassini (*)
Libera Università Internazionale degli Studi Sociali, Roma

1. - Introduction

Strong and imaginative as it may be, the effort to privatise socialist property in the former communist countries is hardly likely to be fully successful. There are a variety of reasons: there is nobody willing to buy some enterprises; it might be seen as politically unwise to hand over a public utility to foreign interests; the closure of a firm might increase unemployment to an economically unbearable level; or, finally, an agreement on price cannot be reached. In other words for a number of years the prevailing model shall be that of a "mixed economy" where private and public enterprises shall coexist.

If the starting assumption is right, it might be worthwhile to explore how the experiences of public enterprises in Western European countries could be used by Eastern European countries to avoid at least some of our major errors. But to do so, we must give a definition of what a public enterprise is and such definition might entail some problems. To try to be clear on this problem I suggest to define as a public enterprise any organization controlled by the central or the local government whose products or services are voluntarily

(*) I am indebted to Professor Enzo Pontarollo for some quite useful comments. I am, however, responsible for any error and opinion.
Advise: the numbers in square brackets refer to the Bibliography in the appendix.

bought and sold for a price in some way related to the cost of the same. In other words, there has to be a market.

Of course, one might think that since the government-controlled enterprises are strongly infuenced by the political and the institutional environment in which they operate, each country has its own experience. There is a grain of truth in such opinion. For instance, in the British political setting, a Minister can refuse to reply to a member of Parliament about a question concerning a public enterprise because it is a problem of day-to-day managerial responsibility. A similar attitude in Italy would be considered almost an attempt to overturn the sovereignty of Parliament. Nevertheless, it is a useful exercise to distinguish what is common to several nations and what is peculiar of particular countries. Moreover since the Eastern European countries are rebuilding from scratch their political systems, they might try to avoid some of the worst Western European experiences.

However, the subject to be covered is so large that a paper can hardly deal with it. I shall, therefore, concentrate on the following topics: how public enterprises are organized; which are their goals and their relationships with government and the political institutions; how they are financed; which policies and rules apply to them. Moreover, I shall confine myself to the non-financial sector, because public banks have their own different and complicated problems.

2. - Three Models

Public enterprises fall in one of three main organizational models: they may be a simple branch of the public administration, a public corporation (or something very similar to it, depending on the legal system), or a joint stock company. The second and the third types are often mixed: shares of joint stock companies are frequently owned by a public corporation.

The public administration model is the oldest and was adopted when governments started to provide services and to charge users a price for them. Thus, Railways and Post-Offices were often only branches of public administration. In Germany, at the end of XIX century, both Railways and Post-Offices had almost a military organisation (Chandler [6]). Even as such, these enterprises had a separate and autonomous budget, but their surpluses or deficits benefited or deteriorated the government budget. Also, investments depended more on Treasury policy than on specific needs.

However, the adoption of this organisational model runs into the problem that bureaucratic rules are not usually very flexible even in countries, like the United Kingdom, where pragmatism dominates every aspect of life. Thus, procurement and personnel policies developed to guarantee impartiality and fairness did not fit with the needs of enterprises which, as time progressed, needed to become more businesslike to satisfy their customers. Moreover, the ultimate responsibility rested with a Minister, giving political aims a dispropor-tionate weight in decision making. We shall see later the implications of such a situation.

Because of the problems outlined, in Western Europe most pre-existing or newly created public enterprises adopted one of the two other organisational models since the early thirties.

The public corporation (Robson [25]) has normally a separated personality from the State (or the Crown), it can sue and be sued and the civil law applies (with a few exceptions) to all its contracts, including the labour ones. Moreover, it has a capital endowment provided by the incorporating law (and its amendments), it is usually governed by a Board of Directors, appointed either by the full government, a group of Ministers, or a single Minister. Only in Italy the appointment of Chairmen and Deputy-Chairmen has to be approved by special Commissions of Parliament. In most cases every public corporation is under the supervision of a specific or parent Ministry. In many cases, though not always, the public corporation can also own shares of joint-stock companies and, as already stated, it is simply a kind of holding company operating through joint-stock companies, whose shares can also be quoted on a Stock Exchange. A classic example of this arrangement are the "State Participations" of Italy.

In theory, when a public enterprise is incorporated as a joint-stock company, it is not different from a capitalist enterprise. In practice, however, there might be huge behavioural discrepancies between the two, because the budget contraints of a government are by no means comparable to those of even the wealthiest and most profligate individual shareholder. Thus, it must be emphasized that the choice of the joint-stock company as the organizational form for a government-controlled enterprise does not provide by itself a guarantee of a behavior similar to that of a capitalist enterprise. The government can always push the management to a course of action which produces substantial losses, even when there are minority shareholders. It should also be pointed out that minority shareholders cannot bring a legal action unless mismanagement is a borderline case between total incompetence and theft or fraud. In this case, the viable legal course is not a civil suit but a criminal action. The only recourse for a minority shareholder unhappy with the way a company is run is to sell his or her shares. But this strategy does not avoid incurring substantial losses, as it has happened many times in Western Europe. For instance, in Italy Finsider, the holding company for the government-controlled iron and steel enterprises, was considered a blue chip by thousands of small investors. Yet, it ended up in liquidation not only because of the early 1980s steel industry crisis, but also because it was not able to take drastic actions such as closing plants. The minority shareholders were left to bear the burden of the losses, though they had never been able to have a say in management.

3. - Multiplicity of Goals

There is at least one point on which almost all Western European public enterprises are very similar. All of them, whichever might be the reason why they have been established or nationalized, have been given more than one single goal by their respective governments.

In some cases they were asked to improve their performance against foreign competitors and to provide employment and better working conditions than private firms. In other cases they were asked to invest under highly risky conditions, while trying to to make a profit or at least break even over an undefined period of time. In some other cases they were compelled to keep prices steady to avoid inflation rate increases, and meanwhile they were required to invest in order to improve demand in a slump. Similarly, firms which were established to be leaders in high technology industry were often diverted to maintaining jobs for those who did not succeed. Moreover, very often these companies had to get loans because their cash-flows were not sufficient to achieve their goals and governments did not provide money while imposing all kinds of burdensome demands.

In the United Kingdom, Mrs. Thatcher apparently only asked British public enterprises to make a profit in order to be able to privatise them at the best possible price. In practice, even she used her government power over public enterprises to reach quite different aims. For instance, the Electricity Generating Board was requested to buy British coal rather than shop around on the international market for better prices. In brief, noneconomic as well as industrial policy aims were pursued through public enterprises everywhere.

So far, we have analysed only economic aims. Yet, as it is widely known, democratic governments need votes to stay in power and public enterprises are often used to collect votes for the governing party. How this takes place depends on the political mores and institutions of each country. Ideology in some circumstances has played a very important role. The various schools of socialist thought have always considered public property as intrinsically superior to private property. Transferring property from the private to the public sector has given happiness to millions of socialist voters in the UK, France, Portugal, and elsewhere in Europe. Likewise, feet on the ground trade-unionists have experienced how public enterprises, barring those under the Thatcher government, are more pliable employers than private firms. They have, therefore, traded their votes for parties or persons favorable to nationalizations or against privatization. Of course, also the reverse is true: there are people who vote only for parties in favour of privatization. In some cases, State controlled firms have often been asked to provide high standards of service because dissatisfied customers, particularly when the supplier is a monopolist, use the ballots to complain. In many cases patronage at various levels, from top management to the humblest runner boy, is a widely used reward for political support (Grassini [12]). Unfortunately, there have been also instances when government controlled firms have been used to fund elections or to create personal wealth for politicians or their friends.

On the whole, the multiplicity of aims given to public enterprises has been amplified by the fact that in democratic countries the chain of command is far from clear. The fact has been mentioned that public corporations usually have a parent Ministry. The same applies to joint-stock companies but very often above the Minister there are the Prime Minister, the Cabinet or a Ministerial Committee. Side by side with the Minister there is the Parliament. Very often many of these actors have conflicting views and an open or *de facto* compromise can be found or has to be found by the firm concerned, trying partially to satisfy the aims of the various parties.

The consequences of the multiplicity of goals for public enterprises are at least two. First it provides management with a variety of choices and in a limited sense an autonomy from the political masters. A manager can say to his or her parent Ministry that a certain course of action could not be taken because the Parliament objected, and viceversa. There have been occasions when a strong person, like the founder of Italian ENI, Enrico Mattei, was able to choose what he wanted by playing one party against the other (Posner and Wolf [19]).

The second consequence is that it is very difficult to judge the performance of public enterprises. Which yardstick should be used? Those who have tried to consider only profits were widely out of the mark (Durupty [9]), but also those who have tried to broaden the picture have often come out with very unfocused results (Nove [18]).

In Italy very recently a Treasury Committee calculated that from 1930 to 1989 government has spent L. 245,000 billions (i.e. almost a fifth of the outstanding national debt) for State Participations. If it would sell the same on the market, it might fetch less a sixth of the said amount: a very poor business fron a capitalist point of view, but nobody can say where the Italian economy would be without IRI, ENI and EFIM.

4. - Maximizing Profits?

Various devices have been conceived and tried to restrain the consequences of the multiplicity of goals for the government controlled firms. We shall later return to them. Now let us consider whether a single goal might be the solution. In our case we could be facilitated by our starting assumption. In the former socialist economies public enterprises are not, at least at the present time, the result of a political choice, but rather they are the unwanted heritage of a collapsed system. Thus, if they are for a large part a temporary phenomenon, we could assume that a single goal might be thrust upon them: maximize profits and behave just like private firms.

In this case, government should resist the temptation to meddle with management and just appoint it and wait for results. It is a rather heroic assumption, but economists are known for their heroism on paper when building models. In fact, there are at least three problems with this assumption.

First of all profit maximizing is a good rule provided we live in a Pareto optimal world. Thus, given available technology, each firm must use its resources to produce at maximum capacity and it must not be possible to increase the output of any product without sacrificing another output. It is also not possible to use the same resources and produce a different output on which consumers might put more value. No consumer could change his or her consumption to feel better off without leaving somebody else worse off.

In such a world, however, there should not be any difference between private and social costs. This situation unfortunately rarely or ever happens in the real world. So some forms of taxation and compensation have to be devised to fill the gap between private and social costs and benefits.

To have a Paretian optimality you have to take the existing distribution of income as given. Each distribution of income produces a different set of outputs, prices and distribution of goods among consumers and services which is apt to satisfy the Paretian optimality. If the existing income distribution is not what you wish because you think that it is possible to make interpersonal comparison of utility, taxes and subsidies have to be brought into the picture dissolving the nicety of the model. There are also public goods like clean air and environmental preservation which cannot be bought and sold in the marketplace like ordinary goods which are consumed collectively. So taxes and subsidies come again to the fore to complicate and dissolve the model and yet, no ideal solution seems to have yet been envisioned. Last but not least, Pareto-optimality is based upon the implicit assumption that economies of scale and of learning do not exist.

As a consequence of all these factors the world offers only second best alternatives. But it is well known that second best solutions are viable only when first best solutions prevail everywhere else. So we are legitimised to have some doubts on profit maximization. Even if, in homage to the economic tradition, one were inclined to bypass such doubts, two other problems mentioned before remain. First, in case of monopoly, unrestricted profit maximization leads the mono-polising firm to charge higher prices and produce smaller outputs than would be socially optimal. The monopolist, if he is a profit maximizer, sells at a price which equals his marginal cost to marginal revenue, and there is a deadweight loss of welfare, unless he is also so strong as to be able to discriminate among customers.

Of course, Schumpeter [27] first, the Chicago School later, and more recently the contestable markets theory (Baumol [4]) have all tried with different and more or less rigorous arguments to show the irrelevance of the traditional concern with monopolies. In a dynamic society monopolies disappear or might also be helpful at least in the long run. There is evidence that in the former socialist countries monopolies exist and it might take time to dissolve them through disinvestiture of single plants or opening to foreign competition. So at last for a certain period and in the opinion of this writer, who believes in natural monopolies, in the long run, the profit maximization rule cannot be applied as a general and easy rule.

The last and much more relevant problem is that profit maximiz-ation rule is a very simple one when written on economics textbooks but very difficult to put into practice.

Leaving aside one of the controversies on which economists have poured tons of ink, namely profit maximization versus satisfaction (Baumol [3], Marris [17], Cyert and March [7], Demsetz [8]), I wish only to point out that it is more important to understand how difficult it is to operate under uncertainty than to worry whether an enterprise controlled by shareholders is or is not maximizing profits. As the discussions concerning the short-termism of Anglo-Saxon corpora-tions, compared to the long-term views of Japanese and German firms have taught us, decisions concerning the time horizon have a deep impact on investments and price decisions.

Moreover, an investment is profitable not whether the *a priori* appraisal of the best rate of return is chosen, but if the projections of quantities produced, costs and prices expected are right or turn out, *ex-post*, not to be too far from reality. Even a price decision, which might seem easiest to take, can in the not too long run have a favorable or unfavorable effect on the enterprise depending on the appropriateness of competitors reaction.

So even a single and simple goal like maximization does not solve the problem of how to manage public enterprises.

Leaving aside theory, Western European experience shows that, multiple goals notwithstanding, a State-owned enterprise submitted to a certain degree of competition makes a more efficient use of resources than one operating under monopolistic conditions. Efficiency, in fact, is fostered when comparisons with other companies are possible.

5. - Governmental Control

As anticipated, governments of different Western European countries have conceived and tried various devices to limit State-owned firms discretion in pursuing the multiple goals thrust upon them.

The United Kingdom is the country probably where more has been done at the official level. Two White Papers, published in 1967 [15] and 1978 [31], a report of the Select Committee on National Industries in 1974 and a full-scale inquiry by the Nationalised Economic Development Office in 1976 tried to put order in the field of public enterprises.

The 1967 *White Paper* attempted to understand and control public enterprises in terms of conventional economics. Allocative efficiency was seen as the major goal. Prices had to be based on long run marginal costs, investments appraised against a test discount rate, supposedly representing the opportunity cost of capital to the public sector, industry performance had to be monitored against pre-established

financial targets. Most important specific *ad hoc* subsides would be
provided to deal with social costs, so that management could no
longer justify losses as social cost. It is widely discussed whether the
system was ever put into practice. Nationalized industries in the 1970s
were used as instruments against inflation, which seemed the prevailing evil. Prices were restrained and investments constrained by the
Treasury. To put it shortly, the *NEDO Report* of 1976 demonstrated
that the framework of rules put forth in the 1967 *White Paper* had
failed.

The 1978 *White Paper* was much less rigorous. Marginal cost
pricing was only very generally suggested and with caveats. The test
discount rate criterion for investment was dropped and a required
rate of return was advocated. It was recommended that measures of
performance other than financial ones should be developed and that
public corporations should be held accountable to such measures.
However, a complete reversal of policy initiated by the Thatcher
government to swich from efficiency to privatisation has upset the
1978 *White Paper* goals.

In France in 1967 a special commission convened by the Prime
Minister produced a well thought report, known as the *Nora Report*
[22] which proposed a series of measures meant to improve the
efficiency, the autonomy and the accountability of public enterprises.
Even in this case, the *Nora report* proposals were abandoned shortly
after their introduction.

Nevertheless France is the country where the nationalized electricity industry (Electricité de France) is more advanced in setting
tariffs based on marginal costs. It may be that this is due more to the
strong technocratic tradition of the French administration, and its
love for rationality, than to conscious political decisions. The same
Electricité de France has, in fact, been instrumental in helping the
development, pushed by the government, of a national nuclear industry.

France's more recent industrial policy envisaged two quite
different roles for nationalized industries: to provide a public service,
as with telecommunications or rail transport, and to guarantee a
French dynamic and relevant presence in the so called strategic
industries such as electronics, chemical and nuclear-power. Steel,
which in the 50s and 60s was considered strategic is under State

control in France because private investors gave it up during the 80s crisis. On top of these declared goals, however, macroeconomic policy plays a role. For instance, although French electricity tariffs are among the lowest in Europe and notwithstanding the rule to keep price increases 1.5 percentage points below inflation, the Minister of Finance has not allowed Electricité de France to increase its prices in order to keep down inflation. So the corporation has lost money in six out of the past ten years.

In Italy, Pasquale Saraceno [26], the most respected theorist of public enterprises, suggested that public corporations pursue profits and that the special endowment fund which the State provided to the holding public corporations controlling a huge number of joint-stock companies should be considered as a limit to choices available both to government and to management. Also a law in 1978 introduced the notion that social costs should be covered by open subsidies approved by the Parliament. Yet, no precise rule existed and multiplicity of goals prevailed even more than in other countries.

The fact that none of the Western European countries where public enterprises are more widespread has been able to find or consistently apply rules capable to deal with the problem of the multiplicity of goals should not be interpreted either as proof that rules are useless or impossible or from our previous critique of a single rule, such as profit maximisation.

All these considerations show that governments, in pursuing both their macroeconomic and their political objectives, are seldom capable of refraining from using the few instruments at their disposal.

I shall never forget that when I was a young economist doing research on the British Coal Board (Grassini [11]), I had the opportunity to confer with such an authority as Austin Robinson, who had been advisor to the Labour Government immediately after World War Two. Quite naively I asked him why they had frozen coal prices knowing that misallocation of resources would result and he quietly replied "nationalised industries were the only ones we could give orders to". The temptation to have a "command economy" within a market economy is too strong to be resisted. To sum it up paradoxically, it might be said that the real problem to maintain at least a minimum of microeconomic efficiency is how to avoid too much power by government over public enterprises without, if possible, eschewing the problem of public accountability.

6. - Limits Imposed by the EEC

A limit to government power over public enterprises might arise, however, by the new interpretation of article 92 of the *Rome Treaty* put forth by the competition Commissioner Sir Leon Brittan. Under the said articke, State aids to any type of firms is forbidden when it results in unfair competition. When we come to public enterprises aid may be disguised as cheap loans, equity injection, losses write-offs, grants or guarantees. There have been two much advertised cases, the sale of Rover to British Aerospace and the cancellation of State loans to Renault, in which the EEC Commission has compelled the two enterprises to give back some of the envisaged aid. But over the years article 222 of the *Rome Treaty* recognizing the principle of State ownership has prevailed over article 92.

Recently Sir Leon Brittan is starting to argue that the Commission is not getting the needed information. He wants annual reports giving full details of provision of capital, grants, loans and guarantees, dividends and the balance sheets of State-owned companies. He also wants details of money transferred from one part of a holding company to another. The proposed rules would apply initially to manufacturing companies with annual turnover of more than ECU 200 millions.

What is more important is how the EEC competition Commissioner wishes to utilize the information collected. He intends to test the legality of State aid by judging whether a private investor would have provided funds on the same basis. Such a criterion is not a novelty for the Commission, as well as for the Court of Justice of Luxemburg but it is not a very easy one to interpret. A recent holding of the Court says: «The private investor behaviour to which the public investor who is pursuing political economy objectives should be compared is not necessarily the private investor who places his capital in relation to its capacity to produce income in the short or even very short term. The comparison is to be made with a private holding company or enterpreneurial group aiming at a structural policy and guided by a long-term income perspective» (*Opinion 21.3.91* Repubblica Italiana EEC Commission). In some cases, this policy has already been put into practice. For instance, state-owned Electricité de France has received clearance by the EEC Commission to supply power at advantageous rates to Exxon Chemical. Under the 6 year deal, a new Exxon ethylene plant in Normandy is to receive electricity at well below the average rates, in return for which it has to stop using power or face a very high tariff for 22 days each winter. Since the problems of any electricity producer is to level off demand during winter peaks, the EEC Commission was satisfied that the electricity price fixed by the contract reflected a commercial price set according to economic considerations «which a national private investor would follow in a similar situation». A very similar agreement has been signed with the US engineering group Allied Signal which will be charged from seven centimes per kwh in the slack summer periods, up to 53 centimes in winter. This is a very wide range and to judge if it is decided upon commercial consideration requires a through knowledge of demand and capacity supply of electricity.

The United Kingdom, which has sold all its nationalised manufacturing companies, eagerly supports the plan and the principle put forwards by the EEC competition Commissioner, while Germany, Holland and Denmark seem to have no strong objections. Italy, supported by the Southern European States, is strenuously opposed to Sir Leon Brittan's proposals. In 1990, however, a general attack on the competition Commissioner's entire approach to policing State aid led by the same coalition was defeated. The French position is less clear. The economically liberal Socialist government has taken an increasingly hands-off attitude to its national industries, but it does not wish to give up its rights.

The outcome of Sir Leon Brittan's proposals is very uncertain. Yet, his proposed legality standard is revolutionary under two different points of view. No matter how subjective the private investor test would be, at least as far as manufacturing companies are concerned, it would destroy all theories purporting a real difference in role as well as in behaviour between private and public enterprises. It is true that, as the above quoted holding of the Court of Justice shows, if the judgement is based upon the time horizon, there still might be a peculiar role for public enterprises. Nevertheless from a theoretical stand the relevant point is that there should not be any difference from a private investor. Moreover, it would transfer strategic investment decisions from member States to the European Commission.

Hence, there might be a shift of power to a less political and more bureaucratic level. Decisions might change over time according to the prevailing cultural or political mood, because of the highly subjective judgement on how a private investor should behave (many entrepreneurs have been considered visionary and unsound when launching a new venture). And since history moves back and forth like a pendulum, there might be times when a bold investment is approved, and others when the same investment would be considered State aid.

It must be emphasized that the private investor standard is quite different from the profit maximization rule we have earlier examined. It assumes that no clear cut norms exists and that sound business judgement is available at a bureaucratic level. We can dispute whether such assumption could be realistic at the EEC Commission level. It seems sure that it cannot be recommended to countries where private enterprise is still a very feeble baby.

7. - Financing

In order to have a clear picture of the problems of the relationships between government and public enterprises, we have to consider how State-owned companies are financed. When public firms are organized as branches or departments of the public administration, the proceeds of the sale of their products or services are, more often than not, used to fund current expenditure, while investments are financed out of the general budget. When, and this often happens, current income does not cover current costs, the difference is made up by the State Budget.

Most State-owned enterprises, however, are not simple branches of the public administration, but public corporations or joint-stock companies, or a mixture of the two. The instruments used in Western

Europe to finance these types of public enterprises are so numerous that it is impossible to cover the full range.

In Germany the railways — Deutsche Bundesbahn — are special patrimony of the Bund (i.e. the Federal Republic to distinguish it from the "Länder") with autonomous accounts. Yet, they are not a separate juridical entity from the State, so they might also be considered a special branch of the public administration. The Deutsche Bundesbahn by law should cover its costs with sales proceeds and should also get from the market the capital it needs for investments. The funding law, however, states that in case of need the Bund provides more equity capital or makes loans through the funds of the Budget. In practice, since the German railways have not been able to cover their costs through their income, the State has provided most of the finance needed to keep them alive.

In contrast, the German Post Office — Deutsche Bundespost — has no right to receive subsidies by the State. Instead, it has a duty to pay into the Budget a 6% of the total income because of the monopoly it enjoys in telecommunications and mail collection and delivery, and because of tax exemptions it enjoys. The Bund as proprietor should inject sufficient equity capital, while the Deutsche Bundespost bonds are treated as those issued by the Bund itself.

Again in Germany, about two thirds of the capital in the electricity industry is provided by local authorities including the Länder, making most of the electricity companies public enterprises. The large majority of the firms not only finance themselves on the market, but distribute dividends and pay canons (going from 12 to 18% of the benefits) for the concessions they have in their fields.

In the UK, the nationalized industries were mostly organised as public corporations which, according to their Statutes, should break-even in an undefined number of good and bad years. The peculiarity of the British public corporations from a financial point of view was a statutory limit to total indebtedness established from time to time by Parliament. Moreover the British public corporations could only be funded by the Treasury, unless the latter authorized them to seek funds elsewhere. Since UK entrance in the EEC, most Statutes of public corporations included an authorisation, always under Treasury control, to get loans from the various official European financial institutions such as BEI, CECA Fund and so on. The theory behind this approach was that the Treasury is able to indebt itself at the cheapest rates available on the market. Also, precise limits for each corporation were considered an incentive to a conservative and prudent behaviour and permitted Parliament to control nationalized industries. In practice this arrangement increased the dependence of State-owned firms on macroeconomic policies. Investments had to be delayed not because of industrial strategy, but because of monetary policy.

In the 1970s a new source of funds was devised for some public corporations, notably the Iron and Steel Board. The source was a "public dividend capital" on which the Treasury gets a dividend proportional to the results of the corporation. This is clearly a much more flexible source of finance, looking very similar to equity. Also in the United Kingdom when a nationalised industry is requested to provide a service whose costs are not borne by the users, there is a government subsidy. This, for instance, happened in the *Railways Acts* of 1968 and 1974 for passenger services (Beesley and Evans, 1981).

In France the variety of financial sources for public enterprises is such that it is almost impossible to describe even a majority of them. Equity capital is provided with a simple decree by the Minister of Finance after the opinion of the Finance Commissions of both Houses of Parliament. In theory dividends should be paid, but in practice, this seldom, if ever, happens. The most important source of funds for government-owned firms is, however, the Fonds de dévelopment economique et sociale which makes loans at very low rates and for long periods, to finance approved investments. In some occasion, when a public enterprise is not able to pay back a loan, this might be transformed in equity.

Special subsidies for investments can be given by the government when public enterprises are organized as joint-stock companies, but also to public corporations when their investmensts produce social benefits. For instance, Electricité de France gets subsidies when it produces hydro-electric power by regulating rivers or improving irrigation. Other subsidies are provided when public enterprises are requested not to increase their tariffs, or are compelled to behave in a way which causes economic losses in their balance sheets. Often capital contributions, loans, and subsidies are included in a so-called "program contract" which is a kind of medium term agreement between a single public enterprise and the government with reciprocal engagements. This type of arrangment underlines the autonomy and responsibility of the concerned firm, while it makes clear to the government the financial consequences of certain political decisions.

In France after the 1982 nationalisation program which increased the share of public enterprises' added value produced outside the financial and agriculture sectors from 13% to almost 19%, two new financial instruments were introduced to provide quasi-equity capital to government-owned companies: the "titres participatifs" (participating negotiable instruments) and "certificats d'investissement" (investment certificates). The former are very similar to stocks: they are issued by a company, are not redeemable and pay to the holder a fixed interest plus a variable part linked to the enterprise results. This variable part cannot exceed 40% of nominal value. The latter are the result of dismembering a share: the voting rights stay with the State or another public entity, while the pecuniary remuneration goes to the holder of the certificate.

Both these negotiable instruments have clearly been devised in order to tap the private financial market aiming at investors not willing to buy government bonds. At the same time State-owned companies are motivated to improve their financial performance in order to be able to issue these new investments when they wish to expand.

In Italy, the so called "Partecipazioni statali" system can be seen as a device to allow government-owned firms to get money from the capital markets, while government retains control.

The structure, in fact, is based upon public corporations (IRI, ENI and EFIM) that get their endowment funds by a law approved by the Parliament. These enterprises can issue bonds, sometimes with State guarantee sometimes without, and get loans from the market.

These public corporations are structured as holding companies, controlling the majority of other holding companies whose shares are often traded on the Stock Exchange. These second-tier holding companies in turn, control other joint-stock companies whose shares again can be traded on the Stock Exchange. In some cases even this third tier of companies control other smaller firms. The result is that, when the system works, every single company can have the right degree of leverage, while the public corporation has provided only a small fraction of the equity capital needed. Thus, there was a time when IRI boasted that the government had provided only 8% of all financial liabilities shown in the consolidated balance sheet.

Of course the system functions at its best when the financial markets have confidence in the single companies as well as in the public corporations. To get confidence from the financial markets companies have to follow sound economic policies. If the financial markets put all their trust in the capability of the State to fund its controlled companies in case they are not able to return the loans, the system fails or at least has no intrinsic merit.

For this reason it has been very important that in 1978 when a State industrial corporation, EGAM, was so poorly managed that the government decided to dissolve it and liquidate it, the Parliament amended the law in such a way that not all banking creditors' claims were repaid. Since then banks have been a little more careful in providing credit to public enterprises and performance has improved.

Analogous considerations can be made for the equity market. To buy and keep stocks of government-controlled companies investors needed to have confidence in the willingness of the same government not to abuse its power to impose a miserable financial performance.

After the disastrous 1970s the Italian government had problems to restore the collapsed confidence, but the recent successful floatation on the Stock Exchange of a number of State-owned enterprises shows that improvements are on the way.

It has already been noted that in Italy the endowment fund of the public corporation must not pay a dividend to the Treasury and, in theory, it may not be written off to cover losses. According to a widely diffused interpretarion, the opportunity cost of the capital should be considered as the maximum allowed losses that the management of public enterprises should accept as a result of social goals imposed by the government. Unfortunately, some public corporations carry on in their balance sheet losses, which might not be recovered, barring major inflation, in the future.

So Sir Leon Brittan is not wrong when be contends that equity injections as well as increases in endowment funds can disguise subsidies.

An extremely controversial way of financing a public enterprise was devised in Italy when a monopoly to exploit gas in Northern Italy was granted to the oil and chemical national company, ENI. Estimates on the real value of these leases, which are not taxed as such, are extremely uncertain. What is sure is that such rents have permitted ENI to become a leading force in the Italian industry even outside of the energy sectors and much more than the endowment fund would have allowed. We have to add here that the already mentioned capability of ENI's founder Enrico Mattei to play one party against the other and to choose by himself the company goals, was consistently enhanced by ENI's financial strength and independence.

Italy provides also an example of full reliance on self-financing. When the electricity industry was not nationalised in 1962, the new public corporation, ENEL, not only was not endowed with a fund at the onset, but it was charged with the service of the bonds issued to the expropriated companies.

Not always are public enterprises bound to be inefficient. For a number of years till the early 1970s, ENEL exploited economies of scale, and was able to invest huge sums and to repay its own equity capital (Zanetti-Fraquelli [33]). Later, to avoid electricity tariff control from deteriorating ENEL's balance sheet, a small endowment fund was provided. However, internally generated resources, mainly depreciation, and medium term loans remained the main way to finance ENEL.

Only very recently a Ministerial Commission is advocating the transformation of ENEL from a public corporation into a joint-stock company that, issuing new shares to private investors, might better finance its huge investment plants for the 1990s.

This very sketchy survey of how public enterprises have been financed shows that there has been a market tendency to rely more on private savings and less on the Treasuries. Even the big privatisation wave in United Kingdom might be interpreted as a step in the same direction.

It may also be said that this tendency was less due to a difficulty of national Treasuries to issue more government bonds or any other type of negotiable instruments to directly finance public enterprises, as happened in the United Kingdom before privatisation, than to a belief in pushing State-owned firms towards the financial markets to increase their efficiency.

It is undisputed that a recourse to private savings through the financial markets puts a constraint on public enterprises. As far as equity capital is concerned, when a government-controlled joint-stock company sells part of the shares to private investors, there might be an incentive to give minority shareholders a dividend or a capital gain, in other words to make a profit. This incentive is stronger in three cases.

First, the company needs more risk capital and government does not have sufficient resources for such an aim, or has different priorities. Second, the management of the company does not wish to ask the government for money or just desires a large autonomy and therefore uses the presence of minority shareholders as a shield against governmental and political interferences into its sphere of action. It has to be noted that the less a government-owned company needs money from the State, the greater is its managerial authority. In France, for instance, in the 1950s, 1960s and early 1970s when the car producer Renault was highly profitable, Mr. Dreyfus and other following chief executives enjoyed a freedom similar to that of the already mentioned Mr. Mattei in Italy. Third, a government wishes to privatise a company but because of some special constraints it prefers to proceed incrementally. In this case the financial constraint is rather strong because managers know that their performances shall influence prospective investors and their chances of keeping their jobs or to find even better ones in the private sector once the company is privatised.

There is' however, the possibility that the managers prefer to stay in the public sector, just because their perks or power there are more enjoyable, or more likely because having got their jobs because of political connections they might lose them in a private company. Only very capable determined masters might detect this attitude and take the rough and tough decision to fire them.

When a State-owned company gets a loan, the loan can be

serviced either from company income or by an injection of money by the government. With the exception of the Italian EGAM case, the Western European experience shows that as a general rule governments do not let their companies go bankrupt. So the constraint is rather weak, unless the government makes it clear that it is not stepping in, to rescue the company in case of need.

Providing capital is not the only way governments have to help the companies they own. Often, State grant officially or unofficially public enterprises a special status as suppliers of the many goods and services they buy. Sometimes public enterprises are the only supplier of certain technologically advanced good and may have been established just for that purpose. In such cases, industrial policy and demand management are mentioned. Some other times, governments affirm that when a contract is granted to a public enterprise, profit accrue to the State. In other cases, a supplier contract is a confortable way to avoid other forms of aid. It has to be emphasized that, as Liebenstein has taught us, whenever there is a monopoly "X inefficiency" develops. The fact that an enterprise is totally or partially State owned does not change this rule. It is this type of inefficiency, more than the unfair competition to private and foreign suppliers, that should concern Governments when granting a privileged status as suppliers to public enterprises.

8. - Principal-Agent Relationships

It is widely known that when an enterprise becomes so large that the owner is unable to control every aspect of the company, a conflict might arise between owners and managers. In private enterprise it is assumed that the main objective of owners is wealth and income maximisation, while managers strive to increase their power, their income and their tenure. A growing number of economists believe that this conflict can be solved in the same way as any case where somebody (the principal) is not able to carry personally a particular business and has to rely upon an agent. This school of thought is fully aware that property and management do not have the same information about what is really going on inside the firm, and managers can try to shirk, are often opportunists, and operate with bounded rationality. Yet, they believe that through appropriate explicit or implicit contracts the conflict can be solved. These contracts imply a departure from a wealth maximising path which is considered as the cost of the agency.

We have already emphasized that multiple goals permit the management of State-controlled companies a wide choice of action.

As Stiglitz [29] has clearly put it: «the ambiguity of objectives provides the managers further discretion to pursue their own interest... Managers can always claim that the reason they are losing money is not that they are inefficient or incompetent, but that they have been pursuing other goals. *And it is virtually impossible for an outsider to judge the validity of those claims*» (italics added). Substitute "losing money" with "making less money than achievable" and you have a clear picture of what might happen when the shares of a State-controlled company are floated on the Stock-Exchange.

In other words the principal is not able to make the right contracts with the agent because it has multiple goals and shifting priorities among them.

Even making two other very bold assumptions, namely that the State is able to make profit the main and permanent goal of its enterprises and that financial markets are perfect, the principal-agent problem for public enterprises could hardly be solved.

The wealth maximisation goal of shareholders is achievable only if there is a market for corporate control. This takes place through the take-over mechanism. Marris [17] has shown that if a company uses its own resources in such a way that a different managerial team would make a profit acquiring those resources a take-over happens and the previous management is fired. Before this happens information on management performance is disclosed by the price of the company's shares. A poorly managed firm is detected by a perfect stock market and will suffer a declining share price, till a take-over becomes convenient (Jensen and Meckling [18]).

According to such an idyllic assumption the stock market provides on top of signals about "where" to invest and disinvest financial resources, information about management and its capability.

However, if a market for corporate control also existed for

State-owned firms, the property would change hands, they would be privatised and could no longer be considered public enterprises. Other economists of the same school put more emphasis on the managerial labour market as an instrument for disciplining the agents an impose an efficient behaviour (Fama [10]). But, as we shall see in the next paragraph, the managerial labour market for public enterprises does not attach much value to an efficient conduct.

The impossibility to solve the principal-agent problem in public enterprises is one of the reasons for their intrinsic weakness compared to private enterprises, because the principal has mainly political and not economic goals. Of course this conclusion does not exclude that there are State-controlled firms which are managed much better than their private counterparts, especially when the latter are family controlled enterprises. But when it happens it is because of chance, or because sometimes (when there is a crisis) political leaders may be interested in a good economic performance and substitute their personal initiative and supervision to the deficiencies of the principal-agent mechanism.

The failure of a clear solution for the principal-agent problem in public enterprises should point to a deeper involvement by the principal in managerial decisions and strict overseeing of their day-to-day life. This is what often happens. Nevertheless, just because the principal, as often repeated, has shown in too many instances political interest, it is probably better to leave the agent more freedom. Even when pursuing their personal interest many managers have proved to be better than their political master in fostering economic efficiency. It is, therefore, convenient that managerial rewards should be constructed to incentivate economic goals. Their salary should be supplemented with compensation conditional on performance (e.g. profit bonuses) including stock market performance (e.g. stock options). Even if envy might arise, salaries in public enterprises should be similar to those in the private sector at all levels.

As a general rule a carrot is always better than a stick. Yet, sanctions for very poor performance should not be ruled out. But they must be used exceptionally and not decided by the direct supervisor, because political interference is often worse than managerial discretion.

9. - The Choice of Managers

We have reached a very delicate point: the appointment of the management of public enterprises. It would be preposterous if I tried to speak about Western European experience in this field.

Research I conducted in Italy some years ago (Grassini [12]), as well as attention I gave to this problem later on, and conversations I had with many foreign colleagues, persuaded me that only inside knowledge could provide sufficient facts on this subject.

Of course one might say that in the United Kingdom board members of public corporations are chosen by the parent Minister and that since most boards had executive responsibilities, the Minister (i.e. the political power) has a stronger influence than in countries where directors have non-executive functions. Also when State-owned firms are organised as holding companies, the degree of political influence is less with the controlled companies than at the headquarters. But these observations would scratch the surface of the problem only. One could also try, as many years ago Robson did for the United Kingdom, to analyze the previous experience of chief executives and Board members. Yet, the results might be that one finds businessmen, managers, trade-unionists, newspapermen, generals, university professors and accountants (Robson [25]). Too large a universe to understand how good they are.

At a deeper level there are two problems that should be investigated: the choice of management of public enterprises and the degree of independence they enjoy once they have been appointed. First of all to quote Stiglitz once again, in a democracy «the electorate chooses leaders for a variety of characteristics; the ability to choose good economic managers is only one of these. Even if the President were relatively incompetent in this dimension he still might be re-elected, given his other strengths... And given the electorate (at least formally) only communicates a vote for Individual or Party A or B, the vote itself communicates relatively little information about the electorate views concerning the quality of economic management» (Stiglitz [29]).

The same author goes on to explain that the electorate not only is poorly informed but has no incentive to become informed, because individuals know their single vote is unlikely to have much effect on the outcome of the election. Moreover, individuals «would have limited private incentives to acquire the information required to make informed decisions concerning economic management and managers, simply because the gains they receive as individuals are such a small fraction of the social gains» (*ibidem*).

For the same reasons, we might add, when an individual works for a State-owned firm and fears he will be fired if the company is shut-down, he has a very strong private incentive to cast his vote for a party or a politician who promises that never public enterprises shall be closed, no matter how much they might lose.

In general relying mostly upon the Italian experience, one might say that government chooses the top managers of State-controlled enterprises on the basis of the three factors:

a) the visibility of the appointment. The more a manager choice is going to be scrutinised by the press and the media at the moment of the nomination and later, the more careful is the choice. At least on paper the chosen manager should have the right credentials.
On the contrary in a minor position anyone can be nominated;

b) the political gain which the political people involved in the choice are expecting from the appointment. I used the words "political people" because especially where there is a coalition government or, as in Italy, the leader of a party is not always the Prime Minister, more than one person can be involved in the choice. This situation complicates the matter because every politician is different from the others. One may be an idealist, another may be interested in votes, a third one may look for a pecuniary rewards;

c) the competence of the political people involved to judge the business abilities of the man to be chosen. Here the problem is very complicated because if a manager has spent most of his career in public enterprises, the multiplicity of goals makes a true evaluation almost impossible. But also if the manager comes from the private sector, results might be misleading. A company might have had profits simply because of a surge in demand. Moreover Napoleon's dictum that "good generals have to be also lucky" applies to managers as well. Private enterprise experience shows that managemet selection usually is a long term process where co-optation by peers plays a most important role. It could be said that the choice of a good management

requires also some intuitive knowledge and a lot of business experience. The latter is seldom available to politicians.

Briefly, there is no way or rule that guarantees the right selection
for public enterprises' management.

As to the question of management independence from political
interference, to broaden out perspective, we might turn to the French
experience which has been studied by Anastassopoulos [2]. He
examined a number of conflicts between public enterprises and
government which existed because State-owned firms care more
about their own balance sheet than politicians or bureaucrats. His
results were summarized in the following table:

COMPANY RESPONSES TO SITUATIONS ACCORDING TO DEGREES
OF SALIENCY FOR COMPANY AND GOVERNMENT

		Issue saliency for firm		
		low	medium	high
Issue saliency for government	high	submission	grievance	intransigence
	medium	lament	tension	protest
	low	vigilance	touchiness	self-confidence

Source: ANASTASSOPOULOS [2], *loc. cit.*, p. 113.

Without going into all details of the table, we may consider some
of the most relevant points: «Special tension begins to appear when
both parties are deeply concerned about the outcome. Although it
may be assumed that government will impose its will in a forceful
way, the personality and influence of the company top manager and
government's spokesperson may be highly significant» (Anastassopoulos [2], p. 114).

Intransigence arises when both parties are convinced that the
decision is essential to their respective goals. "It is not certain at all
that government view will prevail; no government would push one of
its enterprises to suicide. It would be killing the very instrument it
wants to use. Nor it is certain that the company will win; the

government may disagree on the reality of the danger the company faces. Personal attitudes and influence, technical arguments, agreement procedures, utilisation of the media and public opinion, mobilisation of personnel unions. In short, all means of persuasion and action may effect the out-come» (Anastassopoulos [2], p. 115).

So autonomy of public enterprises even if it might result in conflicts is a good thing, because it enhances the microeconomic performance.

10. - Unfulfilled Denationalization

A last question needs to be answered before concluding our discussion.

If the experience is more negative than positive, why have not all Western European governments followed the example of the United Kingdom privatising their own public enterprises? Very briefly we might say that there are at least four reasons. First if we have seen that the problem of multiple goals is theoretically and practically insoluble, it has to be said that the same uncertainity prevails as far as natural monopolies are concerned. Not all the economists agree that natural monopolies exist and even fewer agree on the appropriate rules which regulatory authorities should adopt when overseeing them. Yet, public property is still seen by a number of economists and by a large number of governments as preferable to private property when a public service has to be provided.

Secondly, there are some governments who believe that private enterprise would not have a sufficient long term view to make investments that are needed, either to actively compete in the dynamic world markets (the Japanese ghost lurks behind this vision) or to locate the same or other investments in the depressed or undeveloped parts of their countries.

Thirdly vested interests are very strong and lots of people prefer the maintenance of the *status quo* to the uncertainties of privatisation. Often these vested interests cover themselves with noble reasons: we cannot sell at a price below the true value, beware of private monopolists and so on. I only wish to remember the old Latin proverb

Time Danaos et dona ferentes, which could be translated «Be careful when somebody with a vested interest pronounces noble words».

Finally not every Stock Exchange is willing or capable to underwrite huge issues. Financial markets are far from perfect and they are not always able to make offer and demand meet at a reasonable price.

11 - Conclusions

This very sketchy survey of the Western European public enterprises experience should have shown that some governments and their electors are sufficiently satisfied with their performance that they do not wish to change the situation.

The economic profession, on the contrary, has not been able to reach unanimous conclusions.

The views I have presented are unfortunately highly subjective.

Nevertheless I shall venture to make a few suggestions as to how the Western European experience might be used by the former communist countries in order to avoid some of our worst mistakes:

a) if multiplicity of goals is unavoidable for public enterprises, at least a scale of priorities might be advisable.

And since neither goals nor priorities can be fixed forever, a company strategic plan is the occasion to take decisions.

Western experience shows that strategic plans do not necessarily imply quantitative forecasts, and can be prepared assuming different "scenarios". Moreover, they have to be implemented with flexibility and sometimes the environment changes so much that they have to be completely revised.

Brain more than rules is how to deal with revisions!

The approval of the strategic plan by the government is the right moment for emphasizing that a public enterprise, however autonomous and independent, is not a private fiefdom of its management, and that if the political power has a big say in fixing strategic goals nothing is wrong;

b) one of the more controversial problems is the selection of the management of State-owned firms.

We have seen that democracy does not guarantee the best choices and that political interference may lead to inefficiency.

So a solution might be for the government to appoint an independent panel and thrust upon them the selection of top managers.

We have also seen that business acumen is required to perform this task, while the former socialist countries at present don't have businessmen on whom to rely.

Why not call some former countrymen who during their exiles have been successful in business or other professions?

For every Timisky there should be, I hope, hundreds of well meaning people. And nothing might be more visible than the choice of the panel charged with the selection of public enterprises management;

c) autonomy and independence are a very important asset if public companies are to perform an enterpreneurial role.

To provide them, board of directors of State-controlled firms should have a long and stable tenure.

Since a strategic plan should cover at least four years and one year is the minimum time to prepare one, a five year tenure might be advisable at least for the chief executives.

Other board members might have a five year tenure but be appointed at different intervals in order to provide continuity and to foster *esprit de corps.*

Moreover top managers should have generous pensions so that they should not fear too much not to be reappointed. In Italy one of the best run institutions, the Bank of Italy, pays a life time full salary to past Governors;

d) accountability is one of the public enterprises unresolved problems. Proprietors have to have control according to a widely diffused view. At the same time Parliamentary decisions concerning public funds or reviews of performance and similar tasks are occasion for strong politicians to extend their patronage on public enterprises and make their political or personal interest prevail. Well, most democracies are based upon the division of powers and the judiciary is often selected on a nationwide scale on merit competitions controlled by the existing judges and neither government not Parliament can interfere.

My suggestion is that wherever in a country exists an Account Court or General Control Office, Parliament be expropriated of every auditing function with regard to State-owned firms;

e) with all the limits we have seen, financing State-controlled companies through the market is better than financing them through the Treasury.

For the same reason a joint-stock company is preferable to a public corporation;

f) as we said at the very beginning the former socialist countries might retain the control of enterprises either because nobody wants them and/or because their closure might increase unemployment to an unbearable level.

State aids or subsidies might be required. They should be given in the open and decrease with time.

As in Western Europe, I suppose the former socialist countries might have regional disequilibria. It would be wrong to ask State-controlled enterprises to invest there and provide them with special aid, as we have done in many Western European countries.

Inefficiencies can easily be disguised as social costs.

Much better, therefore, to make an auction among competing firms, giving aid to the one that requests less for making a specific investment or better provides a certain number of permanent jobs.

g) when a public enterprise provides a public service under monopoly the peril that the monopolist and the regulator — be it a Ministry or a special body — come to have coinciding views and disregard the consumers interests are higher than when there is a private monopoly.

If the country has an anti-trust legislation and an authority charged with its implementation, it is advisable to put also public enterprises under this general authority, so that collusion is less likely.

The suggestions here advanced are by no means exhaustive, nor do they solve all the problems that the Western European experience with public enterprises has shown.

There is, therefore, a last suggestion that I would make: as soon as you can, privatise as much as you can. If you are bound to be a mixed economy some enterprises, like the poor of the Gospel, shall stay under the government property forever.

BIBLIOGRAPHY

[1] AHARONI I.: *Markets, Planning and Development: The Private and Public Sectors in Economic Development*, New York, Wiley, 1979.

[2] ANASTASSOPOULOS J.P.: *The French Experience: Conflicts with Government* in VERNON R. - AHARONI R. [32].

[3] BAUMOL W.I.: *Business Behaviour, Value and Growth*, New York, Mac Millan, 1959.

[4] — —: «Contestable Markets: An uprising in theory of industry structure», *American Economic Review*, March 1982.

[5] BERLE A.A. - MEANS G.C.: *The Modern Corporation and Private Property*, New York, Mac Millan, 1932.

[6] CHANDLER A.D.: *Scale and Scope. The Dynamics, of Industrial Capitalism*, Cambridge (Mass.), Harvard University Press, 1990.

[7] CYERT R.M. - MARCH I.G.: *A Behavional Theory of the Firm*, New York, Prentice-Hall, 1963.

[8] DEMSETZ H.: *Ownership Control and the Firm*, London, Basil Blackwell, 1988.

[9] DURUPTY M.: *Le Privatisations en France*, Paris, La Documentation Française, 1988.

[10] FAMA E.F.: «Agency problems and the Theory of the Firm», *Journal of Political Economy*, April 1980.

[11] GRASSINI F.A.: *La nazionalizzazione dell'industria del carbone in Gran Bretagna e Francia*, Roma, Studium, 1957.

[12] — —: *The Italian Enterprises: The Political Constraints* in VERNON R. - AHARONI R. [32].

[13] — —: «Molteplicità di obiettivi ed imprese pubbliche», *l'industria*, 1984.

[14] HARLOW C.: *Innovation and Productivity under Nationalisation*, London, Allen and Unwin, 1977.

[15] HMSO: «Nationalised Industries: A review of Economic and Financial Objectives», London, HMSO, *Cmd* n. 3437, 1967.

[16] JENSEN M.C. - MECKLING W.H.: «Theory of the Firm, Management behaviour, Agency Costs and Ownership Structure», *Journal of Financial Economics*, n. 305, 1976.

[17] MARRIS R.: *The Economic Theory of Managerial Capitalism*, London, Free Press, 1964.

[18] NOVE A.: *Efficiency Criteria for Nationalised Industries*, London, Allen - Unwin, 1973.

[19] POSNER M.V. - WOLF S.J.: *Italian Public Enterprises*, London, Duckworth, 1965.

[20] PRODI R.: *Il nuovo quadro economico della concorrenza europea*, Torino, Fondazione Agnelli, 1971.

[21] PRYKE R.: *Public Enterprise in Practice. The British Experience of Nationalization after the two Decades*, London, Mac Gibbon and Kee, 1971.

[22] — —: «Rapport sur les Enterprises Publique», Paris, La Documentation Française, *Rapporto Nora*, 1967.

[23] REED P.: *The Economics of Public Enterprises*, London, Butterworks, 1973.

[24] REES R.: *Public Enterprise Economics*, London, Weinfeld - Nicolson, 1976.

[25] ROBSON W.: *Nationalized Industry and Public Ownership*, London, Allen - Unwin, 1961.

[26] SARACENO P.: *Il sistema delle Partecipazioni statali nell'esperienza italiana*, Milano, Giuffrè, 1975.

[27] SCHUMPETER J.A.: *Capitalism, Socialism and Democracy*, New York, Harper - Brothers, 1942.

[28] SHEPERD W.G. (eds.): *Public Enterprise: Economic Analysis of Theory and Practice*, Lexington Mass, Lexington Books, 1976.

[29] STIGLITZ I. *et* AL: *The Economic Role of the State*, London, Basil Blackwell, 1990.

[30] STOFFAES C. - VITTORI I. (eds.): *Nationalisation*, Paris, Flammarion, 1977.

[31] ———: «The Nationalized Industries», London, HMSO, *Cmd* n. 7131, 1978.

[32] VERNON R.- AHARONI Y. (eds.): *State-Owned Enterprises in the Western Economies*, London, Croom Helm, 1981.

[33] ZANETTI G. - FRAQUELLI G.: *Una nazionalizzazione al buio*, Bologna, il Mulino, 1979.

II - THE EXPERIENCE
OF SELECTED COUNTRIES

Transition to a Market Economy: the Experience of Hungary

Béla Kádár

Minister of International Economic Relations, Hungary

The global historic changes of our age and the internal decay which had evolved for a longer time crushed, at the threshold of the 1990s, the Stalinist and post-Stalinist systems of Eastern and East-Central·Europe. The decay is a multi-casual process. From the point of view of economic growth these systems could not respond to the challenges of modern technologies spreading around in the last two decades, and they could not exploit the driving forces of technical-scientific and management revolution. The inward-looking attitudes and the autarchic efforts hindered the process of adjustment to the requirements of global development and co-operation in international relations. From the point of view of the regulatory system the established forms of central planning did not offer a solution at the time of accelerated technical-structural transformation and social-economic division of labour, both becoming more and more complex and centrally less and less controllable. From the point of view of the social value system and environment the ideas of egalitarianism and collectivism, otherwise distorted in the social practice, gradually froze the processes of human capital accumulation, innovation and per-formance improvement and, further, wore away and distorted human motivations. As a consequence of the scarcity of resources, the economic model characterised by low or deteriorating levels of in-come-generating capacities was less and less capable of carrying the burdens of Soviet global power efforts and those of non-efficient but still rather wide-scale social services, built out at very low levels of development.

The process of decay was signalled already in the 1970s by the growing technical-structural obsolescence, loss of ground in the world economy; in the 1980s by the growing equilibrium tensions, stagnating growth then finally, by the unfolding general operational crisis.

By the turn of the 1990s politically the one-party system, economically central regulation and collective property, in the field of external relations the *Warsaw Pact* and the social-economic system "gleichschalted" by the CMEA, has collapsed in East-Central Europe (Hungary, Czechoslovakia, Poland) and has been shaken to its foundations in Eastern Europe. Thus the question arises : *quo vadis,* Europe? The countries of the region have begun their march on the uncharted road, albeit at not identical pace, determination, leading to a market economy and a pluralistic political system.

1. - The Scenes of Changes

The unique historical characteristic of East-Central European changes lies in the historical simultaneity of changes at various scenes. This region has simultaneously to change the political system, the economic model, external economic partners and growth road. The changing of the political model creates the legitimacy of power without which hardly any sacrifice can be demanded from the society; further it makes possible the removal of the nomenklatura, the demonstration and realisation of interests which are rather multi-coloured even in countries at medium levels of development, and the elimination of the earlier omnipotence of political power and the realisation of economic legalities. The essence of changing the economic model is to replace the earlier administrative regulation of the national economy by market mechanisms, competitive environment and forms of economic regulation harmonised with given levels of development. The external economic re-orientation is urged by the shrinking of earlier CMEA trade, by the modernisation and replacement of relations and forms of co-operation, disintegrating as a consequence of the East European crisis, by new, dynamic partners and driving forces. The changing of the growth road is the consequence of all these changes mentioned above. The priority given to traditional heavy industrial mass production and military industry, which brought the development processes of the first half of the century to a long-term extreme, reflected: *a)* the power base of the earlier political system; *b)* a relatively simple regulatory technique for the centralised regulatory system; *c)* the requirements of the CMEA in external economic relations.

In the new situation it became obvious that changing only the system and the model itself does not safeguard economic recovery, the modernisation of production and infrastructure, instead, world economic integration requires new production, supply and utilisation structures and a new road of growth.

The situation, and the response to the "quartet of challenges" is complicated by the aggravating crisis phenomena. In the economy the signs of recession replacing stagnation, moreover, in some countries precipitating production levels, were well visible in 1990. The accumulating crisis in the human sphere, the deterioration of the social environment of the national economy (health, education, public security, individual sphere) is less visible but bears even graver effects. When the illusions concerning the immediate improvement of private situation attached to political changes vanish, sometimes the signs of lethargy, now and then those of civil unrest and the new violence can also be identified. The scope of target conflicts, double rationalities resulting from the new situation gets wider since the political rationalities of democratic transformation often collide with the economic rationalities, and the soft tuning technique, the capacity of action of the government has not yet fully come about.

2. - Dangers of Copying - National Roads

Owing to the specific nature of the situation, the danger of the "demostration effect" of the transformation, that of strategic copying is high. Neither the present operational system of the American market economy, nor the action programme of the post-war transformation of totalitarian systems or that of the South European authoritarian systems in the 1970s can be transplanted into East-Central Europe. There is no standardised road, nor a guide-book to, leading from the "existing real socialism" to a market economy embedded into a global system of relations. One cannot disgregard the fact that in a numer of East European countries hardly any developed economic automatisms were established even in the times preceding the Stalinist model. The transformation of the totalitarian systems relied on a much wider market economy base and value system than the Stalinist or post-Stalinist model, further on significant external resources, on the energy-releasing experience of "zero hour" and the survival of the war. The transformation of the authoritarian South European systems took place in the period of economic recovery, was based on wider market economy bases, was carried out without an external economic re-orientation and a more pronounced change in the value system. In order to avoid historic traumas stemming from the dangers of copying, the East-Central European countries can shape their transformation strategies on the basis of the individual endowments, possibilities and limits of their actions.

3. - Hungary: a Specific Case of the Transformation Process

Although the driving forces of the past tend to be forgotten in the second year of transformation, it is hardly disputable that the pioneer role of small Hungary has also been instrumental in the acceleration of transformation in the East-Central European region. As a heritage of world war two, the Hungarian nation received a tougher Stalinist treatment than its neighbours, this is why the Hungarian people responded firstly and explosively already in 1956 to the social-economic order imposed upon, and alien to, the country. As a belated and indirect achievement of 1956, the national elbowroom increased and, with its reforms carried out in small steps, Hungary distanced itself considerably in the course of the last two decades from the Stalinist and post-Stalinist East European system.

Based upon the road covered so far, the new, democratic Hungarian government, formed as a result of the parliamentary elections of April 1990, partly speeded up, partly broodened the process of transformation. It is perhaps worth mentioning that at the beginning of 1991 the share of free prices in the Hungarian price structure is over 90% (compared to 63% in 1989), similarly more than 90% of imports are liberalised (compared to 41% in 1989) — which in practice means convertibility at enterprise level for domestic import-ers —, there are more than 5,000 joint venture companies in Hungary (compared to 1,200 in 1989), and, finally, about 50% of foreign investments made in the East-Central European region are made in Hungary. The external economic re-orientation is pro-ceeding at a relatively orderly pace: in the course of 1990 the share of CMEA countries in Hungarian foreign trade decreased from 42% whereas that of the European Community went up from 24% to 36%. Further, having reached an export expansion of 17% and an import expansion of 9%, the country's hard currency trade pro-duced an export surplus unprecedented in the economic history of Hungary. For the first time in two decades there was no increase of the country's external debt.

When evaluating growth and transformation performances, it is also worth mentioning that the Hungarian government inherited, as short-term economic conditions, a recession getting deeper since the autumn of 1989 and an accelerating rate of inflation. As far as the exogenous factors are concerned, one has only to refer to the 27% in "Eastern" exports, drought and the so-called "Saddam Hussein ef-fect", the combined impact of which meant a loss of 11-12% of Hungarian GDP.

4. - Hungary and the Tetralogy of Transformation

Based upon the limited time-span of historical retrospect and on prognostics, in general terms four phases of the East-Central European transformation process can be distinguished. If the trans-formation is initiated in the political sphere, its speed in the first phase (in case of a non-violent transformation) is lower but the transform-ation is less chaotic since the old state "machinery" is still working, discipline is maintained, and the various forms of stifled tensions do not yet break the surface. In the second phase a "fellow traveller" of the acceleration of transformation is the economic-social pluralisation and the shaking of the previous state "machinary", and at the same time, tensions become visible, chaos and self-interest assertion proliferates and the performaces in the real economic sphere deteriorate. The task of the third phase is to handle tensions, to stabilise the new laws and order and to stop the decline in the real economy. Recovery, upswing, then the structural catching-up can take place in the fourth phase.

According to this system of typology, Poland finds itself at the beginning of the second phase, while the other East European and Central European countries are "calling at the stations" of the first phase. A rather uncertain perspective for a number of these countries is whether the size and time-span of the chaos, inevitable in the second phase, could be limited more expediently by a new type of authoritarian system of a military or populistic nature.

As a result of 25 years of reform efforts, Hungary is approaching the end of the second phase of the tetralogy of transformation. She has a clear advantage, compared to her fellow sufferers, in terms of changing the economic model, external economic re-orientation and the minds of her people. It is a special Hungarian feature, bearing with it a certain degree of disharmony and asynchrony, that the process of transformation in Hungary began by changing the political system. As a consequence of this, the preparedness and organisation of the political driving forces of transformation lag behind those of the economic ones and a disproportionately large part of transformation energies is absorbed by the political sphere, that is, the de-politicised atmosphere based on a relative national consensus, necessary for launching the third phase, is created at a slower pace than would be desired for the sake of the economy. Despite this, the third phase can already be prepared in 1991 in Hungary and the period of the overdominance of domestic political determinations can be left behind.

5. - Lessons

Despite the national efforts in these last decades, not even the Hungarian transformation process covers the optimal road, rather, it has to follow the one which is possible under the given circumstances.

Despite the specific nature of the Hungarian road, some general positive and negative experiences deserve attention.

In Hungary, as in the other countries of the region, the government's interpretation of its own role in the strategic direction or spontaneity of the transformation process is to be clarified. As an understandable reaction to the last decades, a wide influence is exerted, and gets support even from abroad, by the theory and practice of "spontaneous transformation", that is, by the *laissez-faire* type interpretation of government role. Can the liberalisation, the opening of the economy, be carried out in a solely liberal way, can the government shift the responsability (if yes, to what extent) to the other actors of economic life during the transformation process? In other words: can the gigantic transformation be entrusted, in the spirit of the Anglo-Saxon philosophy, to the "big hidden hand", or instead, is the strategic management of the transformation, the participation of an efficient state administration, labour force training, educational, regional development, health, employment, etc. programmes and institutions necessary?

One is advised by the experience of economic history and by theoretical considerations that at a lower or medium level of development the government *a priori* is bound to take a certain responsibility for the regulation of the modernisation process. The responsibility of the government sphere always increases in crisis situations, independently from any levels of development. Finally, the limitation of the size and time-span of the chaos accompanying the accelerated transformation of a distorted social and economic model, the strategic "distribution" of all the torments,social costs of changing the system (bearing in mind the threshold of social tolerance) is par excellence a task of the government. These days this approach characterises the philosophy of the Hungarian coalition government. In terms of the regulatory techniques it means that — after the overdominance of production regulation in the Hungarian economic policy in 1968, that of fiscal management between 1968 and 1988, and finally, that of monetary regulation since 1988 — the requirement of external economic and social policy-based regulation appears in new proportions, based always upon the current real processes.

One of the great political and economic policy debates has been provoked by having to choose between shock teraphy, trying to cut the Gordian knot of the Stalinist heritage at one stoke, and the transition in stages "distributing" the risks, tensions, social costs involved more evenly in time. From the point of view of regulatory technique, the shock therapy is a more simple task for the economic policy-makers since it exempts them from working out the sequencing rationalities, scales of timing, more sophisticated instrumentary of the transition in stages bearing in mind the national characteristics, and the responsibility can be thrown to the mechanisms of domestic policy and the coercive force.

Hungary has opted for the solution in stages. Namely, based on the road covered so far, the most critical phase of the market economic transformation can be finished in 12-24 months, the government received a mandate from those who elected it for carrying out this programme, this is the lesson to be drawn from the destiny of the Mazowiecki government, the costliness of the "blitz-integration" of the GDR, the increasing danger of explosion in the region, the peresent insufficiency of conflict-handling instrumentary but, at the same time, also from the available quantity of internal and external financial resources, adjustment abilities and preparedness necessary for a one-time "big leap forward".

A similar debate (which was not even limited to Hungary) evolved around the character of economic policy, about its demand-restricting or supply-building nature. In developed market economies, the economic policy-makers can successfully operate with the instrumentary of demand-regulation, with its monetary management technique. However, in the distorted scarcity economy environment of monopolistic socialism, the main source of disequilibrium is not the market but, rather, the quantitative and qualitative shortage of supply as a result of this, demand-restriction, monetary rigour are necessary but not sufficient conditions for restoring the equilibrium of the national economy. Its one-sided implementation can waste real economic processes, the national economic equilibrium will be established at an excessively low level of both production and employment and at an excessively high level of social tensions. The comprehensive modernisation, exernal economic re-orientation and the changing of the growth road particularly emphasise the importance of the supply building elements of economic policy.

Economic policy too can be fitted into the system of transformation tetralogy. The mixture of restriction, deregulation, promotion and liberalization must be made according to a special portioning which differs by countries and situations. As far as sequencing and portioning is concerned, after exactly 12 years of one-sided restriction in the Hungarian economy, deregulation must be speeded up parallel with the strengthening of financial discipline since only those economic actors who are free from administrative constraints and prescriptions can survive in the competition which is becoming much sharper owing to the liberalisation process. In Hungary liberalisation, somewhat "stepping out" of the line of rational sequencing, has advanced too quickly, owing to the excessive copying of Western patterns. Its risks and tensions can be countered (without evoking the dangers of withdrawing the liberalising measures) only by reinforcing the promotional elements (encouragement of enterpreneurship, savings, exports and investments).

From the point of view of inflation, the Hungarian economic policy has by 1991 been coerced to aroad it is bound to follow. Although the Hungarian population, having experienced the two highest inflations in this century, hates inflation more than unemployment, the government could not mobilise adequate resistance even in 1991 to curb inherited inflation. Its rate was 16% in 1988-1989, 29% in 1990, and in the absence of greater counter-measures, it will most probably be around 34-40% in 1991. The increase of the inflationary forces is explained by such one-time factors as the shift to hard currency based payments and accounting in "Eastern" trade, falling agricultural supply as an aftermath of the drought, stricter IMF equilibrium limits than in 1989, the accelerated liberalisation while significant monopolistic structures continue to exist. Of course, a national economy can maintain its operating ability under the conditions of differing, sometimes high rates of inflation. These rates are rather different in Switzerland and in Brazil. The Hungarian economy enters this danger-zone in 1991 and therefore, if the critical thresholds are overstepped too much, new approaches in economic policy and budget policy may become necessary.

Last but not least, the size of external support and resources. Until now Hungary has meticulously serviced its international debt, amounting to one-seventh of GDP and 40% of exports, and thus has contributed too to the stability of the international financial system and, at the same time, has transferred a considerable volume of incomes abroad. To my judgement it is not the year 1991, that is the year of shocks, which is most appropriate for enforcing the strict international equilibrium requirements and, further, the practice of support from abroad which is not based upon the transformation performances, on the commitment to market economy, does not have extremely mobilising effects. Today, for getting to its feet, Hungary and East-Central Europe needs bigger, quicker and more efficient external support. Mobilising and redeploying her domestic resources, carrying out her transformation strategy and establishing the market economy environment, Hungary can play a new type of pioneer role, with adequate external support, in the 1990s, which may have a "reverse domino effect" in the process of lifting up again the fallen East-Central European dominos. The *Association Agreement* with the EC will integrate Hungary into the European economic space and this trend is further enhanced by the new type of co-operation with the Central European and East European CMEA countries. If no greater international or East European crisis situations occur, by the second half of 1992 Hungary can get out of the present storm-zone and, later, by the mid-1990s, will adjust to the European and world economic integration process by means of a rapid pace of development resembling that of Southern Europe and the new industrial exporters earlier.

The Development of the Social Market Economy in Hungary and the Opportunities Resulting from Future Entry into the European Community

Otto Hieronymi

Battelle-Europe, Geneva Research Centres

1. - Introduction

The following topics are discussed briefly in the present paper:

1) the three main tasks of the Hungarian government, including the choice of the appropriate «model» for the success or failure of the transformation of the former Socialist economies of Eastern Europe;

2) the relevance of the «social market economy» for the transformation of the Hungarian economy: the term «social market economy» may be used to designate not only the modern German, Swiss and Austrian tradition of economic policy-making, but also, maybe under different names, the economic order in several other Western European countries such as Italy, France, Spain, etc.;

3) the impatience among some Western economists with the speed of transformation of the Hungarian economy is partly due to lack of information and to confusion;

4) the interdependence between the development of the «social market economy» and future Hungarian membership in the European Community: the long-term success of the social market economy in Hungary will depend on the success of integration into the European and world economy. At the same time, without developing a social market economy of the Western European type, full integration and

membership in the European Community would not be conceivable
for Hungary even in the long run;

5) the conditions of success: a brief conclusion mentioning the
principal domestic and external conditions of success of transformation and integration of the Hungarian economy.

2. - The Three-Fold Task of Economic Policy

The governments of the Eastern European countries which have
made a full and determined move towards political democracy (essentially Hungary, Czechoslovakia and Poland) are faced with a well-
known set of very difficult tasks in the field of economic policy. These
can be summed up under the following headings with brief comments
on the performance of Hungary on each account.

2.1 *Dealing With the Inheritance From the Past*

The «loss of the last forty years» is the gravest economic problem
facing Hungary as well as the other Eastern European countries. The
country's heavy external debt (which Hungary is making systematic
efforts to honour) is only one of the many manifestations of the
inheritance of the Socialist economic system. The gap which exists
between Hungary and the Oecd countries is also seen as an opportunity: the «catching up» with Western Europe could become a strong
stimulus for economic growth in the 1990s.

2.2 *The Problem of Change vs. Stability*

One of the greatest advantages of established democracies is the
relatively efficient management of change and the ability to find the
right combination of stability and change at the level of both policies
and officials and managers. In Hungary, as well as in the other two
countries mentioned above, the people have voted in favour of

fundamental changes to be carried out within a relatively short time span. The difficulties involved here also include the need for the newly elected leaders to become familiar with the extent of the problems and with the complexities of day-to-day government. This is a task for which most of them did not have the kind of preparation enjoyed by opposition parties in older democracies. It may be argued, however, that Hungary (the government and the opposition) has coped rather well with this problem so far. Nevertheless, it has been the source of some impatience with the government's economic policies both within the country and abroad;

2.3 *Crisis Management*

The Hungarian authorities, as the Polish and increasingly also the Czechoslovak governments, have to define and implement economic policies under trying, crisis conditions, which would present a serious challenge also for much more experienced policy-makers and would create considerable social strife in the much richer Oecd countries. Three crisis areas may be mentioned here, the management of each of which by itself represents a formidable task:

a) the first one is the necessary contraction of traditional (inefficient) production, and how to prevent a dangerous domino effect. In Hungary, registered industrial production declined in 1990, but so far, Hungary, in contrast to Poland for example, has managed the problem relatively well. Avoiding a cumulative downturn, while at the same time applying pressure for change and increasing efficiency, will remain one of the most difficult problems of Hungarian economic policy-making;

b) the second task of crisis management to mention is inflation (open and repressed). Some of the price rises are the result of the necessary price liberalization at a time when competition is not yet fully effective, sone of them are the inheritance of past policy errors (partly condoned by organizations such as the Imf). In contrast to Poland or Yugoslavia, Hungary has managed to avoid hyperinflation. Nevertheless, the country lacks a fully effective anti-inflationary policy;

c) a third issue to point out is the impact of the economic crisis of the Soviet Union. Hungary's 1990 foreign trade performance was remarkable (due to a sharp increase in convertible currency exports, rather than to import restrictions). Yet, the deterioration in Hungary's terms of trade with the Soviet Union and the threat of a collapse of Comecon trade will require in 1991 an even greater effort of adaptation than the one which occurred in 1990.

2.4 *Change of System and the Selection of an Appropriate Model*

The third, and probably most complex task is guiding the transformation of the economic system and the creation and development of necessary structures for the appropriate functioning of a market economy. This task has three major dimensions: 1) identifying the «model» which correspomds best to the country's economic, political and social objectives and around which a broad consensus can be developed; 2) defining the measures required and adapting the model to Hungarian conditions; and 3) implementing these changes.

3. - The Choice of a Model: Hungary and the Social Market Economy

While there is broad agreement in the Oecd countries and in Eastern Europe that collectivism should be replaced by competition, private ownership, i.e. the market economy, there is relatively great confusion on the meaning of the market economy, on what kind of market economy and the best way to develop it.

The broad consensus about the general goals of the metamorphosis of the economic system is one of the most encouraging aspects of the current political and economic situation in Hungary. Government and opposition agree today that the goal for Hungary has to be development of a European type «social market economy».

In fact, Hungary was the first Eastern European country where the concept of the «social market economy» was first proposed as the model for the transformation of the economic system. The notion of the "social market economy" was accepted with remarkable speed. Yet, one finds very few references to the concept of the «social market economy» in European or American press reports on Hungary and on the Hungarian government's objectives for the transformation of the economy.

If little is written about the concept of the «social market economy» in the Hungarian context, this has to do less with Hungary than with the general state of information about economic policies and with the force of intellectual fashions in our Western societies. In fact, there are very few English speaking economists (and very few economists in the international economic organizations) who are familiar with the term, or, if they have heard it, take it seriously.

Yet, the expression the «social market economy» describes the most successful set of economic policies in modern history. First introduced to describe the policies followed by Germany after the economic and monetary reform of 1948, it is used describe the economic system not only of Germany, but also of Switzerland and Austria. But in a broader sense, the expression also covers the current, modern Wester European tradition of economic policy making. One may argue that the economic system and the policy making framework of many continental European countries (including France, Italy, and even Spain) can be described as part of the common European tradition of the social market economy.

Without going into details, some of the principal relevant aspects of the concept can be briefly mentioned here:

1) the «social market economy» is an open and liberal market economy based on the principles of economic freedom, individual effort and private property. It differs, however, from the extreme nineteenth century type concept of the market economy in that it recognizes that all economic and social functions cannot be fulfilled properly by the market alone, and that some markets do not work efficiently;

2) there is an important division of labour between the market and the State. The State (at the national, regional or local level) has to assume some important functions, not only to assure genuine, fair and effective competition and, thereby, the proper working of markets, but also to assure social justice (which is not an attempt to create

equality or an egalitarian society) and to help correct distorsions
which may result from competition and from the functioning of
markets. This division of labour between the State and the markets is
organized in a pragmatic manner according to the specific conditions
and preferences of each country and it is subject to change under the
influence of changing economic conditions and preferences;

3) the «social market economy» implies growing prosperity (Lu-
dwig Erhard's slogan: «Wohlstand für alle»). Economic growt is not
the result of inflationary policies (fighting inflation is an essential
element of the concept), but of an increasing production and the right
kind of incentives for increased effort and savings. Thus it differs both
from Keynesian demand management policies and from rigid monetarism. It also differs from the economic model represented by the
term «austerity» (whether the British post-war version, or the more
recent Imf version);

4) the social market economy is fundamentally different from the
«welfare state». But it also contrasts sharply with current concepts
which show a profound lack of social sensitivity. In the case of the Imf
this is less due to a «lack of heart» (as the critiques argue), or to the
«necessary economic and fiscal rigour» (as the Imf argues), but rather
to an apparent inability to distinguish between the areas where
competition, market prices and efficiency have to be vigorously
promoted, and areas where even in the most efficient liberal market
economies, market forces and market prices cannot be relied upon
exclusively to bring about economic efficiency and growth;

5) finally, it should be emphasized that the social market
economy is not an approach reserved for rich and successful economies. It is a concept which has made possible the reconstruction and
sustained growth of economies which had been much poorer than
today's Hungarian economy.

At present, rapid and thorough changes are taking place
throughout the Hungarian economy. The process is radical and
irreversible. From a socialist economy (which for years had contained
only limited, but still the most dynamic elements of a market economy
in East-Central Europe) a true market economy is emerging in
Hungary which will be based increasingly on private property and
driven by private initiative.

The following are some of the key features of the Hungarian government's economic program published in September 1990.

3.1 *Privatization*

The Hungarian Government believes that private ownership has to become, once more, the dominant feature of the Hungarian economy. This is necessary for reasons of both economic efficiency and social stability and equity.

3.2 *Welcoming Foreign Capital and Foreign Initiative*

Foreign direct investments are seen as a key factor for the development of the market economy, for modernizing the economy, for introducing modern technologies and methods of management and for stimulating integration with world markets. Thus, foreign investors are also expected to play an important role in the private program.

3.3 *Liberalization, Competition, Deregulation and Market Prices*

Price, wage and foreign trade liberalization have already made considerable progress in Hungary. The government aims at speeding up and completing this process. Providing the conditions for competition, as well as deregulation and the elimination of bureaucratic red tape, for both domestic and foreign businessman are among the high-priority objectives.

3.4 *Encouraging Private Initiative and the Creation of New Companies*

Freeing and encouraging private initiative are the key to increased efficiency and prosperity.

3.5 *Reducing the Role and the Weight of the Government*

Hungary needs an effective economic policy and an efficient government, but one whose direct economic role is and will be much more limited than had been the case in the past.

3.6 *International Competitiveness, Opening of Markets,*
     Promoting Exports and International Economic Integration

Even under difficult circumstances, Hungarian foreign trade has had some remarkable results. In 1990 the trade balance shows a large surplus and Hungarian exports to the OECD countries have achieved a sharp increase. Maintaining and strengthening the international competitiveness of the Hungarian economy are key objectives of Hungarian economic policy. Hungary has made considerable progress towards current account convertibility. Completing and consolidating the convertibility of the Hungarian currency is a central objective of the economic program.

3.7 *Checking Inflation and Maintaining Domestic*
     and External Balance

Inflation is one of the problems inhered from the structure and the policy errors of the socialist economic and political system. Although Hungarian inflation is far from having reached the dimensions seen in some of the other countries in the region, the government considers the task of checking inflation and breaking inflationary expectations as a central objective. Hungary follows a tight monetary policy and is making determined efforts to reduce the budget deficit (which already today represents a much smaller proportion of GDP than in the average OECD country).

3.8 *Meeting International Financial Commitments*

Over the last twenty years Hungary accumulated a large external debt. Notwithstanding the heavy burden of the debt service, Hungary did not and does not ask for rescheduling.

3.9 *Promoting Savings and Strengthening the Banking and Financial System*

Savings are relatively high in Hungary already. The objective is to stimulate savings further, to assure a more efficient and more market-oriented use of savings in the economy.

3.10 *Improving Productivity and Increasing the Mobility of Labour*

The Hungarian labour force is the country's most important resource: in the socialist system it was also among the most wastefully used resources. Hungarians want to succeed, want to work more efficiently, want to live better. This is the key to the success of the market economy and of future economic growth. It is the policy of the government to help increase labour mobility, to eliminate legal or other obstacles which hamper productivity and the most efficient use of our labour resources.

4. - The «Information Gap» and the Impatience of the Western Economists with Hungary

There is a certain information gap among Western economists about the state of the Eastern European economies and about the progress towards the market economy in the individual countries concerned. This gap is usually larger among university economists or journalists than among other professionals involved in economic life, such as businessmen and bankers.

One of the great merits of this volume collecting the essays presented at the Rome conference, organized in January 1991 — at a crucial time for developments in both the Soviet Union and the Polish economy — was to bring a greater sense of realism to the academic debate about the process of transformation of economic systems and the chances of success for this transformation in Eastern Europe.

This information gap can be illustrated with the example of Hungary. Since the Spring of 1990 many Western economists have shown impatience with the allegedly slow «speed of change» in the Hungarian economy. The Hungarian government was often chided for not "moving fast enough" towards the market economy. This essentially faulty perception of development in Hungary was not only due to the poor communications skills of the Hungarian government (and to the lack of sufficient information about the huge package of reform measures being tackled by the Hungarian goverment and Parliament) and to the attention being paid by the domestic and foreign press to the complaints of the Hungarian opposition parties (which is only good party politics). It may be argued that this impatience with developments in Hungary was not only due to a lack of familiarity with the actual developments in Hungary (or Poland for that matter), which in view of the language problems and the difficulties of reliable statistical measures in economies of rapid transition are excusable. It has been due also to a certain confusion about the very process of change towards a market economy and about the very working of the market economy and of mixed economies (the category to which the Eastern European countries will continue to belong for some time to come and a category to which many OECD countries also belong).

Two points should be mentioned here, both of which were discussed at some length in this volume (and both of which are at the heart of the problem of transition and the «impatience» with the Hungarian approach): the first one has to do with the confusion between the need or justification for a «big bang» monetary reform (in some cases), on the one hand, and the need to create the legal and institutional basis for the working of the market economy. It should be obvious to anyone who lives in a market economy, that a big bang monetary reform cannot obviate the need for the much more detailed job of creating the institutions and rules for the working of the market economy.

It so happens that in the case of Hungary there has been much less justification for a big bang monetary reform (in contrast to Poland where there was no other way out of the initial monetary mess), and at the same time there has been considerable (even if not spectacular) progress towards institutional reform, including *de facto* privatization and a sharp *de facto* loss of central goverment control over economic activity. Hungary, like many other countries, is suffering from a very heavy dose of bureaucracy and from numerous monopolistic and oligopolistic markets (which the government is trying to break up as fast as possible). However, it is clearly no longer an economy where the government would have a decisive say in what should be produced, who should produce it and at what prices.

Today, Hungary suffers from a high rate of inflation (although it is much less serious than in Poland even after monetary stabilization). This inflation is partly the result of the necessary correction of the price distortions of the Socialist economy, and partly of policy errors, condoned by the «austerity policies» advocated by the International Monetary Fund. While it is imperative that inflation be brought under control, it also clear that this should not be attempted through a sharp reduction of production and productive capacity and by exacerbating social tensions. Increased production and productivity are as important to fight inflation as tight fiscal and monetary policies.

The second issue, closely related to the nature and the extent of monetary policy and monetary reform, has to do with the dangers of a «scorched earth» reform, or a reform that leads to a *de facto* destruction and disorganization of productive capacity, way beyond the need to clear away «dead wood». Some of the impatience among Western journalists and economists with the new Hungarian government's policies has been due to its refusal to follow a «scorched earth» policy that would have led to a dramatic drop in output (and in living standards). As it is, the stagnation and the decline in GDP, combined with the large income transfer for the interest payments on the country's external debts represent a serious constraint not only on living standards, but also investments and on the speed of modernization of the Hungarian economy. A much sharper further decline in production would not only threaten to precipitate an external payments crisis, but it would also increase the difficulty of dealing effectively with inflation by creating much greater shortages in the economy than is the case today.

5. - The European Community and the Development of the Social Market Economy

One of the principal consequences of the imposition of the Communist economic system on Hungary and its neighbours after the second world war was their isolation from the process of economic integration in Western Europe and in the world economy at large.

Hungary has begun negotiations with the European Community for associate status and it may be expected that Hungary will become a full member of the EC before the end of this century.

The associate status will bring immediate economic and political benefits. Setting the long-term goal of full membership will help shape both the economic structure and the institutional development of the Hungarian economy.

There is a close interdependence between the development of the social market in Hungary and the goal of full membership in the European Community, from the point of view of both Hungary and the Community.

1) *For Hungary* the goal of EC membership will facilitate the full development of institutional models as well as creating the basis for sustained and balanced growth). Conversely, if Hungary had chosen a different model (e.g. the «Korean» or the «Chilean» model, there would be no chance for effective integration into the Community.

2) *For the EC* it will mean that if the social market economy is effectively developed in Hungary, there will be no grounds to fear the diluting of the achievements of the EC through Hungarian membership. If, however, the EC had adopted a negative attitude towards Hungary and the other Eastern European economies, their chances for developing a modern European-type economic structure and policy framework would have greatly diminished.

6. - The Conditions of Success

The chances of success of Hungary appear to be good, despite a certain pessimism prevailing in the country (one of the main causes of which is the uncertainty engendered by inflation).

Among the numerous domestic and external conditions of success, the following should be mentioned as a brief conclusion:

1) *at the domestic level*, the need to create the basis for sustained growth should be emphasized. Without growth neither the social market economy, nor integration can succeed. It is also important to develop an efficient anti-inflationary strategy through the right combination of restrictions and stimuli. Finally, the «social» dimension of the market economy has to be treated very carefully. These are all areas where the EC model can be extremely helpful;

2) *as for the external conditions*, beside all the traditional ones (no war, no depression, no protectionism, etc.) it is important that Hungary's foreign partners should realize that Hungary needs help to digest the one-time costs of the change of economic system. These costs are much smaller than those that can be witnessed in the former East Germany, but it would be a delusion to believe that these costs can be covered exclusively by direct investments or by borrowing abroad.

Inflation Stabilization in Poland: A Year After

Grzegorz W. Kolodko

Warsaw School of Economics (SGPiS) and Institute of Finance, Warsaw

1. - Introduction

The fundamental problem to be considered in this paper concerns the theoretical and practical problems of the stabilization in post-communist economy, in particular the Polish experience, since stabilizations of this type must, by their very nature, differ from the classical stabilization policies (Bruno - Di Tella - Dornbusch - Fischer [1]) (*) in at least two fundamental aspects.

Firstly, in the post-communist economy it is not only the stabilization at a low, controllable price inflation level that matters, but also — and even in the first place — the elimination of shortages. In other words, the goal of stabilization is the formation of a mechanism of prices which, with as low as possible rate of their rise, will help to clear the market.

Secondly, the stabilization is to be perceived in a broader context of systemic transformation from planned, bureaucratically administered economy, to a market economy. In the light of this perception, stabilization is one of the prerequisites and, at the same time, mechanisms of the market-oriented transition, while the systemic transformation is of prioritary importance.

It is from this point of view that the Polish experience of 1989-1990 and the resulting perspectives must be evaluated, since

---

(*) *Advise:* the numbers in square brackets refer to the Bibliography in the appendix.

Poland's case is not unique. Both the process of reaching very intensive inflationary processes and the attempts to fight them under conditions of market transformation are, may be, the most spectacular but still only one aspect of certain more general trends appearing within the post-communist world.

The empirical analysis and certain generalizing theoretical conclusions in this paper will be particularly focussed on the character and sources of the Polish inflation in the period immediately preceding the 1990 stabilization package, assumptions and goals of the package and evaluation of its implementation. This is of particular importance because of conclusions resulting therefrom for economic policies of the post-communist countries are hardly to be overestimated. Many other countries — from Soviet Union to China, from Estonia to Albania — are facing options similar to the Polish dilemmas of 1989-1990. On the one hand — they find themselves in different development stages of inflationary proceses and of attempts at controlling them and, on the other hand, are in different situations as to the pace and direction of the market transition, but the Polish experience should nevertheless be highly instructive for all these economies.

The paper consists of ten paragraphs. The second paragraph shortly discusses the development of inflation in the late 80s, especially the so-called induced inflation of the later half of 1989. In the third paragraph, fundamental assumptions of the stabilization package the implementation of which was started at the beginning of 1990 are presented. The fourth paragraph informs about the announced program goals, while the fifth presents its real results after one year of implementation. In the next, sixth paragraph, favourable economic processes and developments connected with the stabilization and systemic transformation policy are presented. It is against this background that, in paragraph 7, an attempt is made to answer the question what causes have led to such huge divergencies between the assumed targets and the achieved results. Do the causes lie in the assumptions or rather in the program implementation sphere? The eighth paragraph, in turn, poses the question about the applicability of the cold-turkey-type or graduality-type approach to the stabilization in post-communist economies in general and the Polish one in particular.

The ninth paragraph discusses the transition from a shortageflation-type crisis to slumpflation. And, finally, the tenth paragraph, in summing up the discussion, contains a certain attempt to outline the perspectives of stabilization policy in Poland as well as the conclusions resulting therefrom for other economies of the post-communist world. To the paper, a statistical Appendix is subjoined (Graphs 3-12) illustrating the course of inflation and stabilization as well a the accompanying real and financial processes.

2. - Inflation of the Late 80s

In the Polish inflation of the 80s several distinct phases could be distinguished. After the acceleration of price rise pace in 1980-1982, it slowed after the 1982 stabilization and was further falling till 1985. At the same time, the scale of shortages was somewhat reduced too. Then, from 1986 till mid-1989, a renewed acceleration of price inflation rate could be observed. It grew from somewhat less than 15% in 1985 up to about 160% in the former half of 1989. What is more, this time a reversal of the favourable trend from the preceding period with respect to shortages was also noticed, as their scale was growing too. So, we had to do with the shortageflation syndrome (Kolodko-McMahon [12]). This syndrome consists in the fact that, under conditions of socialist economy in the course of reform, still characterized — in spite of market-oriented changes — by soft budgetary constraints (Kornai [15]), a price inflation-versus-shortage trade-off appears in the short run. Whereas in the long run — because of the inconsistent and soft fiscal, monetary and income policies — both the so-called price (open) inflation and repressed inflation with its accompanying permanent shortages simultaneously grow (Kolodko [8]). The shortageflation curve is shifting ever farther from the coordinate system origin towards the upper right-hand corner of the diagram (Graph 1).

The essence of the shortageflation syndrome shows that, in the face of intensification of both the open and repressed inflations above a certain critical level, the syndrome can not be overcome without making recourse to price liberalization, the latter being — as is well

GRAPH 1

SHORTAGEFLATION SYNDROME

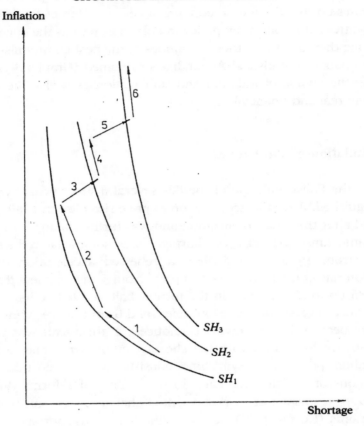

known — contrary to the command-type economy management system. Attempts at partial price liberalization not supported by other necessary measures tightening the budgetary constraints imposed on all economic agents through appropriate fiscal, monetary and income policies, lead in the long run exclusively to an acceleration of open-inflation processes, and by no means eliminate the shortages. Moreover, not only the position of the shortageflation curve in relation to the coordinate system origin, but its slope too, are changing. With time, it becomes more and more vertical. This means that the scope for the specific substitution between the open and repressed inflation is becoming ever less. Reducing the shortage scale by one additional point requires an ever greater increase in the open (price) inflation. This was just the path Poland took since 1985 until, in mid-1989, it reached the situation of extreme exhaustion by the shortageflation syndrome. In spite of the ever faster price rise pace, the shortages not only did not diminish, but were growing too. This resulted not only from a faster increase in nominal incomes than in prices, but also from the fact that, beginning with May 1989, we already witnessed an onset of recessionary developments in the real sphere.

It was against the above background that the transition from galloping price inflation, with the accompanying shortages, to quasi-hyperinflation took place in Poland beginning with August 1989. Till the initiation of the stabilization package, this hyperinflation was accompanied by shortages, so for half-a-year we had to do with hypershortageflation. This resulted from the only partial liberalization of prices, namely liberalization of food prices in August 1989. The huge inflation acceleration was also a result of the introduction of a general income indexation system imposed by the Solidarity. After the power take over by Solidarity in August of that year, indexation rules were somewhat modified, but this change was already unable to stop hyperinflation.

This temporary hyperinflation was of induced character (Kolodko [11]). It was to a certain extent provoked by the macroeconomic policy carried out in the peculiar period of fundamental political transformation in Poland (Fischer-Gelb [4]). The hyperinflation was provoked, on the one hand, by political struggle and, on the other hand, by the conviction that under hyperinflation conditions it would be easier substantially to lower the level of real wages and to depreciate the value of money balances, especially in possession of households. In addition, the induced quasi-hyperinflation perceived in this way resulted from the conviction that hyperinflation would be easier to overcome than the shortageflation syndrome in the form in which it existed immediately before. But above all, the more or less deliberate option on behalf on hyperinflation ensued from the priority given to objectives bearing on the transition to a market economy, since the implementation of this task requires, among other things, an almost full liberalization of prices and a deep money devaluation as

well as a rise in credit costs up to their real level. Under conditions of
such a considerable monetary destabilization with which we had to do
in Poland, the achievement of the above objectives was not possible
otherwise than by passing through hyperinflation phase.

3. - Stabilization Package

The stabilization package was structured so as to induce processes which would lead to: a) first, demand and supply equilibration in
the commodity market or, more exactly, formation of a mechanism of
market-clearing prices; b) second, reduction in the inflation rate to the
lowest possible level; c) third, equilibration of the current account
balance.

Putting aside some technical details (Frydman - Wellisz - Kolodko
[5]), the stabilization program included five main planes of action,
namely: 1) fiscal adjustment; 2) price liberalization and adjustment; 3)
tough monetary policy; 4) wage control; 5) exchange rate unification
and introduction of internal convertibility of zloty.

The fiscal adjustment policy was aimed at balancing the budget.
In the year preceding the stabilization, budget deficit amounted to
6.0% of the state balance and 7.4% of the general government
balance. Subsidies made about 1/3 of state budget expenditures. It
was assumed that, in order to eliminate the budget deficit, their level
should be reduced by at least one half and their share in the reduced
expenditures had to make about 1/5. The improvement of the budget
situation was also to be forested by better fiscal discipline, and
possible temporary deficits were to be covered either with limited
commercial bank credits or by contracting debt in the open market
just being formed. In addition, budget revenues of 2.5% order were
planned from issues of tresaury bonds with option of later conversion
into equities of privatized enterprises. As a result of all the above
measures the state budget had to show an insignificant deficit amounting to 0.2% of expenditures and the general government balance — a
surplus of about 1.6%.

The second main plane of action of the package was liberalization
and adjustment of prices. Contrary to widespread opinions — especi-

ally in the light of the not always justified talk about the so-called Polish Big Bang — the scope of price liberalization performed at the moment of the package initiation was very limited, since the majority of prices had been already previously released, namely in the course of reforms of the 80s or — with regard to food prices — in August 1989. Thus, in the period of making way towards stabilization, the price system considered from the point of view of price control was as in Table 1.

In 1990, free prices of consumer goods and services made 82.6% of total sales value in this category, procurement goods prices were

TABLE 1

PRICE STRUCTURE IN POLAND IN 1989

Category	July	December
Share of contractual (freely negotiated) prices in the total sales		
Consumer goods and services	71	86
of which food	58	93
State purchasing prices of agricultural products	30	41
Procurement goods	86	89
Raw materials and components	89	89
Share of prices subjected to maximum rise index and obligation to inform about intended rise		
a) maximum price rise indices:		
consumer goods and services	12.4	6.6
procurement goods	24.7	21.0
b) obligation to inform about intended price rises:		
consumer goods and services	23.6	21.4
procurement goods	4.6	5.5
Share of fully prices in the total sales value		
Consumer goods and services	35.0	58.0
Procurement goods	56.7	56.5

Source: PRICE DEPARTMENT OF THE MINISTRY OF FINANCE.

liberalized in 89%, and purchasing prices of agricultural products in 100%.

Thus, sources of the huge price explosion which took place immediately after the program initiation must not be sought in first line in the price liberalization scope, since the latter was limited, but in the centrally performed price adjustments and especially in the administratively carried out energy and coal price rises (in the latter case as much as sevenfold). These price rises were aimed, on the one hand, at reducing the subsidies which had excessively pressed on the budget and, on the other hand, at changing the price relations through a stepwise relative appreciation of fuels, especially of the hard coal playing a key role in the Polish economy.

The third main plane of stabilization neasures had to include a tough monetary policy finding its expression in a strict control of money supply and regulation of its growth rate through the use of really positive interest rates. The really negative interest rates both on credits and deposits, typical of the shortageflation period, were to be replaced by positive interest rates. After a short period of the so-called corrective inflation whose rate was assumed to amount 45% in January (in comparison to the average price level in December) and to 20% in February, the interest rate had to exceed the inflation rate in the third month of program implementation already. The tough monetary policy had to bring several effects. First, it should radically reduce the demand of economic agents for credits and, as a result — through limitation of the liquidity of all economy sectors — bring a reduction in demand and, consequently, a decline in inflation rate. Second, it was intended to force the enterprises to reduce their investment demand whose excessive proportions were one of the chronic sources of inflationary processes in the previous period. Third, the really positive interest rates had permanently to increase the households' propensity for saving and overcome their inflationary expectations. It was in such an environment only — i.e. with tightened budgetary constraints resulting from restrictive fiscal and monetary measures — that the price liberalization and adjustment were not doomed to degenerate into hyperinflation.

It was also assumed — and that was the fourth program plane — that, in spite of the general trend towards liberalization, nominal wage rises would be subjected to strict control. In Poland — as distinct from other programs, e.g. the Yugoslav stabilization program carried out at the same time (Coricelli - Rocha [2]) — wages were not fully frozen, but a mechanism of their partial indexation was adopted which provided for the linkage of the admissible wage fund rise in the enterprise to the inflation rate through officially fixed coefficients. In consecutive months of the former half of the year they were set at 0.3, 0.2, 0.2, 0.2, 0.6 and 0.6, respectively. In July, this coefficient was exceptionally set at 1.0 and, then, for the rest of the year, reduced back to 0.6. It can be easily noticed that with this kind of indexation the higher the inflation rate the larger the scale of the drop in real wages.

Finally, the fifth main stabilization program plane was the introduction of internal convertibility of the domestic currency along with simultaneous exchange rate unification. It was provided that enterprises would be obliged to sell to the state at the stabilized exchange rate their foreign currencies gained from export receipts, while banks would be obliged to sell foreign currencies to importers. Also, the foreign currency turnover in the households sector had been already earlier (in March 1989) liberalized. Liquidity was to be guaranted by means of a stabilization loan obtained from OECD countries in the amount of US$ 1 billion. This point of the package also required a devaluation of the Polish zloty. After gradual devaluation (from Zl 1,400 to 6,000 for one US dollar) between September and December 1989, it was decided at the start of the package implementation to drastically devaluate the domestic currency by over one half, down even below the free-market level of Zl 9,500 for one US dollar. And decision was made to adopt just this exchange rate as the nominal anchor supporting the whole stabilization program.

Is is still to be added that very high charges were imposed on imports in the form of duties (mostly of 20% order) and, additionally, in the form of the so-called turnover tax equally amounting to 20% assessed on the above basis (i.e. on the merchandise value increased by duty). As a result, the cost of a dollar in the import was often by 44% higher than the value obtained by enterprise for a dollar earned in export. This was intended to limit the enterprise sector's demand for foreign currencies and, in this way, contribute to exchange rate stabilization and, in consequence, to inflation stabilization at a low level.

4. - Program Goals

The stabilizarion program outlined in the above-described way got the approval of the International Monetary Fund and its basic points were put down in the Letter of Intent. Also, there was an explicit social support for this program, above all as a result of fundamental political transformations towards democratization simultaneously going on in Poland.

Both these facts — international support as well as the indulgence of the country's population or, more exactly, the governments belief as to their scale — led to an unrealistic formulation of program goals and, what was worse, to a general overshooting of the program, since it was assumed the inflation would drop in the middle of the year to 1% in monthly scale. At the same it was assumed that after a half-year period already the economy would once more enter the road of economic growth. But this was to be achieved at the cost of a 20% fall in real wages.

As far as trends in the real sphere were concerned, a drop by 1% (!) in consumption, by 3.1% in GNP and by 5% in industrial production was assumed in comparison with 1989. This relatively — for the project scale — small recession (after an only 1.5% GNP decrease in the preceding year) was to be accompanied by unemployment amounting to 400,000 persons, this being equivalent to about 2% of the total workforce.

With respect to foreign trade it was assumed the stabilization program execution would lead to such exports and imports development that in the so-called I payments zone (unconvertible currencies) a small surplus amounting to SUR 0.5 billion would ensue, whereas in the II payments zone (convertible currencies) — a deficit amounting to about US $ 0.8 billion.

It was also assumed that in the initial program implementation phase the nominal exchange rate of Zl 9,500 for one US $ would be maintained which, in view of the expected inflation scale, was equivalent to a small real appreciation of zloty.

5. - Implementation

Should the formally taken execution degree of the above-present-ed goals be adopted as exclusive implementation criterion of the Polish stabilization program, we would be obliged to ascertain its complete failure. This is clearly illustrated by the comparison pre-sented in Table 2.

TABLE 2

POLISH STABILIZATION PROGRAM: GOALS AND RESULTS

	Assumptions	Results
CPI (%)	20	100 (*a*)
Industrial output	− 5.0	− 25.4 (*b*)
GNP	− 3.1	− 18
Unemployment	2.0	6.3
Trade balance:		
in billions of dollars..................	− 0.8	+ 4.3
in billions of roubles	+ 0.5	+ 4.2

(*a*) In the second *Letter of Intent* to the IMF, approved in August already, the monthly inflation rates for October, November and December 1990 were on the average assumed at 1.5, 1.0 and 2.0% respectively, i.e. at about 20% in annualised scale. The real inflation rate in this period amounts — likewise in yearly scale — to almost 100% (almost 6%).

(*b*) Index for 11 months of 1990 with respect to the public sector whose share in the industrial output amounts to about 90%.

Source: MAIN STATISTICAL OFFICE and own calculations.

Thus, not only the announced goals were not achieved, but what was achieved was obtained at a much higher cost than that originally foreseen in exchange for better results. In particular, the scale of decline in the standard of living and in real wages has been much larger than originally announced by the government, since real wages were reduced by as much as 20% (1), and the real money balances of

---

(1) This fact seems to be still overlooked by one of the foreign experts who earlier foretold a decline in inflation rate down 1% at most for the first month following the package initiation already and later tried to belittle the recession scale brought about by the wrong stabilization policy. Jeffrey Sachs [20] declares: «There has been a persistent — and certainly erroneous — forecast of a 20% unemployment rate, though the unemployment rate stands at 5.5%, lower than in the United States. Similarly, fears of

the households sector were reduced on a still larger scale. The really borne hardly be justifiable, and still less socially acceptable, even if one of the basic goals — i.e. inflation rate reduction down to 1-1.5% monthly on the average or 13-20% yearly — were achieved. More important still, the inflation rate at the end of 1990 and beginning of 1991, when it has been still more intensified, can not be compared with the above-mentioned quasi-hyperinflation, just because of the induced character of the latter. Still more inadmissible is comparing the inflation from arbitrarily chosen months with its highest — after all, completely induced — record level of January 1990 (as much as 79.6% monthly). It is worth remembering here that in the last three-month period of 1989 the inflation rate was already falling, dropping from about 55% in October to 23 and 17% in November and December, respectively. So, if the contention of induced character of the Polish hyperinflation is justified, proper reference point for the 100% inflation arisen as a result of the stabilization package implementation and the accompanying processes (among other things, the recent adverse external developments) in the 160% inflation of the former half of 1989. It is in this perspective only that one can see how poor with respect to inflation stabilization have been the results brought about by the Polish Big Bang.

So, no wonder that in the presidential election in the later part of November 1990, where the governing prime minister running for presidency got a poor 18% of votes, Polish people gave voice to their negative evaluation of the economic situation. It is just because the stabilization program of his team had failed that Mazowiecki's government was overthrown, and not the other way round. It is not true that destabilization caused by the election has made the program implementation impossible, but it is just this program that has contributed to the political destabilization accompanying the election. This is an extremely important ascertainment, as it has a substantial

---

plummeting take-home pay abound, though the average industrial worker earned the equivalent of $131 in October, compared with $108 in October 1989». As I mentioned above, government forecasts of unemployment rate spoke about 2% and not 20%. Besides, comparing the unemployment in Poland which, within one year, has grown from zero to over 6% with unemployment in the United States can not be taken seriously. Finally, suggesting a more than 20% wage rise by converting the wages into dollars, in a situation where they really have fallen by over 20%, is an utter misuse.

importance for the proper assessment of the Polish experience from the point of view of other post-communist economies which will have to undergo a similar antiinflationary and stabilizing therapy.

6. - Stabilization Versus Transition to a Market Economy

An assessment of stabilization program results separately from the broader context of systemic transformation oriented towards creation of market economy would be one-sided and over-simplified. The stabilization package being implemented in Poland must be perceived in a broader perspective of the complex market-oriented transition process. Hypothesis can be framed that, in reality, stabilization has been subordinated to transition in so far as transition in the primary strategic goal to be attained even at the cost of failure of the stabilization policy, inclusive of further destabilization.

What is more, transition is to a certain extent enforcing destabilization, this being especially visible in those post-communist countries of Central and Eastern Europe in which, before the acceleration of the market-oriented systemic transformation, inflationary processes were relatively little developed (Czechoslovakia, Bulgaria, Romania, Baltic republics of the USSR i.e. Lithuania, Latvia and Estonia). This results from the simple fact that market-oriented transition requires, among other things, policy measures such as price liberalization, reduction subsidies, devaluation, significant rises in interest rates, etc. So, in the initial period, orientation towards a market economy brings about an acceleration of inflationary processes rather than their check.

In Poland's case, at the moment of stabilization program initiation, the market-oriented economic reforms were considerably advanced already. One must keep in mind that the Polish economy was in 1989 already in the forefront of the countries — then, not yet called post-communist (post-socialist) — which were progressing towards a market economy. One can however imagine that, in theory, a stabilization policy different from that actually chosen — and similar to the attempt undertaken in 1982 — could have been adopted. However, at that time, it was the inflation stabilization, with simultaneous reform of the socialist economy without any infringement of its fundamental principles, that was intended. It was the stabilization, after which the State was to remain the dominating agent in almost all spheres, and the scope of economic liberalization, inclusive of price liberalization, was limited (Kolodko [9]).

Whereas the 1990 stabilization constitutes not only a fight for internal and external equilibration of the economy, but also for the creation of a different economic mechanism. It is accompanied by construction of appropriate institutional surroundings for the market and the use, especially in the fiscal and monetary areas, of ever more numerous policy instruments typical of the market economy.

Thus, when looking at the Polish stabilization in this perspective, its negative assessment formulated in the preceding paragraph requires relativization. It is true, that the stabilization policy of the first post-communist government has led to the deepest recession in postwar Poland and, at the same time, the deepest one in contemporary Europe, with simultaneous stabilization of inflation on the highest level in Europe in 1990. But it is equally true that the Polish economy is clearly nearer — with respect to institutional changes and economic policy — to a market economy than any other post-communist country. Subsidies have been markedly cut, the budget is balanced and its possible deficit must, by law, not be monetized, prices are to a very large extent liberalized, internal currency convertibility has been introduced, the privatization process has been set in motion, elements of financial markets are being developed, etc.

So, the question arises, did not certain positive effects achieved with respect to transition to a market economy unavoidably require such high costs finding their expression in the destruction of the real sphere and decline in the population's standard of living as those actually finding place? These costs are huge indeed, and attempts to belittle them not backed by any factual argumentation (Sachs [20]) do not change the facts; they at most can purposely present them in a false light. However, detailed analyses show that the huge costs of market institutional transformation and stabilization policy have not been unavoidable. Their magnitude could have been much less — and that with achievement of not worse but, may be, even better effects with respect to systemic transformation — if the numerous errors contained in the stabilization package were avoided and if the package were not evidently overshot (Rosati [19]).

7. - Overshooting

One of the basic wrong assumptions contained in the stabilization package were expectations of a quick positive supply response on the part of the business sector. Enterprises behaved — and this inertia is to a large extent still lasting — differently than it would be the case in a market economy (Jorgensen - Gelb - Singh [6]). The supply responsiveness is very low and the enterprises have generally responded to shock reduction in internal demand not by improving their efficiency but by maximization of prices — which, this time, in the phase of radical departure from the shortage economy, is already limited by effective demand barrier — as well as by reducing the absolute output level. Togegher with this, there is a time lag in employment adjustment; the employment is diminishing much slower than is the production decline. In Poland's case, the former fell in the course of 1990 by about 10% with an about 25% drop in the output of the socialized (state-owned and cooperative) industry (2).

Wrong assumptions with respect to the real sphere consisted in the naive belief that the output would automatically rouse up by itself without interference on the part of macroeconomic policy. Some state interventionism attempts were too late and badly sequenced. For the post-communist economy is not yet a market economy (but not a planned economy any more). It is a certain "systemic vacuum" period in which the known fiscal and monetary policy instruments are functioning somewhat differently than in a developed market economy. The problem consists not only in using an appropriate set of policy instruments, but also in doing in the right time. And this has not been the case; since we have to do — on the one hand — with a general overshooting of the program, and — on the other hand —

_____

(2) This index regards the output of the socialized sector. In the private sector — whose share in the global 1990 industrial production has increased up to over 11% — the output has grown by about 9%, although there are other estimates showing its much greater increment.

with wrong responses resulting from undue insistence on automatic functioning of certain mechanisms. In other words, a kind of "over-liberalization" of the economy has taken place here as, may be, a reaction to its bureaucratization in the past.

The above-mentioned overshooting regards, in particular, the excessive scale of reduction in incomes of the households sector (among other things, in real wages) as well as the excessive limitation of the liquidity of enterprises resulting from the wrong sequencing of the monetary policy. As far as the former is concerned, the adoption of the indexation coefficient permitting the wage fund growth by only 0.2 of the price rise has led to a drastic drop in the households' demand and, in consequence, to a decline in sales and production induced by lack of demand. Whereas the desired stabilization effect could have been achieved through a much-smaller — of 20% order — reduction in real wages, the real reduction in the first two months of the stabilization amounted to more than twice as much.

What is more important, the mechanism for controlling the pace of nominal wage rise has been constructed in such a way that the non utilized limit of the admissible wage rise (upon exceeding this limit, the enterprise is bound to pay a prohibitive tax making from 200 to 500% depending on the scale of overstepping the limit) can be utilized in the following months. And this has been the case, especially in the latter half of the year (Tables 3 and 4). This is a bad mechanism. In the initial period its action was pro-recessionary (through reduction in effective demand and, consequently, in sales and production). Where-as later its action has been rather pro-inflationary, since an acceler-ation of the wage rise rate does not automatically lead to output growth but, in the first place, to acceleration of inflationary processes. This has been particularly visible since September. Thus, the statistical indices of real wage changes can not be averaged, since the excessive drop at the beginning of the year is not neutralized by the excessive rise in its latter half. Because the former has brought about recession whose scale could have been less, and the latter is not able to reverse the situation.

And as to the drastic rise in interest rates in January and their maintenance at a restrictive and processionary level till the end of February, it almost provoked a collapse in the real sphere. It was

TABLE 3

NORMATIVE AND ACTUAL RATES OF WAGE RISE IN FIVE BASIC SECTORS OF NATIONAL ECONOMY

	Months of 1990										
	I	II	III	IV	V	VI	VII	VIII	IX	X	XI
1. Corrective coefficients	0.3	0.2	0.2	0.2	0.6	0.6	1.0	0.6	0.6	0.6	0.6
2. Percentage rates of price rise:											
— projected............	45.0	23.0	6.0	6.0	2.5	3.0	5.5	3.0	4.5	4.0	3.0
— actual	78.6	23.9	4.7	8.1	5.0	3.4	3.6	1.8	4.6	5.7	4.9
3. Actual rates of wage rise	4.6	5.4	10.5	2.5	8.7	5.6	14.4	5.9	8.7	13.8	10.3
4. Normative rates of wage rise											
— by projected price rise	13.5	4.6	1.2	1.2	1.5	1.8	5.5	1.8	2.7	2.4	1.8
— by actual price rise	23.6	4.8	0.9	1.6	3.0	2.0	3.6	1.1	2.8	3.4	2.9

Source: Own calculation based on Gus data.

TABLE 4

NORMATIVE AND ACTUAL WAGES
IN FIVE BASIC SECTORS OF NATIONAL ECONOMY
(in thousand of zloties monthly per employee)

	Months of 1990										
	I	II	III	IV	V	VI	VII	VIII	IX	X	XI
1. Actual wages excluding profit payments	618.3	651.9	720.1	738.2	802.2	846.8	969.2	1,026.3	1,115.7	1,269.1	1,400.3
2. Normative wages (corrected by drop in employment) by actual price rise	738.1	782.2	799.9	823.4	864.8	892.5	939.7	965.3	1,006.0	1,054.1	1,085.1
3. Margin (normative minus actual wages) by actual price rise	119.9	130.3	79.8	85.2	62.6	45.6	−29.5	−61.1	−109.7	−215.0	−315.2
4. Cumulative margin (normative minus actual wages) by actual price rise	119.9	250.1	329.9	415.1	477.7	523.4	493.9	432.8	323.2	108.1	−207.1
5. Hypothetical wages after a single payment of cumulative margin (normative minus actual wages)	738.1	902.0	1,050.1	1,153.3	1,279.9	1,370.2	1,463.1	1,459.2	1,438.8	1,377.3	1,193.2

Source: own calculations based on Gus data.

mainly during these two months that the huge recession — of 30% order — took place and, ever since, the economy has been already staying in recession state. Whereas the explosion of the so-called corrective inflation took place mainly in the former half of January. Then, the high interest rate already exerted a mainly pro-recessionary rather than antiinflationary inflence, since its really negative level with respect to deposits did not contribute to overcoming the inflationary expectations of the household sector. The administrative regulation of interest rates in monthly cycles — after all, having little in common with real cycles of economic and financial processes — was not flexible enough. Appropriate modifications to the interest rate policy were made in November only. Interests on households' deposits have been raised — tough they still are negative in real terms (Table 5). This raise especially regards medium-term (three- and six-month) deposits. And under stabilization conditions these are long terms. But the move was made too late. Because now the inflation, the interest rates and the inflationary expectations are all growing. The increase in interest rates by the central bank and commercial banks only authenticates and additionally strengthens the inflationary expectations of the public. In such a situation, raising the interest to its really positive level can bring about a perverse effect in accelerating rather than stopping the inflation. Whereas if interest rates on deposits had been set at a really high level beginning with the 7th or 8th stabilization week already, this could have overcome the still extremely strong inflationary expectations. It could still be done in the 3rd to 5th month of the package implementation. But in November-December it was a right move at wrong moment, thus an ineffective one.

The third basic aspect of overshooting has been the devaluation scale. The official exchange rate was reduced down to much — even below the market (parallel) rate level. It should in this way anticipate the so-called corrective inflation. And this was what really happened, although the inflation scale was much higher than expected because of the negative feed-back between the scale of devaluation and acceleration of inflation caused by this devaluation. Nevertheless, the exchange rate has been kept over the whole year (initially, a three-month period only was assumed). But, on the other hand, such a deep exchange rate devaluation — with simultaneous additional charges

TABLE 5A

NOMINAL AND REAL INTEREST RATES IN JANUARY - NOVEMBER 1990 MONTHLY INTEREST RATES

| Month | on deposit to PKO Bank in % | | | | | | on credits in % | | | percentage rates of price rise |
	a vista	3-months	6-months	12-months	24-months	36-months	refinancing credit	one year credit minimal	one year credit maximal	
Nominal										
January	7.00	10.00	17.00	36.00	37.00	38.00	36.00	36.00	62.00	79.6
February	5.50	10.00	13.00	20.00	20.50	21.00	20.00	20.00	23.00	23.8
March	3.00	5.00	6.50	10.00	10.25	10.50	10.00	9.00	12.00	4.3
April	3.00	4.00	5.00	8.00	8.25	8.50	8.00	7.50	9.50	7.5
May	2.00	2.75	3.40	5.50	5.65	5.80	5.50	5.00	8.00	4.6
June	1.30	3.00	3.50	4.00	4.10	4.20	4.00	4.00	5.50	3.4
July	0.95	1.81	2.01	2.47	2.50	2.53	2.47	2.47	2.60	3.6
August	0.95	1.81	2.01	2.47	2.50	2.53	2.47	2.47	2.60	1.8
September	0.95	2.01	2.21	2.47	2.50	2.53	2.47	2.47	2.60	4.6
October	1.17	2.47	2.72	3.09	3.12	3.14	3.03	3.03	3.20	5.7
November	1.24	2.80	3.07	3.42	3.45	3.47	3.26	3.26	3.63	4.9
December										
Real by average price index of consumer goods and services										
January	−40.42	−38.75	−34.86	−24.28	−23.72	−23.16	−24.28	−24.28	−9.80	
February	−14.78	−11.15	−8.72	−3.07	−2.67	−2.26	−3.07	−3.07	−0.65	
March	−1.25	−0.67	2.11	5.47	5.70	5.94	5.47	4.51	7.38	
April	−4.19	−3.26	−2.33	0.47	0.70	0.93	0.47	0.00	1.86	
May	−2.49	−1.77	−1.15	0.86	1.00	1.15	0.86	0.38	3.25	
June	−2.03	−0.39	0.10	0.58	0.68	0.77	0.58	0.58	2.03	
July	−2.56	−1.73	−1.53	−1.09	−1.06	−1.03	−1.09	−1.09	0.97	
August	−0.84	0.00	0.21	0.66	0.69	0.72	0.66	0.66	0.78	
September	−3.49	−2.47	−2.28	−2.04	−2.01	−1.98	−2.04	−2.04	−1.92	
October	−4.28	−3.06	−2.82	−2.47	−2.45	−2.42	−2.53	−2.53	−2.36	
November	−3.48	−2.00	−1.75	−1.41	−1.39	−1.36	−1.56	−1.56	−1.21	
December										

Source: Own calculation based on the data of Gus, Pko and Nbp.

TABLE 5B

NOMINAL AND REAL INTEREST RATES IN JANUARY - NOVEMBER 1990
MONTHLY INTEREST RATES

| Month | on deposit to PKO Bank in % | | | | | | on credits in % | | | percentage rates of price rise |
	a vista	3-months	6-months	12-months	24-months	36-months	refinancing credit	one year credit minimal	maximal	
Real by point-to-point price index of consumer goods and services										
January	-48.01	-46.55	-43.15	-33.92	-33.43	-32.94	-33.92	-33.92	-21.28	105.8
February	0.19	4.46	7.31	13.96	14.43	14.91	13.96	13.96	16.81	5.3
March	-2.92	-1.04	0.38	3.68	3.91	4.15	3.68	2.73	5.56	6.1
April	-3.29	-2.35	-1.41	1.41	1.64	1.88	1.41	0.94	2.82	6.5
May	-2.49	-1.77	-1.15	0.86	1.00	1.15	0.86	0.38	3.25	4.6
June	-1.75	-0.10	-0.39	0.87	0.97	1.07	0.87	0.87	2.33	3.1
July	-2.75	-1.92	-1.72	-1.28	-1.25	-1.22	-1.28	-1.28	-1.16	3.8
August	-0.93	-0.09	0.11	0.56	0.59	0.62	0.56	0.56	0.68	1.9
September	-3.86	-2.85	-2.66	-2.41	-2.38	-2.35	-2.41	-2.41	-2.29	5.0
October	-4.73	-3.51	-3.28	-2.93	-2.90	-2.88	-2.99	-2.99	-2.82	6.2
November	-3.67	-2.19	-1.94	-1.60	-1.57	-1.55	-1.75	-1.75	-1.40	5.1
December										
Real by average producer price index of industrial output										
January	⋮	⋮	⋮	⋮	⋮	⋮	-35.18	-35.18	-22.78	109.8
February	⋮	⋮	⋮	⋮	⋮	⋮	9.59	9.59	12.33	9.5
March	⋮	⋮	⋮	⋮	⋮	⋮	10.22	9.22	12.22	- 0.2
April	⋮	⋮	⋮	⋮	⋮	⋮	5.78	5.29	7.25	2.1
May	⋮	⋮	⋮	⋮	⋮	⋮	4.98	4.48	7.46	0.5
June	⋮	⋮	⋮	⋮	⋮	⋮	2.46	2.46	3.94	1.5
July	⋮	⋮	⋮	⋮	⋮	⋮	0.80	-0.80	-0.68	3.3
August	⋮	⋮	⋮	⋮	⋮	⋮	0.42	-0.42	-0.30	2.9
September	⋮	⋮	⋮	⋮	⋮	⋮	0.23	-0.23	-0.10	2.7
October	⋮	⋮	⋮	⋮	⋮	⋮	1.79	-1.79	-1.62	-4.9
November	⋮	⋮	⋮	⋮	⋮	⋮	0.04	-0.04	0.32	3.3
December										

Source: Own calculation based on the data of GUS, PKO and NBP.

imposed on imports — was a successive, additional impulse stimulating both the corrective inflation and the recession. In the latter case the impulse consisted in a clear reduction in imports, this leading to a still deeper drop in production.

A particular kind of overshooting took place not on the economic plane but on the political one. The fundamental political breakthrough in Poland in 1989 which led to power takeover by Solidarity also resulted in a vast popular support for the new government. This fact — as well as a fundamental change in the West's attitude towards Poland — permitted to undertake the extremely difficult and socially painful economic program, inclusive of its stabilization aspects. However, the awareness of vast popular support — and it was confirmed by all public opinion polls — convinced a part of politicians that the limit of social resistance was very remote and that an even farthest-going blow in the shape of a shock stabilization program was feasible. While, in the previous periods, stabilization measures did not go far enough, this time a clear abuse of social confidence took place and the restrictiveness of the fiscal, monetary and income policies was overshot far beyond the dimension capable of obtaining social acceptance. The worst in this ascertainment is the fact that political situation of this type is not likely to happen again in foreseeable future. The overshooting with respect to utilization of the popular support was a fundamental political mistake which made the effectiveness of the contemplated stabilization effort impossible. This has been an irreversible loss.

8. - Cold Turkey Versus Gradualism

There are many arguments for the superiority of cold-turkey-type approach over gradualism. Dornbusch and Fischer [3] stress that a shock therapy is the only one which can gain the necessary credibility. After the initial shock — by its very nature, extremely painful for the population — there is the possibility to obtain spectacular short-term effects in fight against inflation. If so, the shock therapy can be effective if it is not followed by a too early loosening of financial restrictions. For example, in Yugoslavia, after a high inflation (64%) in December 1989, it was reduced down to zero in the second quarter of the following year. This was a spectacular effect which authenticated the cold-turkey approach (Kolodko - Gotz - Kozierkiewicz - Skrzeszewska - Paczek [14]). But soon afterwards a renewed acceleration of inflationary processes took place (up to about 10% monthly in the last months of 1990) which deprived the program of its credibility.

In Poland, the program pratically did not succed at all to gain the necessary credibility, because the inflation rate did not fall — even temporarily — to the level foretold by the government. After December 1989, when the inflation rate was reduced from 55% in October to somewhat less than 18%, it bounced once more up to 80% in January 1990 and 23% in February. Then, a stabilization of the inflation took place at a level several times higher than that announced by the government and — as a result of these announcements — expected by the population. No right conclusions were drawn from this fact and implementation of wrong program assumptions was continued in the illusive conviction that overcoming the inflation was — under the given institutional, structural and political conditions — a function of time only. So, the cold-turkey approach did not succeed. This however does not testify to the superiority of the gradualist approach. It must be clearly stated that in the face of such a scale of disequilibrium and inflation with which we had to do in Poland in 1989, shock therapy was the only justified one. The fault does not lie in its use as general method — since this was not by any means a mistake — but in the wrong implementation of the methodologically right shock approach. The unique chance has been wasted.

Another aspect of the cold-turkey-versus-gradualism dilemma is the necessity to distinguish the three planes on which economic processes in general, and in particular those bearing on transition to a market economy, take place. These planes are: stabilization, transformation and restructuring. From this point of view, the shock approach is applicable to stabilization only. And in cases of especially severe inflationary processes it frequently is the most justified one. Such was Poland's case. Whereas with respect to systemic transformation, i.e. institutional systemic change — although there is need for possibly rapid progress too — the cold-turkey approach is not applicable. With one exception, however, of which I take no account here, namely the one-time German Democratic Republic.

So, there is nothing like a Polish Big Bang in the systemic sphere. The transformation process in this area was subject to an evident acceleration in the framework of the general historic process of changes spreading over the whole post-communist world, and even was feeding back these changes. But here we have not to do with a shock approach but with a gradualism, natural for such cases, although the transformation itself is of revolutionary character. Key importance in the institutional change process perceived in the above way must be attached to a proper sequencing of measures to be taken (Nuti [18]).

The more so, shock policy is out of question with respect to structural changes, since these, by their very nature, require a longer time perspective. Against this background it must be concluded that the rather widespread talk about the Polish Big Bang is exaggerated, since it can at most refer to stabilization — which, anyhow, ended in failure — and not to the whole institutional and structural market-oriented transformation of the economy. Because the latter is a long-lasting, gradually developing process with extremely complex implications.

9. - From Shortageflation to Slumpflation

The societies of the post-communist countries evolving towards market economy think — and often are confirmed in this conviction also by politicians — this will relatively soon be a Western-type market economy. Such illusions are also fostered by transferring the patterns of developed market economies onto the ground of the destabilized post-communist economy involved in deep crisis; in this case the above patterns are not applicable. Underestimating the perspective of the long, arduous road to the market also results from the lack of knowledge of the realities and peculiarities of these economies on the part of some Western experts and, in consequence, from the lack of sufficient imagination and responsibility in framing the goals and outlining the perspectives (3).

On the other hand, this imagination was not lacking to D.M. Nuti ([17], p. 47) when he remarked many years ago: «If Poland were a capitalist country in a similar crisis, painful but fairly automatic processes and policy response would be set in motion. There would be hyperinflation, currency devaluation, drastic public expenditure cuts and deflationary taxation measures, tight money, high interest rates, disinvestment, bankruptcies and plant closures, and a couple of million unemployed. Some external creditors would get very little, or nothing at all, following the financial collapse of their debtors; some of the remaining debt would be offset by the scale to foreigners of financial assets (shares, bonds), land, building and plant. Fresh external finance would be available to the more credible borrowers. Unemployment would keep the unions in check restraining real wages and ensuring labour discipline. The drop in real wage trends and industrial steamlining would eventually promote exports and encourage new investment, attracting foreign capital; in ten years or so the economy would be getting out of crisis».

The above view was formulated on the basis of observation of the 1981-1982 crisis, but it seems all the more adequate to the still larger-scale crisis of 1989-1990. Only that in the latter case the Polish economy already is nearer to capitalist economy than ever before in the post-war times. So it is understandable that it responds in a way similar to that outlined in Nuti's scenario from nine years ago, this time ever more resembling the market economies of Latin American-type rather than those of West European type (Kolodko [10]).

So, expectations of rapid stabilization cannot come true. Especially impossible are quick systemic transformation and rapid institutional and structural changes (Kornai [16]). But with all this, the question about the transition path from one system to another, important for many post-communist countries, still remains unanswered. Poland's example shows the impossibility of direct transi-

---

(3) I have drawn attention to this problem, among other things, in my debate with J.D. Sachs (KOLODKO - SACHS [13]), in pointing out the danger of so-called "latinization" of the difficult process of economic and political reforms. This danger threatens not only Poland but the whole of Eastern and Central Europe as well as the Soviet Union.

tion from a crisis typical of the state-controlled socialist economy finding its fullest expression in the shortageflation syndrome to an equilibrated capitalist economy not involved in crisis. The path is much more tortuous, long and complicated, since it leads from shortageflation to sound market economy in a truly distant perspective only, first passing through stagflation and even slumpflation. It is not possible to enter the road of radical transformation into a market economy under conditions of a relatively well functioning socialist economy. The situation must deteriorate first, i.e. destabilize to such a degree that overcoming the crisis will not be possible without fundamental institutional transformation. Because it is only then that both the population and their governing elites will be ready for indispensable reforms.

But equally impossible is a direct transition from crisis (4) and shortageflation to an inflation-free and growing market economy. On this road there is continued inflation, however this time accompanied no longer by shortages but by recession and unemployment. Their proportions depend on many circumstances of which a part are of specific character typical of the systemic vacuum of the post-communist economy. However, in their majority these are symptoms well known from underdeveloped market economies. Thus, as illustrated in Graph 2, the shortageflation curve passes to the "other side of the mirror", i.e. to the other side of the Y-axis.

The inflation rate is dropping and shortages are being eliminated — though not always and not completely — but, at the same time, unemployment appears (5).

If these processes are also accompanied by recession — or even long-lasting depression — there will be transition from pathology characteristic of the command-type economy (shortageflation) to pathology typical of the market economy (slumpflation). It seems that in the period of transition to market economy it is not possible to avoid this arduous path. But the scale of crisis symptoms which are to

---

(4) I define this crisis as a general crisis of socialism, stressing in this way its invincibleness without fundamental institutional changes (KOLODKO [7]).

(5) Therefore, when assessing the scale of stabilization effects in Poland, one should compare not the price inflation rate of the former half of 1989 (8.5% monthly) with the inflation rate of the end of 1990 and the beginning of 1991 (about 6%) but the shortageflation rate (of 10-12% order) with the stagflation rate (over 12%), respectively.

GRAPH 2

SHIFT FROM SHORTAGEFLATION TO STAGFLATION

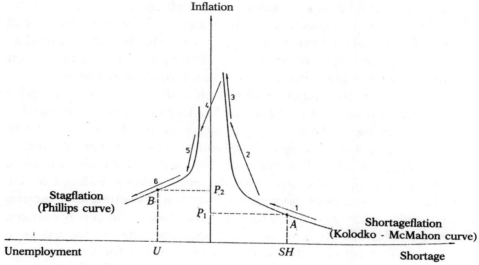

$P_1 + SH$: Rate of Shortageflation (A)
$P_2 + U$: Rate of Stagflation (B)

be met on this path is, in the first place, a function of the adopted policy of stabilization, systemic transformation and structural changes. In the case of the Polish path to a market economy, the errors of these policies led to transition from a particularly intensive shortageflation to an exceptionally big slumpflation. As I have shown, this has not been unavoidable, if the stabilization measures were not overshot.

10. - Perspectives

When talking about perspectives, the problem of time horizon arises at once. Over a longer period — estimated at many years — there is no reason why relatively optimistic forecasts and scenarios should not be framed. But over a short period a progress in the macroeconomic stabilization is hardly to be expected. The departure point — and this results from the hitherto conducted policies — is very unfavourable. Shortageflation sindrome has been replaced by slumpflation — and that with a very high rate of both inflation and recession. The inflation-versus-shortage trade-off has been replaced by inflation-versus-recession trade-off. Because of the above-mentioned time lag in the adjustment of employment reduction scale to production drop scale, the unemployment will continue to grow in the next period, even if the economy regains its growth momentum.

There is also much evidence that the acceleration of price inflation processes observed in the last three months of 1990 and at the beginning of 1991 is by no means bound to be of transient character, if a new complex stabilization package is not initiated.

Moreover, the adverse impact of the external situation must not be overlooked, in the first place the price inflation induced by the change in settlement principles between post-communist countries beginning with 1991 as well as by the rise in prices of energy carriers, in particular oil. It is to be added that the latter factor has been already to a certain extent accommodated during the last months of 1990. However, the uncertaity zone is still considerable and to a large extent dependent on changes in international conditions. Some of them could — and should — have been foreseen (transition from settlements in transfer roubles to settlements in US dollars and the resulting proinflationary and prorecessionary effects), others (oil shock caused by the Middle East conflict) have complicated the situation in an unforeseeable way.

But there also is a feedback link between the internal political situation — on the one hand — and the stabilization and transition — on the other hand. One can hardly expect this situation to be as favourable in the future as it was in the initial period of stabilization program implementation. Therefore, successive attempts at stabilization — since their necessity is beyond any doubt — can be ever more difficult.

The Polish experience of the implementation of stabilization policy should be particularly useful to other post-communist countries. They will face — or are already facing — many dilemmas which Poland has, better or worse, tried to solve. Not that the so-called Polish experiment has entailed such high social costs, it would be well if lessons learned from it were as widely as possible used by other countries.

GRAPH 3

INFLATION, ECONOMIC GROWTH AND REAL WAGES
IN 1981-1989

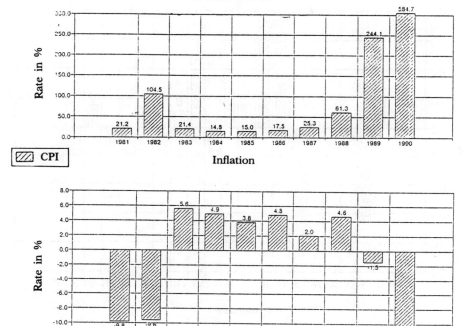

Inflation

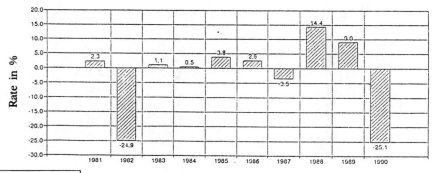

Economic growth

Real wages

Source: CENTRAL STATISTICAL OFFICE (GUS); MINISTRY OF FINANCE, NATIONAL BANK OF POLAND and own calculation.

GRAPH 4*A*

STATE BUDGET DEFICIT

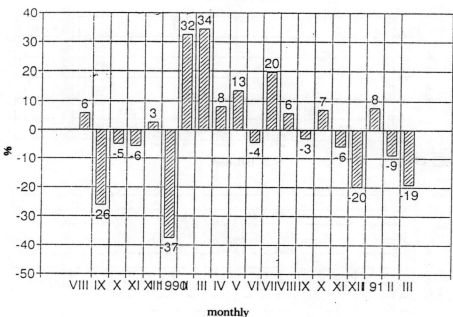

monthly

 Deficit

Source: CENTRAL STATISTICAL OFFICE (GUS); MINISTRY OF FINANCE, NATIONAL BANK OF POLAND and own calculation.

GRAPH 4*B*

STATE BUDGET DEFICIT

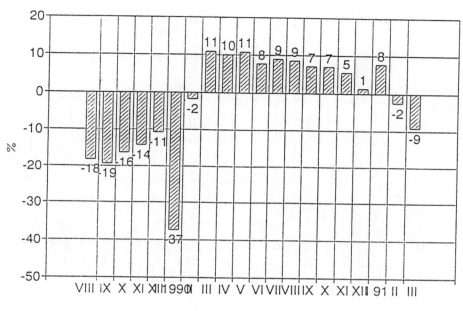

cumulative

▨ *Deficit*

Source: CENTRAL STATISTICAL OFFICE (GUS); MINISTRY OF FINANCE, NATIONAL BANK OF POLAND and own calculation.

Grzegorz W. Kolodko

GRAPH 5

PRICE AND WAGE INFLATION

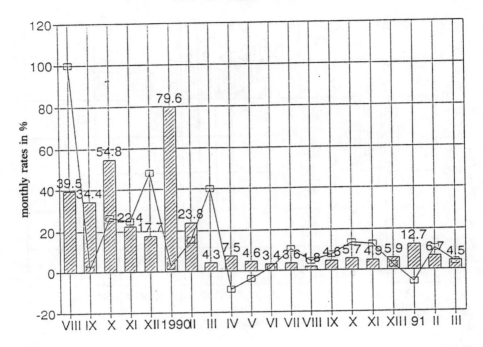

▨ Prices

–▱– Wages

Source: CENTRAL STATISTICAL OFFICE (GUS); MINISTRY OF FINANCE, NATIONAL BANK OF POLAND and own calculation.

GRAPH 6

PRICE AND WAGE INFLATION
(August 1989 = 100)

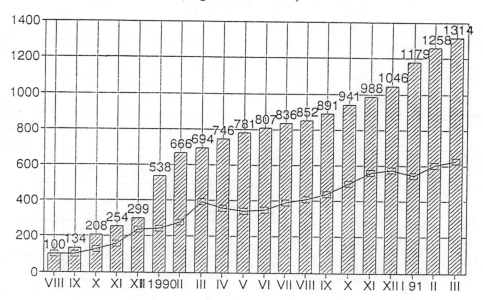

▨ Prices

—☐— Wages

Source: CENTRAL STATISTICAL OFFICE (GUS); MINISTRY OF FINANCE, NATIONAL BANK OF POLAND and own calculation.

GRAPH 7

MONTHLY INTEREST RATES

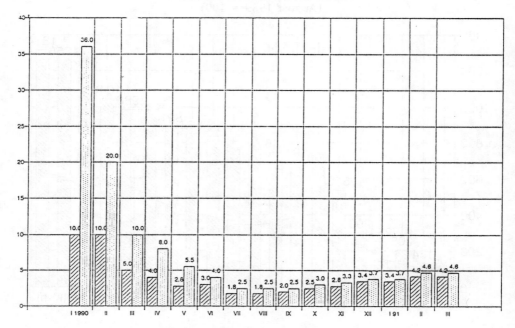

A: 3 month deposit   B: refinancing credit

▨ A
▦ B

Source: CENTRAL STATISTICAL OFFICE (GUS); MINISTRY OF FINANCE, NATIONAL BANK OF POLAND and own calculation.

GRAPH 8*A*

REAL INTEREST RATE BY AVERAGE
AND POINT-TO-POINT INDICES

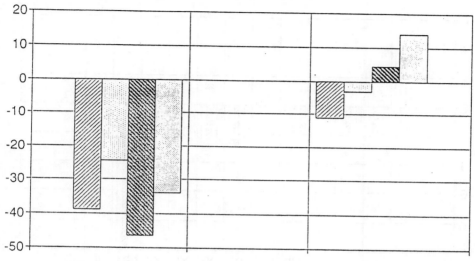

January 1990   February 1990

A: 3 month deposit   *B:* refinancing credit

▨ *A*-average

▧ *B*-average

▨ *A*-point

▨ *B*-point

Source: CENTRAL STATISTICAL OFFICE (GUS); MINISTRY OF FINANCE, NATIONAL BANK OF POLAND and own calculation.

GRAPH 8*B*

REAL INTEREST RATE BY AVERAGE
AND POINT-TO-POINT INDICES

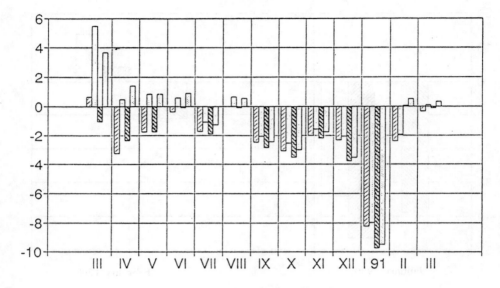

A: 3 month deposit   *B:* refinancing credit

▨ *A*-average

▨ *B*-average

▨ *A*-point

▨ *B*-point

Source: CENTRAL STATISTICAL OFFICE (GUS); MINISTRY OF FINANCE, NATIONAL BANK OF POLAND and own calculation.

GRAPH 9

REAL WAGES AND BALANCES
OF HOUSEHOLD
(July 1989 = 100)

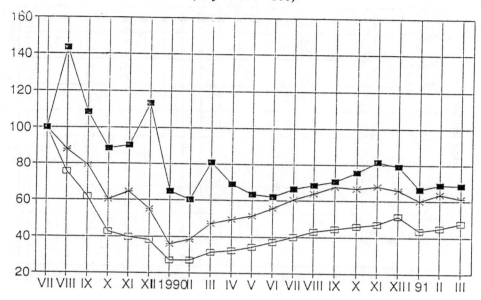

—■— wages

—▱— deposits

—✳— cash

Source: CENTRAL STATISTICAL OFFICE (GUS); MINISTRY OF FINANCE, NATIONAL BANK OF POLAND and own calculation.

GRAPH 10

OFFICIAL AND PARALLEL EXCHANGE RATE
(Current prices)

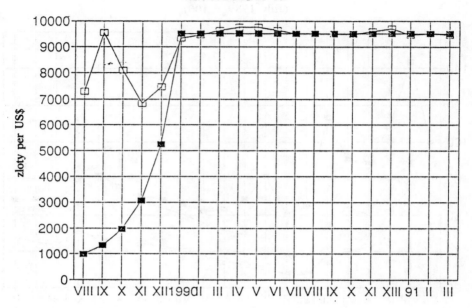

—■— official

—▱— parallel

Source: CENTRAL STATISTICAL OFFICE (GUS); MINISTRY OF FINANCE, NATIONAL BANK OF POLAND and own calculation.

GRAPH 11

OFFICIAL AND PARALLEL EXCHANGE RATE
(July 1989 prices)

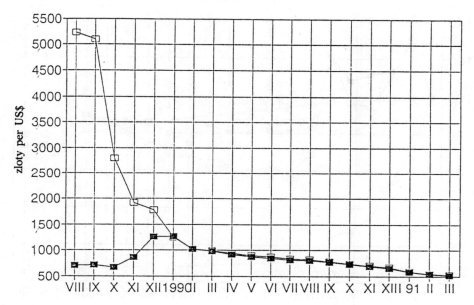

—■— official

—☐— parallel

Source: CENTRAL STATISTICAL OFFICE (GUS); MINISTRY OF FINANCE, NATIONAL BANK OF POLAND and own calculation.

GRAPH 12

HYPERINFLATION AND RECESSION
(July 1989 = 100)

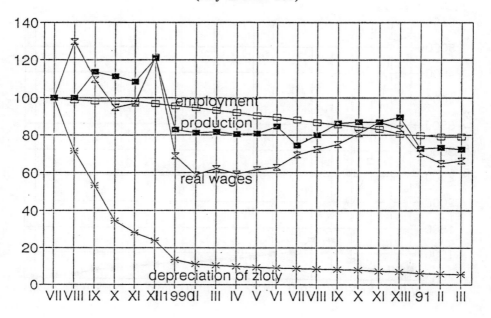

- ──■── production
- ──◻── employment
- ──✳── deprec zl
- ──◻── real wages

Source: CENTRAL STATISTICAL OFFICE (GUS); MINISTRY OF FINANCE, NATIONAL BANK OF POLAND and own calculation.

BIBLIOGRAPHY

[1] Bruno M. - Ditella G. - Dornbusch R. - Fischer S.: *Inflation Stabilization. The Experience of Israel, Argentina, Brazil, Bolivia and Mexico*, Cambridge, (Mass.) and London, MIT Press, 1988.

[2] Coricelli F. - Rocha R.: «Stabilization Programs in Eastern Europe: a Comparative Analysis of the Polish and the Yugoslav Programs of 1990», paper presented to the World Bank conference on *Adjustment and Growth: Lessons for Eastern Europe*, Poland, October 4-5, 1990.

[3] Dornbusch R. - Fischer S.: *Macroeconomics*, fifth edition, New York, Mc Graw-Hill, 1990.

[4] Fischer S. - Gelb A.: «Issues in Socialist Economy Reform», paper presented at the OECD conference on *The Transition to a Market Economy in the Central and Eastern Europe*, Paris, November 28-30, 1990.

[5] Frydman R. - Wellisz S. - Kolodko G.W.: «Stabilization in Poland: a Progress Report», final version of a paper presented at the conference on *Exchange Rate Policies of Less Developed Market and Socialist Economies*, Berlin, Freie Universitat, Berlin, May 10-12, 1990.

[6] Jorgensen E.A. - Gelb A. - Singh I.: «The Behavior of Polish Firms After the "Big bang": Findings from a Field Trip», paper presented at the OECD conference on *The Transition to a Market Economy in the Central and Eastern Europe*, Paris, November 28-30, 1990.

[7] Kolodko G.W.: «Crisis, Adjustment and Development in Socialist Economies: the Case of Poland», Varsavia, National Bank of Poland, Banking and Money Research Institute, *Paper*, n. 1, 1988.

[8] — —: «Economic Reforms and Inflation in Socialism: Determinants, Mutual Relationships and Prospects», *Communist Economies*, vol. 1, n. 2, 1989, pp. 167-181.

[9] — —: «Reform, Stabilization Policies, and Economic Adjustment in Poland», Helsinki, World Institute for Development Economics Research of the United Nations University, *WIDER Working Paper*, n. 51, 1989.

[10] — —: «Un futuro giapponese o un destino argentino per la Poland?», *L'opinione*, October 1990, pp. 21-30.

[11] — —: «Polish Hyperinflation and Stabilization 1989-1990», *Economics of Planning*, n. 1, forthcoming, 1991.

[12] Kolodko G.W. - McMahon W.W.: «Stagflation and Shortageflation: a Comparative Approach», *Kyklos*, vol. 40, n. 2, 1987, pp. 176-97; reprinted Borustein M. (ed.): *Comparative Economic Systems. Models and Cases*, cap. 26, Homewood (Ill.), Irwin, 1989, p. 429-46.

[13] Kolodko G.W. - Sachs J.D.: Comment on «The Patient is Ready», *The Warsaw Voice*, n. 52, December 24, 1989, p. 10.

[14] Kolodko G.W. - Gotz - Kozierkiewicz D. - Skrzeszewska - Paczek - E.: *Hyperinflation and Stabilization in Postsocialist Economies*, Dordrecht, Kluwer Academic Publishers, forthcoming, 1991.

[15] Kornai J.: *Economics of Shortage*, Amsterdam, North Holland, 1980.

[16] — —: *The Road to a Free Economy. Shifting from a Socialist System. The Example of Hungary*, New York and London, W.W. Norton, 1990.

[17] NUTI D.M.: «The Polish Crisis: Economics Factors and Constraints», in DREW-
     NOWSKI J. (ed.): *Crisis in Eastern European Economy. The Spread of Economic
     Disease*, London and Canberra, Croom Helm, New York, St. Martin Press, 1982.

[18] — —: «Crisis, Reform and Stabilization in Central Eastern Europe: Prospects and
     Western Response», in FITOUSSI J.P. (ed.): *Eastern Europe: the Transition*, Paris,
     forthcoming, 1990.

[19] ROSATI D.: «The Sequencing of Reforms and Policy Measures in the Transition
     from Central Planning to Market: the Polish Experience», paper presented at the
     OECD conference on *The Transition to a Market Economy in the Central and
     Eastern Europe*, Paris, November 28-30, 1990.

[20] SACHS J.D.: «A Tremor, not Necessarily a Quake, for Poland», *International
     Herald Tribune*, November 30, 1990, p. 8.

The Problems of Transition from a Socialist to a Market Economy in Yugoslavia

Mate Babić
University of Zagreb

1. - Introduction

The European economies are in the process of transition. West European economies are in the process of transition to monetary unification after 1992. Eastern European economies are in the process of changing structure, trying to make a transition from socialist into market economies.

The changes of economies that the process of transition initiates, cause a lot of problems. Economic problems are always the consequence of changes.

The transition from socialist to the market economy is neither simple nor easy. It has costs and benefits. In the short run, the costs are much higher than the benefits. In the longer run however, it is hoped that benefits would exceed costs.

Among the many costs of the transition, the most visible are uncertainty and unemployment. The increase of unemployment decreases the production.

According to the UN Commission for Europe, the recession in Eastern Europe in 1990 will result in the decline of industrial production by 20%. The intensity varies across countries. In Poland the decline will be 27%, in East Germany 40%, in Yugoslavia 10% etc.

The current account deficit of these countries in their trade with Eastern European countries increased from 4.3 to 10.1 bil USD.

Such high costs at the beginning of the process of transition frightened governments and some of them slowed down the pace of the process of transition.

For Yugoslavia, 1990 was the year of deepest crisis. Industrial production fell by more than 10%. This resulted in the increase of unemployment by 5% from January to October. Exports in the second half of the year were declining and imports rising due mainly to the high overvaluation of dinar, which amounted more than 90% in December 1990. Merchandise trade deficit amounted 4.1 bil USD which is about 50% more than planned. For the first time since 1982, current account balance in 1990 was in deficit. For 1991 the government plans again a current account deficit of 1.9 bil USD. The international reserves are declining, In the last two months of 1990 there was a rush on the banks by people to take out their foreign exchange deposits. When the banks were not able to satisfy their demands, the resulting panic destroyed the confidence in the banking system.

The inflation rate in 1990 expressed as the rise of consumer prices exceeded 120%.

All these developments destroyed the confidence in the stabilization program of December 1989, the main points of that stabilization program were: 1) price and wage freeze in the first half of 1990; 2) restrictive monetary policy; 3) restrictive fiscal policy; 4) fixed exchange rate of 7 Dinars for 1 DM.

In the first half of 1990, the government followed strictly the propositions of the program and everything seemed to be under control. The inflation rate was brought down to zero. But after defreezing prices and wages, in the second half of 1990, inflation revived, exports started to decline, imports to rise, and we had the results that I have just mentioned. The credibility of the stabilization program has been compromized and Yugoslavia is now entering a new inflationary process which could result again in hyperinflation like that in 1989.

Since 1985, every government in Yugoslavia formulated each year at least one stabilization program. All of them failed. We are now in a situation that it will be very difficult to regain the confidence in new stabilization programs no matter how consistent they may be.

In this situation, the transition from a socialist to a market economy in Yugoslavia is even more complicated, But it has to be done. Otherwise the long-term costs of non adaptation will be very high. The process of transition has to start immediately. Delaying it, will make things worse.

In my paper I tried to explain the causes of the problem of transition from a socialist to market economy in order to be able to give some recommendations as how to do it in order to make that process as smooth as possible. The paper is divided six parts: *Introduction*; *The Causes of the Structural Problems*; *The Need for Managers*; *The Problems of Privatization*; *The Role of the Government* and *Suggestions*.

2. - The Causes of the Structural Problems in Yugoslavia

After World War II, the Soviet economic system was totally transplanted to Yugoslavia and remained in force, officially, until 1950. The system was adopted without any regard to the considerable economic, sociopolitical and other differences between the two countries. The transplant did not take.

In 1950 that system was replaced with self-management socialism, which performed better than the transplanted one had. Many features of the administrative system, however, remained: investment decisions were still centralized; non-economic criteria were often used in investment allocations; the selection of managers was the same; goals of the enterprises had a high level of ambiguity; income, and exchange rates were controlled at the federal level. These features appeared to be the main barriers to healthy economic growth. Even though the growth rates in the 1950s were impressive, Yugoslav industry was still inefficient by international standards: Per capita output was low and the quality of goods was inferior.

The reform of 1965 was initiated in the hope of expanding the role of the market as one of the fundamental regulators of economic activity. The reform was to achieve five goals: improved efficiency in the use of scarce resources, modernization of plant and equipment, improved quality of production, increased share of international trade, and faster economic growth. Enterprises were to be granted a greater role in income distribution. A gradual freeing of international trade was to expose domestic industries to stiffer competition abroad and in turn make them more competitive in international markets. Inflation was to be controlled, multiple exchange rates abolished, and the dinar devalued.

Unfortunately the high hopes for the reform did not materialize. The policy measures that accompanied the reform resulted in the surfacing of the deep-rooted structural imbalances in the economy. Administrative price increases for primary products, intended to achieve parity with the prices of manufacturing goods, had a strong cost-push effect. Devaluation of the dinar reinforced these cost-push pressures. The policymakers were frightened by the course of events and by 1968 the reform was abandoned.

Yugoslavia continued attempts to reform the economy several times after 1965, in 1971, 1974, 1976. But the structure of the economy has not been substantially improved. It is the structure of Yugoslav economy that is the most difficult obstacle to the smooth transition from socialist to the market economy. This structure was built for 45 years and it is not to be expected that the structural problems of Yugoslav economy will be solved within the short time period. This is why the process of transition from socialist to the market economy in Yugoslavia will be neither quick nor smooth.

The structural problems of the economy in Yugoslavia as well as in other Eastern European countries, are due mainly to the marxist doctrine. The essence of this doctrine is the faster development of the so-called Section I (the production of the means of production) in the process of economic development. All Eastern European countries strictly followed this pattern of development. The high share of industrial products in their foreign trade (over 90%), which is the characteristic of all these countries is the direct consequence of such development.

The faster development of the sector of production of means of production was achieved by channelling most of their investments into it. So the financial markets were not supposed neither to function nor to exist. Agriculture and the consumer sector were relatively neglected.

The disequilibrium in growth caused shortages of consumer goods on the domestic market with a high degree of instability.

In order to "prevent" the disequilibrium in the internal markets, especially in the market for the consumption goods, the price system was suspended. Central planning was introduced to substitute the price system in its informative and allocative functions. The logical result was complete distorsion of the price system. In order to preserve price stability, the pervasive control of the price system was introduced. But, the stability of the distorted prices meant more the stability of distorted economic system than the stability of prices. The logical consequence of price control, the black market, was able to challenge the stability of the prices but not the stability of the distorted economic structure of the whole system.

In order to ensure the "stability" of the system, the management personnel of enterprises was selected in a special way. The managers to be selected had to be able to realise the directives from above. They were supposed only to monitor enterprise operations. This is why the main criterion in the selection of the managers was their "obediency". By strictly following the directives they helped the smooth functioning of the system. Any initiative of the manager to improve the technological process, cost structure, output structure etc. was not tolerated because this would endanger the whole system of central planning.

Managers of such business are typically not paid on the basis of profitability and cost containment, and therefore have no particular reason to run the business efficiently. The combination of complicated and perhaps conflicting goals and unclear management incentives produced inefficiency and losses.

The relatively high ambiguity of goals in socialist enterprises like in all socially owned enterprises, SOEs, also makes it difficult to link the managers' reward to a well-defined performance measure. Managers attempted to steer the enterprise toward goals that maximize their own utilities.

The best "obedient" managers were the persons of trust of the party in power. The enterprises were an extremely convenient way for party bosses and government officials to provide employment for their friends and supporters. Of course, close friends and relatives were included. So nepotism and corruption were not unknown in this system.

International trade in Yugoslavia was for a long period of time directly or indirectly state controlled.

The main instruments of control were import and export quotas and licences and the system of foreign exchange allocations. Bilateral treaties especially with the so called "clearing currency area" implemented under tight government control have created supply monopolies. New and superior products have been discouraged. Export industries have been locked into an uneconomic output structure and outmoded product and process technologies, which have made them uncompetitive in the hard currency area of the world market. This is the main reason why Yugoslavia now faces severe supply restrictions and lack of export marketing, know-how and infrastructure.

The biggest constraints on competition were inappropriate macroeconomic, trade, and industrial policies. These include over-valued exchange rates, import quotas and bans, foreign exchange allocation systems, high tariffs, price controls, investment licensing, and regulations on entry and exit.

The results of this system are well known: suboptimal allocation of resources, inefficiency in production, decreasing standard of living etc. Such an environment makes the process of transition of the Yugoslav economy into a market one very difficult.

3. - The Need for Managers

The transition from a socialist to a market-oriented economy involves changing attitudes, institutions, and organizations. The most important problem of transition from socialist to market economies is how to assure an adequate supply of innovation and enterpreneurs i.e. how to assure an adequate supply of the new ideas and people who think in a new way.

The success of any enterprise depends on creativity, flexibility, and hard work, particularly of its top managers. Governments should therefore hire top-quality enterepreneurs and managers and should design the organization in such a way as to shield these people from undue political and bureaucratic interference.

The manager is the person who organizes production, introduces new ideas or processes, makes the business decisions, and is held accountable for success or failure. This is why the most urgent need not only in Yugoslavia but also in all East European countries is for good managers. In the short-run, this problem could be solved by hiring teams of managers from abroad. But in the long-run, indigenous entrepreneurs should be ready to take over. They should posses managerial skills and courage to assume financial risk. Therefore a sufficient number of managers should be created. The most efficient aid to these countries would be the education of managers.

4. - The Problems of Privatization

To some extent, the reasons why socialist, as well as public enterprises in market economy, generally do less well than their private counterparts are due to the difference inherent in their ownership. These include the fact that the directors of socialist as well as of public enterprises in market economics have no financial stake in the business. They have limited threat of bankruptcy and reorganization, because of the easy recourse that these enterprises have to government finance. Moreover, there is political opposition to reducing payrolls, even when financial conditions suggest that is needed.

When such a firm is driven into loss, the government injects more and more capital into it and tries to retain staff by paying them higher and higher salaries.

This is also one of the important causes of the poor performance of state companies.

These reasons suggested the solution of most (if not all) problems of Yugoslav economy, as well as the economies of the East European Countries, by the process of privatization of SOEs.

The idea of privatization has become very fashionable in the former socialist economies including Yugoslavia. It has become equally fashionable as the idea of nationalization after the second world war. Sometimes privatization is taken as *panacea* which will solve all structural problems of East European countries. Very frequently a privatization is suggested as the most efficient way of transformation of a socialist into market economy.

There is no disagreement among economists that the Yugoslav and other East European economies are less efficient than the West European market economies due the differences in political and economic systems. The disagreements begin about the ways and means of how to transform the former into the latter.

The privatization of enterprises is an important aspect, but not the only one and not even the most important one in transition from socialist to market economies. In other words, privatization matters, and matters very much, but not only privatization.

We cannot expect that the problems of Yugoslav and other East European economies will disappear simply by handing enterprises over to the private sector. In these countries the private sector is undeveloped and when it exists, it is very imperfect. So we have the choice between imperfect public sector and imperfect private sector, not between economically inefficient public and economically efficient private sector.

Privatization of enterprises should go hand in hand with their restructuring.

Restructuring of enterprises must precede privatization. If enterprises are sold before restructuring, bidders will want a substantial discount to compensate for the uncertainty. The restructuring could be accomplished within a relatively short period, but privatization will take longer, partly because of a lack of buyers, and the need to work out administrative arrangemets.

Privatization is complicated and difficult.

First, there is the problem of finding people willing to purchase firms that appear to private investors that, with a different managment approach, the firm can succeed despite its unhappy history.

Second, there is the problem of the determination of the price of socially owned enterprise. The fair price for an enterprise depends on its future profitability. But what would be the price of loss making (value substracting) enterprises that are in overwhelming majority in Yugoslavia? Namely, the amount of losses exceeded the amount of accumulation in 1990 in Yugoslavia by more than 2.5 times. In this case it is suggested that the price of such an enterprise should be determined on the basis of the value of its assets. This approach faces also many problems, because the book value of a firm in Yugoslavia has usually only historical interest. Therefore, a firm's assets must be evaluated anew. And this takes time and effort.

Even when these problems are solved, some others arise. Investors must believe that they will be able to run business freely as a normal private firm, if they are to be attracted as bidders. In particular, they must be free to eliminate unnecessary workers, have the freedom of price determination according the market conditions, and otherwise pursue the policy aiming at maximization of profits. Namely, very often, a government tries to sell an enterprise for an attractive price and then limit its freedom of operation in ways that compromise its profitability. Moreover, governments often try to sell the losers and not to sell the profit-making enterprises.

The main objective of the transition from socialist economies is to introduce a high degree of competition in order to increase its efficiency. There are two ways to achieve this. Liberalization of imports is one approach, and creating a number of private firms in the domestic economy is another.

The domestic market and domestic business ought to be exposed *rapidly* to international competition. The opening of the economies should be immediate because the slow and gradual approach will *de facto* be chronic insulation from competitive pressures in international markets.

The final problem with privatization is political. Privatization entails change which is often seen as a source of increased uncertainty. The workers and managers often oppose privatization because they are afraid that they may lose their jobs. Some political leaders oppose it because of the loss of their direct influence over part of the economy. Consumers might oppose the process of privatization because they believe that prices might rise. Some political leaders point out that privatization might result in the creation of a new class of capitalists with "exploitation" and the unjust distribution of national income as a consequence.

There are many proposals concerning the techniques of privatization: the selling of shares; the distribution of shares to every citizen or to employees; a combination of the two, etc. Each has its advantages and disavantages.

The solution to distribute shares to the workers and so make them private owners aims primarily at the creation of the ownership incentives. But, due to the differences in capital intensity in different industries, workers would receive very different capital values. Those working in factories will receive more than those in agriculture and services. What about unemployed and those employed abroad? Besides, the experience shows that the workers try to sell the shares for cash. This is why in Yugoslavia the federal government attempted to compel workers by law to purchase shares by deducting their values from wages. That provoked furious reaction on the part of workers and this system simply did not work.

The diffusion of stock ownership among a large number of people tends to protect entrenched management, because it is difficult or impossible for such a large group of investors to organize a majority to force such managers out of the business.

Besides, there is the question whether the workers in the system of self management who (at least in theory) manage the enterprises and distribute the profits, would behave differently when they become small owners. The question boils down to whether this transformation will improve the efficiency of the enterprises.

Another approach is that all firms ought to be transformed into state enterprises in order to sell them gradually to domestic and foreign investors. Due to inferior results of SOE compared to comparable private enterprises, this approach loses grounds. What has to be done is to transform the state firms into independent decision makers, to create an environement for entrepreneurship.

Lastly, the approach to privatize all enterprises has become very attractive. The privatization should be done as soon as possible. But the process of overall privatization should be controlled and conducted very carefully. I prefer the "guided" to "spontaneous" privatization.

A great number of small establishments (village, shops, restaurant, repairshops, service stablishments, appartments), often unprofitable parts of larger firms, could be sold immediately to individuals and cooperatives, perhaps on the basis of installment credit and mortgage. The rest of the firms may be controlled by a certain amount of holding companies owned mostly by banks. For this reason and due to the extremely bad performances of the banks in Yugoslavia, the most urgent need of the aid from Western countries is for good bank managers from these countries.

The main goals that the process of privatization should achieve is to increase the efficiency of enterprises and to get fresh investment funds in order to create new job opportunities especially for workers that will lose their jobs due to the process of privatization. These goals suggest that the increase of the efficiency through the process of restructuring of enterprises should precede privatization and that privatization should take the form of selling the enterprise to private businessmen. The proceeds should be used to generate new jobs to replace those which are being phased out.

5 - The Role of Government

What should be the role of the government in the process of restructuring and transition of socialist to the market economy? The fundamental precondition for economic efficiency is political democracy. Political democracy is necessary, but not a sufficient condition for the increase of efficiency of an economy and for the transition from a socialist to market economy.

The governments have to set the rules of the game which define the use, ownership and transfer of physical, financial and intellectual assets. The more certain these rules, the better they are defined and understood, the more smoothly the process of transition will be.

The governments should set very clear rules for privatization and design the control system as simple as possible. The wider the controls, the harder they are to enforce.

Management must have clearly defined goals to achieve, and incentives to run the business profitably, and the power to make the decisions to achieve these goals.

Although the privatization should be overwhelming, some enterprises should be kept in the ownership of the state (1).

---

(1) The reasons for the maintenance of enterprises in state ownership are: 1) banks are often publicity owned so that the government controls the allocations of loans; 2) natural monopolies; 3) when industries produce sizable positive externalities; 4) valuable natural resources; 5) state ownership is also justified on the grounds of generating savings; 6) a desire to force investment into backward regions of a country; 7) saving jobs in a failing private business is another reason for privatization involvement.

Because of its complexity, the transformation of socialist economy into market economy in Yugoslavia will raise many difficult questions.

The questions to be answered in the process of restructuring in the Yugoslav and Eastern European economies are:

1) how to define the competitive advantage in order to improve the gains from international trade?;

2) how to improve the quality of the products and their competitiveness on the world market?;

3) how to decrease per unit costs, especially the relatively high costs of energy which are twice that in OECD?;

4) how to change the monopolistic structure of the economy?;

5) how to decrease the relatively high environmental costs of production?;

6) how to remove distortions caused by the administratively determined pricing structure?;

7) how to establish a social safety net to mitigate the effects of unemployment and other costs of transition?;

8) how to reform the financial system i.e. how to increase the competition in the financial sector?;

9) how to remove restrictions on private economic activity, i.e. how to change the structure of the ownership?;

10) how to change the fiscal system in order to create an environment to attract foreign investment?

In order to start the successful process of restructuring their economies, Yugoslavia as well as the other East European countries will need assistance from developed Western countries and from international organizations.

The assistance from the West to these countries should be in the form of training of managers to run market economy and in the form of fresh money for investment.

Fresh money is needed in order to create new jobs and thus mitigate the social problems of transition of which unemployment is the most difficult one. Foreign direct investment is crucial for the process of transition from socialist to market economy, because it brings in capital, know-how, management and marketing. But domestic reform must precede any assistance and be the precondition for it. Massive unconditional financial aid to Eastern European countries could be counterproductive because it would allow these countries to delay the transformation of their economies into the market one.

6. - Suggestions Instead of a Conclusion

The problems of transition are here to stay for a long period of time. The governments in Yugoslavia and in other Eastern European countries lack the knowledge, institutions and financial means to perform this process smoothly and quickly. This volume is likely to be one among many that will discuss the problems of transition from socialist to market economies. The result of any such conference should be a set of messages that could alleviate the process of transition. This is the reason why I shall try to formulate such a message from this Conference in the form of a set of suggestions to the Eastern European governments in order to help them to carry out the process of transition of their economies from socialist to the market ones. The suggestions are given in the following twelve points: 1) define the goal of the management as the maximization of profit and hire (or educate) qualified managers; 2) introduce the market for goods, services and factors (labor and capital); 3) make complete price liberalisation; 4) open the economy to foreign competition, and adopt a realistic rate of exchange; 5) privatize the economy in the highest possible degree and as soon as possible; 6) define property rights and bankruptcy laws (and enforce them); 7) change the structure of production according to the comparative advantages; 8) establish a safety net for the jobless; 9) reform a tax system, make it more transparent and make it compatible with the European one; 10) speed up the development of financial markets; 11) speed up the development of a modern banking system with an independent central bank; 12) get new capital (domestic and foreign) to open new jobs and to change the structure of the economy.

BIBLIOGRAPHY

[1] BABIĆ M.: «Yugoslav External Debt. A Constraint for Macroeconomic Policy» in SINGER H.W. - SHARMA S. (eds.): *Economic Development and World Debt*, London, MacMillan, 1989, pp. 219-24.

[2] BABIĆ M. - PRIMORAC E.: «Some Causes of the Growth of the Yugoslav External Debt», London, *Soviet Studies*, n. 1, 1986, pp. 69-88.

[3] LEVY B.: «A Theory of Public Enterprise Behaviour», *Journal of Economic Behaviour and Organization*, n. 8, 1987, pp. 75-96.

[4] PRIMORAC E. - BABIĆ M.: «Systemic Changes and Unemployment Growth in Yugoslavia 1965-1984», *Slavic Review 48*, n. 2, 1989, pp. 195-213.

[5] RAMANURTI R.: «Controlling State-Owner Enterprises», *Public Enterprise*, February 1987, pp. 99-117.

[6] VERNON R.: *The Promise of Privatization*, Washington (DC), The Council on Foreign Relations, 1988.

Planning Authority and Enterprise in the Soviet Transition: A Principal-Agent Model

Claudio De Vincenti (*)
Università «La Sapienza», Roma

1. - Introduction

A key problem in the Soviet economic crisis is increasing shortage in the official consumer markets. This phenomenon certainly stems from the excess dynamics of aggregate demand due to government deficit and monetary indiscipline, which have long characterized the Soviet economy and have worsened in the last years. Yet today it also suffers from the consequences of a sharp disruption in the administrative supply system, which is cutting off the provisions which normally go to the official markets, for sale at controlled prices. Certainly the political situation in the USSR can partially explain this disruption: nationalist conflicts, strikes, difficulties of the Communist Party in mobilizing people for harvesting, the strengthening of illegal organizations, and so on. But it also seems very likely that, above all, specific economic factors have created troubles in the administrative supply system.

The purpose of this paper is to analyze whether the changes in the center-firm relationship, which have been occurring as a result of the economic measures adopted in recent years, could eventually

(*) This research is part of a project on *Ruble Convertibility and Opening Up of Eastern Europe Economies* financed by Università «La Sapienza», Roma and conducted by Prof. Marcello De Cecco. The author is very grateful to C.A. Bollino, G. Calcagnini, M. Gallegati, A.M. Simonazzi, and S. Zecchini, for careful reading of the paper's first draft and for useful comments. Obviously, all responsibility for any eventual error or inaccuracy is expressly the author's.

Advise: the numbers in square brackets refer to the Bibliography in the appendix.

affect the firm's behaviour in an undesired manner, given the USSR's current macroeconomic situation. Such a negative influence would cause an output diversion from the administrative supply system, and from the provision of goods at controlled prices, towards transactions at free prices on official or unofficial markets. If this is the case, a further aim of this paper is to help to devise remedies and ways of further developing economic reform.

Our attention will center on the relationship between planning authority and the State-owned firm, and on the corresponding incentive structure for the enterprise's manager, as this is a crucial point in order to understand the reasons for the disruptions in the administrative supply system. We will not consider herein the problems connected with the development of other forms of enterprise allowed by Soviet economic reform (1).

In order to compare the new incentive structure and the traditional one, we will adopt a principal-agent theoretical framework, with a risk-neutral principal (the center) and a risk-averse agent (the manager). Under some very simplified hypotheses we will obtain a diagrammatic representation, which enables us to clear up the most important properties of the old incentive scheme and the new one.

Paragraph 2 presents a simplified static principal-agent model, which provides a stylized formalization of the incentive structure that traditionally characterized — consistently with the prevalently administrative system for the economy's management — the planner-firm relationship in the Soviet Union, before the recent economic reforms. We will simplify the model using some hypotheses on the feasible levels of effort and outcome, and on the probability distribution of outcomes. Under these assumptions, the old incentive scheme approaches a second-best contract between the center and the manager, namely a contract optimal under the constraint resulting from the agent's invisible action.

Therefore, we can devise a rationale for this traditional incentive structure. Certainly, the administrative system of the economy's management can exhibit several known allocative and X-inefficiencies, which we will not consider here. Yet our principal-agent model

---

(1) For a theoretical analysis of some problems connected with the Soviet liberalization process, see MARRESE [13].

shows that we can expect that the incentive scheme, consistent with this form of economic management, guarantees a reasonably regular functioning of the material supply system.

In paragraph 3 we propose a simplified formalization of the incentive structure which seems to emerge from the present process of Soviet economic reform. It is consistent with the political requirement for a gradual marketization of the Soviet economy, which should have several advantages from the allocative and X efficiency points of view, although we should not underestimate the specific efficiency problems that can also arise in a prevailingly market system. These problems and the policies necessary to face them will not be considered in this paper, which will center only on the consequences of the new incentive structure on the functioning of the administrative supply system during the transitional period. For this purpose, in paragraph 3 we will fit our principal-agent model to the new incentive system and we will verify its effectiveness to ensure regular deliveries from enterprise to the administrative bodies. We will see that, with the new incentive structure, the center loses an informational tool regarding the firm's actual level of output and therefore needs a new informational tool (fiscal system). Failing this additional tool, an information problem arises, yielding several important undesired consequences when there is a strong excess demand for goods at controlled prices: in this case, the positive effects of the new incentive system are jeopardized by the informative loss implied for the planner; a disruption in the administrative supply system can arise, with several negative consequences on the supply of goods at controlled prices.

Paragraph 4 is devoted to briefly deriving some conclusive notes from the previous paragraph's analysis, concerning the economic measures necessary for the functioning of the administrative supply network, during the present transitional period from a prevalently administrative system to a prevalently market system.

2. - A Model for the Traditional Incentive Structure

Here we will adopt a very simplified formalization of the traditional Soviet incentive structure, based on a single success indicator consisting of the quantity produced and delivered to the administrative supply bodies (to simplify our analysis, we are leaving out other indicators such as labour productivity, reduction in average costs, quality of goods, and so on, due to their relatively minor importance in the Soviet experience). Moreover, we will consider the firms as a single agent and the manager's objective-function as the enterprise's objective-function. Finally we will assume that all the bonuses can be reduced in terms of money.

The planning authority fixes an output target y^* for the firm's deliveries to the administrative supply system and a bonus B^* for the manager, contingent on the fulfilment of the target. In the case of underfulfilment, the bonus is sharply reduced to a basic level $\underline{B}$, which can also equal zero. In the case of overfulfilment, instead, the bonus grows with the output delivered to the administrative bodies, according to a simple linear function:

$$B = B^* + \beta (y - y^*)$$

Therefore, this traditional incentive structure combines a dichotomous part of contract with a linear one.

Let us analyze what may be seen as the rationale of this traditional structure. First, we will consider the incentive problem in a general principal (planner) — agent (manager) framework. Then, we will introduce some very specific assumptions which will enable us to handle the model in an easier diagrammatic form, and then to compare in the next paragraph the properties of this traditional incentive scheme with those of the new one.

Our basic general hypotheses are: the firm's equipment, material inputs and labour are given; output y is a function of the manager's effort e and of a random variable Θ, with a density function known to both parties; the effort affects the density function, increasing the probability of high output levels and decreasing that of low output levels, but not the "floor" y_L and the "ceiling" y_H for y; the authority observes outcome y but not effort e and the actual value of Θ. Therefore, we are adopting a cumulative distribution function for y such as $F(y; e)$ on $[y_L, y_H]$, with density $f(y; e) > 0$. We assume that: for $e_2 > e_1 \ F(y; e_2) < F(y; e_1)$, namely $f(y; e_2) > f(y; e_1)$ for the highest output levels and $f(y; e_2) < f(y; e_1)$ for the lowest ones.

The principal's optimization problem, when he is risk-neutral, will be:

$$\max \ EW = Ey - EB = \int_{y_L}^{y_H} [y - B(y)] \, f(y \, ; e) \, dy$$

s.t. $EU = EU[B(y), e] \geq U_o$ (participation constraint)

     $e \ = \text{argmax} \ EU[B(y), e]$ (incentive-compatibility constraint)

where $B(y)$ is the reward function for the manager expressed in terms of purchasing power on output, $U[B(y), e]$ his utility function — assumed strictly concave in B according to an income risk aversion hypothesis for the agent — and U_0 is the reservation level for manager's utility. It is known that solving this problem is, in general, a very complex task and that few general results can be derived without some specific assumptions (2). A standard result in the agency literature is that, under the hypothesis of an increasing likelihood ratio f_e/f, the optimal reward is an increasing function of observed outcomes (3).

In order to analyse in a diagrammatic form the properties of the traditional Soviet incentive structure, we will adopt some highly simplified hypotheses such as: there are only three feasible values for y, that is $y_L < y_M < y_H$, and only three feasible levels of effort $e_1 < e_2 < e_3$. Let us indicate with P_L, P_M and P_H the respective probabilities of the three hypothesized levels of y, where obviously: $P_L + P_M + P_H = 1$. Let us indicate with P_{1L} the probability value for y_L when the effort level is e_1, with P_{2L} the probability value for y_L when $e = e_2$, and so on. We will assume:

$$P_{1L} < P_{1M} = P_{1H}$$
$$P_{2L} < P_{1L} < P_{1M} = P_{1H} < P_{2M} = P_{2H}$$
$$P_{3L} = P_{2L} < P_{1L} \leq P_{3M} \leq P_{1M} = P_{1H} < P_{2M} = P_{2H} < P_{3H}$$

---

(2) See Grossman-Hart [4].

(3) See Holmstrom [5], Milgrom [14], Grossman-Hart [4], Rogerson [20], Tirole [21], pp. 51-5. For an interpretation of the general theoretical role played by the principal-agent approach, see Arrow [1].

Assuming that the target fixed by the center for the firm is $y^* = y_M$, the center's objective-function can be written as:

$$EW = P_L\,(y_L - \underline{B}) + P_M(y_M - B^*) + P_H\,[y_H - B^* - \beta\,(y_H - y_M)]$$

Let us assume that the manager's utility function is additive-separable in income and effort, is homogeneous in income, and that, indicating with $v(e)$ the disutility of effort, we have:

$$U = u\,(B) - v\,(e)$$
$$u\,(0) = 0 \qquad u' > 0 \qquad u'' < 0$$
$$v\,(e_1) = 0 \qquad v' > 0 \qquad v'' > 0$$

The manager's optimization problem is then:

$$\max\, EU = Eu\,(B) - v\,(e) =$$
$$= P_L\,u\,(\underline{B}) + P_M\,u\,(B^*) + P_H\,u\,[B^* + \beta\,(y_H - y_M)] - v\,(e)$$

Under our simplifying hypotheses, the agent's optimization problem comes down to the choice between only three feasible levels of effort and of his expected utility:

$$E_1 U = E_1\,u\,(B) - v\,(e_1) =$$
$$= P_{1L}\,u\,(\underline{B}) + P_{1M}\,u\,(B^*) + P_{1H}\,u\,[B^* + \beta\,(y_H - y_M)] - v\,(e_1)$$

$$E_2 U = E_2\,u\,(B) - v\,(e_2) =$$
$$= P_{2L}\,u\,(\underline{B}) + P_{2M}\,u\,(B^*) + P_{2H}\,u\,[B^* + \beta\,(y_H - y_M)] - v\,(e_2)$$

$$E_3 U = E_3\,u\,(B) - v\,(e_3) =$$
$$= P_{3L}\,u\,(\underline{B}) + P_{3M}\,u\,(B^*) + P_{3H}\,u\,[B^* + \beta\,(y_H - y_M)] - v\,(e_3)$$

The agent will prefer e_3 to e_2 when $E_3 u\,(B) - E_2 u\,(B) \geq v\,(e_3) - v\,(e_2)$ and e_2 to e_1 when $E_2 u\,(B) - E_1 u\,(B) \geq v\,(e_2) - v\,(e_1)$.

Let us examine how the center can find the values for $\underline{B}$, B^* and β, which induce the manager to choose the level of effort which maximizes the center's objective-function. We can solve this problem using a two dimensional diagram and proceeding through two analytical steps. First, we can identify on the (y_M, y_L) plane the optimal levels for $\underline{B}$ and $\tilde{B}$, where $\tilde{B}$ can be interpreted temporarily as a hypothetical bonus which the manager can achieve when output is y_M or alternatively y_H: in the subsequent step we will see that $\tilde{B}$ must be interpreted as the certainty equivalent for the manager, given $P_{2L} = P_{3L}$ and $\underline{B}$, of the prospect $[P_{3M}, P_{3H}; B^*, B^* + \beta(y_H - y_M)]$.

Graph 1a shows the agent's indifference curves between $\underline{B}$ contingent on y_L, and $\tilde{B}$, contingent on the achievement of y_M or y_H. The agent's origin is O_A and the principal's origin is O_{PM} when the horizontal dimension of the box is y_M, and O_{PH} when this dimension is y_H. $U_0{}^1$ represents the manager's indifference curve showing pairs of value $(\underline{B}, \tilde{B})$ which yield for expected utility the reservation level U_0 when effort is e_1. Its slope on the agent's certainty line $O_A C_A$, in absolute value, is $[(P_{1M} + P_{1H})/P_{1L}]$. $U_0{}^2$ and $U_0{}^3$ are the indifference curves for $U = U_0$ when effort is respectively e_2 and e_3. Their slope on the certainty line is $[(P_{2M} + P_{2H})/P_{2L}] = [(P_{3M} + P_{3H})/P_{3L}]$ (for hypothesis, $P_{2L} = P_{3L}$ and, therefore, $P_{2M} + P_{2H} = P_{3M} + P_{3H}$).

Point b gives us the pair $(\underline{B}, \tilde{B})$. It is known from the agency theory that the optimal (second best) contract can be found at a point such as a, where it is just equivalent for the agent to exert effort e_2 rather than effort e_1 and risk-sharing is the closest to the first best one (which would be along the agent's certainty line) (4). A point such as b would be not optimal if bonus $\tilde{B}$ is offered to the manager both when he achieves y_M and when he achieves y_H: indeed in this case the agent will prefer to exert effort e_2 as in point a. Yet point b can result as optimal if the meaning of $\tilde{B}$ is not that of a warranted bonus both for y_M and for y_H but that of the certainty equivalent for the manager of the prospect $[(P_{3M}, P_{3H}; B^*, B^* + \beta (y_H - y_M)]$, given $P_{2L} = P_{3L}$ and $\underline{B}$.

Graph 1b shows the manager's indifference curves between B^*, contingent on y_M, and $B^* + \beta(y_H - y_M)$, contingent on y_H, given the bonus $\underline{B}$ obtained in Graph 1a and contingent on y_L. If bonus $\tilde{B}$ is offered to the manager both when he achieves y_M and when he achieves y_H, he is on his certainty line $O_A C_A$ at a point such as d, where the indifference curve $U_0{}^3$ crosses the certainty line with a

---

(4) See for example RICKETTS [19], chapter 5.

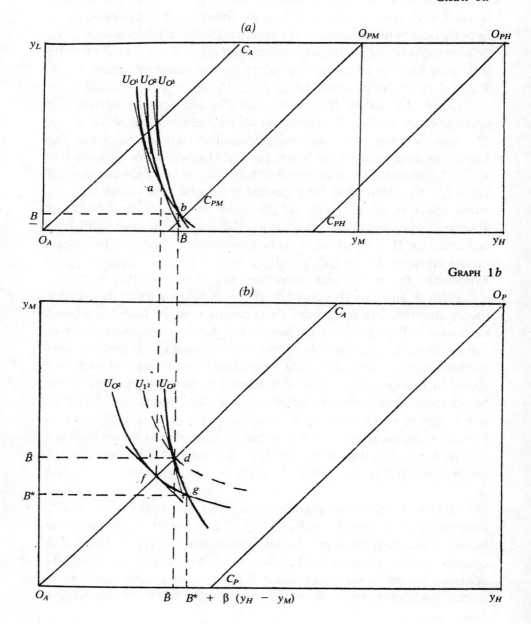

slope equal, in absolute value, to (P_{3H}/P_{3M}). In this case, the agent prefers to exert e_2 because the corresponding indifference curve U_1^2, which passes through point d with a slope $1 = (P_{2H}/P_{2M}) > (P_{3H}/P_{3M})$ (for hypothesis), involves a utility level $U_1 > U_0$. The indifference curve, involving the reservation utility level U_0 when the effort is e_2, is U_0^2, which crosses the certainty line in point f. If the center wants to induce effort e_3 it has to offer the manager a contract such as point g in Graph 1b, fixing a bonus for y_M equal to B^* and a greater bonus for y_H. Point g allows the principal to fix coefficient β for the target's overfulfilment. The indifference curve U_0^3 in Graph 1b shows that $\tilde{B}$ obtained in Graph 1a has to be considered as the certainty equivalent of the prospect $[P_{3M}, P_{3H}; B^*, B^* + \beta(y_H - y_M)]$, given $P_{2L} = P_{3L}$ and $\underline{B}$:

$$(P_{2M} + P_{2H})\, u\, (\tilde{B}) = (P_{3M} + P_{3H})\, u\, (\tilde{B}) =$$
$$= P_{3M} u\, (B^*) + P_{3H}\, u\, [B^* + \beta\, (y_H - y_M)]$$

The previous analysis shows a result quite analogous to that standard in agency literature: the agent's reward is an increasing function of the realized outcome. We do not yet have an explanation for the dichotomous part of the incentive scheme: why should the bonus be sharply reduced for any $y < y_M$, with a step from B^* to $\underline{B}$?

A first, limited answer to this question can be found by observing that in Graph 1a, given the slopes of indifference curves U_0^2 and U_0^3 (that is the $(P_M + P_H)/P_L$ ratio resulting from an effort greater than e_1), the stronger the slope of indifference curve U_0^1 is (namely the $(P_M + P_H)/P_L$ ratio when effort is at its lowest level e_1), the more point b shifts downward and to the right. So, the greater the slope of U_0^1 curve is, the greater the probability is that $(B^* - \underline{B}) > \beta(y_M - y_L)$, with an asymmetric bonuses' response to the output level and a kinked reward function at target y^*: indeed, in this case the difference between $\tilde{B}$ and $\underline{B}$ increases, and therefore the difference between B^* and $\underline{B}$ also grows (5).

The economic interpretation for this result can be the following:

---

(5) In Graph a both point a and b shift downward and to the right, with a increase in the difference between their abscissa values. So, in Graph b points f and d shift to the right on the certainty line, with an increase in the difference between their abscissa values, and point g must also shift to the right and upwards. Given a utility function

the lower P_{1L} is, the lower the difference with $P_{2L} = P_{3L}$ is, namely the lower is the effort's effect on the probability value of the "floor" y_L; in this case, the agent is less afraid of underfulfilment, and at the same time he knows that his effort is less effective in reducing the probability of underfulfilment; therefore, in order to force the agent to exert $e > e_1$, the bonus for $y = y^*$ and penalty $B^* - \underline{B}$ for underfulfilment must be greater. Moreover, we can see that in this case the target y^* plays a key role in the incentive scheme: at y^* there is a corner in the reward function, and bonuses exhibit a strong reduction for an output lower than the target, which sharply helps to reduce the probability of the lowest levels of output. Thus, through this diagrammatic analysis we obtain an asymmetric reward function which is optimal under the constraint resulting from the agent's invisible action. Therefore we can consider the Soviet traditional incentive scheme as approaching this second best contract (6).

---

homogeneous in income, point g' (of intersection between the indifference curves U_{O^3} and U_{O^2} applying to the reservation level for manager's utility when the bonus $\underline{B}$ for y_L in Graph a is lower because of the lower level of P_{1L}) must lie to the right of g on the straight line passing through the origin 0_A and point g. In this case, B^* and $B^* + \beta\,(y_H - y_M)$ are growing in the same proportion, and the distance between B^* and $\underline{B}$ increases more than that between $B^* + \beta\,(y_H - y_M)$ and B^*.

(6) This result is consistent with that reached by KEREN [8] which, under more general hypotheses on the probability distribution of outcomes, concludes that a linear contract is superior to a dichotomous one, when effort is effective on the probability values of the extreme levels of output; otherwise a dichotomous contract should be superior. On our part, we have a case in which a mix between a dichotomous contract and a linear one approaches the optimal reward function, when the "productivity" of effort is low for the lowest levels of output and high for the highest ones. So, our analysis suggests an explanation for the coexistence, observed in the Soviet experience, in the same incentive contract of a dichotomous part and a linear one or, at least, for the asymmetric shape of the reward function with a corner at the target (for a different interpretation of the target, as the most important tool in the planner's hands in order to force the manager to enlarge the production feasible set known to him and to reduce the X-inefficiency, see DE VINCENTI [3], chapter 2).

The Keren model is an extension, under more realistic assumptions about the cumulative distribution function and the planner's bounded rationality, of the seminal model proposed by MIRRLEES [15] to show that a dichotomous contract, with a very strong penalty for underfulfilment, can elicit the first best effort by the agent. Unlike Mirrlees's assumptions however, in KEREN [8] as in our model, $F\,(y_L\,;\,e)$ cannot come down to zero for $e = e_{max}$ either. Mirrlees's approach has been used in several articles that have applied the principal-agent methodology to the Soviet framework. See OSBAND [17] and BROWN-MILLER-THORNTON [2], which polemize with the principal-agent model for the Soviet economy proposed by LIU [12]. However, it is noteworthy that the rationale for a dichotomous incentive structure had already been investigated in KEREN [7], anticipating some of the results subsequently obtained within the principal-agent framework.

This analysis leads to the following general conclusion. It is known that the traditional incentive structure links bonuses with actual deliveries to the administrative supply bodies and is consistent with the prevalently administrative framework, which characterized the Soviet economy up to now. Certainly, this administrative system exhibits several known allocative and X inefficiencies. Yet our principal-agent model shows that we can expect that it warrants a reasonably regular functioning of the material supply system: the center can find an appropriate reward function, which elicits a good level of managerial effort, turned to deliver to the administrative supply system the greatest output that is obtainable by the firm within the administrative framework.

3. - The New Incentive Model for the Soviet Firm

During the *perestroika* period, several changes have been introduced by the political authority in the State-owned enterprise's juridical *status* and, consequently, in the center-firm relationship. Today's incentive structure for State enterprises seems very different from the traditional one. The process of changes has not yet finished and the incentive structure is still "in motion". However, the most important features that have been coming out during the last few years seem to be the following.

The key role in forming the firm's incentive funds is played by profit: first, Sumy and AvtoVAZ's experiments in 1985 (7), then instructions for the *12th Five-Year Plan (1986-1990)* (8), Law on State enterprise approved in June 1987 (9) and finally new instructions for the last three years of the *12th Five-Year Plan* (10), have asserted — although not always in a univocal manner — a rule that grants to the firm, for the incentive funds, the availability of its residual profit, after making the payments to the State budget (11). The new law on the

---

(7) See MOSKALENKO [16].

(8) See *Ekonomicheskaya gazeta*, n. 8, 1986.

(9) See *Ekonomicheskaya gazeta*, n. 28, 1987.

(10) See *Ekonomicheskaya gazeta*, n. 7, 1988.

(11) For a comment, see OXENSTIERNA [18], KUSHNIRSKY [11], IASIN-MASHCHITS-ALEKSASHENKO [6].

enterprises' taxation, approved in June 1990 and in force since January 1991, provides for a general tax rate on profits with only limited exceptions (12). The mandatory output targets for enterprises have been replaced by State delivery orders, and at the same time firms have been allowed to negotiate a greater part of their deliveries with each other, developing a network of nearly free contractual relations (13).

Passing over the partial implementation of these guidelines, for our purposes it seems appropriate to adopt the following, quite simplified, hypothesis about the presently prevailing incentive scheme. The center fixes the basic quantity of goods that the firm must deliver, at fixed prices, to the administrative supply bodies (which in turn will supply, at fixed prices, these goods as inputs to other firms and to retail stores); if the enterprise meets these delivery orders, it can itself sell the surplus of output under market conditions and retain the extra-profit, after deducting the sum due to the State for taxes; otherwise, it is subject to a certain penalty — in our model the penalty is monetary in form and reduces the firm's retained profit.

This system for the management of the State sector of the economy can be considered as a market system with an administrative constraint, specific of the necessary transitional period from a prevalently administrative system to a prevalently market system. We assume that marketization has several advantages from the allocative and X efficiency point of view, although we should not underestimate the specific efficiency problems that can also arise in a market system. These problems and the policies necessary to face them will not be considered here. We will center only on the consequences of the new incentive structure for the functioning of the administrative supply system during the present transitional period.

Let us call y^* the level of output that the firm must deliver to the administrative bodies. If the authority can observe the global firm's

---

(12) For an analysis of the recent Soviet measures about profit taxation, see TRUPIANO [22].

(13) See the «Decree on the Improvement of the Economic Management in Light Industry», *Ekonomicheskaya gazeta*, n. 20, 1986; the law on State enterprise and the further interim regulations to limit State orders issued in July 1988. For an analysis of the role of contracts in the Soviet economy and in Gorbachevian reform, see KROLL [9] and [10].

output y, it can verify if the firm actually did not attain $y \geq y^*$ when it does not fulfill the delivery y^*. Under this hypothesis, and assuming for simplicity that there are no taxes on the profit resulting from the delivery of y^* to the administrative bodies, the gain for the firm when it produces exactly $y = y^*$ is:

$$G^* = p_a y^* - C$$

where p_a is the price for the output delivered to the administrative system and C is the firm's total cost (which is given). For $y < y^*$ the gain is sharply reduced to a basic level $\underline{G}$, but for $y > y^*$ it is:

$$G = p_a y^* - C + (1 - \tau) p_m (y - y^*)$$

where p_m is the market price for y and τ is the tax rate on extra-profit (14).

The general interpretation of this incentive model is quite different from that of the traditional one: the latter entails an income argument of the manager's objective-function (bonuses deriving from deliveries to the administrative bodies) which is completely linked to his performance within the administrative system; the new incentive structure, instead, entails a manager's gain related to his market performance, with a delivery constraint to the administrative system.

Yet the formal structure of the new incentive model is very similar to that of the old scheme: a mix between a dichotomous contract and a linear one (if p_m is given for the firm). Knowing the market price p_m, the principal can handle the moral hazard problem manipulating the parameters $\underline{G}$, p_a (and then G^*), namely the price for administrative deliveries, and profit tax rate τ. The optimal (second best) levels for them can be found through a diagrammatic analysis such as that proposed in paragraph 2 for the old incentive system: assuming $y^* = y_M$, point b in Graph 1a gives us the values for $\underline{G}$ and $\tilde{G}$, where the latter is the certainty equivalent of the prospect $[P_{3M}, P_{3H}; G^*, G^* + (1 - \tau) p_m (y_H - y_M)]$, given $P_{2L} = P_{3L}$ and $\underline{G}$; point g

---

(14) More precisely, p_a and p_m are the prices in terms of a weighted average of the administered price and the market one, so that the gain G can be considered as expressed in terms of its purchasing power on output.

in Graph 1b shows the optimal values for G^* and $G^* + (1 - \tau) \, p_m \, (y_H - y_M)$, so that we can obtain p_a and τ (15).

So, we can conclude that, under the observability hypothesis about the firm's actual output, the new incentive scheme — which is consistent with a policy turned to gradually open the economy up to the advantages of marketization — can also provide the planning authority with a viable tool to guarantee proper functioning of the administrative supply system during the transitional period. Indeed, handling $\underline{G}$, p_a and τ, the center can elicit a level of managerial effort sufficient to increase at the desired value the probability of the delivery orders' fulfilment.

However, in this case the output observability hypothesis can be sharply questioned. Under the old system, the incentive structure was linking the income argument of the manager's objective-function to his performance within the administrative system (bonuses resulting entirely from the output delivered to the administrative bodies), and so it was the same incentive structure that was forcing the manager to reveal (*ex-post*) the actual production to the center. Under the new system, the income argument of the manager's objective-function is the profit, and the manager is interested in concealing the actual output in order to increase the part sold at market price, which is higher than the administered one: the center has lost an informative tool, and the observability of actual output is limited by the agent's having an interest in concealing it.

This problem could be overcome by observing the enterprise's profit, which is linked to actual output and sales, but for this the center needs a good fiscal system able to assess the firm's actual profit. In the present Soviet situation the planning authority does not yet seem provided with a similar system, which is still under construction at the date. Nor do the branch ministries seem the suitable bodies for this task: on one hand, today it is necessary to reduce, not to amplify, their residual power over firms; on the other, the so-called "departmentalism", which traditionally characterizes the Soviet industrial management, based on branch ministries, prevents the center from entrusting the ministries with checking the enterprises' actual

----

(15) We do not consider herein the problems that can derive from the likely existence of some allocative, distributional or just political constraints on p_a and τ.

profit (they are not interested in observing delivery orders to the other branches' firms, and they may be interested in leaving the profit at their enterprises' disposal). In short, it is possible that the new incentive structure is causing an informational gap for the Soviet planning authority regarding the actual productive performance of the firm.

In such a case, we have two undesired consequences: first, the manager will try to conceal the extra-profit $p_m(y - y^*)$ to avoid taxation; secondly, and more important here, the actual fulfilment of the delivery orders by the firm, when it produces enough to meet them, depends on the manager's gain resulting from such fulfilment. In order to choose between meeting delivery orders or not, the manager will weigh the profit from selling more than $(y - y^*)$ on the market against the penalty for the breach of planning orders.

In our model, assuming that the "floor" level y_L for the output is known to the center, the necessary condition in order that the manager is interested in orders' fulfilment is that gain $p_m(y_M - y_L)$ (16) — resulting from the sale on the market of the output which should meet the State orders (net of the minimum level of output which in any case the firm must deliver to the administrative supply system) — is lower than the penalty ($G^* - \underline{G}$ for underfulfilment. When this condition is satisfied, the values obtained above for $\underline{G}$, p_a and τ affect managerial effort in the desired manner and guarantee a proper functioning of the administrative supply system. Otherwise, the manager will prefer to sell on the market $(y_M - y_L)$ also, thereby underfulfilling his delivery target, although the firm is producing enough to meet delivery orders. In this case, the incentives offered by the center are ineffective to ensure the regular functioning of the administrative supply system, which is crowded out by the market.

As we have seen above, in our model the penalty for orders' underfulfilment is not unbounded and this seems a reasonable result connected with the assumption that effort does not reduce to zero the probability of obtaining the "floor" level of output (17). Therefore, we

---

(16) Obviously, given the assumption about unobservability of profit by the center, we did not take away the taxes from the manager's gain considered here.

(17) See KEREN [8]. Apart from our several simplifications about the density function, this seems the main qualitative difference between our hypotheses and those adopted by MIRRLEES [15].

cannot exclude practical situations in which the gain from trade $(y_M - y_L)$ on the market exceeds the penalty. This can be well the case under the present Soviet macroeconomic conditions characterized by a large, increasing excess of demand for goods at controlled prices: the prices on the free (official or unofficial) markets are much higher than those for deliveries within the administrative supply system. Therefore, it is very likely that several firms are finding it more profitable for themselves to underfulfill orders so as to sell their commodities on the market at free prices. The consequence of this is a breakdown in the administrative supply system and, therefore, in the provisions to the markets at controlled prices.

Concluding this analysis, it is easy to verify what the consequences resulting from such a situation on the managerial propensity to effort would be. When the gain $p_m (y_M - y_L)$, resulting from selling on the market the output which should meet the State orders, is greater than the penalty $(G^* - \underline{G})$ for underfulfilment, the gains for a manager who reports the falsehood about his firm's output to the center are:

$$G^F = \underline{G} + p_m (y_M - y_L) \quad \text{for} \quad y = y_M$$
$$G^F = \underline{G} + p_m (y_H - y_L) \quad \text{for} \quad y = y_H$$

where:

$$[\underline{G} + p_m (y_M - y_L)] > G^*$$
$$[\underline{G} + p_m (y_H - y_L)] > [G^* + (1 - \tau) p_m (y_H - y_M)]$$

The three expected utility levels are:

$$E_1 U = E_1 u (G^F) - v (e_1) = P_{1L} u (\underline{G}) +$$
$$P_{1M} u [\underline{G} + p_m (y_M - y_L)] + P_{1H} u [\underline{G} + p_m (y_H - y_L)] - v (e_1)$$

$$E_2 U = E_2 u (G^F) - v (e_2) = P_{2L} u (\underline{G}) +$$
$$P_{2M} u [\underline{G} + p_m (y_M - y_L)] + P_{2H} u [\underline{G} + p_m (y_H - y_L)] - v (e_2)$$

$$E_3 U = E_3 u (G^F) - v (e_3) = P_{3L} u (\underline{G}) +$$
$$P_{3M} u [\underline{G} + p_m (y_M - y_L)] + P_{3H} u [\underline{G} + p_m (y_H - y_L)] - v (e_3)$$

GRAPH 2

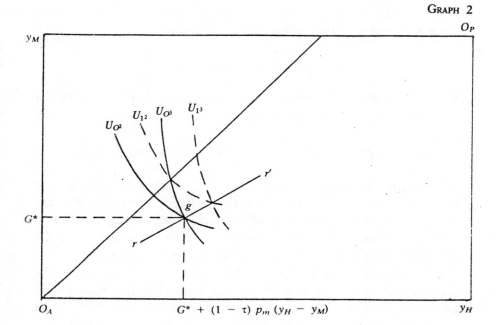

In this case, for $\underline{G}$, p_a and τ graphically found in Graphs 1 (a) and 1 (b) we have:

$$(P_{3M} + P_{3H})\, u\,(\tilde{G}) < P_{3M} u\, [\underline{G} + p_m\,(y_M - y_L)] + $$
$$+ P_{3H} u\, [\underline{G} + p_m\,(y_H - y_L)]$$

and in Graph 1a the manager finds himself at a point to the right of b. The manager's propensity to effort e_2 is strengthened. Moreover, because:

$$[\underline{G} + p_m\,(y_M - y_L)] > G^*$$
$$[\underline{G} + p_m\,(y_H - y_L)] > [G^* + (1 - \tau)\, p_m\,(y_H - y_M)]$$

in Graph 1b, the manager is at a point above and to the right of g. Line rr' in Graph 2 shows the locus of the intersection's points between the "with effort e_3" and "with effort e_2" indifference curves applying to the same utility level: when point

$$\{[\underline{G} + p_m\,(y_M - y_L)],\, [\underline{G} + p_m\,(y_H - y_L)]\}$$

falls to the right of this line, the manager prefers effort e_3; otherwise, he prefers effort e_2. The difference

$$[\underline{G} + p_m\,(y_M - y_L)] - G^*$$

obviously equals the gain $p_m\,(y_M - y_L)$, net of the penalty for underfulfilment, and the difference:

$$[\underline{G} + p_m(y_H - y_L)] - [G^* + (1 - \tau)\,p_m\,(y_H - y_M)]$$

equals the sum between the gain $p_m\,(y_M - y_L)$, net of the penalty, and a term $\tau\,p_m\,(y_H - y_M)$ which increases when τ increases. So, the lower τ is, the lower the probability is that the manager will find himself at a point to the right of locus rr', namely the greater is the probability that the manager will prefer the lower effort e_2.

The economic interpretation of this result seems quite direct. The gains obtainable on the market are so high that the manager is induced to prefer the level of effort which cuts the probability of an output inadequate to sell something on the market; at the same time, the lower the tax rate on profit is, the lower the incremental gains resulting from the sale of $(y_H - y_M)$ are, with respect to the situation characterized by the observability of output, and therefore the lower the manager's propensity to exert the highest effort e_3 is.

4. - Concluding Remarks

In the previous paragraph we have seen that the incentive structure which seems to emerge from the present process of Soviet economic reform can have several positive effects, preserving proper functioning of the administrative supply system and gradually paving the way for the marketization of the Soviet economy. Yet, because under this new incentive scheme the center has lost an informational tool, the necessary condition in order to actually obtain these positive effects is that the planner have an additional informational tool at his disposal: a good fiscal system able to assess the firm's actual profits. Because in the present Soviet situation the planning authority does not yet seem provided with a similar system, it is likely that the center is today facing a very sharp informational gap regarding firms' actual performance.

Two undesired consequences result from this: first, the enterprise's manager will try to conceal the actual profit to avoid taxation; secondly, and more important here, the actual fulfilment of the delivery orders by the firm, when it produces enough to meet them, depends on manger's gain resulting from fulfilling. We have seen that, particularly in a macroeconomic situation, such as the Soviet one, characterized by a large, increasing excess of demand for goods, the prices on the free (official or unofficial) markets can be so high as to make more profitable for the enterprise's manager to underfulfill central delivery orders, and to sell output on the market at free prices: the resulting profit is higher than the penalty for the breach of planning orders. In this case, the incentives offered by the center are ineffective to ensure the regular functioning of the administrative supply system, causing a breakdown in the provisions at controlled prices to the markets.

Two straightforward conclusions result from this analysis. First, the proper functioning of the new incentive scheme for State-owned enteprises requires an adequate fiscal system, so that the planning authority can observe the single firm's actual profit and derive from it the actual level of output. As long as such a system is yet to be built, the present large excess demand for goods prevents the appropriate functioning of the new incentive structure, causing a sharp disruption in the administrative supply system and cutting provisions at controlled prices to the markets. Therefore, the second conclusion deriving from our analysis is that an effective stabilization policy is today a necessary condition for the proper functioning of the new incentive structure, the aim of which is to preserve regular functioning of the administrative supply system and, at the same time, to open the economy up to the advantages of marketization.

364 *Claudio De Vincenti*

BIBLIOGRAPHY

[1] ARROW K.J.: «Agency and the Market», in ARROW K.J. - INTRILIGATOR M.D. (eds.): *Handbook of Mathematical Economics*, vol. III, Amsterdam, North Holland, 1986.
[2] BROWN P.C. - MILLER J.B. - THORNTON J.R.: «An Optimal Incentive Scheme for Planning with Targets», *Journal of Comparative Economics*, vol. XI, n. 4, 1987.
[3] DE VINCENTI C.: *L'economia di tipo sovietico. Impresa, disequilibrio, ordini e prezzi*, Roma, NIS, 1989.
[4] GROSSMAN S.J. - HART O.D.: «An Analysis of the Principal-Agent Problem», *Econometrica*, vol. LI, n. 1, 1983.
[5] HOLMSTROM B.: «Moral Hazard and Observability», *Bell Journal of Economics*, vol. X, n. 1, 1979.
[6] IASIN E. - MASHCHITS V. - ALEKSASHENKO S.: «Trinadtsataia Piatiletka: ot Ekonomicheskikh Normativov k Sisteme Nalogooblozheniia Predpriiatii», *Voprosy Ekonomiki*, n. 3, 1989.
[7] KEREN M.: «On the Tautness of Plans», *Review of Economic Studies*, vol. XXXIX, n. 120, 1972.
[8] — —: *Optimum Incentive Contracts for Large Centrally Planned Hierarchies: the Static View*, Atti del V convegno scientifico annuale dell'AISSEC, Pavia, 14-16 September 1988.
[9] KROLL H.: «The Role of Contracts in the Soviet Economy», *Soviet Studies*, vol. XL, n. 3, 1988.
[10] — —: «Property Rights and the Soviet Enterprise: Evidence from the Law of Contract», *Journal of Comparative Economics*, vol. XIII, n. 1, 1989.
[11] KUSHNIRSKY F.I.: «The New Role of Normatives in Soviet Economic Planning», *Soviet Studies*, vol. XLI, n. 4, 1989.
[12] LIU P.: «Moral Hazard and Incentives in a Decentralized Planning Environment», *Journal of Comparative Economics*, vol. X, n. 2, 1986.
[13] MARRESE M.: «Entrepreneurship, Liberalization, and Social Tension», *Jahrbuch der Wirtschaft Osteuropas*, vol. XIV, n. 1, 1990.
[14] MILGROM P.: «Good News and Bad News: Representation Theorems and Applications», *Bell Journal of Economics*, vol. XII, n. 2, 1981.
[15] MIRRLEES J.: «Notes on Welfare Economics, Information, and Uncertainty», in BALCH M. - MCFADDEN D. - WU S. (eds.): *Essays in Economic Behavior Under Uncertainty*, Amsterdam, North Holland, 1974.
[16] MOSKALENKO V.: «Samofinansirovanie Kak Metod Ratsional'nogo Khozyaistvovaniya» *Voprosy Ekonomiki*, n. 1, 1986.
[17] OSBAND K.: «Speak Softly, but Carry a Big Stick: on Optimal Targets under Moral Hazard», *Journal of Comparative Economics*, vol. XI, n. 4, 1987.
[18] OXENSTIERNA S.: «Bonuses, Factor Demand, and Technical Efficiency in the Soviet Enterprise», *Journal of Comparative Economics*, vol. XI, n. 2, 1987.
[19] RICKETTS M.: *The Economics of Business Enterprise*, Brighton, Wheatsheaf Books, 1987.
[20] ROGERSON W.: «The First-Order Approach to Principal-Agent Problems», *Econometrica*, vol. LIII, n. 6, 1985.

[21] TIROLE J.: *The Theory of Industrial Organization*, Cambridge (Mass.), MIT Press, 1988.

[22] TRUPIANO G.: «I prelievi sui profitti e le recenti riforme dell'imposizione diretta delle imprese nei paesi dell'est Europeo», *Comunicazione alla XXXI Riunione scientifica annuale della Società italiana degli economisti*, Roma, November 2-3 1990.

Interconnections Between World Markets and Soviet Economy

Nikolai P. Shmelyov
Economic Commission of the Soviet Parliament

1. - Basic Problems

1.1 In the nature of any normal economy there is nothing that could require autarchy, fencing-off from the world economic life. The long-time striving of the Soviet Union for maximum self-sufficiency was dictated first of all by political circumstances. These circumstances have changed.

A profound *perestroika* of the Soviet economic is impossible without an active participation in the international economic exchange, without using the advantages and benefits of the international division of labor. The Soviet Union is aiming at the creation of an "open economy". This means that in the long run, in evaluating possible options for internal economic strategy in such areas as production, investment and technical progress, it is absolutely necessary to take into account opportunities that exist in the external market. This also means that the export and import of capital should become not an exotic or occasional phenomenon, but a norm for the Soviet economy.

1.2 In the whole range of economic problems of the Soviet economy the most acute are: insufficient saturation of the domestic consumer market, the threat of inflation and the intolerably high amount of the budget deficit. All these are interrelated problems and their solution is possible only in a package. Of course, internal sources have been and still are the main basis for the restoration of equilibrium in the domestic market and the elimination of the budget deficit. But the external factor can, undoubtedly, play a considerable role in resolving these problems.

According to different estimates the "hot" money (i.e. that which is "waiting" for the appearance on the market of required goods) now amounts to 160-200 bln. roubles in this country. At the current level of the profitability of consumer imports for the state (800-1,000% and even more) this means that a one-time import of industrial consumer goods worth up to 20 bln. could fully alleviate the acuity of this problem. Afterwards, to keep the consumer market in balance and increase the revenues of the budget so as to eliminate the deficit, we need a stable regular import of consumer goods from the West of up to $5-6 bln. a year (my estimates). This is especially urgent during the forthcoming 2 to 3 years, until the time when the new structural policy of the state and the new economic mechanism encouraging competition, quality and high technological standards of manufactured products will begin to pay off, i.e. will start to yield tangible results.

Where to obtain funds for such an increase in imports, taking into consideration the deteriorated world situation unfavorable for our exports and the difficulties of its restructuring in favor of products with a greater degree of manufacture? With appropriate effort, in my opinion, it is possible to find these funds. *First of all*, on the export side, there are the policies for stimulating all possible kinds of exports and freedom for all enterprises (state, cooperation or private) to export. On the import side, there are policies aimed at the reduction of our imports of grain and other kinds of foodstuffs, which may be carried out due to various measures, stimulating domestic production and reducing losses of agricultural produce. *Secondly*, there may be a temporary but rather considerable reduction of our imports of industrial equipment for large-scale projects in heavy industry with a long repayment period and shifting of the saved funds towards imports of machinery and equipment for the light and food industries. There is, *thirdly*, the use of our gold and foreign exchange reserves and the reduction of our international assets in various geographic areas (credits granted to developing countries). There is, *fourthly*, the opportunities to borrow in the international credit markets not only for imports of equipment for consumer goods industries, but also for imports of consumer goods themselves.

Under the existing conditions, in my opinion, a short-term international credit can hardly be the most efficient way of solving the problem. The preferable way is medium- and long-term international borrowing and, of course, not government credit, but private international credit on generally accepted commercial terms under appropriate guarantees. The funds for servicing such an increase in indebtness can be obtained, first of all, due to noticeable cuts in imports of grain, as well as of some other kinds of our traditional imports including pipes. One also should not ignore opportunities for the expansion of our exports as a result of measures being undertaken now to enhance the interest of Soviet industrial enterprises in export activities.

1.3 A full "opening" of the Soviet economy is a long-time objective and it can hardly be reached before the end of the next decade. To achieve this objective, it is necessary to create a number of preconditions which are either do not exist or they are only starting to be shaped now.

1.3.1 It is necessary to weaken the attachment of our exports to such commodities as energy and raw-materials and to ensure an increase in the share of industrial goods with a high degree of manufacture. The problem in this case is associated not only with investments into export-oriented industries, first of all into high-technology ones. A qualitatively different level of competitiveness of Soviet manufactured products is necessary, as well as of their maintenance and marketing. An important step towards the accomplishment of this aim is to grant the Soviet State and cooperative enterprises the right of free access to the external market and as well as the right to use their trade hard currency earnings independently. It seems to me that it is about time to create powerful and competing with each other trade associations, intermediaries of the "trade houses" type. Among other promising methods of improving competitiveness of Soviet exports one should mention industrial cooperation with foreign firms, joint ventures, the formation of regional or industrial "free economic zones".

1.3.2 The reform of domestic wholesale and retail prices which is being prepared now will make it possible to establish a true and, what is equally important, single exchange rate for the ruble. This will create conditions for direct linkages and objective proportions between domestic and world market prices.

1.3.3 A gradual shift during coming years towards a wholesale trade in the means of production will create the preconditions for a domestic convertibility of the Soviet ruble. Soviet and non-resident holders of rubles will obtain, at last, a real opportunity to spend their money on the Soviet domestic market, buying what they need.

1.3.4 The establishment of a reasonable rate for the ruble and the transition to free wholesale trade will make the ruble partly convertible, i.e. convertible for our enterprises and their foreign partners. In principle, there is another opportunity of the transition to convertibility of the Soviet ruble and it is lively debated now: the creation, as in the '20s, of a parallel "chervonny" (high-carat) ruble freely convertible into foreign currencies and a gradual substitution of the present non-convertible ruble by a new one in the monetary circulation. Both these ways lead to the same result, but it is difficult to say right now which of them is more efficient.

1.3.5 A partial convertibility of the ruble will provide necessary economic conditions for the development of industrial cooperation, joint ventures and "free economic zones", or, in other words, for stable regular imports of foreign capital into the Soviet economy on generally accepted commercial principles. Today, unfortunately, such conditions are lacking and our long-time cooperation with foreign partners rests mainly on mutual enthusiasm rather than on mutual economic interests.

1.3.6 The shift towards a convertible currency, especially at its early stages, raises the issue of additional sources of funds for regulation of temporary fluctuations in foreign trade and payment balances. All these sources are known and international crediting does not rank last among them. As one of such opportunities, I would not exclude the prospects of a closer cooperation by the Soviet Union with international monetary and financial institutions.

1.4 Of course, the prospects of "opening" the Soviet economy depend mainly on ourselves. But not only on us. A fullfledged participation of the Soviet Union in international economic affairs, the opening up of its vast domestic market for international cooperation is also in the interests of our foreign partners. It seems that now, in view of obvious positive changes in the international political climate, the time has come to eliminate those artificial barriers for economic cooperation that were inherited from the period of the "cold war". And there are quite a lot of them. In my opinion, the most significant among them are, *first of all*, trade and political discrimination of the Soviet Union on the domestic markets of certain Western countries, including the USA; *secondly*, unreasonable restrictions imposed by Cocom, which include not only military-oriented products (this is more or less natural), but a broad range of high-tech products designed for purely non-defence purposes; *thirdly*, political evaluation of normalization of economic relations with the West mostly in terms of a sort of a new *Marshall Plan*, though today East European countries are not all that needy of such a plan, as they mainly seek usual generally-accepted commercial norms of international business partnership; *fourthly*, political attemps to hinder access or, at least, a more active cooperation of the Soviet Union with such international organizations as GATT, IMF, the World Bank.

Does the *perestroika* of the Soviet economy need assistance on the part of the West? Yes, it does. But the point is it needs assistance, not charity. Assistance differs from charity in that the later is mutually beneficial. Today these are not only Soviet problems that really matter, but also new opportunities opened up by the *perestroika* in global economic and scientific-and-technological cooperation from which everybody will benefit.

2. - Current economic situation

It looks like the major policy directions for economic restructuring are now taking their final shape. The Soviet leadership has at last recognized something that should have been recognized at least 3 years ago: there is no other alternative to a market economy except a national catastrophe. And there is nothing that can save the country from degeneration and falling apart except common sense, i.e. except the market, if one speaks about economics.

The government is clearly moving currently in the right direction, elaborating plans for economic reforms, But what really matters today, is not plans or intentions. The real problem is whether the government has a possibility to put the planned reforms in practice. And most important — whether the government would be able to overcome its ideological commitments in pursuing the economic strategy, whether it would manage to suppress the feelings deeply embodied in the large part of Soviet population towards the "leveling-out" of any noticeable income differentiation.

Here are some crucial but still unresolved and still rather vague issues, that, as I see it, will have key implications for the success or failure of the proposed reforms.

2.1 The need for unrestricted freedom of all types and forms of entrepreneurship in all legal areas of economic activity — privatization of the major part of the state sector through the creation of shareholding companies, leasing state enterprises, development of cooperatives and private businesses (with a right to hire up to 50-200 employees). Besides the well-known advantages of these non-state companies in economic efficiency, product quality and technical progress, it is probably the only way to resolve the emerging problems of mass unemployment without reviving our tragic experience of labor camps and labor armies. Everybody is aware now of the large parasite strata of Soviet bureaucracy, but most people do not, probably, recognize that no less than 1/4 of total labor force in the USSR is in fact abundant, that is to say, these workers may very soon lose their jobs as the emerging market pushes inefficient companies out of business.

2.2 The government definitely does not have any more time: it is not years and months, but really even weeks, which are of crucial importance. The reforms cannot be delayed even for half a year: the consumer market may fall apart completely even this year if urgent measures to reduce the government budget deficit, to stop the money emission and to liquidate the monetary overhang are not implemented. There is a need for an urgent budget for 1991 with urgent cuts in government expenditure. And there is a need to proceed from declarations to real policy measures in selling individuals everything that the government may sell. It is also essential in my view to avoid the lure of imposing the rationing of basic consumer goods, as it is not going to resolve out problems, but, on the contrary, may call into question the whole strategy of the transition to the market.

2.3 Today I'm already not the only specialist convinced that we missed a chance that probably existed 2-3 years ago to get out of depression by our own efforts alone, without assistance from abroad. Given the desperate current situation in the consumer market, it is doubtful that the population can withstand the expected increases in retail prices. Hence, it is absolutely necessary to use all natural and artificial ways to assure a large-scale injection of imported consumer goods (first of all those, that are highly profitable for the budget) in order to saturate the consumer market in the coming 2-3 years, which seem to be most painful. Right at a moment we are the only country in the world that is pursuing a policy of exports restriction instead of exports stimulus (though it is not a matter of free choice). A reevaluation of the whole set of four external economic policies, and a shift to exports stimulation by all ways and means are badly needed. The priorities for providing aid to other countries should be urgently reexamined. And it is quite urgent to proceed with borrowings abroad, using all kinds of possible collaterals, including the political ones, such as, for instance, "Gorbachev's program".

There are not only good economic reasons for an urgent injection of imported goods to the consumer market, but political and psychological ones as well. It will not be possible to avoid strikes and wide-spread unrest if the planned economic reforms are carried out while the store shelves remain empty. Unlike Poland, our people do not trust the leadership, and do not have the same kind of confidence in the government.

2.4 It is my belief that there are no good reasons to envisage an increase of agricultural output this year, unless the government dismantles the system of obligatory production quotas for farmers and unless it shifts to taxation as the predominant instrument of agricultural policy. Also, no later than this summer it is necessary to lift all prohibitions on the free transportation, sales and marketing of agricultural produce in any place in the country. Besides, the government must find the courage to dismantle the hopelessly inefficient and non-competitive collective and state farms (that means, no less than half of them), transferring their land to small coops and independent family farmers.

2.5 It is important to use all the power and the authority of the State and the President himself to persuade the people to bear the economic sacrifices, inevitable in the course of reforms, during the transition period. In addition to a decent discussion of the existing opportunities for the compensation of price increases and other costs, it is also necessary to explain the basic ideas of the reforms without any hypocrisy and double-thinking. We've already come to the point, when people simply don't believe anybody. Probably, there is no need for repentance (though there were mistakes and mismanagement that the government should admit!), but it is no longer possible to deceive the people, talking to them dishonestly.

We need not only to protect the low income families (i.e. about 80 million people) from unacceptable costs and damage in the period of transition to a market economy, but also to elaborate a special government program for retraining employees of inefficient enterprises and industries and their migration to other regions and industrial sectors.

2.6 An important separate issue is the struggle against the mafia that is now merging the interest of government bureaucrats and illegal trade millionaires with those of traditional criminal activities. It looks like the mafia is becoming so powerful, that it is losing a sense of reality. The only way to undermine this mafia is, no doubt, to saturate (or better, to oversaturate) the consumer market and to allow free trade in the means of production. The inflow of imported goods in such quantities that the mafia will not be able to "digest", independent entrepreneurship and open auctions for buildings, business space and new construction, equalizing the rights of state companies, cooperative and private companies in such areas as supplies and marketing of their products, leasing government shops and stores to individuals on a large scale, etc. all these measures are certainly going to yield quick positive results. But, I believe, the President and the government may begin a direct and open war with the mafia right now.

I also believe that beginning from next year all industrial departments should be abolished and substituted by a single Ministry of Industry and Commerce. The State Bank should become completely independent, being subordinate only to the Parliament. It is also necessary to begin dismantling the huge administrative pyramid in agriculture, which has already nearly ruined our farm production.

Until now the very best intentions of the leadership never materialized due to bureaucratic resistance and also because of the "leveling out" attitude of the crowd. It is time for the government to take a definite stand: whether it is together with the common sense minded and reform-oriented forces of our society or with those, who push us backwards.

The Soviet Union
on the Road to Market Economy

Oleg T. Bogomolov
Academy of Sciences, USSR

1. - Profound Historical Changes

Up to 1989 the administrative system in the Soviet Union underwent partial changes. The basic principless remained intact: the leading role of the Party, domination of the state form of ownership, monopoly of Marxism in the ideological life, fear as an instrument of political power. The first attempt of restructuring did not satisfy the society, nor did it resolve the State of crisis. On the contrary, it only aggravated the situation.

In the light of recent events in Eastern Europe and of our own experience it has become clear that the existing system cannot be improved by a partial perestroika, that it has fully descredited itself. It is necessary to form a qualitatively new social organization which would ensure a true social and economic progress. It implies disassembling of the command-administrative system and of the unitarian empire, formation of a new Community of republics, liberation from dogmatism and utopianism, establishing the rule of law, granting freedom to individuals, integration into the world economy. Many people and some radical representatives of the ruling circles are getting more and more aware of this necessity, but the tenacity of dogmatism and utopianism in policy and ideology, as well as the resistance of the bureaucracy, party apparatus and military-industrial complex remain the main obstacle in the way of transformation.

Nevertheless, many facts indicate that the '90s will become the period of the transition to a new social arrangement in the Soviet

Union. Its basic features - the market with its immanent plurality of forms of ownership and their equality, freedom of entrepreneurship and competition, a broad democracy and glasnost, political pluralism including a multi-party system and a parliamentarian opposition, ideological and philosophic-outlook diversity, restoration of rights of common human values of freedom and humanism, openness towards the external world.

The transition period in our multinational state which is experiencing an acute economic crisis and a sharp collision of confronting forces will be inevitably painful and long-lasting.

The economic and political situation in our country continues to worsen. Despite a very good yield of crops, many essential foodstuffs are not available in shops, especially meat, butter, sugar, cheese. This year GNP and industrial output decreased by 3-5 per cent. We face a considerable drop in oil production. The budget deficit is huge — it amounts to 10 per cent of the GNP. The enormous money overhang completely destroyed the consumer market where prices are mostly fixed and inflation manifests itself through disappearance of goods one after another. The transportation system does not work properly. The shadow economy and organised crime are getting stronger and distort distribution.

One should not understimate populistic anti-reform movements, even protest of a significant part of the population against the hardships of perestroika, to say nothing of the resistance of obsolete political structures. During the transition period political instability is unavoidable. Even attempts to use the discontent to establish a dictatorship regime cannot be ruled out. However, the zigzags of the transition period can hardly change the general tendency towards the market and democracy.

Would the Soviet Union take the road of Western development? Of course, the achivements of Western civilization are very impressive. But does the Western pattern fit into our realities? One should take into consideration the ideas of social justice, collectivism and egalitarianism deeply rooted in our society, and also the urge of masses for preserving the "protective umbrella" of the State. It is very difficult to transform the state property which in reality belongs to nobody into other property forms, distribute the wealth between collectives and individuals without challenging the habitual principles of social justice. In short, the society which is being shaped now in the Soviet Union will be drastically different from the former Stalinist or neo-Stalinist one, but it will not fully resemble the society of the West.

In contrast to the West, this transitory society, at least in the foreseeable future, will be characterized by a more substantial controlling role of the State, lack of political culture and slowly differenciated social forces, preservation of certain constraints of a free market, by the influence of egalitarian moods on the policy. But it can be assumed that the basic differences between the West and East will gradually disappear.

2. - Contradictions and Inconsistency of Transition to the Market

There is no relevant historical precedent of transition from totalitarism to democracy, from a command-administrative economy to a market-oriented one. The trial-and-error approach and the heavy legacy of ideological prejudices explain the inconsistency of the process of democratization and marketization in the Soviet Union, the indecision of our leadership, its half-way measures.

The Soviet Union as a unitarian state is being decomposed. Its constituent parts strive for their own state organization and national sovereignty. One by one the Republics have adopted declarations of their full sovereignty and supremacy of their laws over the Union laws. The "war of laws" is going on because the Centre is not likely to recognize the declarations of sovereignty and upholds the necessary of preserving State unity. But it is clear that in its previous form this is not possible any more. The imperial foundations of such unity are already shaken, while the new ones, common economic interests and common security, are still insufficiently understood. The desire to gain greater independence from the centre is stoked by the impotence of the latter to stabilize the money system and the market, to stop the process of degradation of the economic and social life. The transition towards the market is intimately interrelated with the radical reform of the State, its transformation into a true federation and, probably, into a more loosely structured confederation or even an economic community with elements of a common political superstructure like, for example, in the European Community.

It is already impossible to preserve unity by using the strength and power which are still available at the centre, although many politicians appeal to exercise this strength against separatism. It is likely that Republics and territories shall first partake of the fruits of their independence before their interest in the development of integration and readiness to delegate a part of the acquired rights to the centre are revealed to the full. One should hope that already now it would be at least possible to come to provisional agreements for the Union budget and interrepublic deliveries of goods for 1991, of a single command over strategic forces of centralised management of transport, communications, environment protection and of a commonly governed monetary system and customs union. The new *Union Treaty* is under discussion. Its concept was approved by the last Congress of People's Deputies, but many republics do not accept the right of the Centre to determine the volume of republican competences. They insist on their right to delegate voluntarily some competence to the Centre and to determine its role in the future Union.

The principle declared by Republics — all that is on the territory of a given Republic is an exclusive property of its people — looks rather anachronistic in the light of the world's experience. While the land and its entrails are rightfully considered the property of citizens dwelling on the territory of respective national-territorial formations, numerous industrial enterprises of Union subordination, systems of power supply, transport and communications, defence facilities and the like have been created at the expense of all Republics and this should be taken into proper consideration in the division of property.

The best mode of solution of this problem known to the contemporary world but excluded from the practice of our country and other CMEA countries is internationalization of property in the form of the establishment of multinational or transnational joint-stock companies. The activity of such corporations is associated with a rapid proliferation of up-to-date technologies, the success of European integration and the impressive break-through of the so-called newly industrialized states. That's why it is important to preserve in this country the trans-Republican production structures, to make them a joint property. The trans-Republican company can be one of main pillars of political integration.

The deeping economic crisis in the country and discontent of people in the results of perestroika substantially complicate the choice of the best option of transition to the market. Lately, public opinion was attracted to two different concepts: the governmental one and the *500 Days* concept. The latter was born in Russia and, by common consent of Gorbachev and Eltsin, completed by a group of experts and then adopted by Parliament of Russia. The difference between them is principal in character. The government held that it would retain in its hands the power over the greatest portion of the national economy, would continue to regulate on its own the money and credit emission, prices as well and to dispose over all hard currency reserves. The *500 Days* concept envisaged autonomy of the Republics and voluntary delegation, by them, of some of their duties to the centre.

The Supreme Soviet did not approve any of the concepts and entrusted the President of the USSR to synthesize them. However, the worsening situation forced the President and the government of the USSR to make decisions on the most urgent economic issues without waiting for approval, by the Supreme Soviet, of the program of transition to the market. In fact, the government, still having no powers from the Supreme Soviet of the USSR, started to implement its program of overall considerable price increases under state control as a first step to economic stabilization.

The Decree by the President of the USSR on the priority measures of transition to market relations also bore a high inflationary charge. In fact, it buried another alternative approach to the market which put forward, as a precondition, the healing of the money system, bringing the country's finances in order, tieing of "hot money", introducing the common management by the Republics of money emission and credit policy. Prices should be liberalized only after implementation of these measures including a possible currency reform.

Since the centre proved to be impotent in restoring trust in money, it clashed with the desire of the Republics to introduce their own currencies and prices. The President tried by his Decrees to

freeze the existing commercial relations between regions and enterprises. It turned out to be a hopeless task. In the absence of sound
money, barter exchange becomes the basis of economic relations.
With money swiftly losing its weight it is impossible to expect
enterprises to fulfil contractual liabilities.

Administrative compulsion becomes less and less effective. It is
ever more frequently ignored by producers and republican economic
bodies. Will the economic disorder make the administrative
commands be supported by the authority of the military force and by
fear of repressions? The wider presidential power conferred by the last
Congress of People's Deputies makes it more possible. It is very likely
that some of the leaders would be so tempted, but there is little
chance that this way of getting out of the crisis would succed. This is
also evidenced by the experience of martial law in Poland. It is
economic interest, effective material incentives that must start to act.
This was the focus of the *500 Days* concept which provided for
beginning movement towards the market not with the price increases,
but with stabilization of the money system. Of course, it had a number
of weak points and the proclaimed time limits looked unrealistic. But
the direction and sequence of changes were indicated, in general,
quite properly.

The accord between Gorbachev and Eltsin on pooling efforts in
the preparation of the market reform was greeted with great hope. It
is clear that without the alliance with Russia any attempts by the
centre to stabilize the situation and ensure the economic unity of the
country are doomed to failure. In fact, the events are still developing
in another direction. Meanwhile, the elaboration of coordinated
approaches by the Central and Russian leadership for overcoming the
crisis and the actuation of market mechanisms is absolutely indispensable for the future of our country and its unity.

The Supreme Soviet adopted in the autumn of 1990 the *Main
Directions of Economic Stabilization and Transition to a Market
Economy* proposed by Gorbachev as a compromise concept. It provoked a very critical reaction from Eltsin and leading economic
experts. They believe Gorbachev's approach to a market economy will
whip on the inflation spiral. Indeed, Gorbachev, using the wording of
the *500 Days* program, retained substantially by intact the essence of

the governmental program and thus violated his previous agreement with Eltsin to use the *500 Days* program as a base. Thus the most painful and unreliable way to a market was chosen. In recent weeks we could observe the strengthening of administrative leverage in economic management and distribution of commodities.

The politically weak authorities are not in position to put state finances in order because it requires unpopular measures and affects the interest of the military-industrial complex.

What do the radicals and democrats suggest to get out of crisis?

a) A political agreement between the Centre and Republics on distribution of economic power based on recognition of their sovereignity.

b) Healing of the monetary and credit system, abolishment of the budget deficit and restoration of sound money.

c) Privatization of the State ownership and the creation of real and equal freedom for every kind of property. The government plans to sell some state assets to the population and use this money to cover the state debt and expenses. It is necessary to burn this buy-back money and not to put it back into circulation. A considerable part of the state property has to be given to the adult people in the form of vouchers which can be used for buying land, houses, shares. Abolishment of monopolies and the creation of conditions for competition. Gradual liberalization of prices. Effective social security measures to protect the people (first of all those with low incomes) against the hardships of transition to a market. Conversion of military industry to civil production, radical structural changes in favour of consumer goods and services.

3. - Overcoming Isolation from the World Economy

Analysis of the ongoing changes in the social life of the Soviet Union leads to the conclusion that our country can become more open and adapted to international cooperation and exchanges.

Despite the measures recently taken to make the Soviet economy more open to the external world, real improvements will take time. The foreign turnover is even more drastically decreasing. This unfavourable trend, of course, has to be counteracted. In the first place, the export potential of Soviet industry and science is to be enhanced. It is not utilized to its full capacity because of the bureaucratic centralization of management, widely spread xenophobia and insufficient information about its achievements in other countries.

An important potential source of expanding Soviet export is the vast stock of scientific and technological achievements accumulated by the Soviet Union in basic and applied research. The conversion of military industries will also give access to high technologies in the military-industrial complex. Commercial exploitation of these would make it possible to export principally new articles. This is one of the promising areas for joint enterprises with Western companies.

The expansion of imports of machinery and equipment from the West on credit terms cannot, however, be considered a promising way to promote external relations. Today the cost of these credits is very high. Taking into account the inefficiency in putting into operation this imported equipment and its profitable exploitation (which, unfortunately, is characteristic for us), the growth of foreign indebtedness will lay a heavy burden on the Soviet economy. It is likely, therefore, that preference will be given to other forms of collaboration such as industrial cooperation, joint ventures, direct foreign investments and free economic zones for joint enterprises organized on Soviet territory.

Several scores of joint enterprises with Western companies have already been set up. Several thousands are registered, but only a few hundred have became operative, mostly in services. The economic, financial and legal conditions of their establishment and functioning are being improved. The Western approach to investments of this kind is rather cautious. The restraining factor in the progress of this form of business relations is the political instability and the requirement for Western participants to take their profits and to repatriate the capital in convertible currency form. There are also some contradictions between the interests of the partners, since Western firms seek to expand their sales on the Soviet market, while we want to increase our incomes in freely convertible currencies by means of such joint ventures. Difficulties also include the lack of information about the available possibilities for the organization of joint ventures and about the levels of demand for particular products. Joint enterprise activity is also hindered by the lack of a free market for raw materials, difficulties in ensuring trouble-free chains of supply and shortcomings in the quality and technological level of components, parts and materials. However, the greatest problems lie in the difficulties of adapting joint ventures to the internal economic mechanism of the USSR, and their incorporation in it, as well as the non-convertibility of the Soviet ruble and its unrealistic exchange rate.

The obstacles to the formation and functioning of such enterprises can clearly be overcome to a great extent through the provision of special tax-free zones enjoying a preferential legal and economic regime. Enterprises operating in such zones would be given the opportunity to carry out their transactions in freely convertible currencies and at Western market prices (except for wages, land rental. etc.) which might eliminate the problem of the poor adaptability of their operational activity to the internal Soviet economic mechanism. The possibilities for the creation of such zones on the Baltic and Black Sea coasts, at the Soviet-Finnish, Soviet-Polish borders and in the Far East, as well as the mechanism of their functioning and self-management are currently being studied by the Soviet government.

In assessing the prospects for a greater involvement of the Soviet Union in the world economy, another significant circumstance should be taken into consideration. An important role in the integrational processes occurring in the world economy is played by transnational corporations. Despite all the controversies over their activities, from the perspective of national interests of the countries in which they have their affiliates, these corporations contribute to the proliferation of technological progress and enhance interdependence of different countries. They have an ever-growing influence on the dynamism and geographical flows of world trade. The Soviet Union has no large transnational companies with affiliates around the world, nor has it divisions of Western transnationals on its territory. Joint ventures will clearly contribute to the transnationalization of production in the Soviet Union. But at what time and in what form this development will take full shape is difficult to foresee now.

4. - Western Support?

The principal means and resources for improving the economic situation in the USSR which should be unleashed by perestroika are, of course, domestic ones and they lie mainly in the sphere of politics, rather than in the economic sphere. The democratization of society, emancipation of the people's consciousness, awakening of talents and moral and cultural upgrading of society are the most crucial factors for our rebirth. One of the main obstacles on this path is the immaturity of civil society in our country, the lack of confidence in the leadership.

The West could substantially facilitate the renovation of the Soviet society by showing readiness to reach compromises over the reduction of conventional and nuclear arms, to continue a political dialogue with the Soviet Union and to expand contacts and cooperation in all spheres. However, a measure of restraint can be seen on the part of some Western countries in respect of supporting perestroika in the USSR.

It is understandable in the light of the consolidation of reactionary forces in our country. In case of their political backlash any material help from abroad will be counterproductive. The inflow of Western goods can postpone the collapse, but not create sound conditions for economic development. In my opinion, the West should promise to provide a generous assistance in the form of low-cost credits, direct investments, grants, transfer of high technology, retraining of the labour force at the moment when the Soviet Union or its constituent Republics have proved in practice their firm intention and ability to introduce a socially-oriented market and passed to a rule-by-law State. It has become clear that massive and coordinated Western help is indispensible for the success of perestroika. What the European Community and other international institutions do in this respect for some East European countries must be highly appreciated.

It is important not to miss the historical chance for a radical improvement of the situation in Europe and in the world offered by the democratic renovation of the Soviet Union and Eastern Europe.

Political Change and Economic Evolution in the Soviet Union

Eugenio Ambarzumov

World Economy Institute, Moscow

Political changes in the USSR are important in shaping economic developments. I should like to point out the characteristics of such changes.

First point: the de-legitimation of the governing Party and of its leader Gorbachev. The Party has ceased to perform its social and political functions and instead has put its efforts into developing and defending its own egotistical interests. At the same time, the Party is still the only vertical political structure existing in the entire country, and in the entire State. For this reason it will endeavour leadership in periods of future political and economic crises which are now developing and deepening.

Second point: the erosion of state power. Even if the monopolistic State structure, which is vast, has remained essentially the way it was, it has become partially paralized. This is confirmed by the chaos in the economic system where the centralized structure today is on the verge of collapse.

Third point: the distruction of para-Marxist ideological myths, the loss of the ideological monopoly of the party and the adoption of Glasnost, that is transparency, have been important, However, Glasnost is being increasingly limited, and recent decision about news broadcasting have confirmed this. The resignation of Mr. Shevardnadze, in fact, was not even televised. A paradoxical situation exists: while the people have enjoyed the possibility of knowing the actual state of things and the true condition of the country, the society's actual state, above all its economic situation, is worsening day by day. The people have access to the truth, and even more, to the liberty of choosing among different truths, different interpretations of their situation, whereas before they were locked into their habitual Spartan lives and their meager existences.

Fourth point: the loss of political influence of the governing Party has not been matched by the strengthening of democratic forces. There is a superabundance of new political parties each of which, however, has relatively few members and does not attract popular mass support. However, among these parties there are some that are relatively larger, like the Democratic Party, led by former factory worker Travkin, which has a strong populist bent although it has nothing in common with the United State's Democratic Party, and the Republican Party which is also much different from the American Republican Party. At the same time, certain weaker parties can be considered puppets of old structures like the Liberal Party, which is, in fact, considered to be linked to the Kgb.

There is the possibility that the formation and reinforcement of a large democratic movement may take place which, some months ago, was successful in bringing the Democrats into the Republican parliaments. I have had the honor of having been one of the elected members of the Russian Parliament which was very much influenced by, although not dominated by, democratic forces. Some months ago, this democratic movement was weakened and lost active popular support as a result of the worsening of the economic situation. A confirmation of this phenomenon took place with the partial elections held in autumn 1990 when only 20% of the electorate went to the polls with the result that many democratic candidates, even if they had good chances of being elected, were not.

Two scenarios can be made out of this: there is the prospective of a resurgence of a popular movement in the event of a hardening of the regime and the establishment of a paramilitary dictatorship. But it is also possible — and this is the second scenario — that the people will feel so disillusioned by the economic and social situation that they will not support anti-dictatorial political groups. This situation can be compared with the well-known events that took place during the last century when the anti-republican *coup d'état* by Louis Bonaparte succeeded without any reaction whatsoever.

Fifth point: in the last few years there has been a sudden strengthening of reactionary forces. More precisely, I am referring to the substitution, in terms of political influence, of the traditional apparatus with alliances between the new, more aggressive, political apparatus and the military. Even though the armed forces and the military officers are more or less evenly divided on political questions, there are many radical officers among the democratic forces who are very active not only among the military but also among a good part of the managers of the industrial-military system. This symbiosis, this alliance, can be referred to, as Gramsci did in one of his notes from the *Quaderni dal carcere* («*Prison Notebooks*») as Soviet fascism.

During the latest elections last spring, the Russian chauvinist forces were not able to obtain popular support. No one was elected to the Russian Parliament. However, given the contradictions and the crises in the Baltic Republics and other national republics on the borders of the Soviet empire, these conflicts could increase and strengthen the influence of the Russian national chauvinist movement, although I am confident that the rationality of the Russian people will ultimately prevail.

These forces of "Soviet fascism" are trying to bury democratic reforms and attempting to bring about the privatization of large state-owned businesses in order to appropriate them themselves. There are cases of old ministries and State departments being transformed into new concerns and new trusts but still managed by the same people within the government's economic establishment. These are the forces which have obtained an increase in military spending in the Soviet Union budget, even risking a worsening of the USSR's relationship with the West. There has been a barely concealed attempt to recreate the image of the West as an enemy because this would be their only reason for being. They are the ones who, taking advantage of Gorbachev's political weaknesses, have made him their prisoner, destroying his past alliance with the democratic Left and with the popular movement.

They are the ones who have forced the dismissal of some people who are among the most highly regarded of Gorbachev's associates, people of liberal orientation: like Shevardnadze, and have imposed a vice-presidential candidate who could easily represent a personal challenge to Gorbachev, even as his possible successor.

Sixth point: the true counter weight to the totalitarian party and to the excesses of centralism is currently represented by the national republics where the democratic movement has shifted. It is indicative that the famous *Shatalin Plan*, which could be rightly called the *Javlinskj Plan* (since it was formulated by the former Vice-President of the Russian Council who later resigned) was in fact elaborated in the Russian Republic.

According to the most recent survey of last December, 41% of those interviewed indicated Yeltsin, the leader of the Russian democratic movement, as the most popular political leader of the year while Mr. Gorbachev obtained only 22% of the popular preferences.

Particularly important in this respect were not only the survey's results in Russia but also in the Baltic Republics, in Georgia, in Armenia, in the Ukraine and in Byelorussia. Instead, in the muslim republics the democratic movement is very weak, pratically nonexistant, since it is far removed from an oppressed population which is politically passive and ignorant. There, the dominant force is always the Party's apparatus which is allied with extremist islamic nationalists who are increasingly gaining influence.

Unfortunately, however, in other republics, as in the Baltic or in the Ukraine, there were and are situations of national extremism, the neglect of the justified interests of other nationalities such as, for instance, the Russians in the Baltic Republics. Despite this, lately there has been a greater understanding of the interests of these minorities. Fascist or conservative Soviet forces were, however, able to take advantage of these errors of the national liberalization movements in the republics in order to find, if not a consensus, at least a partial support by these minority groups for military intervention in these republics.

Acts of anti-nationalist violence on the part of the central government, imposed by Soviet fascist forces as a counter-offensive move, signify the end of perestroika because they indicate that the movement towards an authentic economic reform in the direction of a market economy has in fact been abandoned. The continuation of the reform movement will greatly depend on the position which Mr. Yeltsin and the Russian leadership will assume in opposition to Mr. Gorbachev with respect to armed intervention in the Baltic Republics, intervention which could in the future be extended to other republics.

In my opinion, the plan elaborated by Yeltsin was important. It consisted of a horizontal agreement among four republics: Russia, the Ukraine, Byelorussia and Kazakhstan. Toghether, they make up 90% of industrial output and productive forces and could replace some central structures which are becoming increasingly inefficient.

Point seven: even if the perestroika is interrupted or postponed for a while or altogether eliminated, the para-military dictatorship of the forces of so-called order will not last forever. There will be a dictatorship analogous to the one established in Poland after the so-called *coup d'état* by Jaruselsky in 1981. A legal basis for the eventual return to democracy is expressed, in my opinion, in the *Constitutional Project of the Russia Republic* promoted by Yeltsin. This text which is widely discussed in Russia is the most democratic constitutional text in Russian history.

Point eight: according to these same surveys the most dominant characteristics of the popular psychology of this movement are tiredness, anger and aggressivity. 42% of those interviewed put, in fact, these characteristics in first place, while 22% indicate "fear" and only 13% say that they have maintained "hope".

Point nine: prospectives. It would be desirable to restabilize the center-left alliance: Gorbachev and the democratic movement with the forces of the so-called left. In the Soviet Union these notions are reversed: left not in the extremist Western sense but in the progressive, liberal and democratic sense. There are, however, few possibilities that this prospective will prevail. It is with regret that I must say that, in my opinion, Gorbachev's options appear to be exhausted.

The center of attraction for the democratic forces is Yeltsin whose political position has considerably evolved from a fairly traditional populism to democratization and to his resolute support of a market economy and economic pluralism based on private ownership.

The last point: which conclusion should, in my opinion, the West draw from all this? *a)* Don't put all the eggs in Gorbachev's basket; *b)* bear in mind that in the future, if it has not already happened, the centers of economic decisions will be based in the republics, although I exclude the possibility of a total breakdown of the USSR and rather envisage a reorganization of the Soviet system in the sense discussed above; *c)* Western aid should continue because the consequences of a return to the old regime would cost the West much more; *d)* it would be more reasonable to concentrate assistance and aid on ways of transferring modern experiences, organization, management and technology rather than on direct financial aid; *e)* it could be useful to impose certain conditions concerning the utilization of aid so that it is not wasted or used against democratic forces supporting the free market.

In my opinion, it was an error by the West not to have exerted a certain amount of pressure on Gorbachev in this sense. In conclusion, western isolationism towards the USSR could backfire and this would be even more dangerous for the Russian Republic and many other republics which are an integral part of the world economic culture, above all, European economic culture, which represent, after all, possibility for and movement towards progressive development in the Soviet Union.

Index